Sonia Florens is a writer and translator based in London. She has previously appeared in *The Mammoth Book of Erotica* series and has been published in various SF and fantasy magazines. She lived in France for many years.

The Mammoth Book of

Women's Erotic
Fantasies

Edited and with Introduction by
Sonia Florens

ROBINSON

RUNNING PRESS
PHILADELPHIA · LONDON

Constable & Robinson Ltd
3 The Lanchesters
162 Fulham Palace Road
London W6 9ER
www.constablerobinson.com

First published in the UK by Robinson,
an imprint of Constable & Robinson, 2004

This edition published in the UK by Robinson,
An imprint of Constable & Robinson, 2011

A copy of the British Library Cataloguing in Publication
Data is available from the British Library

UK ISBN 978-1-84901-451-9

3 5 7 9 10 8 6 4 2

First published in the United States in 2004 by Carroll & Graf Publishers

This edition published in the United States in 2011 by Running Press Book Publishers

US Library of Congress Control number: 2009943394
US ISBN 978-0-7624-4002-3

Running Press Book Publishers
2300 Chestnut Street
Philadelphia, PA 19103-4371

Visit us on the web!
www.runningpress.com

Printed and bound in the EU

Contents

Introduction

Sonia Florens

What do women want in their deepest, darkest dreams?

This book will give you a few clues. And you might be surprised at some of the answers. The world has moved on since Nancy Friday's groundbreaking *Secret Garden*; and women's fantasies have moved on, too.

Women fantasize about all sorts of things. Many start with the familiar – going shopping, having lunch with a friend, sitting at your desk at work on a dull day – and one tiny change will suddenly spin life into the exotic. In *It's All in the Mind*, a hen night with your girlfriends turns into seduction by a sexy stranger. The simple act of making breakfast, in *Breakfast With Tiffany*, showcases the erotic potential of food. Visiting a good friend for the weekend, in *Lessons Learned*, turns into erotic revelation.

Some themes are exactly what men might expect: women thinking about sex with a powerful man such as their tutor (*Poetic Licentiousness*) or their boss (*A Holiday Treat*). Thinking about how to spice up a jaded marriage (*Butterfield 8 for 5*), having sex with a stranger (*The Watcher*) and initiation into new and perhaps forbidden pleasures are also common women's fantasies.

The taboo or forbidden plays its part. Women fantasize about different sorts of couplings – making your husband watch you have sex with his best friend, as in *Cuckold Heaven*, letting your boyfriend and his best friend pleasure you, as in *Jessie's Girl*, or even watching your boyfriend have sex with *his* best (male) friend, as in *Three-Way Play*. Women think about their female friends, their colleagues and bosses, and wonder:

what *would* it be like to seduce or be seduced by them? Find out, in *Thursdays at McKinney's*. Or maybe they'd take it a step further and try a threesome, as in *Happy Birthday, Mr President*. Some take it further still, into areas they might not explore in real life but fascinate them in fantasy, such as S&M in *Puppet* and fetishes in *Tell-Tale Toes*.

Power play is another common theme. There's the man who tells you what to do, in *Dirty Girl*: perhaps because more women are working in senior positions and supervising staff, being told what to do by a man becomes an erotic possibility instead of something to fight against. Then there's seeing the power you can have over someone else, in *At the Window as He Watches* – though who's the one who *really* has the power, there?

Women fantasize about sex at work – with a colleague, a customer, a friend, the gorgeous hunk who makes your heart turn over. They think about sex at parties: strangers can turn into lovers, and maybe after a drink or two you'll hear a friend whisper something you didn't expect or show you a secret side you'd only ever dreamed about. They think about sex when they're driving in a car, or riding on a bus or train: perhaps the modern equivalent of being swept away by a muscular man on horseback (and who hasn't fantasized about the knight on the white charger, and wondered what exactly is under that armour?). They think about sex and shopping - check out *Skirts and Shoes*. And technology definitely isn't a male preserve any more – *Toothin' It* is as up-to-date as it gets!

Some see their sexual fantasies in the form of a movie, as in *Unicorn's Ravine*. Others are well aware that there's a huge gap between their real lives and their imaginations, and they know exactly what flicks the erotic switch:

When it comes to real-life sex, I'm about as straight-laced as my Minister's untied running shoes. But when it comes to fantasy sex, I'm a girl gone wild! I see a guy or gal that turns me on, and right away he or she becomes a character in one of my wicked sexual imaginings.

Work is Play (Karen - Albuquerque, USA)

I've spoken to women throughout the UK, Europe, the USA, Canada, Australia and beyond. They gave me glimpses of their deepest fantasies – and, after a little persuasion, wrote them down for me in the form of a story. Some may surprise you, some may make you laugh – women *definitely* like their sex spiced with a dash of humour – and some may shock you. But within these pages you'll find women like you and me, you'll eavesdrop on their dreams – and maybe see some of your own reflected in their imagination.

Sonia Florens

Him, at My Feet

Ann (Hartford, USA)

When I'm online, men tell me I'm a rare gem, that there aren't many like me. They tell me they wish their wives and girl-friends were like me. They wish they'd take the reins like I do.

These men give me too much credit. I'm just like them, a pretender who's only as real as they believe me to be. I might be curious and adventuresome, haughty and fierce, but I'm a pretender all the same. Oh, I want this, this desire to be on top and in charge. I want to act on these fantasies of mine, but if the online world has taught me anything, it's that the number of submissive men waiting for someone like me in real life makes for a daunting and overwhelming prospect.

But I do wish I had a willing man, a naked willing guy who would fall to his knees when I snap my fingers. He'd find me astonishing as I stand before him, dressed in black – sheer, dark hosiery offset by severe heels, black panties, and a waist cincher. I'd leave my breasts exposed to tantalize him with promises of either reward or punishment, either of which hinge entirely on his ability to concede to my whim.

With his hands clasped behind his back, he'd use his teeth to pull down my panties. Oh, it wouldn't be easy, you know. My panties aren't just going to slide off my hips as if by magic. If anything, they'll hug my hips and they'll resist abdication. He'll have to work at it, tugging at the waistband, pulling at the crotch, manoeuvring to set free that which he longs to worship.

And once he does, once my panties are at my feet and I step from them, he'll be there, at my feet, ready to ply his tongue to the patent leather that covers my feet. That's where he begins his pursuit of me, at my feet, and what begins with a tentative kiss progresses to that full tongue licking that makes me hot.

Think about it: a naked man at my feet, crouched down so tightly on all fours, he's in like a foetal position on knees and elbows. His protruding, rounded butt entices me as he faces my feet. I can't see the look on his face, but when he commences to shine my shoes, the little grunts and groans of abasing pleasure that rise from him tell me he's thrilled to follow my command. The more he licks, the more he slobbers, and the wet noises that issue from him remind me of sloppy sex. I wonder if his cock drips from the lust he feels.

I don't have to wonder whether his cock is hard, however. I know it is. It always is when he's at my feet. In the deepest of my fantasies, his cock's trained to stay hard in my presence. It never loses sight of its reverence for me. But the man attached to that appendage is more human and in his desirous haste, he forgets his place easily. He starts for my ankle, kissing and caressing it with lips and tongue – without my permission to proceed. He takes a liberty I haven't granted.

Without hesitation, I raise my crop and lay the full brunt of his misdeed across that rounded rump of his. It's a harsh smack and he answers it with a startled moan. His body quivers – not just his ass but his whole body, as if the impact resonates throughout him. It's not the surprise of the crop upon his ass alone that makes him cower like a timid mouse, nor is it just the pain. It's the knowledge that he's done something to warrant the crop, something wrong.

Before he can surmise his mis-step, I speak.

"Did I give you permission to kiss my ankle, slave?"

He shudders at the sound of my voice, at my bark. "No, ma'am." At least he's able to eke that admission out.

"Then what were you doing at my ankle? Answer me!"

"I–I – don't know."

"Start again and don't you dare leave the leather of my shoe until I tell you to. Understood?"

He grunts affirmatively and, as his tongue touches my patent leather once more, I ply the stinging crop to his backside again, just for good measure.

"Don't try anything slight," I tell him. "If I so much as get a hint that you're sabotaging my intentions just to get a beating with this crop, this scene will end faster than you can say 'I'm a worm.' Got that?"

His head nods as he slathers my shoes anew.

Oh, I've played this scene out in my head so many times, but that's how fantasy works, isn't it? You get an idea and you dwell on it, each time building into it new details, new twists and turns. You yearn for its realization and your longing grows each time you visit these thoughts. Fantasy – it snowballs on itself, doesn't it?

At this point, I let him work on my shoes for so long that the entire matter becomes tiring for him and tiresome for me. But it's best that way because, no matter how dull it might seem, I know he's learned his lesson. He's learned not to move without my explicit direction. He's learned he's to do things at my behest, not at the behest of his cock or his desire. He's learned this is all about me and that he's an afterthought. Or better yet, a tool. A tool for my pleasure.

When I finally allow him to stop, he's panting. I suspect his diligence has left his throat dry, but I don't have time to show him mercy. Being nice is the last thing on my mind. Reinforcing the message is first and foremost.

"Do you understand now that you're not to take it upon yourself to make decisions about what your tongue should be doing?"

"Yes, ma'am."

"And who should decide how you employ your tongue?"

"You should, ma'am."

"Good. See to it that you remember this lesson well. Forget yourself often enough and I'll look for another slave to serve me. That wouldn't be hard to do, would it? After all, your type's a dime a dozen and I bet I could even find one who wouldn't think to forget himself."

He's quivering and moaning again. Threats do that, you know, no matter how hollow they may actually be.

I extend my left leg before him and tell him that he can kiss my ankle. I instruct him to slowly work his way up my leg.

"But you're to stop at the lace of my thigh-high stocking, slave. Go further without my permission and you'll run the risk of being dismissed from my sight."

These words are harsh but I know they're part of his fantasy, part of his desire to be treated roughly, punitively, perhaps even cruelly. He moans at what I tell him and again when his lips first touch my ankle, yet he adheres to my instructions. Slowly he kisses his way up my leg, savoring each spot as if that one spot of hosiery is the center of his existence, as if he lingers there long enough, he'll feel skin through the nylon barrier.

Barriers. That's what this scene is all about – creating barriers to his pleasure while slowly opening the gates to mine. Denying him is such an arousing, hot way to gift myself. Watching him work so conscientiously when I know his dick would like nothing better than to force me down and plough into me – having that level of control is sheer diabolical pleasure.

His lips reach just past my knee. He has risen up from the floor, and, still kneeling, has almost wrapped himself around my leg. His hands, long tired of being behind his back, embrace each side of my leg as he straddles it to reach beyond the curve of my knee, to reach towards that sacred place at which he longs to worship. Yes, my cunt is a place of worship to him and no matter how vulgar mere words might make it sound to others, to him it will always be a shrine.

He strains forwards to close in on the border of my stockings. Tempted, I raise my foot and press it into his cock. Hard resistance meets my foot and, as I press harder and rub rougher, I can feel the skin of his cock roll over its erection. The sensation makes him moan and he pulls ever so slightly away from me, lost in the intensity of feeling my foot against his hardness.

"Like that, slut?" I ask him.

He pants affirmatively, slack-jawed, eyes fuzzy with lust.

"Just how much do you like it, hm?"

I expect him to mouth something worshipful or meek, but words fail him completely. His cock, however, doesn't. And next thing I know, I feel it humping my leg. *He* is humping me – like a dog and with a lolling tongue, no less!

"Beast!"

I push him from me and grab him by the hair. I push against his chest and attempt to wrestle him to the ground. It's a messy affair, full of stumbling uncertainty on his part and inexperience on mine, but I get him there. I get him on his back. Quickly, I straddle him, planting my lap firmly over his cock. Oh, I'm not going to fuck him. I have no intention of enjoying the thick penetration he's capable of at this moment, but I do want him to feel my wet luscious cunt lips against his firm erection. I want him to feel what he's not getting. I want to taunt him.

"Hump me like an animal, will you!" I castigate. "Always the dog, aren't you?"

I don't wait for an answer as I grab my forgotten panties from the floor.

"I bet you could smell me when you kissed my thigh, couldn't you? That's why you couldn't answer me in words, isn't it? Because of my smell. It's my smell you like."

"Your perfume," he offers worshipfully.

"Perfume, schmerfume," I counter. "You like cunt, pure and simple, don't you?"

He stammers a "yes" while I find the inside crotch of my panties and bring it to his nose.

"It's this you like, isn't it?"

He barely has a chance to inhale before I mash it into his face. I can only pretend to smother him with this bit of well-worn, well-scented fabric, but I do overwhelm him with my force and cunning, and my effort leaves him gasping and panting as if I had actually robbed him of air. He tries to rise, but I push him down with as much force as I can muster. I grab the crop and, reaching behind with it, slap whatever thigh muscle I can find as fiercely as possible. The slaps are sharp, as staccato as little firecrackers, but as I apply the crop, I focus on words so castigating they have their own smarting slaps.

"This is what you like," I repeat myself. "Cunt smell."

It's an insult to him, this observant worshipper of mine, to call his place of worship a cunt, but I love to thwart him. I love to push the sacred into the profane while the crop stings red and painful.

"Yes!" he admits. "Yes! That's what I like."

He trembles as he admits his coarse desire. Which makes me smile. I feel like a wily fox that's outwitted the rooster and expelled him from the henhouse. But it's premature to gloat; I've yet to catch the chicken.

I cast aside the crop and pull my panties over his head, roughly, swiftly, leaving the "perfumed" crotch at his nose. One hole of one pant leg allows him to see while the other dangles from his chin. He looks ridiculous and a soft laugh from me is all it takes to make him blush, humiliated.

I climb off of him and, taking my crop, return to my chair. I spread my legs as he rises to kneel before me.

"This is what you want?"

I point to my cunt with the crop. He nods, weak, submissive, and conquered.

"This is what you want?" I repeat as I use the crop to play with myself. I rub its flat bat over my clit, use it to spread wide my generous labia. I use it to toy with myself until I gleam. And, finally, slowly, I insert the handle into my hole.

His pantied face watches me. Slowly, I masturbate with the handle and a finger from my free hand to my clit. It feels delicious.

I moan and suggest, "Maybe I don't need you. This feels so good that maybe I just don't need you."

That's when he breaks and literally begs me for the opportunity to please me.

"Please, no! Please let me serve you. Let me taste you and bring you pleasure."

His words form common cliches. They're what every hopeful submissive says, online or off. But here, in my fantasy, my panty-compromised slave speaks them in desperate sincerity. He longs for access, for permission, and whatever I grant him will be his bliss. He won't care if, as portrayed in countless female domination fantasies, he never gets to fuck me. He won't care if I never suck his cock. Those typical male fantasies don't have a place in his desperation. The only thing he's focused on is whether I'll permit him or deny him.

"Please allow me, ma'am."

He's whimpering as he speaks. He looks sad and near defeat, like a mama's boy who's been scolded into staying away from the cookie jar yet clinging to one string of hope, one final chance at a cookie. It's delicious and it's my teasing that puts him there.

If I were a greater woman, I'd keep him there all day, hanging onto my every move for the slightest permission, but my lust weakens me and makes me impatient. I beckon him to me. I remove the crop from my wet depth and make him lick it clean.

"Do you think you can lick me as good?"

The taste of my juice upon his tongue makes him speechless. He can only nod.

"Then I want your tongue on my clit. Make sure it keeps to its target. No wandering. And put your hands behind your back."

It's difficult for him to balance himself, to perch his tongue on my clit while placing his hands behind his back. He bobbles back and forth on his knees, struggling to find his balance, but as he finds his footing, he leans forward and his tongue touches me at last. That first touch is electric and I'm almost instantly delirious, it feels so good. I lose myself in the sensations he imparts as he presses, strokes, and laps at me.

He sucks lightly every now and again, so sweetly that I deem him diligent, proficient, and worthy. I won't ever need to send him away; I won't *want* to. My cunt agrees; it tightens and throbs, responding to every flick of his tongue, every circle he makes, every grab and release of his little sucks and nips. Yet it's not enough. My cunt yawns and begs to be filled. I want him in me.

"Your tongue," I whisper. "Fuck me with it."

As he shifts lower, I reach for my clit. Wet with his spit, it lurches under my finger and, as he enters me, my cunt clutches at his tongue. His tongue works in concert with my finger and although the tightening within tells me I won't have long to wait, I want still more. I am greedy with lust.

"Stroke yourself," I decide. "And be a pig about it."

Together, we masturbate in mutual raunch. My hand and his tongue curries me while he pulls and strokes on his cock. We utter sounds of sex gone wild; we're lost in our realm of commands and compliance, and as I near my own orgasm, my mind runs wild with images: of his cock, bound tight; of a dildo anchored in his mouth and me riding it, hard; of caning him while he beats off; of locking his dick away and denying it any freedom for days on end, of that rounded rump of his awaiting the approach of my strapped-on dick. They're mad thoughts, formed in lust. They're ideas and intentions, bold and brilliant.

They're my greed let loose. I want to tease him and use him and deny him, and these raw desires drive me right over the edge. Orgasm seizes me and rips through me, strong enough to leave me weak and breathless, limp.

But I'm not so out of it that I fail to hear him nearing. He's working his cock fast now, panting with every stroke. A huge groan tells me he's there, then little whimpers of "oh my, oh my" escape his lips as he spills his seed at my feet.

I make my final gestures of decadence when I examine the little white puddle that lies thick at my feet, then command him to put his nose in his come, leaving him abased one last time as my fantasy fades and my mundane reality returns.

Yes, this is my fantasy, to demand his compliance, to command my pleasure. It fuels me when I touch myself and it never fails to satisfy me. But over time, it has grown stronger and with it, my need has grown great, insistent. It's a powerful potion and I suspect that someday soon I'll overcome my hesitance. Someday soon, I'll act on this fantasy and answer my needs for real. It scares me, but I tell myself the same single word each time, after I come: Courage. Because that's what it takes to realize your dreams. Courage. No matter how wild those dreams may seem, no matter how long it's taken me to embrace them.

Breakfast with Tiffany

Madeline (Toronto, Canada)

Lust has a hundred aromas and a thousand flavours. Whether my lovers are men or women, it's the savory tastes of their bodies that I recall with the greatest pleasure. My open mouth passes over heated skin, vacuuming its bouquet. My tongue relishes the sweet-salt of sweat, lapped from intimate creases. I dote on the spicy saliva I suck from beneath an amorous tongue. The slippery, slightly lemony musk that oozes from the labyrinthine folds of an excited vagina delights me. When a man anoints my mouth with the hot wet cream-and-leather proof of his passion, I am transported.

Perhaps it is strange then, that in my fantasies, I dwell more on my lovers' oral pleasures than on my own. My favourite mental accompaniment to my solitary play is an appetizing little scene I call, "Breakfast with Tiffany."

"Tiffany" is a composite of every slender young blonde I've ever lusted after. She's somewhere in her late twenties, with vanilla skin and enormous, creamy-lidded, espresso-brown eyes. Her lips are raspberry cream; her nipples cones of milk chocolate.

My fantasy starts with me laying a table for breakfast. I set out a dish of thick sweet cream that I've whipped to stiff peaks and a bowl of fresh fruit. It is very important that the fruit be perfect, without a single blemish, and arranged aesthetically. Setting the table is an act of seduction. My selection is always the same – two large thick, definitely phallic, bananas that are a few days away from being ripe – a pair of Jaffa oranges that mimic the shape and size of Tiffany's tender breasts – a bunch of big black seedless hothouse grapes and one glorious peach that is juicy-soft to the touch but not squishy – just past "ripe".

The fruit knife is silver, inlaid with gold. There are no napkins or fingerbowls. If either is needed, my tongue and mouth are ready to serve.

With the table prepared, I sit to one side and wait. What I am wearing doesn't matter much. Sometimes I imagine it's a short satin slip, sometimes a tailored shirt or perhaps the tops of a pair of pajamas. Usually, I don't even think about what I have on. I might as well be invisible, except to Tiffany. The fantasy is about her, not me. When, in the fantasy, she looks at me, I'm seeing her looking, not what she sees.

When Tiffany comes down from upstairs she's perfectly made up, cotton-candy hair artfully tousled, wearing a tiny white lace bed jacket that frosts her slender arms like a dusting of icing sugar. Sometimes she has mules on her feet, sometimes not. I tried imagining hose on her legs once but they didn't add to my pleasure so I don't bother any more.

She ignores me, but not from haughtiness. Tiffany is enraptured by the banquet I've spread for her. With her butter-smooth little bottom perched on the edge of a delicate cafe chair, she gorges her eyes on the feast that awaits her. Her mouth waters. I can't *see* that it does but we have perfect empathy. I can *taste* the saliva that pools in her mouth.

A willowy arm reaches out. Her elegant hand hovers above an orange, over a banana, close to the peach. It is as if her fingertips test the textures of skins and rinds without actually making contact. She traces each fruit's contours with air-caresses.

I hold my breath. Which of my offerings will she choose first?

When she makes her selection, her hand moves with predatory speed. She snatches up an orange. With the fruit nestled securely in her left hand, she takes up the knife and bisects it with one deep swift slash. One half falls to the table. She strikes again, and again, criss-crossing the pulpy interior of the other half with a dozen precise cuts. Juice, the orange's blood, wells up. The lacerated hemisphere is lifted to her breast. Tiffany squeezes. Pale sweet droplets fall in a slow steady stream, *exactly* onto her left nipple. She shivers. The juice is chill.

Her left hand bears the other half orange to her mouth. Her

face transforms. Tender calm dissolves into ravenous ferocity. Her lips curl back from tiny white teeth. Almost snarling, she tears into the succulence. Slurping, sucking, *devouring*, Tiffany gobbles shamelessly. Pulp smears her lips and chin. Juice flows.

And yet, even as she falls on one half of the fruit like a rapacious beast, her other hand continues its slow controlled squeezing of the other half. Orange juice drips from her left nipple. My thirsty eyes follow its descent. Drops splatter a creamy thigh. Tiffany lifts her knee until her heel rests on the cross-bar of her chair. With her leg angled thus, the sticky fluid runs down into the crease of her groin.

I groan in anticipation.

Half the orange is reduced to gnawed pith. The other half is concave from losing juice. Tiffany arches back and clamps the hollowed half over her breast. Her hand revolves it, pressing it as one might on an old-fashioned juicer, with her nipple the spike that impales it. Like some sort of fruit-sadist, she grinds and compresses. Little translucent juice-sacs smear her delicate skin.

I half-rise, thinking to nibble those tiny nectar-filled gobbets off her loveliness, one at a time, but subside. There is a full bowl of fruit. My darling has sampled but one, so far.

Her hands open. Ruined orange-halves fall to the floor, discarded. Tiffany's avid eyes are on the peach. *I* am that peach. I lie in my bowl, almost over-ripe, almost trembling with anticipation. How will Tiffany choose to consume me? Will I be ripped asunder and gulped down? Or?

One finger strokes, savouring the texture of delicate fuzz. The peach is cupped and lifted on a palm. Tiffany takes up her cruel knife. Its gleaming blade rests on the peach's skin too lightly to indent it. Her wrist lifts, angling the cutting edge. Slowly, with a surgeon's precision, Tiffany *slices*. Flesh parts. The incision is fine and deep, running a third of the peach's circumference. She prepares to cut again. The blade *slithers* through fruit-flesh, mostly parallel to her first cut but meeting it at the top and at the bottom. The twin points of the knife lever the new-moon sliver free and discard it. A once-perfect fruit is now slotted but is not marred. It is as if peaches were *meant* to wear thin tight smiles, displaying hints of the yellow wetness of their lush interiors.

Tiffany cradles her fruit in both palms. The nails of her thumbs rest in the wound. They press, move, press again. She is turning the raw edges of the cut inwards, creating lips for it. From time to time, as she works, she looks down into her lap. I understand. She is a sculptress. The fleshy slit that nestles between her thighs is her model. She is transforming the lush fruit into an effigy of her own, more luscious, sex.

Edible. I mouth the word, tasting it, tasting the peach, tasting the flesh. Succulence. The true meaning of that word is revealed to me.

Tiffany glances my way with naughtiness sparkling in her eyes. I understand. She is telling me, "This is for you."

Holding the peach in her left hand, Tiffany scoops cream from the bowl with the forefinger of her right. She smoothes it into the slot, leaving a dab at its apex. I recognize the image. When clever fingers tease me until my sex weeps and gapes, its lips ripe and plum-purple, and those fingers stoke the urgent hunger between my thighs until only ferocious abuse will serve to sate it, and those fingers fold into vicious spikes that plunder me deep and hard and fast, they whip my clear dew into a thick white froth. So it is with Tiffany, for she is me and I am her.

She is showing me my, our, sex, as it is when most avid – in that excruciating nanosecond when climax is inevitable but not yet achieved. It is Tiffany's sadistic practice, when she has driven me to that peak of expectation, to pause, withdraw her fingers and slurp up the ambrosia I have leaked, suspending me in a delirium of desire.

Tiffany is reminding me.

Twisted on her seat so that she can maintain avid eye-contact with me, she extends her tongue. Hers is a tongue among tongues. All tongues were meant to be like Tiffany's, but fail. It is narrower than mortal tongues, and longer. Its tip is a supple arrow-head, bluntly pointed. Her tongue is pink, pink, pure pink. It is prehensile. I fancy that she could pick small objects up with it, if she wished.

She rolls its width into a "U". She flattens it and curls its tip up. Stiffening it, she trills, vibrating its end. Her hand brings the peach closer. By stretching her tongue to its incredible limits, she is able to take cat-laps that *just* touch the fruit's skin, a fraction below the slit.

My thighs squeeze together. I know what that lick feels like. I've felt it, when my thighs have been spread achingly apart and the skin immediately below my *own* sex has been pulled drum-taut.

The tantalizing tongue drags up, up to where the slit parts the flesh. It twists, insinuating itself into that narrow slot.

Where *my* slot's lips unite, there is a little lip that forms a subtle cup. It is in that little depression that my juices pool when my sex weeps. The nectar inside Tiffany's peach is a mixture of peach-juice and cream. Its flavour is different from mine but will suffice as a substitute.

Tiffany's fresh-from-bed skin has the aroma of apples baked with cinnamon. *Her* pussy-dew always reminds me of pina colada – pineapple and coconut. We are all different. I once had a lover, a Mexican barmaid, appropriately, who tasted like salty-lemon and Tequila. I push her from my mind. This is *Tiffany's* breakfast, not hers.

Held rigid, a spike of flesh, Tiffany's tongue stabs. With its tip buried, it vibrates. She drags it upwards, still quivering, until it "flips" free at the very top of the slit. My sex feels each fraction of an inch of its progress, vicariously. It remembers the vibrant pressure of her tongue's tip on the softness of its floor. It recalls how delicately it trills the edges of my inner labia. It knows what her tongue feels like on the firm smooth plane, between my outer lips but above my inner ones. That even curve is crowned by the pink pea of my straining clitoris. When she subjects me to that particular caress, at the moment of the "flip", her tongue's tip *flicks*.

I moan.

Tongue still stiff, Tiffany moves the peach away and back, each motion impaling it, stabbing low, high, between. Its juices, as mine would, run. Her hand moves faster. Her tongue pierces deeper.

The peach is fucking Tiffany's tongue.

She returns the assault. Her fingers tighten, bruising the softness. Her tongue flattens and slavers, running up and down the full length of the drooling slot. She sucks hard, then curls her lips back from her even white teeth.

Once more she looks at me, with erotic threat. Gazing into my eyes, she turns the peach sideways. Her lower teeth are inside the slot. Her upper ones rest on the delicate skin. Fascinated and squirming, I watch as her teeth slowly sink into peach flesh.

She *bites!*

Poor peach! Poor vulva! Savage and slavering, grunting her greed, Tiffany *devours* its sensitive vulnerability.

My legs cross and clamp. I vibrate. Pity and envy consume me. The thought of it, of her feasting on my flesh, of being eaten alive by this lovely young girl, even with a peach as my proxy . . .

The thrill of it is too much. I surrender to the gleeful paroxysms of a convulsive, gut-clenching climax.

When my mental eyes focus again, Tiffany is looking at me, smug. We know that breakfast is not yet done. My first orgasm always leaves me on a plateau, ready to scale higher peaks once I've caught my breath and my legs have ceased their trembling.

She arches a brow at me and beckons. I saunter to the table, hitch my bottom up on it and spread my thighs. Tiffany has to stretch round me to reach the fruit bowl. She takes her time selecting the next treat by touch. My navel is inches from her eyes. The tip of her nose is even closer to the roundness of my lower belly. Tiffany's breath warms my mound. When she inhales, the aroma of my climax fills her mouth.

She has chosen the other orange. Looking up at me, she peels it. Orange curls drop between my thighs, to the floor. When it is bare, orange flesh showing through white pith, her thumbs dig in and rip it apart. Precise fingers separate one section. She lays it on my bare thigh, ready, and reaches for a banana, which she sets on the table between my thighs, one end just touching the wrinkled lips of my sex.

For the first time, in the fantasy, Tiffany touches me. Two fingers, forked, press on my mound, one to each side of my clitoris. My slit opens. My clit's engorged head protrudes from beneath its hood. Holding me like that, my naked clit exposed,

Tiffany lifts the orange section to her mouth. Delicate little bites clean the pith away. A nibble exposes the tiny sacs of juice along its narrow edge. She rests that naked oozing slice between my parted lips with the raw edge gently pressed to my clit. Her fingers slide it, up, down, up, frotting my clit delicately. Her free hand guides my fingers to take the segment and continue the subtle teasing. Once I am moving the slice to her satisfaction, not too quickly, without too much pressure, just enough to tantalize, she lets me take over.

It's the banana's turn. Tiffany pushes back half a foot. Her left fist wraps the base of the firm yellow stalk. The nails of her right hand slit the tip, vertically. She peels the sections of yellow skin down slowly, baring the ivory column. Three strips of skin dangle over her left fist.

Tiffany changes her grip. Holding the very base of her fruit in her fingertips, she makes a ring with the fingers of her right hand, around the stalk, below the skin. Her hand runs upwards, smoothing the banana's foreskin back into place, then down, exposing the flesh once more. As she slowly masturbates the banana, she lifts it, an inch at a time, towards her open mouth.

Were I a man, and the banana my cock, I'd have been sore pressed to resist grabbing handfuls of her hair and dragging her parted lips down, hard. As it is, my pressure on my orange slice increases. I feel tiny plump sacs burst, each "pop" a minute kiss. Juice runs down, trickling into my sex.

Tiffany's raspberry lips purse on the tip of her banana. She kisses it. It presses upwards, forcing entry. Half the banana disappears into her mouth. Her cheeks hollow, then relax. She sucks rhythmically, in time with the banana's thrusts into her mouth.

She removes the banana, glistening wet, and slurps up its underside with a flattened tongue. Holding it still, she bobs on it, fucking it with her lovely mouth.

My orange slice disintegrates under my fingers. I shrug and reach for another piece. As I separate it from the remains of the orange, Tiffany takes the first pulpy piece from me. It replaces the banana, in her mouth. Her eyes roll with pleasure as she sucks the mixture, orange juice and *my* juice, before spitting the mess into her palm. Grinning, she reaches between my thighs and prods the sodden and crushed segment *into* me.

Insistent fingers slide the pulp between my inner labia, then press it up behind my pubic bone. They rotate it on the engorged mass of my G-spot. Citric acid tingles until my seepage dilutes it.

Smiling sweetly, Tiffany takes a third segment, then a fourth. Each orange-slice is poked and prodded until it is snug and secure, packed into the slight internal cavity. Not content yet, she selects grape after grape. Each is wetted, cleansed, in her mouth, before it is added to the fruit cocktail she is preparing.

I relax my internal muscles to make room. Although I twitch inside, I resist the urge to squeeze. The fruit becomes a weight that distends me and threatens to slither lower. I frown in concentration. My unspoken instructions are to *hold* the soggy mass, but so gently that not a single grape is crushed; no whole segment of orange bursts.

Her fingers pinch the lips of my sex together, taking some of the strain. With six quick neat bites, she devours her banana. Tiffany hands me the second one to peel for her. When it is bare flesh, she takes it from me. Her tongue laves it. Sweet lips purse to smear her drool over its length. When it is glistening wet from end to end, she presents it to my sex. The pinching fingers part. I feel the mess of fruit move but before it can extrude, the banana blocks its path.

The banana prods. The fruit is forced back up. With the bulk of the banana added, I am gently but firmly distended. A third of the banana disappears, then a half, three quarters, and at last, the entire length. I am *full*.

Tiffany takes my hand and guides it to cup my sex to keep the mess confined. She takes a napkin and leisurely wipes her fingers. My need to expel, to *evacuate*, becomes urgent. She knows that. That's why she takes her time, moving her chair away, taking a cushion and arranging it precisely on the floor and laying down, on her back, with it supporting her head.

"I'm ready," she tells me.

Holding my sex, legs spread awkwardly; I hitch myself off the table. I duck-walk to my lover and squat, knowing how obscene a picture I make, lowering my sex towards Tiffany's face. When the lips of my sex are three inches from the lips of her mouth, her finger touches my thigh, halting my descent.

"With cream," she says.

I bite my lip and nod. The heel of my clutching hand moves aside. I wet one finger of my free hand. It finds the pink pea of my clit. I flick, left-to-right, right-to-left. My clit's nerves scream for more, more, more . . . I obey. Faster and faster, I whip that morsel of pulsating flesh, driving it, and me, into no-thought, no will, just raw need. Likely, my face screws up in concentration. No matter. Tiffany can't see my face. Her eyes are focused on my bulging, fruit-filled, vulva.

It becomes too much. My twin needs, to climax and to void, peak. Deep inside me, an inexorable hand squeezes. Orange slices are crushed. Grapes pop. I can *feel* their small explosions. My vagina squirts tears that add to the lubrication.

I can resist no longer. With one mighty *clenching*, I eject the fruit mass in a long lumpy stream, directly into Tiffany's avid, open mouth.

And Tiffany eats her breakfast.

The Watcher

Kate (London, UK)

I've always had exhibitionist tendencies, I suppose. From my earliest days I can recall becoming excited by my own nakedness, particularly when someone – an unknown, unseen someone – could also see it. I remember as a young girl, probably about eight or nine, lying in the garden on an old rug and looking at the windows around me. There weren't many, only about three or four houses in a row, but each window, anonymous and dark, held the promise of an unseen observer and I grew very excited as I imagined who might be watching. I folded the blanket over me and slipped out of my clothes, feeling a tremendous rush of what I now know as sexual energy as I peeled off my final sock and lay completely naked beneath the blanket, in full view of the neighbours. My nakedness – or at least the excitement it engendered – was almost physical, making my body tingle with anticipation. Anticipation of what I had no idea, being so young, but even then I knew that displaying my body was something I enjoyed.

That day I didn't dare pull the blanket from me to reveal myself fully – that landmark in my sexual development came a few years later. I was a student in my first year at university, virginal and shy. I had had a sheltered upbringing and so, while in retrospect I can see I adapted and matured very quickly, at the time I felt gauche and inferior in comparison to my more experienced friends.

It was a particularly fine day, I guess at the end of September or early October, one of those days when autumn forgets itself and mimics the gentle promise of spring, with fresh sun and warm breeze and gentle, vivid air. I had taken myself out for a drive, investigating the craggy countryside. Avril, who had the room next to mine in our six-bedroom student flat, had brought a man home the previous evening, and I discovered for the first time how thin the walls were. The sounds of their lovemaking had gone on into the early hours and I lay next door, frustrated and curious, desperate for knowledge. Listening intently, I stroked my slit in rhythm with the lovers next door, but didn't dare take myself to climax for fear of letting out a moan and alerting people to what I was doing. I can laugh now, but at the time I didn't see any incongruity in my reticence.

And so, the next day, I was still feeling aroused and dissatisfied. As I drove I pressed my hand over my crotch, pushing my palm over my clitoris. I could feel the excitement filter through my body, raising my nipples erect and sensitive, flushing my face and neck and tingling down my arms and thighs. In my distracted state I feared I was becoming something of a traffic hazard and pulled over into the next layby.

I was highly sexually charged, and yet very inexperienced. I think that was a factor in what I did next: I had so much excitement running through my body I had to release it somehow and, not having experience of more conventional methods, invented my own. My initial thought was that I was going to masturbate in the car, bring myself off so I could continue with my drive unaffected by libidinous overload. There were lots of cars and lorries passing, however, and it felt impractical and unsatisfying. I had parked next to a wooded area, dark and secluded, and somehow the thought entered my head to go there to conduct my solo lovemaking. It'd be quieter and more sheltered than doing it in the car, I thought.

As soon as the idea entered my head it took over. My excitement doubled, trebled, my body trembling at the thought of masturbating outdoors. Although my first thought had been that the woods would offer more privacy than my car, it was the notion of being outdoors, in the open, which really galvanized me. I got out of the car and jumped over the crumbling wall into the wood. It was overgrown and unkempt, broken branches and the crumbly, fragrant residue of several years fallen growth scattered over the ground. I scrabbled through, fighting against increasingly dense undergrowth, beginning to regret my decision and trying to convince myself that I wouldn't do what I had set out to.

But I knew I would.

As I walked on, deeper into the wood, I stroked myself through my jeans. I was tingling with anticipation, imagining playing with myself while sitting in the open woods. I undid my button and slid the zip down, feeling the air against my panties. With my hand pressed against my mons, fingers sliding across my slit, feeling my lips swell beneath the cotton of my panties, I walked on determinedly. My initial thought had simply been to find a broken tree to sit on while I frigged myself, but I was growing more horny with every step.

I'm going to strip, I thought. Completely naked.

I conducted an argument in my head, alternately convincing myself that I would indeed go through with it and that there was no need to worry because I would never do anything so foolish. Deep down, though, I think I knew what would happen, I think I knew which argument would prevail.

I came to a clearing. There was a big, fallen tree resting across it, offering a perfect perch. I looked around. Nothing, no noise but for the rustle of the remaining leaves and the solitary cries of a couple of birds. If I was going to do it, this would be the place. Negotiating with myself, I tried to reach a decision, all the while resting on the tree and pressing my palm against my clitoris. Quietly, I slid my jeans over my bum and dropped them to my knees. Unrestricted, I could now part my legs and settle my fingers against my slit. It was soaked, my juices oozing into my panties. I wanted to take them off, to reveal myself to the world. Looking round, feeling very exposed, I raised myself from the tree trunk and slid my panties down, gasping as the cool wind drew across my pussy lips for the first time.

My body began to respond as I stroked up and down my lips and played my thumb around my clitoris. I became flushed and aroused, quickly losing sight of common-sense. I wanted to be naked. I wanted to be exposed. Looking through the clearing once more, I gripped my T-shirt and raised it over my head. The coolness of the wind against my skin was electrifying. Reaching behind, I unclasped my bra and let it fall to the ground, and instantly my nipples swelled more stiffly than I had ever experienced. They were almost painfully erect, my puckered areolae enhancing the effect and making my nipples appear to stick out much further than ever before. By now I was concentrating almost exclusively on my clitoris, stroking my index finger round and round, dragging the nail against it, squeezing it between thumb and middle finger.

I stood up. This was the moment of no return. I knew now that I would go through with it, that within moments I would be completely naked. I undid my shoes and heaved them off, followed by my socks. Stopping for one final – and by now pointless – look around the clearing, I slid my jeans and panties down and stepped out of them.

I was totally naked.

An overwhelming rush of sexual arousal flew through my veins and nerves, leaving me gasping. I was senseless by now, overcome by the knowledge that I was completely naked, outdoors, and that anyone could see me. Somehow, it didn't seem enough: I wasn't exposed enough, because my clothes were at hand. If someone were to come I could make myself decent relatively quickly, and that wasn't good enough. I was coming to understand the nature of my exhibitionism.

Picking my way gingerly over the rough ground, I walked to the far end of the clearing, away from my clothes, away from safety. The air against my skin was delicious, each gust of wind adding a frisson of excitment. Some thirty yards from where I had undressed I stopped and leaned against an old oak, bending and sitting on my haunches, legs spread wide. I closed my eyes and pressed my thumb hard to my clitoris, stroking my fingers furiously against my engorged lips. I began to moan and scream as an extraordinary set of reverberations, vibrations and whirling, whorling eddies began in my belly and womb and alighted across my arms, legs, fingers, toes, bursting through my head and hijacking my brain with visions of ecstasy and notions of lust.

My climax came, my body ripped asunder by wave after wave, my skin alive with lust. I continued to stroke myself gingerly, forgoing my now too sensitive clitoris and sliding against the sticky moistness of my lips. I opened my eyes.

And saw a man.

He was old, around fifty, I guess. He was watching me intently, making no attempt to conceal himself. I screamed and jumped up, my nakedness no longer an exciting indulgence but a fearful, humiliating encumbrance. The man appeared startled by my sudden movement and backed away. Stopping for one final look he turned – reluctantly, I fancied – and walked away.

But it was too late. I knew I should have felt ashamed. I knew that it should have taught me a lesson. But I also knew, deep in my soul, that what had occurred was the most exciting thing I had ever encountered. I had been caught, and I loved it.

I went back to the woods three times in the next couple of weeks. Each time, I tried to stop myself but I couldn't. In rational moments, surrounded by my unsuspecting friends and the totems of normality, I knew what I was doing was foolish, and in those moments I could easily persuade myself that I would not succumb again; but then, alone and tortured by memories of the excitement of exposure, my resolve crumbled and I would find myself driving once more to the woods.

Of course, what I really craved was for the man to return. That would make my exhibition complete. Those three return visits were satisfactory, but failed to live up to the drama of my first encounter: without the denouement of discovery, they were merely a taster, foreplay before the main event. As I stripped and cavorted around the clearing, I would look for him, hoping beyond hope that he would reappear.

Finally, he did.

By my fifth trip to the woods, I had started to strip off as I walked. Barely beyond the wall beside the layby I peeled off my T-shirt and bra and sauntered, topless, into the depths of the wood. It was well into autumn by now, and the sharpness of the air added an extra dimension to my excitement, a frisson of coldness shivering around my body. I found my way to the clearing, my jeans and panties sliding over my backside, and settled on the toppled tree.

I was overtaken by the wanted sense of danger and adventure. My heart was racing, my ears pounding, and in my stomach the steady stirrings of excitement were presenting themselves. There are times when you know, an instant before it occurs, that something is about to happen. This was such an occasion: for some reason I knew the man was there. As I bent to untie my shoes I saw a movement in the distance. An immediate stab of panic speared my chest and my heart stopped for an instant. Without raising my head, I looked up and searched the trees.

It was him.

He was standing, as before, watching me impassively. I felt afraid, instantly cursing myself for my stupidity. But at the same time I felt a surge of sexual release, an intense excitement which was almost overwhelming. My heart was hammering in my chest – I fancied I could even see it – and I knew my face was flushed with embarrassment. It was difficult to understand the emotions welling inside me: part of me wanted to run away from this terrible situation, fearful and repulsed in equal measure; but another part of me was drawn to the danger and stimulation. There was no doubt, finally, which emotion would triumph. Slowly and methodically, I continued, forcing myself to do what I knew to be wrong. I slid off my left shoe and then the right, then peeled off my socks. Still giving no indication that I had seen my observer, I stood up and slid my jeans down to my ankles and stepped out of them. I didn't know if he was still there or had disappeared as he did the time before, but somehow that uncertainty increased my excitement.

This was the moment of truth. I hooked my fingers in the waistband of my panties and pulled them down, bending and slipping them over first my left and then my right foot. Holding them in my right hand, I stretched my arm and let them dangle to my side. I looked up directly at where he had been, praying he would still be there.

He was.

Our eyes met and I smiled. I shook my panties provocatively and let them drop to the woodland floor and stood completely naked before my watcher. I walked away from my clothes, never letting my eyes leave his, towards an upturned tree stump and draped myself across it, leaning back and feeling the cold, hard edge of wood rasp against my skin. Drawing my hand towards my crotch, I let my fingers explore, seeking out my slit, parting my lips, coating them with my moisture, dragging upwards, up towards my swelling clitoris.

All the while, the man remained immobile, watching me. I felt such a peak of excitement that I fancied I was becoming detached from reality. The clearing began to spin and turn, twisting around me, until I felt I were floating, rising above myself, shucking free from my own body. I began to feel as though I were a spirit, watching myself – watching myself being watched, an observer of the observed. My body was electrified, my senses heightened to an unprecedented pitch. I thought I had achieved the ultimate satisfaction.

And then the man started to move. He began to walk steadily towards the clearing, treading carefully while still keeping his gaze on me. Panic and excitement can be almost indistinguishable emotions, firing the same neurons and afflicting the same senses. I don't know which I felt at that moment – probably both. I knew I was in danger: I had no idea who this man was and yet I had allowed him to observe me masturbating and now remained still while he approached me. And yet, the danger was thrilling, inspiring in me an intense and deep-rooted sense of fulfilment.

The man was approaching my clothes, about twenty yards from me. He stopped beside the untidy pile and we stared at one another silently. I was still stretched back on the tree stump and I twisted myself to the right so that I was facing him directly. Slowly, I parted my legs. He nodded slightly, but made no other response.

I had no idea how things would resolve. I was afraid that he would approach, that he would wish to touch me, to join me. That wasn't part of the game. With increasing agitation I watched as he bent and began to pick up my clothing. He took my panties and stuffed them into a pocket, then grabbed the rest of my belongings. Gathering them to his chest, he stood before me silently, almost challengingly, then turned and began to walk away.

I resisted the temptation to shout out, but only just. The situation was sliding out of my control but, I realized, wasn't that exactly what I wanted? The man was toying with me – watching silently and then helping himself to my clothing. We both knew we were engaged in a game, and the excitement was derived from not understanding what the game was. Or how it would finish.

My hands were shaking and a constant tremble had settled in my thighs as I rose from the tree stump and began to follow the man. It was hard going, as I had nothing on my feet, but he walked slowly, looking back every so often. He was drawing me towards him and I was helpless, with no option but to follow. We were headed back in the direction of my car and gradually the wood began to thin, increasing shafts of daylight penetrating the high cover and basking us in cold sun. With each step my exposure felt more extreme and it was becoming increasingly difficult to prevent myself from shouting out to him to stop. He was leading and I wanted to follow, but my courage was slipping.

Still he marched on, and I realized that he intended to go all the way to the edge of the wood. As he reached the little stone wall at the layby he turned and faced me. I stood still, completely exposed, fear coursing through my body. The man felt in the pocket of my jeans and picked out my car keys. Mimicking the way I had dangled my panties before him, he swung them in front of me for a moment, then turned and climbed over the wall, out of the wood.

I almost screamed at that point. Fuck, I thought, he's going to take my car, leave me stranded, with no clothes. I scrabbled up the slope towards the wall. I heard my car door open and close and began to cry as thoughts flashed through my mind of how I was going to extricate myself from this. I reached the wall and looked over, willing myself not to hear the sound of the engine starting.

The man was in the passenger seat, watching me. My clothes were piled on the roof of the car, on the far side nearest the road. Instantly, fear became excitement, those twin emotions alternating once more in my mind. The game was still on.

I readied myself and summoned up my reserves of courage. Listening for the sound of approaching traffic, I climbed over the wall and scrambled back onto the layby. As I did so a car passed, but it was travelling too fast and I was standing too far back in the layby for the driver to see me. Emboldened, I stood tall and walked towards the car. The man was watching me closely, observing my reactions, and I was determined to show no fear. I slowed my walk to a crawl, the fear of discovery by a passing vehicle creeping across my skin, but I refused to let it dominate me. I walked round the car and onto the main road, stopping by the rear passenger door. I looked up and down the road. There was a car approaching, a couple of hundred yards away and instinct yelled at me to get in my car and hide. The game dictated otherwise, and I made a great play of gathering my clothing from the roof of the car, securing it carefully to my breast before proceeding. As the car neared I opened the back door and slid in, out of sight. I was closing the door as it passed.

I looked up and faced the man in the passenger seat. He smiled.

He was in his mid-fifties, craggy-faced and impassive. Deep set eyes, brown and hard, appraised me carefully, his wide, thin mouth fixed certainly. He was handsome in the way that all confident men are, self-assurance ascribing a nobility to the features that, individually, they might not warrant. He was dressed casually, in browns and greens, a countryman with no sense of fashion. His body was strong, with a broad chest and enormous hands and long, thin legs. He watched me sardonically, but chose not to say anything. I was glad about that.

I felt immensely self-conscious, almost humiliated, seated in the back of my own car, completely naked while a stranger sat watching from the front. His gaze wandered over my body, and I felt his eyes bore into my breasts and down my stomach, towards my bush and the hidden features below. My body was tingling. My nipples were hardened and erect and my stomach was churning. I wanted him to see. I wanted him to see everything. I didn't understand it, but it was important to me that I exposed myself completely to the watcher.

I slid down the seat and settled myself. Our eyes met, and slowly I looked downwards towards my pussy. His eyes followed and when he was staring directly at me I slowly began to part my legs, stretching them wide, opening myself before him. I slid forward once more and lay before him, totally exposed. An involuntary sigh rose from my chest as I played my hand towards my slit, running my fingers the length of my lips and parting them, easing them aside, opening up the pinkness and moistness within. All the while he stared intently, drinking up the vision before him. I began to stroke my fingers up and down my lips, sometimes outside, sometimes inside, feeling them swell with excitement, while my thumb circled my clitoris, round and round, tantalizingly, exquisitely. Hooking my left arm under my thigh, I stretched towards my backside and pressed my middle finger against my hole, probing and teasing, while my right hand continued to draw me towards a climax.

I forced myself not to close my eyes as the moment approached – I was determined to see the watcher's reaction. My middle finger was in my arse by now, probing and twisting, and my thumb was pressed hard to my clitoris. I began to squeeze it and slide my fingers either side, pushing myself to the boundaries where pain and pleasure meet. I gasped as the first wave of my climax jolted out of my womb and down my thighs and into my toes. Another followed, and another, and then they began to merge into one another as my body was consumed by the fire of fulfilment. My eyes were closing automatically, but I forced myself to watch the watcher, an additional shiver of satisfaction sliding through me as I saw the sly contentment on his face. I was panting like a dog, mouth opened wide, the trauma of my delight etched in my expression, as the waves flooded through my veins and nerves, flesh and bone.

Slowly, the rush began to subside and I was left, tingling, hot and flushed, on the back seat. My inclination then was to cover myself, the moment over, but I chose not to. Rather, I stretched myself even wider apart, hooking my leg over the front seat and pulling my arse cheeks apart, so that the watcher had a clear view of everything. Somehow, that felt even more erotic. Before, I had been performing, indulging in a sexual act. Now, I was just wanton, spread casually before a stranger. It gave me the most extraordinary sense of humiliation and liberation, all at once. And at that moment – only at that moment – I felt complete, and satisfied.

The watcher seemed to sense this. He nodded, his expression unchanged, and yet I knew he was pleased. He took my panties from his pocket and kissed them. Watching me, following my expression, he slowly returned them to the pocket. I nodded.

The watcher opened the door and without looking back walked back into the woods.

Of Thee I Sing

Krista (San Diego, USA)

I'm totally afraid of anal sex, but I still want it. I secretly want a man to ram it in good without being sensitive to my needs. I want him to hammer into me without bothering with whether I like it or not. I'm not whacked out or anything, I just dream of being able to withstand rough sex.

When I play with myself I close my eyes and think about a man I've known that's had power over me. I visualize him luring me into his car and taking me to some remote place where he ends up giving me exactly what I deserve.

He's an acquaintance, an old professor of mine. He calls me names like, "Cunt, Bitch and Whore". He makes me say things to him like, "I'm a cock-sucking whore that loves to suck cock." He tells me after I blow him for a while that I did a shitty job and to do it over, again and again, till I get it right. He fucks me up the arse, with his dick and his fist till I can barely walk, long after I beg him to stop. And when he's done driving into me, he takes me to his friend's house where a couple of guys are waiting to gang-bang me. They're professors too, smart men that possess a dictionary's worth of words inside of their heads. I can't always understand what they're saying. They say words like, "peritoneum" when they're making me swallow their come. They ask me things like, "Does that touch your peritoneum?" when I'm giving them blow jobs.

So there I am, willingly kidnapped, fucked to exhaustion and about to be devoured by three professors. The bald-headed one with bulging biceps (from all the manual labour he does around the yard for his wife on the weekends) carries me over his shoulder. As I look down at his cowboy boots I notice that the seams on the back of his jeans are tattered. I press my face into his Levi-covered arse and feel the bulk of his wallet pressing into my mouth. I beg him to let me down, but he darts a "Shut the fuck up" at me while squeezing my legs. I'm butt naked. His juice is still trickling down my thighs and my nipples are sore from him tugging on them. I reflect back to him pulling on them with his fingers as he pounded into my virgin arsehole. I begin to whimper. He tells me to "Shut the fuck up" again, that I deserved it.

It all starts out with him pulling up next to me in his pick-up, while I'm walking to my car. He asks if I want a ride, I get in. I don't need a ride, but I get in anyway and when he goes the wrong way, I keep quiet. Afraid a little of where he's taking me but, holy shit, I have a bad crush on him so thinking about being with him excites all the fear out of me. He drives ten minutes away from campus to a car park behind a recreation centre. He knows that it'll be empty. All that's around are baseball fields. There's nothing but dirt, bleachers and dug outs between us and the rest of the world. I'm a little scared, but my desire to have him between my legs is greater than my fears.

He reaches over and combs my hair with his fingers. I close my eyes, smile and tell him it feels good. "You like this?" he asks as he keeps finger combing my hair.

"Yes," I answer, wanting more. I'm growing a little apprehensive, but I know it's too late for backing out.

"You've been teasing me ever since you first came into my classroom. You know how much I want you?" I keep looking down at my hands as he combs my hair. "I like being able to touch you. Do you mind me touching you?" I shake my head no, smiling a small, but nervous smile. "How about you taking off your top for me so I can get a better look at you, I'll help you." I pull my sweater over my head. "Nice, you didn't wear a bra. I like natural women." He cups my breast in his hand. "How about we climb in the cab?"

I crawl between the seats and get in back. It's a tight fit, but we both adjust to the small space comfortably. We start to kiss with greed, our mouths pressing hard into each other's lips. "I'm hot," he says as he pulls his shirt over his head. Seeing his bare chest makes everything real. When I reach out to touch him he asks if I like his chest and I smile and shake my head then reach for his zipper. "You want it, huh?" I shake my head again. He grunts a little as he pulls his pants and boxer shorts off. Undressing in the cab of a pick-up isn't one of the easiest things to do, but we both undress. When he's done I reach down and take his full cock into my mouth. I'm slurping it in, spitting on it, keeping it nice and wet. "Bend over," he tells me. I take his warm cock out of my mouth and do as he says, climbing onto all fours. He's standing up on his knees, hunched over my back with his hands softly touching my arse cheeks. "Pull yourself apart for me." I turn around and look at him from over my shoulder and tell him, "I've never done it there before." He pushes on my upper back till I fall onto my hands again and as he spreads my crack open he says, "First time for everything." Then he begins pumping his swollen cock into my tight hole. I groan in pain, but he keeps going deeper. "Stop, it hurts," I plead. But he keeps pressing deeper into me with a, "Shh, you wanna get us in trouble?" as he pounds. I'm being dominated, with him plunging into me and this is what I want, remember, this is what I want.

His bigness in my arse is hurting, adding a tinge of night-mare to my fantasy. It continues to hurt more than I thought it would. I feel like I an ripping in two, but it's a good hurt like when you're stretching muscles you've never used for the first time.

"Tell me you're an arse-fucking whore. Tell me, tell me," he says.

"I'm an arse-fucking whore," I say.

He moans with a soft, "That a girl, that's what I want to hear, now turn around and suck me." I do everything he asks of me as if I were his student again fulfilling an assignment. But I hesitate, thinking about my shit being on his cock. He sees my hesitance then adds, "Clean yourself off of me, baby." I start to take him into my mouth but before I know it he's pushing himself to the back of my throat, making me gag a little, but I like it, I want more of him. "Now sing, 'Our

Country Tis A Thee.'" I start to take his cock out of my mouth, "No, keep it in there and show me how well you can sing with it in your mouth." I hum. "Hmm, Hmm, Hmm, Hmm, Hmm, Hmm . . . Hmm, Hmm, Hmm, Hmm, Hmm, Hmm . . . Hmm, Hmm, Hmm, Hmmm." I lick the tip of him, look up into his eyes, while happy for giving him exactly what he wanted. "I'd give you an A if you were being graded but, since you're not, I have another surprise for you."

We're back to him carrying me over his shoulder. We're only a few steps away from entering a house where two other professors will fuck me. His wallet is a hard leather, not the soft kind that costs more, but a cheap leather and every time he takes a step it presses into my lips, hurting them a bit. His boots are ridden with dirt. He is dirty and I like it that he's not smelling of cologne, but of a natural odour instead. I can smell his sweat through his jeans while knowing that remnants of my shit are still on his dick. As he carries me in the dark, up a flight of stairs, my head dangling upside down, I hear a man say, "You brought her here? You crazy?" It's a cowardly voice. I can hear a high-pitched whine in it and begin to think of how students probably make fun of him because of it. I know that he'll be fucking me too, maybe not up the arse, but he'll be trashing me out in his own style. I am their entertainment. I am their trip back to their fraternity years. I am their wild girl, willing to do anything asked of me and I will do it willingly.

"Put her on the couch." There's three men all together, one for each hole. I sit naked on the couch. A man with long hair for his age hands me a glass of water. I reach out to take it then he pulls it away and says, "For a little suck, a little sip." I unzip his pants, take out a rather pencil thin, but long penis, and begin sucking. "That's good." He pulls away and hands me the water, "Where'd ya find this one, Boss? She's submissive as hell." I swig it back then sit the empty glass on the floor, waiting for my next order. The whiny voiced man walks over and tells me he wants time alone with me. I stand up and say to him with my eyes that I'm eager to please him. He takes my hand and leads me to a bedroom, but my arse-fucker professor shouts out, "Not so quick there, she's for all of us to share. You want a romance, you can go home to your old lady. Bring 'er back here." We turn around and join the other two in the living room again. I am pleased my ass fucker is territorial.

The long-haired professor walks over to me, takes my hand away from the whiny guy then tells me to lie down on the card table. I walk over to it then lie back on its cold surface. He climbs on top and jams his thin prick into me. "You like this, little lady?" he asks while pumping me. I answer with a quiet, "Yes." My arse-fucker walks up and puts his dick into my mouth. I have Pencil Dick in my hole, Arse-Fucker in my mouth and Whiny Boy looking at us from across the room while jacking himself off. "Tell me how much you like having two cocks inside of you," Arse-fucker says.

"I love having two cocks inside of me," I say it with a warbled voice, with his dick still in my mouth. "Prove it," he says as he plunges to the back of my throat.

"Tell me you love it like you *mean* it," he demands, plunging deeper in the back of my throat as he says the word "mean", making me wetter than I've ever been before.

With as much sense as I can muster up I say, "I *love* having two cocks and would love it even more if I had all three of you inside of me." Arse-Fucker is pleased. "D'ya hear that, get over here." He motions for Whiny to join us. He walks over to the card table, still whacking his meat, then the long-haired man gets off of me, turns me over like a Rotisserie chicken, or a hog on a stick, while Arse-Fucker's cock is still in my mouth. I'm slurping while climbing onto all fours so that every hole is accessible. Whiny asks to get on the bottom. He gets underneath me. I slip his short chubby dick into my pussy, still sucking on Arse-Fucker's woody, only seconds before Pencil Dick pushes his thin prick into my sore arsehole. I keep sucking. I'm being fucked in my mouth, in my arse and my pussy while on a card table.

"Will it break before we're done?" Whiny asks.

We move to the floor. We slide off of the table, but my territorial arse-fucker won't let me take his cock out of my mouth. He has claimed his spot and I love sucking on him, so I keep blowing him while the other two men find their way back into my holes.

Arse-Fucker says, "Tell me you're a whore, tell me."

"I'm a whore," I say.

"Say it again, I wanna hear it again."

"I'm a whore, I'm a whore," I say as clearly as I can with his cock still in my mouth, while the three professors pump quicker and harder into me.

"You coming, baby?" Arse-Fucker asks me.

"Yeah, I'm coming," I moan.

"I'm close," Whiny adds.

"Ahhhh, Theeerrrre," Pencil Dick says while grabbing onto my hips, while coming into my ass.

With a half whisper caught between silence and screaming I repeatedly say, "I'm coming, I'm coming, I'm coming," until Whiny and Pencil Dick explode into me. The two fill me up with their jism, but Arse-Fucker pulls out of my mouth then takes his cock into his hands and continues to stroke it in front of my face.

"You want a little bling bling, Baby? Say you do, cause here it comes." I get his cream in my mouth, on my lips, cheek and hair. I'm soiled with sex juice. I swallow everything that lands on my tongue. When I stand up it's dripping out of me like individual pearls falling off a string. The men's juice drains down my thighs, drops onto the floor, then Arse-Fucker tells me to lick it all up. I get back down on all fours and begin to lick the come drops off of the carpet then scoop up the rest with my hands and lick my fingers clean as if I were starving and this were the only thing I had to eat.

"I've got to piss, baby." Arse-Fucker walks over to me. I'm still on all fours. I open my mouth and he begins urinating into it. I let the piss fill my mouth till it begins to overflow then I swallow it. The other two Professors laugh and hum and haw about how Arse-Fucker's gone too far. I smile at them and shake my head, no, because I'm willing, totally willing to please, to be the object of their desire, at their disposal, because I want to know in every fibre of my being what it means to be lesser, what it feels like to be trashed, reviled, completely undone, completely woman.

Arse-Fucker brings me my clothes and asks if I want to shower.

I say, "No. Thank you, but thanks for the offer." I don't
want to wash the experience away so quickly. I want to wear
their come home with me like a badge of honour. I want to feel
them dry up inside me, on my thighs to where I see a clear layer
of their come sticking to my body as if I were a child again
playing with glue and watching it dry, peeling it only when I'm
ready, liking the way it feels as I unpeel it from my skin.

"Can I drive you to your car?" Arse-Fucker asks.

I smile, then burst into laughter, remembering that that was
how the night began. He smiles, asks me for a hug, asks if I'm
all right.

I answer, "I'm perfectly fine," and as I say that to him I
begin to feel it happening, all the "equal opportunity" bullshit
that hovers over the psyche of men these days and how awfully
accommodating they've become towards women. I think for a
second about how men probably truly feel and about how
awful it is that they can't be their complete desirous flirtatious
selves anymore. I become saddened when I think about how
much honesty is lost inside of the whirl and twirl of "political
correctness". I think of him and his politeness, his offers and
how dry it all feels in comparison to the juiciness of his
dominating ways. I begin missing Arse-Fucker's madness. I
want to feel like a sexual being, not shunned, to feel that sense
of sexuality alive and kicking in every pulse I walk by. I mean,
why not? So I embrace the fantasy world, forgetting the graces
of men, their smooth safe talk. I tell him, "I don't want you to
ask me for a hug, if I want a ride or a shower. I want you to
force me into letting you fuck me up the arse again even though
I'm sore. I want you to make me hum patriotic songs with your
dick in my mouth."

So with that, my fantasy ends with me humming, "Oh,
Beautiful," with Arse-Fucker's cock in my mouth. "Hmm,
Hmm, Hmm, Hmm . . ." He smiles, liking the music that's
being played with his penis while Whiny and Pencil Dick pop
beers and wait their turn.

Unicorn's Ravine

Catriona (Caledon, Canada)

This is my movie. I direct it and form it. I am the cast and the writer and the producer. It is all mine.

My life, how should I say? Leaves a lot to be desired. In fact, it could be called dull, boring and not fulfilled. Usually I paint but this time I am painting a movie in my mind.

This is what I need.

Frame 1: See the unicorn, his head hanging low and his body close to the ground. Tiredness numbs every cell of his body. Instead of doing the many useful, constructive things needing to be done by busy unicorns, he sits heavily, rests his head in the smooth warm hollow of his favourite rock and basks in a circle of sun. Light dapples the dense black of his coat. A blue jay beside him screeches, raucous and wide-awake. His is the Canadian forest. He is king and I am about to be queen.

Frame 2: He rubs his horn against the bark of an elm and scratches at the earth, digging with his hoof, until, as if bored, he looks up at the sky and yawns.

The best part of spring is the pink trillium. He loves to put his nose right into the trumpet and breathe in the Ontarioness of the flower.

He has walked through a carpet of camomile and the air is full of the bitter-sweet smell of the herb.

He curses the world, and spring, and pink trilliums and this strange sweet and bitter smell. He ambles to the stream, kneels into the soft sand and laps the clear, babbling water. Grazes for a while then eats a few trilliums, though generally he never eats them.

All round him a bad aura touches everything. It is in my purples, mustards and navys; it is in the way my shapes are square and sharp and hard. People ask me what the shapes and the lines and the colours mean. Why should a painting have a meaning? It means whatever they want it to mean. It is a feeling. This one is the feeling of a unicorn and the ravine and the trilliums and the shapes and colours in my paintings are the life of the unicorn and my own breath in him. My paintings are the flowers my grandmother scattered here and the herbs she grew and the spring of camomile under my feet.

The ravine is mine. It had been my mother's and her mother's. All mine and I love it. It's as if I have to hold it and take it into me, just as woman has to take the body of a man she loves into her.

Frame 3. Alan and I amble down the gentle path leading to the bottom of the ravine. It's easier to walk here than to walk down the path of this marriage. Three children make it important to keep on the path. I rub the rough, hard barks of the walnuts; finger the tips of the yellow-green sprouting plants and soak in the thin spring sunshine which shines through the bare branches.

This is also a picture painted by me: Alan is forty, tall and thin as one of the bare poplars, stooped, with a halo of fair blonde hair. He always gives the impression of being deep in thought. That kind of glazed expression most men have as they are about to come. I'm younger than Alan but not much. And so short I barely reach his shoulders. One of the things he liked about me was my size. His "little dwarf" he used to call me affectionately and I called him my "gentle giant". We used to be quite the cliched couple.

My bad habit of putting every situation and every experience into a picture.

"What do you think?" I say.

"About what?"

"You know . . . about widening the path so we can take a garden tractor down and bring up fire-wood. If we could bring up the dead and useless wood it would improve the health of the remaining trees."

"Come on, you've been reading too many leaflets put out by the Department of Agri. You sound like one of them. You know as well as I do the work of making a proper path wouldn't be justified. Not worth the cost of any wood we may, or may not, use."

"Not just for the wood – for fun too. It would be nice to come down and smell the herbs and . . ."

"Your kind of fun, I don't need," he says, his face still blank. "And as for your herbs! Look where all that rubbish got your mother. Ended up in the nut-house."

"What about me? I'm not my mother. Come on . . ." Smile. Paint a picture of a smiling woman. He walks ahead. Keep smiling.

"We shouldn't be too long," he says over his shoulder.

"Why hurry?"

"Have to be in the city by four."

"Forgot."

"Oh, you had a lot to think about." He laughs, an insincere, dry laugh. "What do you, of all people, have to think about? Oh, yes, you have to make sure you have some paint, the odd canvas and as long as you have a couple of hours a day dabbling you're happy. The artist, the great artist, is then satisfied."

"I *am* an artist. I *do* sell my paintings and I almost keep myself by my work. I make a contribution."

"You whine too much." My immediate subjects are gallows, firing squads and electric chairs. What is wrong with him? We box in shadows. For some months I have suspected the colours of another woman round him and then brushed them off as a reflection of my own overabundant shade of green. Yet . . . we hardly make love now and when we do it's a mechanical run to the end, not a process in itself. Images of men with soft hands and tender lips and armpits smelling of sweat.

Move past him and stop to face him. "Odd, isn't it, that after all this time, you still think my painting is some kind of game?"

"Don't get on that high horse again. Making a point, that's all. Some of us have to be in certain places at certain times; some of us have to do certain things, though we don't want to do them. You don't *have* to do anything."

"I see. I have nothing to do, I have nothing to think about?"

Once upon a life this used to be my magic place; a place where nothing could hurt me.

We walk on in angry silence until we reach the stream. He stops, clasps his hands behind his back, stoops as he says, "The great artist. Ha!"

Will not react. Paint a picture of a unicorn hanging by its hooves, blood dripping from his mouth. In the cavity I will put Alan.

Cress grows lush and appetizing. It is the first of the plants I harvest in the ravine. Salad tonight. Perhaps a cold cress soup. Pick an armful. There should be some nasturtiums at the fence which separates this land from McLaren's. A hoofprint.

"Look, there's been a horse here. Imagine! A horse drinking at our stream." Trace the mark with my finger just as if I was drawing it in the form classes in art school.

He doesn't look at the print. "Probably one of McLaren's horses broke through the fence."

"Never! This couldn't be one of those ugly, scraggly, great mulching-bags of riding-school horses; it has to be the print of a gentle stallion, full-maned, flowing tail, nostrils flared and breath billowing before it like a tunnel of steam. Yes, that's how I see the horse which made this print." Giggle in spite of my mood. Romantic idiot. He ignores this, or he didn't hear. Just as well.

Bunch my cress with some dead grass. No, the nasturtiums are too small for picking. We walk back to the house in silence. The day is yellow and bitter. It has the taste of overcooked meat.

Frame 4. Another week on this damned unicorn. It's solid. Dead. No magic, a mundane glibness.

So, take a walk, girl, go and find the magic in your special place. Look at the rocks, feel the humid damp, wallow in the rotting leaves and stick your nose into a damned trillium. Pink or white.

One colour, one movement, one shape, and it could make everything come alive. Sure it could.

Find the spot where the cress grows. Funny, the cress has all gone. See a unicorn eating my cress and he's welcome to it. Set up my easel, spread my blanket and line up the paints. The ground is spotted with camomile flowers. I lean against an elm and meditate, clear my mind, become the forest. Float. Huron woman waits for her man to welcome him onto a bed of fine moss; early settler picks ripe tomatoes from her vine as the bread rises; farmer disappears into the heavy corn to see if it's ready for picking.

Clear morning light changes to midday hazy softness as I paint. Colours swirl round me. Forms join and separate.

Need a rest. Bend down to the stream for a drink. More prints in the soft mud. Touch them. They are fresh. What horse this?

Frame 5: Deep inside the forest the unicorn blends into the dappled shadows and vibrating leaves and spotted rocks. He's behind the elm where I work. His breath brushes my bare shoulders, no more than a breeze. He strokes me with his nose. Yes, this shining black horse with the fine turned horn which explodes out of the bone of his skull. Reach out and stroke the horn – dry, hard, rough. Fondle his hot, furry nose. Curl my fingers round the nostrils and with the other hand rub the tip of the horn.

"I can see you're friendly."

He nuzzles my cheek with his mouth.

"You are a silly old horse. I think that you could be almost human." Keep my hand on his neck and the touch of him is as comfortable as the touch of a child. His breath on my face. Lean against the tree. He rubs my face with the side of his horn. Now his head is in the angle between my head and shoulder. I hold his head in my hands; his breath is fresh, like grass. This gentle, huge animal. This silky, warm animal. Nothing in this world but the heavenly darkness of this animal. Lovely darkness.

He licks me clean. Kisses me all over my face and brushes my lips with his horn. He tidies the rug and I sleep.

Later I notice he's left the tip of his horn embedded in the bark of the tree.

* * *

Frame 6. Alan does not like the painting. Says it's rubbish. Says I'm getting more and more off the wall. Who says artists had to be accessible – whatever that means?

Frame 7. July, and I float on the heat. Hate summer. Love fall and spring. At times hate my life. It is certain that the colours of another woman blot out his own colours. I don't know the man I married. He is scarlet. All scarlet, an angry frantic scarlet. I pretend blindness, deafness and no sense of smell.

We again walk down to the ravine. We have company to-night and I need some cress. At least at midday the mosquitoes should be sleeping. I hope. The house is too hot to bear. We walk silently for a while; eventually, as if he's been waiting for the right time, he says, "Been thinking: we may as well sell and move into the city."

"What?"

"Saw Watkins yesterday. I'm going to be more and more in the city. Can't get on with all this travelling, it isn't good for me. We should get a good price for this place and pick up something convenient for the subway. The children would prefer the city too."

"You think so? Have you asked them?"

"No point in asking – we've no choice."

"There's always choice."

"Not for us."

"Is that what you really think? You really think I have no choice and the children have no choices?"

"Have to be in the city; nothing more to say about it."

"It's you that has to be in the city, not me, and not the children."

What is this man talking about? Do I know him? My painting is a grey canvas with huge blotches of red as if someone has been shot through it. We're at the same spot where I had painted my unicorn. The grass is still flattened.

He says, shaking his head, "I don't understand you at all."

Anger bubbles. "I think you do. When it suits you – then you understand me very well. You can go to hell. You can go to your city and leave me and the children here."

"Can't be done."

Something funny in his voice: there's a dead certainty, a sureness, an authority even greater than is usual for him.

"And why can't this be done?" Be patient. Give him time. Let him speak.

"I need the money from the house."

"What?"

"Said I need the money from the house and we have to sell it. There's no question or choice for any of us."

"Go and find an apartment somewhere – like others do when they find family life too much."

"I don't understand any of this. I don't know what's wrong with you, it's as if I'm the one who's being illogical and stupid." He stands right in front of me and looms above me. I'm a fly waiting for the swatter. "This is silly. Only yesterday you were normal. Today you're acting like a goat." He smiles and his eyes become blue and clear as the stream. "All this rubbish about you keeping the children and the house, and me finding an apartment. . . . I don't know where it comes from." He laughs in a friendly, normal manner. Strokes my face. He strokes the cat the same way. Harder and harder all the time until the cat jumps away.

I move his hand from my face. "It sounds a sensible thing for people to do when they're splitting up."

"Wake up, and stop this stupidity!" The bully in his voice. I do not like this painting. Will change it and start another.

"I think I have just woken up," I say too loudly.

I'm a tiny speck compared to his elephantine size. That white, blank face . . . Have seen this look twice before and each time he struck me. I brace by pushing myself against the tree. I swore I would leave if it ever happened again. Silence!

"Bitch! Don't know who or what you think you are. Think you're something special. Think you can turn my life upside down, and I can't do anything. You know what I think?" He doesn't wait for an answer. "I think I'm not going to let you get away with it this time. Not this time."

His leaden hands on my shoulders. Bark cutting into my back and his fingers move up to my throat and . . .

"You think that you can take everything I've worked for from me? Think this: I could squeeze the life from you right

now and leave you here. I could do that. Say you went on a trip
. . . you were having an affair . . . went away. I could say
anything at all and no one would miss you. Bury you here and
you would never be found. Never."

I whisper, "Where would that get you?"

He laughs. "Where would it get me! I'll tell you where it
would get me. It'll get me my children, and my home, and my
house and everything I've worked for all these years."

His fingers tighten the pressure. Discomfort changes to
pain. Must not fight.

Frame 8: Branches gather, come together. It's dark as black
velvet. Through this night is one shaft of light. It shines on me;
it's my circle, my spotlight. My face is red hot in the light while
the rest of my body freezes; it's getting colder and colder as the
hands on my throat turn into a tourniquet.

Now the circle of light on my face gets larger and larger.
Reach up behind me and find the piece of horn and grip it.
Power flows into me. Release the piece of horn and take his
hands in mine and gently lift them off my throat.

Unicorn. Footman. 905 874 1414

Frame 9. "That was a silly thing to do, wasn't it?" I'm
speaking to a wicked child. His eyes bulge, pupils huge. He
looks about and trembles.

"I don't know what happened," he stutters.

I start walking up the path and mumble, "We had best be
getting back. It's getting late."

As I walk I pick foxgloves and white bryony and black
nightshade and monkshood and aconite.

"What's the flowers for?"

"For the dinner arrangement. We have company. Remember? They smell good. Granny scattered the seeds. Wanted
them to be wild as they should."

"Yes, yes, of course. Your grandmother and her flowers.
Her herbs."

Birds sing once more and sun floods into the darkness.

This is how things should be.

"Nice Tits"

Olivia (Ann Arbor, USA)

In my sexual fantasies, my breasts are like a cock. I don't mean
they look like a cock or that I use them to fuck people. But the
images that get me really excited are men and women admiring
my breasts, which represent my sexual power. I imagine a
woman's breathless whisper as she slides her hand into my
blouse: "You have the nicest tits I've ever seen – would you let
me touch them?" she asks shyly. Or I picture a man's rough
hand pulling my nipple up ever so slightly over the border of
my bra, closing his eyes in pleasure as he lowers his face to kiss
it. I have quite an active imagination and my fantasies range
from the mundane (sex with a rock star, for example) to the
taboo. And yet my most treasured imagined scenarios, those
that have driven me to frivol away countless afternoons feverishly orgasming over and over, involve some good dirty talk
about my tits: so big, so soft, so hot, oh turn me on so bad,
baby.

My first serious boyfriend figured out my fetish. When I
first met him halfway through college, he loved to touch my
breasts, to suck on them before my shirt was even off, pulling
at the cloth of my T-shirt with his teeth until he could close his
lips around my hard nipple. He would reach his strong arm
around my ribcage to hold my breasts protectively as he fucked
me from behind. I loved the contrast between his soft, reverent
touch on my tits and the rough, desperate thrusting of his hips
against my arse. If this is what sex is all about, I thought at age
eighteen, I see why people like it so much.

Now let me tell you a bit about this boyfriend. Like me, he
was a big fan of tits. I know this because he freely pointed out

pairs that he liked especially, either on TV or when we passed them on the street. This made me a bit jealous, and I often fantasized that I was one of the women he admired. I would imagine him pulling my shirt open, button by button, to slowly expose inflated silicone breasts like those of the actress or model. But I never seriously minded his wandering eye, because he used to give a lot of attention to my breasts, too. That is, until he realized how much I liked it. It took him a while to notice; in fact he often apologized for focusing so much on my breasts, evidently believing that I merely tolerated his fetish. But one day while he was trying to give me an orgasm my own breast fetish became obvious. I had always orgasmed easily when I masturbated but had not yet been able to with him. This troubled him and scandalized my sexually liberated friends, but it didn't bother me too much. Orgasms were something I could have by myself. Many of the sensations I felt with my boyfriend – being fucked, licked, sucked – did not seem to lead my body toward an orgasm but were horribly, torturously pleasing in themselves. I loved being penetrated from behind, feeling so full of his cock that I thought I'd burst. And I loved riding on top of him, watching his face contort into an expression of so much pleasure that it looked like pain as I slid slowly up and down his shaft.

But my favourite thing, our least common position, was when I lay on my back, vulnerable to the whims of this large man hovering just above me. With just one of his hands, he would grab hold of both my wrists and pull my arms up above my head. He liked to use his boxer briefs to tie my arms tightly to the bed frame. His excited cock would approach my face as he worked, and I would strain upward to run my tongue along its length. Instinctively he would press it into my mouth and let me suck on it for a moment, but then would pull back, denying himself the pleasure he was saving for just later. But the best part came after he finished tightening the knot. Hungrily he would admire my stretched, exposed body for a moment. I would not dare to look down at myself, but I would imagine what he saw: the delicate ribcage, the round, full breasts swelling up from the curve of the waist, the rosy pink aureolaes against creamy white skin. Gently he would

lower his head and graze his lips over my nipple – then he
would pull his head back in surprise, as though he had not
meant to lower it. He would stare at me, his face intense with
desire, until he could no longer bear it; then he would attack
my breast like a starved dog, growling and biting. My back
would arch and my hand would stir instinctively, trying to
move to the back of his head to control his motions. "No," he
would say with a wicked smile, "you can't stop me." His pelvis
would grind against mine as he stabbed his cock all around my
pussy until finally, with a great groan of relief, he slid it inside.
This all was too much for me, and I would moan with the
despair of unbearable, unimaginable pleasure. I remember
whispering to myself, "I can't stand it!" I think perhaps at
those moments I was close to coming, but it was a very
different, more intense type of orgasm than the ones I gave
myself, and I didn't recognize it. So I tried to focus on his
pleasure, matching his thrusts and pauses, until with a final
shudder he came, crying out loudly enough to wake his roommates through the flimsy walls of their apartment. He lay his
head down between my breasts, and I wanted to embrace him,
stroke his hair, but couldn't – my arms were tied above my
head. Lying still and bound, his cock pulsating gently inside
me, I felt just a little jealous of this orgasm that seemed so final
and satisfying.

At other times he worked diligently to try to give me an
orgasm, but none of the tricks in his twenty-year-old repertoire
did anything for me. They were the same things that my female
friends recommended: fingers, vibrators, and oral sex. This
last was the hands-down favourite of all of my friends. "If he
were doing it right," they told me, "you would come." But
watching his head disappear down into the nether regions of
my body did not interest me in the least. I imagined that
anybody might be down there – perhaps a useful possibility for
women who were bored with their partners, but I wanted to see
mine. I had never believed in penis envy until I realized how
much I would prefer a blow job. That seemed like the hottest
imaginable experience, to watch as my enormous, engorged
genitals slid completely inside my lover's mouth. I could watch
his face as he concentrated on my pleasure, see my cock

disappearing between his rosy, parted lips. One day during foreplay, as he lay on top of me kissing my lips and stroking my pussy, I suddenly realized what would be the next best thing – maybe even a better thing. With one hand, I pulled my shirt up over my breasts. Grabbing the back of his head, I pushed it toward my nipple. "Suck my tits," I told him urgently. Surprised but compliant, he began to move his lips to my breast. His hand moved from my pussy as he focused attention on my chest. But I pushed it back, sliding it up under my skirt. "No, don't stop," I told him. Watching his mouth filled with my breast, the pink nipple matching the pink lips, my clitoris come to life as it never had under his touch before, I came in minutes.

At first my boyfriend enjoyed this new discovery, that I could come as long as he sucked my tits. Soon, however, he seemed to realize that he was, in fact, giving me a blow job. Sucking my tits suddenly ceased to be his self-indulgent fetish; now he could seldom maintain interest for the several minutes it took to bring me to orgasm. Soon we stopped having sex altogether. One evening as I napped on his bed, I awoke to find him sucking on my exposed breast. I watched for a moment in disbelief – for weeks I had been longing to see his face at my breast.

Excited, I ran my fingers lightly through his hair. But when he realized that I was awake, he froze. "Don't stop," I whispered. "That was nice."

Instead he sat up on the bed, turning his back to me. "No, I don't want to any more," he said brusquely. He emphasized the final word hostilely – evidently I had ruined his fun by waking up. Over the next few days, I pondered this episode, growing increasingly angry that he would desire me only when I was unable to enjoy it.

Once I broke up with him, my breast fetish grew more intense. Often, as I undressed in front of my mirror, I noticed how good my tits looked. Many of my more flat-chested friends had admired my picturesque curviness in underwear or bathing suits, and I often thought of their compliments as I viewed myself. The sight of my tits filling up the cups of my bra was in itself enough to make me want to come. They had a nice fullness and plumpness and curved seductively where they met to form my cleavage. Looking in the mirror, I would arrange my clothes like the women in men's magazines. One of my favourite pictures in my old boyfriend's porn collection was of a giant-breasted woman wearing a T-shirt that extended only as far down as her armpits. Her huge creamy-coloured tits stuck out provocatively from under the half-shirt, almost as though she were unable to find a shirt large enough to fit. Thinking of her, I would roll my own T-shirt up over my breasts, leaning forward so I spilled gently out of my exposed bra. When the round weight of my tits had fallen nearly all the way out, I would reach around to slowly unhook my bra, causing my chest to jut outward as my arms stretched back. I wouldn't take the bra off right away; instead, I would slide each strap off and, with one hand, hold the now functionless article of clothing against my breasts, just covering my nipples as I leaned forward, my tits seeming all the more exposed against the T-shirt above them and bra dangling at their tips. Finally I would let the bra drop to the floor, and my nipples would pop into view. I was always impressed with this view of myself – I looked as hot as one of those models baring their breasts in the magazines. My breasts were not so melonous but they were full and quite pretty, with soft pink aureolaes and nicely turned-up nipples. It thrilled me that I was as turned on by my own image as by the women in magazines – and I thought of how stupid my boyfriend had been not to appreciate such good-looking tits. With my breasts still exposed, I would lie down on my bed, rub my vibrator across my nipples, and then lower it to my pussy while I imagined elaborate fantasies of people admiring my breasts.

Many of the fantasies were inspired by real events in which people had lusted after my tits. My friend Jackie, for example, really did run her hand over my exposed cleavage as she waited our table at the bar. Jackie is a dedicated lesbian but looks like a sorority girl. She wears tight black pants or little tiny skirts, both of which show off her lean legs and pert arse. She probably has nice tits but generally wears rather high-cut T-shirts that detract attention from them – working at the bar, legs increase your tips but cleavage attracts stalkers. I also generally kept my breasts well-covered. On this particular night, however, I wore my tight T-shirt over a long, shimmering burgundy slip that I had bought at a thrift store and wore as a dress. "What a pretty skirt," she told me. I lifted my shirt to show her the top of the slip. The neckline was shaped like a butterfly, its wings cupping my breasts so tightly that I didn't need to wear a bra. It was quite low cut, however, a fact that was not lost on Jackie. Before this, she had never exhibited any signs of attraction towards me, which is not surprising considering she generally dates boyish, muscular women. But seeing my chest decorated with the slinky butterfly she gasped, reached out and ran her hand lightly across my cleavage. "You look so good," she murmured. "I've never seen you in anything like that." Embarrassed at this unexpected attention, I lowered the T-shirt back down. "I know you like butterflies," I told her awkwardly. But she was undaunted, and attempted to show off my chest to the rest of our friends. "Have you guys seen Olivia in this dress?" she asked them. "She should wear stuff like this all the time." She badgered me until I lifted it to show the table, after which she provided a free drink.

Since Jackie's girlfriend was sitting at the next table, I'm pretty sure she wasn't actually trying to sleep with me. But as I thought about this event later that night, I became increasingly turned on remembering her appreciation of my tits. In my imagination, after she runs her hand across them, she leaves her hand holding my breast, exploring it gently with her thumb. It reaches down under the edge of the slip and teases my nipple until it grows hard and pokes out indecently through the cloth. Then, realizing the inappropriateness of the setting, she leads me by the hand to the back room. There she wraps her arms around me and begins to make out with me, rubbing her hands across my tits and leaning down to suck on them. She doesn't lower the top of my slip but pulls my breasts out of it so that the butterfly wings lie crushed just below my nipples. As she stands with her pretty face pressed firmly into my breast, her girlfriend enters the room. I think she'll be angry, and I start to step back from Jackie. But the girlfriend has evidently been invited, because she walks right over, grabs me from behind, and kisses the back of my neck. She leans over my shoulder toward Jackie, and soon the two of them are kissing passionately just next to my ear. I feel the girlfriend's hands slide over my breast and then lift it to Jackie's waiting lips. The girlfriend caresses my tits as Jackie sucks on them – even in a fantasy, this is too heavenly for me to believe.

Soon they have me sitting on the table, underwear off, Jackie's head buried in my pussy while the girlfriend kisses my face and tits. As in all my fantasies, the admiration of my breasts is ongoing: "Oh, your tits are so hot," the girlfriend murmurs. Jackie raises her lips from my clit long enough to say, "I told you they were hot." Looking me straight in the eye, she adds sweetly, "I've been telling her for weeks how you have the nicest tits I've ever seen." If I make it past this point, I add another scene: Jackie's girlfriend undoes her pants to release a strap-on dildo. She sits me on her lap facing away from her, and I can feel my clit under her fingers jutting forward like it does when my pussy is totally full and turned on. Jackie spends some of the time sucking my clit, but then cannot resist my tits. She climbs up onto the table so that she is straddling me and her girlfriend. Then she lifts her shirt, exposing her own small, round breasts. Shaking slightly from excitement, she rubs her small firm nipples against my larger, softer ones, grinding her body against mine until – well, if I haven't come by this point I always do right then, both in the fantasy and in reality.

Another of my favourite fantasies never happened at all, in any form. I'm not really sure what made me think of it, other than perhaps it derived naturally from my sessions staring at my tits in the bathroom mirror. In the fantasy, I am in my pajamas brushing my teeth at the sink. My breasts are particularly large, larger than in real life, so that as I brush my teeth they obstruct my arm motion a bit. They also completely fill out the thin, worn top of my pajamas, bulging against the soft cloth. I haven't closed the bathroom door, and a male roommate enters the bathroom to grab something or other. He is vaguely good-looking and entirely made-up; he doesn't even resemble anyone I know. He, too, is in old, worn pajamas. As I continue to brush my teeth, he makes some small talk, then falls silent for a moment. I wonder why he isn't leaving the bathroom already. Looking over at him, I see his hand is at his crotch. A giant erection fills the front of his pants.

"Olivia," he asks, "would you mind if I beat off?" But he does not wait for a response; he has already pulled out his cock and is stroking it slowly.

"Why can't you do that in your room?" I ask him.

"No, no, you're the one who made me hard," he responds. "I want to look at your tits. You don't have to do anything. They just look so nice as you brush your teeth."

Grudgingly I comply, resuming brushing my teeth and trying to ignore him. In the fantasy I am slightly put off, but in real life I am extremely turned on imagining this man so aroused by my breasts. As he gets more excited, he begs me to lift my shirt, and I agree. By the end, he is fucking me over the edge of the sink. I can see his face contort in the mirror as he comes. My cleavage swells seductively as I lean forward like a teenage singer in a publicity photo.

Perhaps my dearest breast fantasy, though, is the one that really happened to me, from beginning to end. I still think about it frequently, and it brings me to orgasm every time. It was a one night stand – but with a man I'd known for some time, a friend of a friend whose expression of cocky intelligence I'd admired for quite a while. One late, drunken night, he ended up in my apartment. Of course there was a lot of kissing and groping, but in the fantasy I skip that part; in fact, I skip to after each of our first orgasms that night. I begin the fantasy as we laid in bed, sweaty and sticky and naked, tangled in the bed sheets and our discarded clothing. I sat up suddenly, planning on getting a drink of water. But before I could ask him if he'd like some, he lifted his hand to trace the outline of my breast. "I don't know if this is bad to say," he began. I didn't respond, mesmerized by the sight of my round, firm breast filling his outstretched hand. "You have really nice tits," he finished. His other hand slid across my other breast, and I felt too turned on to speak. "I guess you're offended," he told me as his hands continued to move across my nipples, into my cleavage, out along my upper ribs, "but I just really wanted you to know."

Shaking myself out of my daze, I responded, "No, no, you

didn't offend me at all." After a moment I remembered my manners and responded to the compliment: "Thank you."

With this sign of permission, he rose to devour my breasts and collarbones ferociously. He wrapped his arm tightly around me tightly with one arm and began to make out with my left tit – it pressed softly against his cheeks and chin as he sucked. I could see the outline of his cock as it lifted the sheets still stretched across his lap. I leaned in close to his ear and asked, "Do you want to fuck them?" Perhaps this was an unusual offer, because he seemed pleasantly surprised, even slightly incredulous. "Really?" he asked. I lowered myself onto the bed and pulled him up over me so that his cock aligned with my cleavage, pointing enticingly toward my mouth. As I pressed my breasts upward and he filled the space between them, I took the nice, firm, mushroomy tip of his cock into my mouth. He moaned more and more loudly, seeming to enjoy this more than the intercourse we had just finished. As I arched my back and circled my tongue, he began to talk dirty. "Can I come on your tits?" he asked, and when I nodded he continued. "I want to come on your tits," he repeated breathlessly, "Oh, I'm going to come on your tits!" His balls grew hard against my hand and I knew his prediction was about to come true, so I released his cock from my mouth and raised my upper body. He kneeled over me and took himself into his hand, vigorously stroking until he began to shoot long spurts of semen all over my breasts. I repeat that image over and over – the come erupting from the pretty pink head of his penis, hitting my jutting breasts, sliding down their curved slopes in creamy white streams. As we lay back down together, in a lazy, fatigued motion, he rubbed his hand over my slippery breast. "I can't believe this feels so good," he murmured drowsily. "What?" I asked. His response was mumbled, and I'm not sure whether he said, "Coming on tits," or "Come on tits." I thought about asking him to repeat himself, but then realized that either way, I agreed whole-heartedly.

Poetic Licentiousness

Rachael (Toronto, Canada)

I'm in my mid-thirties and single, with a successful career in film and media. I love my job, but it demands long hours and leaves little time for serious relationships. I have had a strong sex-drive since my early teens and a very active tendency for using sexual fantasy while I masturbate. When I was twelve, I discovered my older brother's hidden stash of porno magazines. The photos were instructive for showing me where things were "down there", but it was the erotica and fantasy letters that really caught my imagination. Through them, I learned how to masturbate. I started off with inquisitive fingers, but eventually graduated to penetration with the handle of a hairbrush, and then – most thrilling of all – I experimented with the electric toothbrush against my clit, and have been hooked on fantasy and self-pleasure ever since. Over the years, I have grown to appreciate just how uncommon this is for a girl. Imagine my horror, having figured out how to come at the tender age of twelve, to find that a lot of women don't orgasm regularly – and some not at all! I feel very lucky to have learned to take control over my own pleasure when I was so young.

Since my job takes up so much time, sexual fantasy has been a real sanity-saver over the years. I don't like sleeping around, but at this critical point in my career I also don't have much time to develop the kind of relationships with lovers that I want. I know myself more intimately than any partner could ever hope to, and can give myself stellar orgasms, either with busy fingers or by using one (or more) of the many sex toys I've acquired. My imagination has always been my greatest tool when getting myself off. I easily have a hundred different scenarios I use to jack off with, but the following is an old favourite of mine.

During my undergrad years in Ottawa, I had a professor I absolutely adored. He wasn't particularly handsome or flashy; in fact, he was fairly short with a careless style of dress. But he had these amazing blue bedroom eyes, and a seductive voice that often had me secretly wet during class. I lusted after him throughout my degree, but he was married – and my instructor – and nearly twice my age . . . in other words, very taboo. But that made him all the more fun to dream about.

In my fantasy, I am going to his poetry tutorial. It is the final class of the year before exams, and I want to leave a lasting impression. Though I have never been so brave or foolish as to declare my feelings, I'd sensed a mutual attraction from the outset of my first year, and thought that, at the very least, I could look my best for him on our last day together. That morning, I wear a flattering dress – casually sexy with a full skirt and a low neckline which shows off my large breasts.

My pulse is racing by the time I reach his office at the top of the staircase. His secretary calls me over to her desk just outside his inner door.

"Oh, Rachael . . . Professor MacLeod has been called away. He left a note asking if you would lead the tutorial."

She hands me a file of notes and, as I read over the familiar scrawl for my instructions, I can almost hear his sultry voice in my head:

Hi Rachael –

Sorry I won't be there today, but I have some urgent business to take care of that I've been putting off for too long, and it simply can't wait. I've cued up a tape recording of the final poetry assignment. Please play it for the class, and then lead a discussion. I'm sure it will be fine – you're a star.

Good luck with your exams.

I walk into the tutorial room, glad I'm the first one there so I can take a moment to get over the pang of disappointment I feel at not seeing him. He has a huge old desk, with a long table pushed up flush against it creating a "T" shape. I go around and sit in his leather desk chair, catching a faint whiff of his cologne. Maybe I can pretend to need help with my final paper and book a private session, just to be alone with him . . . but would I ever have the nerve to act on my feelings? The thought makes my face flush red.

The others drift in and take their seats around the table, including my ex-boyfriend Brad who raises an eyebrow at me when he sees where I'm sitting. His disdainful reaction when I stupidly confided my secret crush on Professor MacLeod was the main reason I'd broken up with him. I couldn't bear his teasing. Even in bed, he wouldn't leave the subject alone. Slipping into me, he'd whisper things like, "Are you thinking about MacLeod right now? Wishing this was his cock fucking you?" The sex had been fantastic with Brad – he had a long cock and amazing stamina, but the mean-spirited way he made fun of my feelings was too much, and I'd ended it before the start of the spring term.

"Hi, guys. Professor MacLeod is away and he left a note for me to lead the class."

No one seems surprised. I am an A student, and I had taken over once before when he was ill. Brad smirks at me and I ignore him.

I pull the chair closer to the desk so I can reach the tape recorder and feel my leg brush up against something warm. I peer underneath to see Professor MacLeod grinning up at me and I nearly jump out of my seat. His hand flies out to grab my knee, steadying me, and he winks and raises a finger to his lips to tell me not to give him away. At first, I figure it is some kind of weird last day joke, so I go along with it.

But his real motive is soon made crystal clear.

I feel his hands gliding up my legs to slowly push my dress up until it is around my waist. His fingers trace along the waistband of my panties and begin to tug at them. I don't dare move and clear my throat.

"Let's get started. Brad, could you get the door? We're going to listen to Eliot's *The Four Quartets*, then have a general discussion."

I lean forward to press the play button, raising my ass off of the chair enough to allow Professor M. to pull my panties down. I lift my feet as I sit back, and he slides them completely off. He nudges my legs open.

I can feel my juices beginning to seep onto the leather chair as he starts kissing his way up between my inner thighs. I'm so excited I could explode. The kissing stops. His face is right in my crotch now. I can sense his hot breath on my damp skin, but he just hovers there – a maddening inch or two shy of my cunt. I can feel myself swelling and opening to him, juices pouring out of me in a cascade. *Oh, God . . .*

I look casually around the room. Everyone is listening intently to the reading and following along in their books, making notations in the margins with pencils. With one hand, I hold my paperback text up to hide the lust on my face, and sneak the other hand under the desk to grab my professor by the back of his head and press him urgently into my desperate cunt. It is all I can do not to scream as I feel that tongue start to lap up the seeming gallons of liquid running out of me. He swirls his mouth around my opening, sucking up the juice. Out of the corner of my eye I see Brad's head turn towards me. Did he hear the slurping sound? I reach out and turn up the volume on the tape recorder. I slump back slightly lower in the chair, my legs open as far as they'll go under the confines of the desk.

I can smell myself now, hot and musky. Can anyone else? I risk another peek at Brad. He's looking at me with a strange expression, but drops his eyes back to his book. I don't care any more. It feels too amazing. I want to throw my head back and scream my lover's name – not Professor M., but his first name, John – order him to lick me. I want to pinch my nipples, grab his head with both hands and guide his wonderful mouth to my bursting clit . . . but all I can do is sit back and act calm with my dream lover lapping at my cunt in front of my oblivious classmates.

The tape is nearly over, and yet he is still just teasing me, keeping me on the edge for the entire agonizing length of the reading. He licks all around, but has not touched my clit even in passing. The bastard isn't going to let me come before I have to lead the discussion!

The final line of the poetry dies away. There's a moment of silence as the class absorbs the last image – and finally he begins slowly, lightly tonguing my clit. I give a stifled moan that quickly becomes a cough, and ask in a husky voice:

"Any observations?"

Luckily, the two other class keeners immediately dive into a lively banter on Eliot's use of melopoeia. I don't even hear what they're saying. Professor M.'s tongue is increasing its pressure, dancing a wild rhythm on my clit. I grab the arms of the chair until my knuckles turn white. His finger is at my entrance, poised to plunge in. I tense my legs and in he thrusts. He cocks his finger around until he is hitting against my swollen inner pleasure point and begins to pound and vibrate against it with the same tempo as his darting tongue.

I feel a tingling heat begin in my clenched toes soaring up and down through my body like someone has poured a shower of hot water over me. I bite the insides of my cheeks hard enough to taste blood as the throbbing gives way to crashing spasms. My cunt clamps around his gifted finger and mouth again and again until the pulses subside. I want to weep from joy and sweet relief.

I realize I've closed my eyes, suddenly aware that the discussion has trailed off. I open my eyes to see that people are starting to pack away their books into knapsacks. Class is over. I recover slightly.

"Okay. Well, I hope you all found that to be as illuminating as I did. See you at the exam next week." I can't help but smile. "It's been a true pleasure."

(Usually by this point in the fantasizing, I'm coming all over the place. But sometimes I need more to get me there, or else I want to put off the big moment so that when it hits, the orgasm is truly mind-blowing. My variation on the longer version – the director's cut, you might call it – goes like this:)

Brad hasn't moved. He's staring at me. I wink and pretend to take some notes as Professor M. lovingly cleans me off with his clever tongue. I can't wait until Brad leaves so I can lock the door and thank John in kind. Finally, Brad gets up and goes to the door. But he doesn't leave. He closes and locks it.

At the sound of the door closing, John pushes my chair back and gets up from under his desk. He straightens up and looks at Brad with mild surprise. I still can't move. The orgasm was shattering and I'm luxuriating in the afterglow. I wait to see what will happen.

Brad looks at me like I'm a hateful stranger.

"How long has this been going on, Rachael? Is this the real reason why you broke it off with me?"

I can't answer, but John does.

"Don't be so jealous, Brad. You had your turn. And don't blame Rachael. I just couldn't bear the idea of her graduating and moving on – not without enjoying a taste of her obvious charms."

Meantime, he's pulling me to my feet and taking my dress off. I'm left standing in front of two fully dressed men in nothing more than a bra.

"And you, Rachael. I think you enjoyed that, didn't you?"

I pull him in close to show him just how much, kissing all over his wet face and diving my tongue into his mouth to suck up the flavour of my own juices.

John's hands are fumbling with the fastening on my bra. He frees my breasts and cups them in his hands, lowering his head to flick his tongue over the nipples. I press his head against me as he sucks each nipple, nibbling them into hard peaks. I sigh and glare over his shoulder at Brad. Why is he still here? I want him to go so I can finally get down to fucking this incredible man.

"You can leave any time now, Brad. Show's over."

"Oh, I don't think so."

My eyes widen as he starts to get undressed.

"If you make me leave now, I'll go straight to the Dean's office."

Both John and I freeze and stare at him. He seems serious. He's also as hard as I've ever seen him. I look at John. He shrugs and steps away from me.

Brad comes around the desk and grabs my arm. I resist, but he pulls me over to the couch along the far wall. He pushes me so that I'm bent over with my ass arched up at him. I crane my neck around to appeal to John. He's leaning against his desk with his arms crossed, watching.

"The boy has a point, Rachael. If you don't do as he asks, we're both in a big mess."

"John! You can't mean –"

"Sssh, Rachael. I'll be right here. Brad, do I have your word that nothing that goes on here today leaves this room?"

"Deal," says Brad as he paws at my ass. I hear John heave a sigh.

"Then I'm afraid we have no choice but to give in. You win, Brad. Fuck her."

Brad grabs my hips and rams his cock into me in one huge thrust that lifts my feet off the floor. I cry out and bite into my own arm to stifle my groans as he starts to pound in and out of me. His cock is long and hits just the right spot deep inside of my cunt. I hate him in this moment, but at the same time being fucked in front of John is wildly exciting. I've never felt so out of control. I have had no say in the matter of what would be done to my body since I entered the classroom earlier, and now I completely abandon myself to the wishes of both men. Brad is panting hard as he swirls and thrusts deeper and harder.

"God, Rachael – you've never been so wet."

"No one has ever . . . oh! . . . done that to me before – not that way." (Of course, I mean John and his licking my cunt under the desk, but I don't know or care what Brad thinks.)

John has come over to join me. He sits on the couch, still dressed, watching me closely. He gently brushes my hair away from my face, locking his bedroom eyes with mine as I jerk with the motion of being fucked.

"You look beautiful, Rachael. You like being fucked, don't you?"

He starts to toy with my breasts, pinching at the nipples. I moan.

"Answer me, young lady. Tell me how you feel."

"I . . . oh! . . . love being fucked in front of you. I love that you are watching me –"

"Are you going to come soon?"

"I want to come with *you* inside me! Hurry up, Brad . . . I can't hold back for much longer."

"Oh, no! *I'll* make you come, you bitch!"

Brad starts to fuck me even harder. I can't speak now – just moan, holding back with every muscle, saving myself for John. He stands up and gets undressed. Unhurried and elegant in his movements, he goes to stand behind Brad.

"You heard the girl. Finish up now. I think you've made your point."

I clamp down and milk Brad's cock with my muscles, pushing back hard against him with every thrust. He could never resist that, and he shudders and spurts into me, gripping my hips hard enough to leave imprints of his fingers in my flesh. I feel him slide out and John gets into position in his place. He is much more sensual, stroking my back and the sides of my breasts like a virtuoso. My cunt is distended, oozing liquid, clutching at air . . . aching for his cock. I can feel the head of it straining at my entrance, slipping around in all of that hot juice.

But first, he makes me beg.

"Tell me what you want, Rachael."

I practically scream: "For God's sake, fuck me John! I need you to make me come!"

With a groan, he complies and eases his cock up into me inch by inch. I gasp in joy: this is what I've dreamed of for the past four years, and it's really happening. He is Brad's match in length and hardness, but has infinitely more finesse. I wriggle against him, primed and ready.

He hits the wall inside and stops, holding himself for what seems an eternity before sliding back out so that only the very tip of him is still inside, then – just a little faster and harder – he dives back in. I am moaning continuously now. Brad is panting, watching, hating us both – but he has given away any power he had over us by fucking me. John is igniting me in ways he could never hope to, and I am swooning in ecstasy.

"Ah, yesss . . . fuck me, John. Show him how to make me come."

He murmurs and strokes me . . . my entire body is ablaze with want and the impending fulfillment of all of my forbidden dreams. I actually fight to hold back, to make it last, but now John is losing control . . . pounding away with double the power of Brad's fucking. He is starting to gasp my name over and over and I know he is close, so I give in. I buck back against him, shouting and moaning, as the waves explode through me with incredible force. (I have rarely achieved an orgasm through intercourse in real life, but the memorable times that I did have been like that – being rammed from behind or with me riding on top, taking charge.)

My climax sets John's off, and he squeezes me close to him as his cock gives a leap and spurts into me. I can feel every individual gush. We collapse onto the couch and curl up together in a naked, sodden heap.

I peer up through half-closed eyes to see Brad doing up his jeans. He gives me a look that is both sad and a little bit triumphant. I smile at him. Nothing has happened that I can't live with. It felt too good. As the door quietly opens and closes, I turn to my greatest fantasy figure and lazily give into a long sweet session of melting kisses.

I have never felt such a strong desire to fuck anyone before or since my professor. Pity it couldn't happen in real life, but even now, he is such fun to fantasize about. I haven't seen him for over a decade, but who knows? Maybe by chance he'll pick up this book and read over my thoughts and recognize himself in it. The idea turns me on more than I can say.

These wild dreams are harmless, sexy fun – but I have found to my dismay over the years that men seem threatened by my voracious fantasy life. Do they honestly think I would really want to be blackmailed into fucking an ex-lover while my professor eggs him on, waiting his turn? Very few men seem to understand that the edgier a fantasy is, the hotter it gets me. This one is relatively tame compared to some, and I have all but given up telling them about any of my lusty scenarios. I have made a couple of male friends online with whom I exchange fantasies via e-mail. They live in other countries, so the temptation to meet is not an issue. The distance gives us the safety to share these kinds of thoughts with each other – at times, they are my sex life when I am between lovers and, except for the lack of physical contact, they are in many ways the best lovers I've ever had. Both of these men are very creative and work in artistic fields where story-telling is important, and they get off on trying to outdo themselves in telling me wilder and wilder scenarios. They love it when I tell them how excited they get me, and how wonderful my orgasm is when I read their letters. Fantasy is wonderful, alone or shared – if one is lucky enough to have a partner who can handle it. There is no point in being jealous of dreams and shadows, and they can awaken a depth of passion that surprises and delights, if one gives in to their power.

Cuckold Heaven

Margot (Nottingham, UK)

I do love my husband. I want to make that clear from the start, because it may not sound like it at times in this fantasy. I don't know how much of this I could do in real life, even if I were to get the opportunity, but fantasizing about it makes me more excited than anything I've ever known.

He's a good man, my husband. That's the only way you can really describe him: good. He's considerate and careful. He runs after me in the house, doing all the washing-up, sharing the laundry and ironing, doing chores without being told. He always asks if we can make love, and if I agree his big spaniel eyes of gratitude make me want to puke.

And that's the trouble. He's just too nice. It's boring. I'm bored.

I have lots of fantasies which I run through when he's at work and our daughter's at school, most of which revolve around not being nice. Sometimes it's Brian who loses his temper and finally lashes out. I have him rip my clothes off and throw himself upon me, spearing his cock inside me before I can protest and fucking me hard. But mostly those fantasies don't work: the trouble is, I just can't imagine Brian really doing that, and I dissolve into a fit of giggles.

And so in the fantasy it becomes someone else. I prefer it to be someone I know – it makes it kinkier somehow. I don't need to fancy them in real life, and in fact it's better if I don't. There's Dave, for example, a regular in the bar where I do evening work. He's a bit of a shag monster, going from woman to woman in a constant cycle, and I never understand how he does it because he doesn't turn me on at all, but the very fact he doesn't makes him all the more powerful as a fantasy figure. He traps me in the loos and forces himself on me, his mouth all over my face and his hands gripping my tits. He unzips his cock and makes me touch it, then pulls up my skirt and twists my panties aside and before I know what's happening he starts to fuck me.

It's a good enough fantasy, but in the end it leaves me kind of cold. I feel that it's Brian's relentless niceness which forces me to fantasize the way I do: I like to dream about roughness as an antidote to his gentle approach. But those Dave fantasies go to the other extreme – they simply replace gentleness with force, and there's no scope for sharing the moment. That's what I crave – a fantasy in which nasty things happen, but where everyone enjoys it.

So my fantasies turned to Brian dressing me up as a school-girl and spanking me, or chaining me to the bed – games where I was a willing participant – but they didn't work either: I still couldn't imagine Brian doing it. The very fact that in reality I would never dare broach such a subject with him rather proved my point. And that's how my favourite fantasy came about.

If he wouldn't do it to me, I'd do it to him.

Once the idea of dominating Brian took hold it swept all other fantasies away. I loved the idea, the notion that I could bully and cajole him into doing things he would never choose to do in real life. But always, in my fantasies, it was important that however much he protested, he really did enjoy what was happening. As I said, I do love him.

They start out gently enough, these fantasies. I imagine a situation where he has annoyed me for some reason – sprayed all over the bathroom, for example (which is something he never does, he always sits down to pee). In the fantasy I scold him terribly and he apologises, but I refuse to accept it because I am so angry. "Stand in the corner," I tell him, more in exasperation than with any genuine intent, but to my amaze-ment he obeys. I leave him to see what he does next, but fifteen minutes later he is still there, facing the wall. I'm astonished, but slightly intrigued. If he will do that, what else will he do?

At first none of my demands are sexual – they are purely to test his obedience – but he complies with everything I ask. I tell him to scrub the kitchen floor and he does it. I tell him to wear my pink (well, peach – it's the nearest I have to pink) apron and he does. I tell him to eat his tea outside, in the rain, and he trots into the garden with his plate. Whatever I ask, he always obeys. So far this is probably completely true to life: if I was to ask Brian those things I'm sure he would look quizzical and a bit hurt, but would do them nonetheless.

But now my fantasies begin to adopt sexual overtones. Seeing him scamper after my every command makes me horny and I get the sudden urge to use him. "Brian," I yell, "come here." I'm lying on our bed, naked, and he blanches as he enters and sees me. "Lick me," I tell him. He tries to say something but I tell him to shut up and get on with it. The tartness of my reply shocks him and he immediately folds himself between my legs and sets his tongue to work. He isn't very good. In reality, he has only done this to me three times, and I haven't had the heart to tell him he was doing it wrong, but in my fantasy I have no such compunction. I make him concentrate on my clitoris and explain how he should roll his tongue round and round its hood, sucking gently and occasionally drawing his tongue directly over the clitoris itself, slowly and softly. As I approach a climax I order him to speed up and to suck harder. "Harder, harder," I instruct him, gripping him between my thighs and pressing his head into me.

My fantasy climax is usually accompanied by one in real life, this thought alone enough to bring me off. But then Brian would come home from work, Mr Nice Guy again, and my frustrations with him would grew ever stronger. Those frustrations have been instrumental in the development of my fantasies.

In them, I progress to sitting on him. I force him to lie on the bed and straddle him, pressing hard against his face, making him push his tongue inside me. I force him to stare into my eyes as he does, so that he can see who is making him do these things. His face begins to go red as he runs out of breath and I shift slightly to allow him some air before settling on him once more. Riding back and forward – sliding his nose against my lips and feeling his tongue probe inside me – quickly brings me to the point of climax and I push down so that he can suck my clitoris to finish me off.

Sometimes I vary the action and have him lick my arse. That's delightful and the idea of it always makes me come in real life. I flatten myself against him and spread my cheeks so that his tongue is pressed hard against my hole. I order him to push inside me and feel his tongue, wet but suprisingly cold, slither into my back passage. I don't need to dream about that for long before fireworks start to explode in my head and my stomach starts to churn with lust.

Everything I've fantasized about so far I would, given the chance, enact in real life. I've tried to drop subtle hints to see if he is interested, but so far he has not risen to it and I don't want to try too hard and offend him. But it adds to my frustration, and in my frustration my fantasies get kinkier. I don't believe I would ever do any of the following in real life, but dreaming about it certainly gets me going.

In my fantasy (and in real life too, to be honest) I get irritated by his passivity. He never fights back, he never shows any dismay at what I force him to do. So I decide that I need to test how far he can be pushed before he starts to fight back. That's when I resolve to take a lover. I do it openly, telling him in advance that I am going to look for someone. His eyes go all hurt, but he doesn't shout or forbid it, or even ask me not to: because I have said it, he accepts it. This annoys me and I push him a little harder: I ask him to recommend someone.

"You must have some nice friends," I say, "well-hung guys, good looking. Who could I chat up? I want to fuck one of your friends, Brian. Who should it be?"

Finally, I find his breaking point. He refuses, crying and pleading with me. But not for long. I press my hand against his crotch and slide my thigh across him, snuggling close.

"Come on," I say, using my most seductive voice. "It'll be exciting. I'll tell you all about it afterwards." I slip my hand inside his trousers and feel his cock. It is fully erect. "And then after that, maybe *we* could have some fun together." A quick squeeze, a lingering snog and a promise of a good time later and he agrees. He gives me a name and sets up a meeting.

The good thing about fantasies is that you don't have to

bother with boring detail. I get fixed up with Gary (in reality a workmate of Brian's and very good looking) and we go out for dinner. When I'm masturbating, I don't usually linger on this bit – it isn't an important part, really – but occasionally I build the scene. I have Gary fuck me in his flat after our first date, taking me from behind and mounting me like a dog, fucking me hard and rough. He calls me a bitch and a whore and a fucking cheat and I swear back, yelling at him to fuck me, fill my cunt with his hot prick. I like to make it as rough as possible, no romance or sensitivity at all. I make him scratch and bruise me, so that I have trophies to show Brian later.

When we finish fucking I hurry home as quickly as possible. Brian is waiting up, as I have ordered him to. I tell him about my evening, describing everything that happened in intimate detail. I tell him the length of Gary's cock, how it was much wider than his and stretched and filled me so well. I explain how he threw me on the bed and fucked me from behind, how he was hard and rough and made me feel used. I begin to strip and show him my bruises and scratches.

"That one," I say as I point to a livid graze across my thigh, "that was when he came inside me. I could feel it pulsing from his cock into me. It was like an explosion. You never come that hard, Brian, you just kind of squirt it out a bit." He nods morosely as he inspects my graze. "Can you smell him?" I ask. "Can you smell his body on me?" I force his face against me, pressing his nose to my skin. "Can you?" He nods and tells me he can.

"There's more," I crow. "I've probably lost most of it, but there's still some of his come inside me." Carefully, I peel off my panties. "Want to see?" He tells me he doesn't, but I ignore him. "Lie down," I order. Despite his protests he complies and I straddle him once more. "There," I tell him. "My cunt's still all wet and messy and dirty from his spunk. Isn't it?" I look down and it is. I can smell it myself, the smell of sex. "I'm all dirty, aren't I?" He nods. "So clean me up, husband, clean all my lover's spunk out of me." I press myself against his mouth and know that he is licking a curious concoction – my stale juices from earlier, the remains of Gary's sperm and the fresh secretions of my current excitement. I ride his face for half an hour, sometimes smothering him for a minute at a time, revelling in the act I have forced upon my husband.

"And just think," I tell him afterwards, "every time I fuck Gary you're going to have to clean it up like that."

Like I say, I don't think I could do these things in real life – not unless Brian said he wanted me to, and since he doesn't talk about sex that's unlikely. I'm not even sure I'd enjoy it in reality: I'm not big on hurting people's feelings. But the fantasy is wonderful. I strip myself completely naked, open the windows wide so that I can feel the afternoon breeze on my skin and stretch myself out on the bed. Sometimes I use a vibrator, but mostly I just use my fingers – they're more delicate, more sensitive, and I've got them well trained over the years. Sometimes when I'm fantasizing about sitting on Brian's face I'll get up on my knees and adopt that position, imagining him below me, looking down on where his reddened face would be, but mostly I lie back and think of cuckoldry.

It's a wonderful word, cuckold, so derogatory. In my fantasies I relish using it on Brian. "How's my little cuckold tonight?" I enquire after a night out with Gary. "Does the cuckold want to swallow up our juices now?" I imagine Brian's crestfallen face, silently nodding, readying himself, sliding into position below me.

Recently I have developed the fantasy a bit further. Brian and I have been going through a rough patch, and we haven't had sex for a couple of months. Even now, though, he is still so solicitous and caring, and it drives me mad. It makes me want to punish him more in my fantasies, and that's exactly what I do.

I decide that it isn't enough for me to have an affair with his friend: I have to let Brian watch it. In real life, I'm not sure there would be many "Garys" who would agree to this, but in my fantasy he is eager and joins me in goading Brian. The three of us sit on the settee, Gary's arm around me, his hand lodged on my tit. He looks directly at Brian.

"I'm gonna shag your missus in a while, Brian. That's okay, isn't it?" Brian makes no reply, but watches Gary's snaking hand over my breast. "I love your wife's tits, Brian. Don't you? When did you last see them? Probably weeks ago, I should think. Tell you what, mate, why don't you get them out for us?"

Brian looks confused and I laugh, shaking my chest provocatively.

"Come on, Brian," says Gary. "Get on with it, mate, I want a feel."

Brian leans over and slowly begins to unbutton my blouse, undressing his wife for the benefit of his friend. He peels the blouse apart to reveal my white, lacy bra, carefully chosen because it is front-fastening. Gary indicates with a nod and Brian unclasps me, releasing my breasts to open view. Gary grips my right nipple and squeezes, while I croon in delight and rest my head on the settee back, watching Brian as he watches Gary. He swallows hard as Gary lowers his head and takes my breast in his mouth, but says nothing. Gary's left hand is wandering over my body, across my naked stomach, down my thighs and back up to my crotch, where he rests his palm, fingers pressing into me. At length he raises his mouth a fraction from my breast.

"Be a good chap, Brian, take her jeans off for me, I'm a bit busy here."

Brian sinks to the floor and wrestles with my button and zip. I raise my bum from the settee and he begins to drag my jeans down over my hips to my knees. Immediately, Gary places his hand on my panties, fingers rummaging against them, while Brian completes the removal of my jeans. He sits back on his heels and watches, as Gary's fingers seek out my lips through the cotton panties and slide up and down, gathering their moisture against the fabric, creating a damp patch to reveal my excitement. I groan.

Gary gestures once more. "Take her panties off, mate. Let me at her snatch." Brian reaches forward and slides them from me, revealing my completely shaved pussy. I open my legs wide. "When did you last see that, Brian?" Gary goads. Brian doesn't answer.

"He never gets to see it any more. He has to lick it, every time I come home with your spunk inside me, but I make him do it in the dark. He's not allowed to see anything. I'm buying him a blindfold tomorrow."

"We want him to see this, though."

"Too right. Every last piece of action." Gary is fingering my pussy, his middle finger sliding between my lips and his index finger circling my clitoris. Brian, sitting beneath me, watches every move.

"Brian, I'm getting a bit uncomfortable here. Got a hard-on which is threatening to poke a hole in my trousers. Take them off for me." At first, Brian looks like he will refuse, but not for long. He reaches towards his friend and undoes his jeans, yanking them down and revealing blue boxer shorts with a large, sex-laden shape hidden beneath them. "The shorts too, mate." Brian eases them down and Gary's fine, chunky erection bounces into view. Immediately, I grip my hand around it and begin to wank him, feeling it grow even harder in my hand. All the time my eyes are on Brian, while his waver between my face and my hand, following the action, observing my reaction. It is delicious.

I want Gary's cock in me. I want to be fucked while my husband watches. I pull Gary on top of me and settle him into position, gripping his cock and sliding its silky, purple head against my lips, pushing forward as I press him towards me, and I sigh as I feel him entering me. I look over his shoulder at Brian, who is watching, dumbstruck.

"Fuck me," I cry. "Fuck me. Show me how it's done." Show Brian how it's done, more like. Gary begins to thrust into me, hard, long and fast. I always imagine this to be rough, almost to the point of being painful: again, I'm not interested in romance, just sex, pure animal sex. He pounds into me, his face pressed to my cheek, biting my neck, fingers scratching at my shoulders and back. He comes quickly, grunting loudly as his spunk spurts deep inside me and I squeal with delight as I watch a pained expression pass over Brian's face. Gary slides off me, exhausted and I clasp my knees together, panting with exertion.

"Guess what, Brian?" I whisper.

"What?"

"It's feeding time, baby." His eyes widen, silently pleading, but I smile and roll off the settee. "Lie down, cuckold," I say. Without a word, he does as he is told and I stretch myself over him. Already, Gary's sperm is flooding out of me, some of it landing on Brian's nose and in his eye. I settle myself above him and part my lips, watching in delight as a string of silver sperm slides from me into my husband's waiting mouth. He swallows and opens again to receive another drop. When most of it has fallen into his mouth I press myself against him. "Lick," I tell him. "Lick out every last drop."

This never fails to bring me to a climax. The thought of my helpless husband hoovering up another man's sperm from his wife's pussy leaves me trembling with lust. Yesterday, I had the most shattering climax of my life as this fantasy came to a conclusion. And as soon as I've finished writing this I shall be going upstairs to strip off and do it again.

What's next for my fantasy cuckold? I'm not sure yet. The best ideas come to me in the middle of masturbation so I shall probably find out very soon. I know my treatment of Brian is getting nastier all the time, and yet in real life I still love him dearly. I don't think I could ever do this to him, but perhaps it would be best if I never have the opportunity to find out.

Meanwhile, I will continue to use my fantasies to spice up what is already becoming a drab, middle-class housewife and mother's existence. Thank you for letting me share this with you. Writing this story has been a terrific turn-on.

Puppet

Lili (San Diego, USA)

When he is gone from me, I miss him. When he is gone from me, I await his return. But I also indulge myself in thoughts of him and in these thoughts, we are naked and he is hard, aroused at the sight of me, aroused by the knowledge that he can take me and use me however he wants to. Always, I crave that, to be the object of his desire and his appetite, and when he is away, I dwell in the memories of how he has used me.

I remember how he puts the leather cuffs on me, how he locks the collar in place. The feel of leather against my skin, its tight grip around my wrists, my ankles, my neck, captivates. But no more so than what he does to me once he runs a rope through their o-rings, connecting my appendages, making me a puppet to his whims.

He lays on his back and tells me to climb on top of him. "Get me inside you," he says simply enough.

I straddle him, spreading myself above him. I take his hard cock into my hand, aim it between my lips, and slowly rock him into me. Because he has ordered this at the start of our lovemaking, I've had no foreplay to prime me, but I know that our brand of foreplay isn't far off. I know it'll start when he's fully in me and when he draws that rope taut through the cuffs.

I grow wet as my cunt devours his cock. He feels huge inside me and it makes me want to ride him vigorously. But before I can, he stops me. He tells me to hold still.

That's when he draws the rope taut. It forces my hands behind my head, forces my feet close together – and forces me to straddle wider. It opens me and makes me vulnerable.

You would think he'd want to take me right then and fuck me viciously, but he doesn't. Instead, he reaches for my breast. When he cups it, his grasp is sure and confident. I can feel determination in his grip, a determination that turns to steel as he squeezes my breast. Hard.

I cry out at the pain and squirm. His hand slips to my nipple. He pinches and pulls, once, twice, thrice, before he stops. I continue to struggle against the pain, whimpering and shuddering.

He laughs at me, but what he declares is far more wicked than how he laughs. "That feels good on my cock."

And he pinches me again.

Yes it hurts, but paradox that it is, it also feels wonderful. I crave this intensity, this mix of pain and passion and prerogative. It is a dance of macabre pleasure – dark but thrilling, thrilling but luxurious. My cunt, so ready to respond, clenches at what he does, and it's all the validation I need to know I like the sexual trials and tribulations he designs for me. Impaled on him, forced to hold this position by the ropes, I am at his erotic mercy.

But this is what makes fucking wonderful. Lacking control, I never know what his next move will be, what his next twist of fate will be. It's like riding a roller coaster blindfolded.

When we first met, our S/M scenes were long and drawn-out – mini-series of sexual sharing and discovery. He would tie me to a post in his basement. A spreader bar would force my legs open while my head was forced upright by a length of string that ran mere inches from the leather head harness to the post. And while he played rough with my body – while he whipped my cunt and tits or simply teased and tormented them with the force of his own grip – a bit gag exaggerated every facial expression I made in response to his manipulations. Often, I'd be so aroused that when he pressed his finger to my clit, I'd pop like a firecracker.

But heat fades. It exhausts itself. And so did we to some extent as our relationship matured, as we worked through all our untried possibilities. Now, we take our time. We play often but in a brief, episodic fashion, and our appetites are more easily sated. Where we used to feast, we now snack.

And when he's away, I dream of the junk food that he feeds me. Thus, the memory of being his sexual puppet stays with me.

I remain lodged on his cock but the more he pinches and teases, the less I feel his cock inside me. My cunt has accommodated it thoroughly and short of riding it, I will not be afforded the pleasure of its presence.

But he can feel me, clenching and clutching, my cunt giving every clue to what his manipulations do to me. Soon, though, this game comes to an end and he tells me to climb off. As I do, I long for him to lay me down and take me, but I suspect he hasn't toyed with me enough. I know better than to think I'll get off that easily. Just as pain and pleasure are paradoxes, immediate desire and delayed gratification have their own strange mutuality and, as much as I ache to be fucked, I also long to see what he'll do next.

He blindfolds and gags me using lengths of denim fabric cut for those purposes, then leads me away from the bed. Unable to see, ropes hobbling me, every step feels like a stumble waiting to happen. It's a clumsy, uncomfortable procession and never have a few steps felt so uncertain.

This is why I miss him, why I fantasize in his absence: because I want to relive what he does to me. What he does for me.

He sits down, puts me over his lap, and re-routes the rope so it runs under the chair. It still runs from my wrists to my ankles and he pulls it tight the way an equestrian would "tighten up" on the reins. The effect is astounding. Draped down, my arms and legs drawn together enough to feel the stretch in my muscles, I feel played. Like a puppet.

Few puppets, I suspect, find themselves bottom up across their master's lap, but there I am, acutely away of the cock that presses into my belly, sticky from the juices of his earlier manipulation.

I know what is coming: a spanking. His hand will strike my fleshy bottom, sending shivers of pain into me, a sensation that will cull arousal from the depths of my pleasure centers. What I don't know – what I never know going into a spanking – is how strenuous it will be. Will he start out slow and sensual and acclimate me to his hand, then crescendo to an intense and thoroughly arousing climax? Or will he start off hard and swift without a care for finesse or subtlety, just so his cock can feel my body squirm and suffer? But that's where the thrill lies: in not knowing.

His first six strikes tell me everything. They are mild and no two strikes hit the same spot twice. They're meant to warm cold flesh, to condition it for more. He is warming me up, slowly and methodically. Six strikes make a pass and, between each pass, he strokes my skin, lightly and with care, as if to pace me, and each time he reaches these reprieves, I go limp across his lap. I can't help it; his touch is golden.

And it arouses me. As my body responds, I become aware that, rounded over the edge of his lap, my arse allows my naked cunt to peek out from between my thighs. I can imagine its slit-like appearance and I know that the more he spanks me, the more it will grow engorged. Soon, it will glisten.

Now his strikes become more intense. His volleys sting and send pain deeper into my flesh. Initially, I groan and take it but by the sixth, seventh, eighth strikes, the sting has accumulated in such unrelenting pain that I can't help myself. I cry out. I squirm. I buck across his lap. And I feel his cock lurch underneath me in response.

His hand caresses me again. I have reached another reprieve. His soft touch competes with the burn left behind from his hearty hand, a light tickle over stinging skin. But as the burning lessens, his touch becomes delicious, so luscious that I moan. It makes me want more – more intensity, more arousal, more of him – and my cunt begins to throb. I suspect that my vulnerable slit has begun to glisten and I hope he will notice my wetness.

Another volley begins and its sudden viciousness replaces kind respite, signaling a grand finale across my ass. It's swift, cruel, and hurried, and I can no better tolerate this round than I could the last. I lurch across his lap, shooting forward as if I'm trying to escape his hand. Perhaps I am. Perhaps the instinct to flee has overtaken me, even though I love what he's foisting on me. But he knows how to keep me in my place – he clamps his free arm down across my back and pins me. I can struggle but I can't escape.

Relentlessly, he continues. The blows merge and I can barely tell where one ends and another starts. My ass is a thing of stinging pain and the pain's so great, it feels like it's leapt into my throat. Consumed by pain, I'm choking on the lump that has formed there.

And, just as swiftly as the volley descended upon me, it ends. Abruptly. My sprint through pain is over. I want him to caress me again, to hold me and tell me I've done well. But his hand finds my cunt instead and its first touch sends a shiver through me.

Fingers probe me and discover just how aroused I am. My labia smack in wet delight and my cunt tightens, begging for attention. I long for his fingers to stroke the length of my lips, to coax and tease me, to explore me in nuanced, subtle movements.

But he is too pedestrian for that. He pries me open and sticks his thumb into me. It's a crude gesture, one meant to remind me that I'm just a wet, ready piece of meat. He never has to tell me I'm a slut; my own cunt does that for him.

His fingers spider up from my slit and find my clit. While one finger massages it, the others grab and pull at my mons. He manipulates me yet again, except now I'm a puppet to his hand – and that hand wants to grope me until I come.

I'm surprised to find my cunt tight and heavy; I'm far more aroused than I expected and, as his hand probes and pokes and strokes, I shudder. Where his touch once soothed, now it coaxes, drawing me into a spiral that will culminate with my orgasm. It's so lusty – lecherous even – that I try to writhe in concert with the hand that strokes me. I want to ride the thumb that plumbs me. I want to feel my hard little clit against a knuckle. Or better yet, against the callous of his rough fingertips. I want him to feel how aroused I am, how I've forgotten all decorum, all passivity. I want to hump until I come.

Except that's not what he wants. His fingers close around my cunt flesh and he pinches me. Sharp pain shoots across my cunt.

"You're not to do that," he orders. "*I'll* make you come."

I collapse under the pain and comply. When he loosens his

grip, I throb from within fiercely. He feels its against his thumb and he laughs. Like a cruel puppet master, he laughs.

The whole incident leaves me conquered and compliant yet its drama brings me even closer to coming. He puts that callous fingertip I longed for against my clit and strokes me hard and fast. I moan and feel close, so close, and the more I reach towards coming, the harder he breathes. Lustful, he sounds lustful, and, in tandem, his cock swells beneath me. And, like my cunt telling me I'm a slut, his breath and his cock tell me the same thing: I'm a slut.

Slut. I'm a slut.

The knowledge pounds in my head, its message is more than I can bear. My cunt clenches as my clit explodes in delight. Pleasure and release and sensation and resolution converge and overtake me. I come. Throbbing, I come. Again and again and again, orgasm rakes me in hard contractions and, when it subsides, I'm left dumbfounded.

Good sex does that to me.

I must admit: Here is where things get fuzzy in my recollections, where my longing and fantasizing become disorganized and incongruous. Like a dream where the storyline all too easily jumps from making sense to going surreal, my fantasy loses its sensibility. Maybe longing has fatigued me. Maybe the very thought of such hefty sex play and such a big orgasm leaves me needing to simplify things. Maybe because no matter how heady the memory or how ingenious the eroticism, I still need to end it with simple penetration.

And that's how I end this fantasy: I'm naked and half-asleep, spent from all he's done to me. Maybe the cuffs and collar are still in place, but there's no longer any elaborate bondage or pain play. Just me, lying there and available.

Drowsy, languid, I am barely aware. But I feel him near. He parts my legs, moves my arms to my side. As he climbs on top of me, his hand goes to my breast and squeezes it. He lowers himself onto me and his hard cock searches me out. When it finds its mark, it pushes. It pushes me apart, pushes itself into me. He takes me.

He fucks me efficiently, concentrating only on what my body provides, on what his cock feels, on what fucking culls up in him. And then, he spits into me. He's gruff and fierce when he comes, as if he must conquer me even as his orgasm conquers him. He stabs me, fills me, spills into me. My one response is to shudder.

He doesn't linger over me after coming. He pulls out and leaves me as I am, still drowsy and ever available, an object to passion. And the only thing I'll feel before sleep overtakes me will be his warm come leak from me. It will wash from my slit and over my labia, evidence of my objectification. Finally, I will slumber.

Just as I sleep alone now, wanting his return. I long for him and though he is gone from me, I count the fantasies until he comes home.

Happy Birthday, Mr President

Donna (Montreal, Canada)

I'm a thirty-five year old woman, married to a great guy. Even though we've been married for almost ten years, our sex life is still pretty steamy! We keep it that way by sharing our fantasies with each other. Not too long ago my husband confessed to me that he'd always fantasized about watching two women go at it together while he is tied up!

Well, seeing as we were in true confessions mode, I told him my big fantasy is to have sex with a woman while he watches and that sometimes I meet incredibly sexy women at the fitness club, and I daydream about bringing them home to him as "gifts".

He was stunned that I'd actually "give" him another woman to enjoy. I told him I didn't think I'd be able to handle doing it for "real" but it was fun to fantasize about it. In my fantasy it seems like the ultimate way to express my love for him and absolute trust in our marriage. Don (my husband) got rock hard talking about it. That night we had the best sex we'd had in ages. This is the fantasy:

I meet a girl in the sauna after my spinning class. She is lying naked on the bench – a beautiful, young cocoa-brown girl. Her long dark hair is twisted into hundreds of tiny braids framing her come-hither face. She is always young and sexy with smouldering brown eyes that pull me right inside her. Her lips are nice and full, the way so many black women's lips are. She even has a shaved snatch (which Don loves) and I can see her clit all moist and swollen, bulging between its folds. Just imagining what she looks like gets me excited and a warm tingle rushes through my body. But I don't stop there. The daydream goes on!

For me to get turned on there always has to be conversation, even in my fantasies. So the girl props herself up on her elbows to talk to me. This gives me an eyeful of her great tits. They're always big, at least a 36D, and for sure the *real* thing! No silicon! She looks me directly in the eye and says:

"I saw you in the spinning class. I was right behind you."

I figure she must like my arse. In spite of having two kids, I've gotten into shape with daily spinning classes. It's my escape from motherhood. While the kids are at school, I go to the gym. My efforts have paid off, and now I have a nice round, firm arse. Thinking about my nice arse also turns me on.

The young girl and I talk about how cute the spinning instructor is. I start thinking about tugging and sucking her nipples and making her moan while my Don watches – helpless! Pretty soon my nipples are tingling and hard and my own clit starts to swell. I always get wet thinking about us sucking each other's tits.

I imagine her wrapping her long muscular legs around Don while he rides her like a young colt. Me sitting on her face getting sucked by those big, fat lips, and then I'm gone on the biggest sex fantasy I can dream up!

We're still in the sauna when she looks straight at my tits and licks her lips. Then she looks right at my shaved cunt and sticks out her tongue, wiggles it, and makes a sucking noise. Right about here my heart starts pounding with excitement and I think I'm gonna come on the spot! But I go deeper.

She stands up to leave the sauna, and I think she's just been teasing me. Then she glances over her shoulder and says: "I'm in the first shower. You can join me if you like." I can hardly believe my ears. Is she saying what I think she's saying? Is she inviting me to have sex with her? I lay in the sauna for a couple of minutes while my cunt squeezes with excitement. Without giving it another thought, I follow her to the shower.

She's soaping up, rubbing her nipples making them big and fat. She smiles and gives me the soap and I start to rub her all over. I keep imagining Don standing there watching us. This gets me so wet and horny I think I'll explode. I keep dreaming.

Soon I am on my knees, my face right in her snatch. I lick it all over, then part the folds and slip my tongue along her clitoris. I suck it right into my mouth. She starts to moan. So I reach up and rub and squeeze and tug those big nipples on those oh so perfect tits. She loves it and grasping my head, grinds her cunt into my face so hard I can hardly breath. Then with a big moan she shudders to a climax. When she recovers she pulls me to my feet and kisses me long and hard on the mouth. "Thank you," she says, "That was wonderful. Now what can I do for you?"

I can't believe my ears. She's asking what she can do for me? I'm thinking about Don and how much he'd enjoy watching what we'd just done so I take a chance and say: "Well, I'm married and I'd love to take you home and give you to my husband for his birthday."

"When's his birthday?" she asks. "I hope it's soon!"

"Ohhh," I groan. "Three weeks! But maybe just as well, I can arrange for the kids to go to my parents for that weekend."

"I'll come to your party, but can't I do something for you right now?" She asks, sliding her fingers into the folds of my dripping cunt. Before I know what's happening, her fingers are inside me and her mouth is on my nipples, biting and sucking like a hungry kitten at its mother's teat. She pushes me against the wall of the shower and ravishes my body. She chews and sucks long and hard on first one, then the other nipple, all the while her fingers playing with my clit and cunt. She has two fingers inside me, wiggling and thrusting while her thumb rubs my clit and her mouth chews and sucks my tits. She brings me to the edge of climax, then says: "No way, not yet baby. I'm gonna give you the orgasm of your life."

Her tongue leaves my nipples and licks its way to my cunt and those big fat brown lips suck my clitoris right into her mouth while her fingers work me inside. She has one hand on my tits, pulling and twisting my nipples and one hand finger-fucking me with two fingers while she chews and sucks my clitoris is if it's chewing gum. I bite my lip to stop myself screaming. It's such a curious mix of pain and pleasure. This young girl is a vixen!

I grab her head and press it into my snatch. In response, she sharply pinches each nipple then slaps and squeezes and scratches my arse, spreading the cheeks so wide I feel my anus open. Then, without any hesitation, she slides her finger right inside and fucks me front and back. When her fingers are working in and out real good, she goes back to chewing my nipples, biting and stretching them till I cry out in pain and explode with a shuddering climax. My knees give out. She presses me hard against the wall, her fingers deep in my cunt and anus and her teeth sunk into my nipple.

"Wow! You are one experienced young lady," I pant.

"I had an expert teacher," she says coyly. "She's about your age." Then she takes my head in her hands and kisses me deeply on the mouth. "I just love doing older women, and I'll come to your husband's party as long as you'll let me do you every time I see you here." I can't believe my ears.

I imagine that after that day, Tanya and I meet regularly at spinning class. Between our "practice" sessions in the shower, we plan Don's party, and go shopping for our outfits. In my fantasy, I even go to her place a couple of times to work up our "routine".

The day of Don's birthday, I get him to drive the kids to my parents just before supper. When he gets home, I'm wearing a new black leather mini-skirt. It is so short it shows off my garters and the tops of my net stockings. I wear a matching leather and fishnet corset-style bustier. The demi-bra holds my tits high and pushes them together while my nipples poke through the fish net trim. Stiletto-heeled leather boots finish the costume.

"Holy shit! That's some outfit!" exclaims Don. "I don't know where to start." In seconds his hands are all over me, rubbing me up and down, exploring every inch of my costume. He slips his hand under my skirt and grabs my bare bum. I'm not even wearing a thong. "Is that costume made for fucking or what!" he says as he pushes me against the wall, squeezing my arse, and kissing and nibbling my tits. Then the doorbell rings.

"Ohhh, that must be the pizza!" I say, knowing it is my special birthday treat for him. "You better get it, I don't think I should go to the door dressed like this."

Don groans and tears himself from me. "Who needs pizza?"

I just smile and say: "I ordered your favourite." The doorbell rings again. "Better get that. You don't want it cold." I can hardly contain my giggles. I am so anxious to see Don's reaction.

He answers the door, and sure enough there's Tanya – holding three pizza boxes. She's wearing a long leather coat open in the front so Don can see her matching outfit. He can hardly believe his eyes. Here is a stunning young cocoa-brown vixen all dressed in a leather outfit just like his wife's.

He fumbles in his pockets for the money, then calls to me: "Honey, do you have the cash?" I come down the hall and, right on cue, Tanya steps inside and closes the door firmly behind her. As I take the boxes from her, she slips off her coat and lets it fall to the floor. Then she rubs her tits against Don's chest and grabs his crotch saying: "Happy Birthday, Mr President." (Oh, yeah, I forgot to tell you, Don has this thing about being called "Mr President.")

She pulls him to her and locks him in a deep, French kiss. Just then, I sneak up behind him and start rubbing his butt and kissing the back of his neck. As he reaches round to grab me, I lock a set of handcuffs round his wrists.

"Happy birthday, Don," I whisper in his ear. "This is Tanya. She's your birthday present. We have a little party planned for you."

"Wow!" is all he can say.

Tanya and I lead him into the bedroom where I uncuff him. Tanya pushes him onto the bed, climbs on top of him and starts lap dancing. As she unbuttons his shirt with her teeth, I get his hands over his head and cuff first one, then the other to the bedposts. By the time I'm finished, Tanya is licking his nipples.

"He's ready!" I announce.

"He sure is!" she replies, as she unzips his fly and pulls out his erect cock. "Wow, you didn't tell me he's *that* big!" she says as she teasingly wraps her big lips around the tip of his cock. While Tanya gets him started with a mini-suck, I pull off his trousers. Tanya works him up good. She licks his prick all the way from the base to the head, then wraps her lips round the tip and sucks it until he tries to push it into her mouth. But before he can get it between her teeth, she pulls away, saying:

"Un huh, not yet!" Then she licks him up and down again, giving him little sucks all along the way.

Don just lies back, moaning, saying over and over: "Yes! Oh, yes!"

His panting gets really intense, the way it does just before he comes, when Tanya teases: "Not yet, lover boy, I want you to shoot your load like you've never shot it before!" Then she jumps off the bed and starts to work me over.

Don groans as Tanya French kisses me, running her hands all over my body, squeezing first my tits then my arse. When she starts licking and sucking my tits, Don cheers like he's watching a football match! "You go, girl! Give it to her!" Then she slips her hand under my skirt and starts to work my cunt with her magical fingers. Don cheers like a goal has just been scored! "Yeah! Hip-hip hooray! Make her want it! I wanna hear her beg!"

Tanya unzips my skirt and it falls away exposing my freshly shaved snatch. She runs her hands over my hips and falls on her knees in front of me, teasing my clit with her tongue. More wild cheers from Don!

By now my pelvis is circling wildly and I'm rubbing myself all over. But my fantasy girl makes me wait while my fantasy creates more conversation. "I've got a surprise for you! Don's not the only one getting a birthday treat!" Tanya says. "Time for pizza!"

Tanya opens the first pizza box and pulls out a short black leather cat o' nine tails whip. She starts stroking herself with it. "You wanna get bum-fucked while Don watches? Or shall I just whip you?"

"You better not hurt her," says Don, from the bed. Tanya groans. "Well, make it hurt, but don't – you know – mark her," he adds.

"Don't you worry, lover boy. I know all about your spanking parties! She can take it. Besides, I'm an expert whip handler."

"Wow!" Exclaims Don. "This is turning out to be one wild birthday party! Donna, sweetheart, I love you."

Crack. Tanya snaps the whip across the bed, narrowly missing Don! "Bend over the foot of the bed, sweetie," she says to me, purring like a cat as she strokes the strands of the whip with her long fingernails. "You'll like it. I promise. Now be a good girl and bend over." And, to make sure I understand, she gives my arse a playful slap with the whip. "Now that didn't hurt, did it?" she purrs. "Bend over!" The purr changes to a slight growl. I obey.

I lean over the foot of the bed, letting my tits dangle where Don can see them and position my head so we can look into each other's eyes. I love his eyes – and will do anything he asks when he looks at me the right way. Then Tanya starts. She strokes my arse a couple of times with the whip. "Mmm, you have such a nice creamy white-girl butt. Let's see how red I can make it!" Then she snaps the whip across my ass. A cry escapes my lips and my hips jerk of their own will. Don sucks in his breath. She goes easy and only gives me a few lashes.

Don lies back on the bed, rolling his head from side to side, saying over and over: "Oh, wow! *Wow*! Oh, what a pair of vixens. Whoa! Ouch! Oh! What a picture!" And I swear his erection grows an inch. I imagine us looking like something from an S&M porn film, what with Tanya all dressed in her leather outfit and me bent over the bed getting whipped. I imagine this is the most exciting moment of Don's life. Even more exciting than when he bought his first Harley. This makes me feel so special.

After about ten lashes, tears are trickling down my cheeks. "Ooh, that's a nice red arse," says Tanya as she kneels behind me and starts kissing and licking my behind, murmuring: "That didnt hurt too bad, did it?" I think I will explode. The mixture of pain and tenderness is indescribable. She slips her tongue along my anus and pushes her thumb inside it while her fingers work my clit. "Nice! What a nice tight arsehole you have. I'm gonna get it ready for Don. Would you like that, Don?" she teases as she pulls out her thumb and dances over to him, circling her hips inches from his head. "Or would you rather lick me?" she asks, as she unzips her skirt and it falls to the floor, revealing her big shiny, shaved cunt. Then she slips her finger inside herself, slathers it with juice, and holds it just out of reach of Don's mouth. He lifts his head and licks the air with his tongue, but she won't let him taste it, taking it into her own mouth and sucking it herself. Then she finger-fucks herself a couple of times, pulls her finger out and lets him suck it. He lifts his head right off the pillow and sucks that finger like a baby at its mother's breast. "Or would you rather watch me and Donna suck each other?" she says as she pulls her finger away from him and dances back to me.

I start to stand up and she snaps the whip across my arse. "You stay put, girl." She commands. Ten more lashes and I am crying and begging, and she is once again all over my behind with her licks and kisses, her thumb up my anus and her fingers rubbing my clit. Then I feel something strange inside my cunt – fucking me in and out – and I realize she is fucking me with the whip handle. She pulls her thumb out of my anus and thrusts two fingers deep inside. I start to buck and pant like I have just finished a race. Between pants, I scream: "Oh, *yeees*!" and rub and pinch my nipples.

Don struggles in the handcuffs and Tanya brings me once again to the edge of orgasm.

"Oh, give it to me, give it to me, fuck me, Tanya."

Don is once again cheering like a football fan. "Make her beg! Make her beg!" No sooner do I scream than Tanya stops fucking and licking me and pulls the whip handle out of me. "What did you say, white girl?"

"Oh, Tanya, fuck me. Give it to me."

The whip stings me, right across my butt.

Fifteen lashes this time before the tears come and I beg her. "Oh, stop, please stop. Fuck me, fuck me, fuck me."

"I think you're ready now," she says, and she brings me round to the bed. "Straddle him. Rub your clit on his prick, but don't let him inside." And she lashes me with the whip.

I do as I am told. Don is groaning and really struggling in the handcuffs. I lower my hot, dripping cunt towards his big fat rock-hard prick and he cries: "Oh, sweetheart, fuck me! Fuck me! Fuck me" And I start to press myself onto his prick that is standing up straight as a flagpole.

"Oooh – you're both good 'n ready!" croons Tanya. "But you're not gonna get it just yet. Don't you fuck him, girl." And the whip cracks hard across my vulva.

"Oh, I want him. I want him."

"Whaddya want more? Your little white-boy husband's

prick in your cunt or my whip handle up your arse?" As she teases me with her words, she licks my behind, spreading my cheeks and working the tip of the whip handle into my anus. Slowly but surely she gets the whip handle all the way in.

"Now girl. Fuck him, now!" she says as she works the whip handle in and out of my arse. I drop my hot cunt onto Don's prick, and he slides inside so easily. The feeling is indescribable. Tanya is pumping the whip behind me, while Don's prick presses deep inside me. Within minutes both Don and I explode with the most powerful orgasms we've ever had.

Tanya unlocks the handcuffs and Don instantly wraps his arms around me, saying over and over: "Oh baby, I love you! I love you." He holds me so tight I think I'm gonna crack. Then he kisses me deeply on the mouth.

Tanya slips out the door while we are locked in our embrace. We fall asleep and when we wake up I still have the leather tail up my arse and Don gently pulls it out.

"Did it hurt?" he asks.

"Not as much as it felt good," I reply. And he playfully strokes my arse with the strands of the whip.

"I'll have to try it sometime – when my hand's sore," he says, playfully flicking the whip in the air.

And that's how it ends. Don and I really got off on this fantasy. Sometimes I think we really should try it. I don't think I could do it for real with a woman. We do get into spanking. Sometimes I think I should buy him a cat-o' nine tails for his next birthday. I know he'd never hurt me. Maybe we could try that part for real.

A Holiday Treat

Allison (Dallas, USA)

I'm a nice girl, really. I have a good job, take care of my pets, send thank you notes, give directions when asked. I am always prompt and efficient at work, and dress to impress but also to blend in. But sometimes, well, often, I get sick of being that nice girl and instead of being Allison Meadows, Official Nice Girl, who everyone tells their problems to and then looks right through me, I want to be Allison Meadows, who everyone admires and wants to find out more about. I want to be the kind of girl who turns heads, who gets gossiped about, who's wild and reckless. Who'd dye her hair purple just for the fun and novelty of it, who'd book a trip overseas leaving tomorrow. Who'd have an affair with her boss . . .

He was completely wrong for me, on so many levels, but that just made him more attractive. I don't just mean that he was my boss, although that was a big part of why he was wrong for me. I mean our personalities. We were total opposites, him a corporate, suit-wearing, rather quiet family guy, at home on the golf course or behind his big, imposing desk, and me a loud, fun-loving, party girl working her day job to support her art and outlandish social life. The truth is, if he hadn't been my boss, I wouldn't have looked at him twice. He'd have been just another guy in a suit, with no distinguishing characteristics, of no interest to me whatsoever. Those kinds of guys all tend to blur together to me, with their short similar haircuts and pasted-on smiles and neat, conservative little lives. I see them all the time – on the street, in bars, driving by in all their macho glory, and I hurry past, eager to escape to my own world where people think for themselves and attract others not with money but with wit and style. Even if one of them had the potential to be interesting, I never gave guys like that a second glance, forgiving myself the snap judgments because the few times I'd tried to chat them up or even go home with one of them, it never worked out.

He was all of those things I couldn't stand, but he was different, at least to me. He was more human, less macho. His soft skin and pudgy belly made me want to take him in my arms. The way he treated me, kindly, with a touch of amusement, like he wasn't my boss but my babysitter, tolerating my silly antics, like the time I hung Christmas lights around the entire office or prank-paged our most hated partner. He was soft and fleshy and sweet. Sometimes I thought of him as a curvy, sexy woman in the body of a male corporate exec.

I was his secretary, the biggest cliche in the book and, if I'm known for anything, it's not doing the expected. But that didn't stop me from lusting after him. It wasn't an immediate attraction; the first week I summed him up and threw him into the same category as all the others, but his charm grew on me. In fact, the more I saw what a kind, gentle, truly nice, guy he was, a devoted husband and father, the more I wanted him. It wasn't that I wanted to corrupt him, I just wanted a little of him to be a part of me. I wanted him to myself in the most intimate of ways for just a brief time, not to live with or cook for or do any of those wifely duties, but simply to connect with on the most intimate of levels, to know what he was like away from the office, stripped down to his purest form. It was never an affair or relationship I sought, but a capturing of his spirit, a brief taste of his body. I would lie in bed and fantasize about him fucking his wife, wondering how they did it, who initiated it. The next morning I could never look at him, had to avert my eyes at the office lest I get immediately wet upon recalling my fantasies.

It wasn't the kind of thing I could tell anyone else at work either. It would have been frowned upon, or could've lost me my job but, even more importantly, nobody would've understood. A young, attractive, fun-loving woman interested in an older, pretty boring, not-much-to-look at guy? Dan Braxton and Allison Meadows? How could I have explained the thrill that ran through me every time our fingers touched when he handed me papers to copy, or I had to lean near him to reach something? I couldn't even explain it to myself. Most people would probably say it was the power dynamic between us, him being my boss and all, but it wasn't that. I could see that even though he was my boss, he didn't have much power in our company overall. With the chain upon chain of command and useless corporate titles, he didn't really measure up. But it wasn't his stereotypically bossy behaviour that drew me to him, it was precisely the opposite – his kindness, his under-standing, his way with people. He was like a sweet little boy offering me a dandelion, and that endeared him to me. I didn't want him to enter my world, or me to enter his; we wouldn't have fit in or felt comfortable. I wanted to take both of us to some other kind of world, away from the pressures of the office or the drama of home life, to a purely innocent place where we could tear each other's clothes off and claw at each other for an hour or two, then put ourselves back together and return to our regularly scheduled lives.

I finally made my move at his annual holiday party. I didn't plan it in advance, in fact I almost didn't go to the party, but I finally ended up going, after digging up a perfectly low cut v-neck sweater and cute short black skirt and telling myself I wouldn't even go near him (but I wanted to look good just in case). Seducing him would never have worked if I'd planned it out too closely; when I plan things precisely, one little snag throws me completely for a loop. I figured I'd see what opportunities presented themselves.

He had no idea of my infatuation. I kept it safely confined within my mind and bedroom, and nobody else knew or even suspected, so that gave me some cover to spy on him covertly across the room. At the party I chatted with all the guests, played with his kids, feasted on the delicious spread of meats and fish and desserts and delicacies. I also had a few glasses of wine to calm my jitters at the thought of talking to him, alone. It was my deepest fantasy, but that's what made it so nerve-inducing.

After dinner, most people drifted outside to smoke or enjoy a brief breath of the chill winter air. I noticed that he was sitting alone in the living room enjoying his dessert, while everyone else was outside. I walked over to him, making sure I stared directly into his eyes. "Want some champagne to go with your cake?" I asked smoothly. I wanted him to look at me like a woman, a potential lover, not just a convenient waitress. At his nod, I went back into the kitchen and poured it, the cold liquid fizzing in the fluted glass. Before heading back to the living room, I tugged my shirt down slightly, providing an even better view of my cleavage. *This is it*, I thought. I walked back to his seat on the couch, but instead of handing the glass to him, I stood directly in front of him, leaned over so my cleavage was right in his sightline, and looked intently into his pale blue eyes. I handed him the glass, making sure our fingers touched. If someone had come by at that moment, I would have turned around and taken a piece of cheese from the tray on the table, and in the process given him a nice view of my ass all shoved into my short skirt. But everyone was too busy talking and chatting and didn't really want to make small talk with the boss anyway.

"Where's your bathroom? The one down here is full. Maybe you could show me where the one upstairs is."

"Okay," he said a bit shakily, putting down his plate and draining his glass. "Follow me."

He led me up the lavish carpeted staircase, and down a long, sumptuous hallway. When we reached the top of the stairs, I deliberately sped up so that I bumped into him. "Oops," I said as my breasts brushed against his back. I stepped back and continued walking quietly. At the end of the hallway, he opened a door, flicked on the light and said, "Well, here it is."

I stepped into the doorway and grabbed his hand. "Please stay with me." He looked at me sceptically, obviously torn between escaping my crazed plan and joining the others, and following through on my taunting dare.

"I really shouldn't," he said, with very little regret in his voice, as his eyes zoomed up and down my body. He shut the door and leaned back against it.

"Excuse me," I said, as I gently rolled down my panties and lifted my skirt before sitting down on the toilet. I started to pee, the liquid making loud splashes against the silence of the room. Suddenly, I didn't know where to look. A little of my bravado left me, and I looked down at my toes.

"You're a pretty wild girl, do you know that? I can't believe you brought me up here to watch you pee."

"Well, that's not exactly true, you know. You can't actually see me peeing, can you? Besides, I have better things for you to do while you're up here." I stood quickly, wiped myself, and pulled up my panties. I walked over to the sink and began washing my hands. He walked over and planted himself behind me, grabbing my waist and pulling me towards him. I could feel his hard cock pushing up against my ass, and let out a little moan. As the water washed over my hands, he pushed himself against me, rubbing his cock against me.

"Feel what you've done to me. I had to follow you up here or else I'd have been sitting there eating my cake with this huge hard-on. What are you going to do about that, little girl?"

I turned around and brought my wet hands up to his face. "Are you sure you want me to do anything about your hard-on, *Mister* Braxton? You have all those guests down there waiting for you."

"Oh, I'm very sure. I want to see those pretty little tits you've been teasing me with all night."

"So you noticed, huh? I thought you were immune to my charms. Is this what you're looking for?" I asked, placing his hands under my shirt so they cupped my breasts. His fingers quickly found my hardened nipples and began pinching them. I spread my legs farther apart, sinking down a little lower, leaning back against the sink. He brought one of his hands under my skirt, fingering me through my flimsy panties.

"I'm not immune, darlin'. You're very cute, of course I noticed that, but I don't make it a practice of fucking around on my wife, nor of messing with my employees. And I didn't exactly think a pudgy, boring old man like me would be your type. But since I apparently am, sweetheart, I'll make an exception." His fingers became more insistent and my breath came faster and faster. For a "boring old man," he certainly knew what he was doing, expertly working me in a way I thought I'd have to rely on myself for in the immediate future. Most guys I'd been with thought fingering was something obligatory they needed to do before sinking their dick into me, whereas Mr Braxton seemed to get off on how wet he was making me, his face a mixture of amusement and determination. When I was looking at it, that is; I soon had to close my eyes as the pressure became too much for me. My face started to contort and I felt on the verge of coming, but I grabbed his hand and pushed it away. This wasn't the right time for me to come, for me to lose myself in him. I sensed that if I let him continue, I'd never get him out of my system, despite my wishes for a hot one-time fling. I wanted to fulfill my fantasy my way.

"Not now, I don't want to come now. No offence meant by that – in fact, it's because that felt so good that I need to stop for a minute. There's something else I've been thinking about; I want to have some fun with you." I brought my hands up to his chest and pushed him backwards towards the bathroom wall. Then I lifted his shirt and began undoing his belt buckle, moving in slow motion so I could savour every moment. I could see his cock straining right underneath me, big and solid beneath the denim. I paused to stroke it, then went back to the belt, alternating in a way that was clearly driving him crazy. He stared down at my mischievous hands. Finally I'd reached the piece de resistance, his zipper. I slowly unzipped it, smiling at the quiet sound of the teeth sliding against each other. I got down on my knees on the coral tiles and tongued his cock through his briefs. It moved slightly, almost jumping towards me. He groaned and grabbed for my hair. My pussy was starting to ache the way it does only when I come in contact with the perfect cock, but I continued with my mission. I pushed his pants down to his ankles and then slowly lifted the waistband of his briefs, unveiling a rather large cock. "Mmmm," I moaned as I looked at its impressive size, its pink, smooth bulging skin, everything I'd imagined and more. I licked the tip, tasting the slight saltiness, the warmth and softness there as I held the hard shaft of him in my hand.

Then I ran my tongue up and down the length of him, while his hand remained on my head. I sat up a little, opened my mouth and slowly brought it down around the first few inches of his cock. I could feel his cock stiffen even more and I sucked on it before letting my mouth slide down so more of him could enter me. I started rocking back and forth, my knees in rhythm with my mouth as I moved up and down the length of him. I placed my ankle between my legs, my pussy pounding against it every time I rocked backwards, torn between bringing a hand down to my clit and fondling him. I leaned back, rubbing my ankle as hard as I could against myself, while bending his cock slightly away from him and sliding my mouth up and down along its delicious length.

I know some girls find it a chore, but for me, sucking a man's cock is sometimes even better than sex, one of the most sensual things anyone can do. I like the way it tickles my throat, the way it works its way into the crevices of my mouth, the way I can smell and taste every morsel of him; nothing else allows me such sensory overload, such pure, raw, indulgent sex. I moved slowly, wanting to prolong the pleasure, and felt a few tears slipping from my eyes; part happiness, part something that often happens when a cock is pressed all the way inside my mouth, as if it's pushing out the tears to make more room. I cried from the beauty of it, from the sheer joy of having him hard and helpless in front of me like that, at my mercy every bit as much as I was at his. My cool, competent boss, this friendly people-person who could command a room of hundreds without a microphone, reduced to his throbbing cock and the need to have it down my throat. I smiled a little, as much as I could in that position. I could hear him stifling his moans, and making a tortured sound when I'd manage to get his entire cock inside my mouth, its tip stroking the back of my throat and my lips brushing against his pubic hairs. I wrapped my hand around the base of his cock and held it there, bringing my mouth up and down, slower and slower, then faster and faster, trying to figure out which he liked better. Then I began sucking in earnest, pulling him into me with my mouth, relaxing so I could go as fast as I wanted. I rocked faster, gliding up and down the slick surface of his dick, sliding my lips along his delicate skin, until he couldn't keep quiet any longer. "I'm gonna come," he managed to say before his come burst into my mouth in a fast, hot stream, making almost a direct pathway down my throat. In one quick swallow, it was gone, and I leaned against his hip, both of us panting, slightly dazed and awed.

We sat silently for a few minutes, breathing, recovering, then stood up and smoothed our clothes. Once that moment passed, and we moved away from each other, it hardly mattered that we were in the same room; we'd never be quite that close again, and we both knew it. I splashed some water on my face, toweled off, and looked at him, feeling incredibly tender and unsure of what would happen next. He went downstairs first, and I followed a few minutes later. Nobody seemed to have noticed we'd been gone, and I went home with only my body's memories of our encounter.

By the next holiday party, I had thankfully moved on to another company, one where nobody held quite the attraction of my old boss. We didn't keep in touch after I left, but I did get a holiday card from him that year. "May you enjoy this holiday season as much as the last one," he wrote, and I imagined his cock hardening as he wrote the words and relived the memory. I never saw him again.

Every Christmas I think of our might-have-been brief bathroom fling, the one I was too much of a "nice girl" to ever truly follow through with (the closest I got was kissing his cheek), and it never fails to turn me on.

Tell-Tale Toes

Melody (Brighton, UK)

I guess you could call me a fairly typical housewife, if there is such a thing these days. My husband, Neil, and I wanted to have a traditional family, so when I finally got pregnant with our first child, I quit my part-time job and went into the Mum business full-time. Two kids later, and I'm still at it.

With the children around, and Neil on the road quite a bit, our sex life has become fairly typical as well – hurried, vanilla intercourse whenever we can sneak it in, which isn't often these days. My fantasy sex life, however, has become anything but typical. In the fantasy world that I inhabit almost every spare moment I can grab, I have stunning, steamy sex as many times as I want, for as long as I want, with anyone and everyone of my choosing – and always with very satisfying results.

My fantasies have even veered off into the fetish realm – an area I wouldn't normally touch with a ten-foot dildo in real life – with feet figuring prominently in my latest hot and hazy mental sex pictures, women's slender, shapely, succulent feet . . .

I saunter into the book/video store and casually browse through the shelves and shelves of X-rated lesbian reading, the racks upon racks of explicit, all-girl videos, trying not to look as nervous as I feel. There's a skater girl parked behind the cash register at the back of the store, reading a magazine and chewing gum, watching me every so often with her black-rimmed eyes.

Anxiety, however, only serves to heighten the excitement for a certifiable foot-freak like myself, so, as my palms and pussy grow wetter and wetter, I draw a deep breath and walk up to the Avril Lavigne-wannabe. "Hi," I squeak, then hastily clear my throat.

"Hi. What can I do you for?" the black-eyed and blue-haired girl replies, her lip and nose rings keeping rhythm with her jaw.

I show the clerk the membership card I begged and borrowed from a recent one-night stand gone weekly, when the lover in question told me stories about "shoe-shine stands" in the back of a bookstore. She'd whetted my sexual appetite with tales of illicit foot love only after I'd sucked on her toes, individually and all together, tickled the sensitive soles of her feet with my fingers and lips and tongue, jammed a big toe into her dyed-blonde pussy and vigorously foot-fucked her to shattering orgasm. After I'd demonstrated my all-encompassing love for women's feet, in other words.

The grunge girl grins, shows off her Bubblicious and tongue-stud. "Club Ped, huh?" she says. "Go right on through."

I give her a shaky smile and fumble the card back into my pocket, then walk past her, part a set of heavy, black curtains and find myself facing a blue wall with two doors in it. One of the doors has a red foot painted on it, the other a red hand. I turn the knob on the hand door.

The room I enter is long and narrow – really half of a larger room bisected by a hanging, red curtain, like a gymnasium cut in two by an accordion wall. The room is further divided up by blue, four-foot-high panels placed every five feet or so, perpendicular to the curtain, creating a series of small cubicles. My hand trails along the wall after me as I walk further inside, then I stop, lean back against the wall, my breath catching in my throat as I see what's taking place in cubicle one – a woman is on her knees, frenziedly licking at the wiggling toes of a beautifully turned foot protruding from beneath the curtain.

The crimson barrier hangs down to within two feet of the floor, hiding the foot's owner, but allowing enough space for her to stick her feet underneath and get them worshipped by the woman on my side of the curtain. I hear the hidden lady emit a low, muffled moan, as the woman on her knees squeezes her tongue in between the pale, outstretched toes, each in turn, before cramming the whole blessed lot of them into her mouth and excitedly sucking on them.

I swallow hard, creep further along the wall, my heart racing, my pulse pounding; this is sweet nirvana for an un-repentant foot-fetisher – like me. I pass three more cubicles occupied by foot-hungry women giving sole satisfaction to lucky gals on the other side of the velvet curtain, and then I come to the final shoe-shine stand and find it empty. I slip inside and duck down onto my knees, and wait.

There's a small, padded, wooden platform, like a confessional kneeler, just on my side of the curtain. It's covered with a sanitary strip of paper that I assume is supposed to be replaced after each session from the dispenser bolted onto the portable wall. There's also a low-level, padded stool tucked away in one corner – for those extra long waits, I guess, when even the plush carpeting gets a little too hard on the knees.

I adjust my butt-length skirt, repeatedly, rub the damp slabs of meat that were my hands up and down on it. I shift my knees around, my legs trembling with anticipation. And as the minutes crawl by, I grow more and more anxious, the entire situation growing weirder and weirder in my mottled mind – anonymous women coming together in a dimly-lit backroom to rub and kiss and lick and suck the toes and feet of equally unknown female partners. How weird is that? The muffled moaning and groaning all around me seems to grow louder and louder, filling the hot, stifling air, filling my ears and brain and body with strange thoughts and feelings. I finally become so discombobulated that I jump to my feet, ready to bolt the booth and flee the store.

Then I hear a door open and close, hear soft footsteps on the other side of the curtain, and I kneel back down and hold my breath and blink the sweat out of my eyes; almost jump out of my skin and scream when a pair of feet suddenly appears like magic from under the curtain, displayed on the footrest. I stare down at those twin, pale apparitions – exquisitely shaped feet flowing poetically out of ultra-slim ankles, clothed only in open-toed, black stilettos, toenails psychedelically painted every shade of the rainbow save violet, silver bands encircling the slender big toes. My wooden tongue scrapes across my cracked lips, but I boldly reach out and touch one of the toes on the right foot, and watch in amazement as the foot jumps in reaction.

I let the stale air out of my lungs in a long, heavy sigh, and my stiff body is suffused with heat. I know what to do now, and I know that I'm going to richly enjoy doing it. I grasp the unknown woman's right foot, run my hands all over and around the beautiful ped and sexy footwear, lace the shapely ankle with my fingers and stroke up and down on it. The woman on the other side of the curtain gasps, feeding my smouldering fire.

I feel up her feet, first one, then the other, stroke the shiny, black leather of her dangerous shoes, the sharp, silver-tipped heels, swirl my loving hands all over the silky-smooth, ivory skin of her twitching feet. Then I replace hands with tongue, anxious to taste the supple leather, the hot skin. She cries out with joy when I hold her feet up by the heels and lightly brush each wriggling, spectrum-tinted toe with my tongue, then slowly drag my thickened tongue across all of her delicious toes.

"Yes!" she hisses, breaking the club rule that forbids talking.

I picture her hand in her panties, two fingers buried to the knuckles in her soaking wet pussy, while she desperately rubs herself off as I attack her feet, and the thought of the owner of those gorgeous peds excitedly finger-fucking herself stokes the fire burning within me into a raging inferno. I tongue the sides of her shoes, lap at her high heels and bare feet at the same time, plunge a spike heel into my mouth and suck on it, tug on it, twirl my tongue all around it; do the same with her other erotic shoe dagger.

I hastily unfasten the strap that binds her luscious feet to her wicked stilettos and pull the sexy foot gear off her peds, bury my nose in her shoes and inhale deeply, and then fling them aside, so that I'm skin-to-skin with her naked feet. I balance them in my hands, admiring the rainbow-hued toenails (running from red on her big toe to orange to yellow to green to blue on each foot), and then I bring her toes up to my mouth and swallow them.

"Oh, my God!" she cries, as I wantonly suck on all ten of her foot-digits at once.

I tug on her toes with my mouth, buff the underside of them by wagging my tongue back and forth, suck long and hard on the delightful, edible ends of her feet. Then I slide her multi-colored toes wet and dripping out of my mouth and softly kiss each of them in turn, before snaking my slimy tongue in between her toes and scouring the sides of them, slathering hot spit all over her feet.

I tongue and suck her toes for a good, long while, and then I lick at the soles of her delicate peds, lap at the arched, ticklish bottom of her feet. She moans, her feet dancing around in my hands as I paint their smooth, tender bottoms with long, slow strokes of my tongue. I hold tight to her feet, never releasing them from my grasp, always licking and kissing and biting them, tenderizing her succulent tootsies even further.

"I'm going to come!" she shrieks, her feet trembling violently.

I urgently lap at the rounded tops of her peds, suck some more on her toes, and then get really carried away; I drop her feet onto the platform, fumble my skirt up and my panties down, and jam the big toe of her left foot into my sopping pussy. I begin frantically fucking myself with her big toe, while I chew on her other foot.

"Jesus!" she yelps.

I gobble up that woman's right-foot toes and desperately pull on them, as I pound big red into my tingling pussy over and over and over.

"Mmmm!" she groans, bringing herself to orgasm as her feet push me over the edge.

I bite into her toes and close my eyes and a heated wave of ecstasy wells up from my toe-fucked pussy and engulfs my quivering body. I'm devastated by foot-induced orgasm, my anonymous lover's big, metal-clad toe relentlessly pumping in and out of my gushing pussy, her other adorable toes brushing mercilessly back and forth against my pulsating clit.

My feet and toes still tingling with after-taste from the licking they've taken from a nameless foot fanatic, I receive the shock of my life when I report to work at my accounts payable job, when my boss, just back from vacation, walks up to my desk clad in a pair of open-toed sandals, her toenails sporting polish covering five of the seven shades of the light spectrum, her big toes twin bands of silver!

"Glad to see me back, Melody?" she asks, smiling cheerfully; then glancing down at her feet, where my eyes and jaw are located. "You like my new toe fashions?"

My mouth opens and closes like a beached flounder. I can hardly wrap my dizzy head around the fact that my boss, Cynthia, was the one I'd frantically foot-pleasured. I've had the hots for the lush, forty-something brunette for a long time, mind you, but never did I expect in my wildest dreams that fantasy and reality would come crashing together so wickedly.

I've been planning to make a move on the hot-looking, big-breasted babe for months and, now that I knew she was my kind of righteous foot-disciple, I quickly make up my mind to put my sensual thoughts into action. So, without saying a word, I grab her hand and tow her down the hall, into her office, slam the door shut with my heel, wrap my arms around the startled beauty, and plant a sloppy, wet one square on her glossy pucker before she can even react.

"Jesus, Melody! What's gotten into you!?" she reacts, jerking her head back, but not attempting to free herself from my bear-hug.

"Your toes, among other things," I quip. And then I tell her all about my foot fetish, my session at the shoe-shine stand, about what I've done to her gorgeous feet, and what they've done to me. The words spill out of my mouth in a burbling torrent, and at the end of it all, I confess my long-held lust for the sultry manageress.

She stares at me for an awkwardly long period of time, and then slips out of my grasp and walks over to the window and twists the Venetian blinds shut. Then she's back in my arms, confessing her own secret cravings for my young, tight body, my blonde cunny, before sealing her lips to mine.

We mash our mouths together, devour each other's lips, my naughty hands roaming all over her curvy body, down to her plump, rounded bottom cheeks – which I grip and knead, while her own fingers riffle through my long, golden locks. I gasp for air, fight to keep my head from spinning off into orbit as wet dreams become wetter reality, and she darts her tongue in between my parted lips and explores the interior of my mouth, till I meet her tongue with my tongue.

I squeeze her body against mine, her large breasts and swollen nipples pressing hard and soft into my smaller boobs, and we slap our slippery, pink tongues together over and over. Finally, I break away from her mouth, push her back, and implore her to tear off her clothes and show me her over-ripe body. I've one thing in mind, of course. "I want you and me to foot-fuck!" I shout. "Face-to-face – no curtain between us this time!"

She gives me a strange look, but rapidly disrobes, leaving her flower-print dress and satiny pink bra and panties strewn on the floor along with her sandals, and any remaining inhibitions. Her body is just as I've pictured it in so many masturbatory fantasies – voluptuous, curvaceous, her golden-brown tits huge and heavy-looking, her mocha nipples thick and jutting, her glistening pussy sprinkled with downy, brown fur.

"Your turn, Melody," she says, waking me out of my trance.

"Yes, miss," I respond, quickly shedding my tight, purple halter top and tiny, black skirt. I was planning on visiting my favourite bookshop directly after work, so I'm sans underwear.

"You're a very beautiful young woman," Cynthia breathes, her warm, brown eyes travelling all over my lean body, my long, supple legs, my high breasts and protruding nipples, before fixating on my shaved cunny.

We melt back into each other's arms, wildly kiss and French some more, our hot nude bodies fitting neatly together like we're meant for each other. I suck on her extended tongue, excitedly bob my head back and forth on it, then escape her embrace and skip over to the huge oaken desk that dominates her office. I brush the business paraphernalia off its gleaming surface with a couple of swipes of my arm and climb on top.

"Time for some foot-lovin'," I state, plopping my bare arse down on the cool, varnished wood and beckoning my boss over.

She joins me on the desktop, sits down opposite me, and I stick out my leg and hold my foot only inches away from her pussy, my toes pointing directly at her slickened sex. She hesitates for a moment, teasing me, my leg starting to shake, and then at last she grips my arched ped and rubs it between her hands.

"That's more like it," I murmur when she pops my big toe into her mouth and starts sucking on it. She has my right foot in her hands and mouth, so I scoop up her right foot and reciprocate her love. I tenderly stroke her ped, then lightly rake my purple-tipped fingernails up and down the vulnerable bottom of her foot.

"Yes, Melody," she mumbles from around my toe.

I kiss her cute, multi-colored piggies one at a time, then tongue the tops and bottoms of them, dart my tongue in between her toes and eagerly scrub them with my velvet-sandpaper tongue. Then I latch my lips onto her big toe and suck it, getting it all nice and wet for my cunny.

"Toe-fuck me, Cynthia!" I bleat, pushing her foot down to my pussy and pressing her toes against my moistened lips. "Toe-fuck me like you did at the shoe-shine stand!"

She slides her big toe into my pussy, starts pistoning her sun-kissed leg, pumping her toe in and out of my sex, her other painted foot-digits caressing my electrified clitty. I pull my own foot out of her hands and mouth and shove it against her pussy, reveling in the hot, damp feeling of her engorged lips.

"Yes, Melody, yes!" she hisses, staring fiercely at me as I feel up her wet labes with my toes, then slip my big toe into her pussy.

We pound each other's cunts with our toes, foot-fuck one another faster and faster, harder and harder, relentlessly, until Cynthia throws back her head and screams my name and her hot juices cascade all over my ped. I grasp her ankle and frantically help her plunder my pussy with her toes, biting my lip and whimpering when my own cunny explodes and a blistering orgasm rents my quivering body, followed by another, and another.

It's only when we're licking our come off each other's feet that my boss admits that she's never heard of the shoe-shine stands, or the bookshop in which they're located. Apparently, she picked up the idea for her rainbow-hued toenail design and silver toe-jewellery from a friend of hers.

"Maybe you'd like to meet her sometime, Melody?" she comments, a satisfied smile on her shiny lips. "If you haven't already, that is."

Now, I don't have a clue if "shoe-shine stands" actually exist or not, and my former boss was anything but a "hot-looking, big-breasted babe" (she was actually a flat-chested, horse-faced sixty year-old with more corns on her feet than toes), but a lady is entitled to a "ped"-estrian dream every now and then, isn't she?

Marital Aids

Kate (Athabasca, Canada)

After ten years of mostly happy marriage to my husband, Jim, sex has become more of a chore than a joy lately – something to do once a week, like changing the sheets on the bed. Our love life has become stale, boring. It isn't that Jim isn't a good lover, it's just that with the kids and the jobs and the new house, sex has become secondary, and, sadly, it doesn't look like the situation is going to improve any time soon.

For that reason, I often wish that I had a really close girlfriend, someone I could talk openly and honestly to about things like sex, maybe get some advice on how I could spice things up with Jim. But, alas, all my women friends in the small town we recently moved to are rather prudish when it comes to things like that, or any other subject that can't be discussed in open church.

As a result, I've had to use my imagination and invent a girlfriend, Marianne, who I can have intimate chats with. I don't actually talk out loud to her, like a six-year-old with an imaginary buddy, but I do converse with her in my mind. And she has, I have to admit, begun to figure more and more prominently in the evermore frequent sexual fantasies that I've come to rely on to retain my sanity. I often combine the two – a helpful talk and a healthful fantasy with Marianne – like I did when I broached the subject of my stale sex life. We were sitting at the kitchen table, and . . .

Marianne twirled a strand of her long, black hair around a slim, silver-tipped finger. "Roger and I had a very similar problem," she said, her glossy lips breaking into a sympathetic smile. "I think all couples do eventually. You get completely over-whelmed by the day-to-day activities of living and striving to get ahead, such that sex doesn't seem so important any more."

I gazed into her crystal-clear blue eyes and blatantly in-quired, "And how did you guys handle it?"

"Well . . . you've got to do something to, um . . . shock the sexuality back into your marriage, so to speak. For Roger and me, it was, uh . . ."

I leaned closer.

"Spanking," she blurted.

"What?"

She looked me directly in the eye, her pearl-white, perfectly made-up face composed. "Our sex life had dwindled to vir-tually nothing, and it was just routine whenever we did make love, so Roger and I tried some new things, experimented a bit . . . until we found that spanking turned both of us on. Really turned us on."

I gulped down my amazement. "You mean that Roger spanks you?"

"Roger spanks me, I spank Roger. We spank each other. It's completely revived our sex life."

"But isn't it, um, painful?"

"There's a very thin line between pain and pleasure, Kate."

I almost spilled my coffee as I took a small sip, my hand was shaking so hard. "And w–what do you, you know, use to spank each other?" I spluttered.

Marianne shrugged her shoulders. "Well, it depends on what we feel like. Our hands, of course, brushes, paddles, rolled-up newspapers and magazines, dildos –"

"Dildos?"

She nodded. "Why don't I just show you our collection of disciplinary devices?"

"Why don't you?" I almost shouted, my face turning red and my body hot as I had a mental flash of beautiful Marianne savagely spanking hunky Roger's bare bum with a dildo. Roger is a big, blond, macho type of guy, and the thought of him getting disciplined with a plastic cock by his petite, polite wife left me light-headed and tingling all over, and wondering if Marianne wasn't on to something here.

"Follow me," she said, pushing back and gracefully sliding out of her chair. She winked at me and then strolled out of the kitchen and down the hall, her hips swaying suggestively under her shark-coloured dress.

I slammed my coffee cup down in its saucer, cracking both, and hurried after her, the two of us colliding just inside her bedroom door. She laughed and steadied me, her smooth, slender hands cool on my hot, sun-burnished skin, and then she guided me over to an antique dresser that crouched against a wall in the tastefully appointed room. She pulled the top drawer open, and we stood there, bare shoulder to bare shoulder, looking down at a neatly arrayed collection of butt-warming tools: switches, yardsticks, steel batons, paddles, hair brushes, a riding crop, and, yes, dildos.

"Wow!" I exhaled. "How long have you and Roger been doing this? Spanking each other, I mean?"

"Oh, about a year now, I suppose."

I picked up a monstrous, blue-black double-dong and held it in my hand, marvelling at its length and thickness, its heft. Then I whispered, as if I was holding a sacred object in a place of worship, "How does getting whipped with this thing feel?"

"There's only one way to find out," Marianne replied matter-of-factly.

I jerked my head sideways and gaped at her. "Huh? Oh, no . . . I couldn't . . . I –"

"You want to reclaim your sex life, or not?" she said bluntly, her soft, sweet voice grown decidedly harsher. Her eyes were hard and intimidating, her full lips parted slightly as if she was having trouble breathing.

I was having trouble breathing. I dropped the heavy-duty, two-pronged dildo and took a step backwards. "I guess maybe I better get –"

"You're not going anywhere!" Marianne barked, scooping up the lewd sex toy and roughly grabbing my elbow.

I glanced anxiously from her hand to her face, and her expression of unbending determination told me that I'd better play along. Plus, my own blossoming desire to find out just what that dildo did feel like kept me rooted to the ground.

"Okay, okay. I–I'm willing to give it a try," I stammered. No risk, no reward, right?

"Good," Marianne replied crisply. She let go of my arm and walked over to the large canopy bed that dominated the room, sat down stiffly on the side of it. She held the wicked-looking cock-substitute in her right hand and patted her tiny lap with her left. "Come over here and accept your punishment. Now!"

Sweat grew on my forehead and the palms of my hands, and my legs turned into two overcooked noodles. My whole body was numb and my head was spinning, but somehow I managed to stagger over to Marianne. I stood in front of her like a nervous schoolgirl, my hands trembling, my breath coming in shallow gasps.

"You've been a bad girl, haven't you!?" she rebuked me, slapping the giant dildo hard across the palm of her small, delicate hand.

The warm, caring woman I had known only moments before was gone, replaced by a cold, aggressive, and aroused dominatrix (I could clearly see her rigid nipples indenting the thin fabric of her dress). I suspected, as well, that her pussy was probably as wet as mine. She grabbed my hand and pulled me down onto her lap, bent me over her knees as if I was a ten year-old girl who'd just been caught smoking.

"This is for your own good," she declared, and then smacked my bottom with the rubber hose.

"God!" I shrieked, instantly amazed at the intensity of my reaction. It hadn't really hurt, but everything, every feeling, every action and reaction, seemed incredibly magnified in the crackling, sexually tense atmosphere of that bedroom. I was wearing only a flimsy summer dress and a pair of panties, and the thin fabric of those two garments provided sweet little cushioning for my bottom against Marianne's wicked love-stick.

She gripped my neck to hold me securely in place, and then whacked my bum again with the dildo, harder this time. I fought to catch my breath and blood rushed to my head and thundered in my ears. She smacked my butt again and again with her heavy spank toy, harder and harder, faster and faster, pounding my arse in an ever-more vicious rhythm.

"Fuck!" I groaned, and twisted my dizzy head around to steal a look at Marianne. Her sky-blue eyes were wide and glassy, her face crimson, her white teeth biting sharply into her pink tongue. I dropped my head back down and stared blindly at the carpet, the searing pain in my ass being fanned into flames by Marianne's relentless spanking.

She beat me unmercifully with the ebony pussy-plunger, and yet, even as she flailed away at my burning bottom, something clicked in my overwrought brain, and I mentally switched gears and the pain suddenly and unexpectedly began to dissipate. It became something I could control as I realized that Marianne would never really hurt me. I channelled the white-hot anguish from my throbbing bum into my drenched pussy, so that each time she smacked me, a jolt of raw sexual energy blasted my pussy and permeated my body.

"You're not hurting me!" I screamed defiantly, slobber spilling out of my mouth and onto the carpet, my transformation from victim to spank-vixen complete.

She angrily pushed up my dress and pulled down my panties, her long nails scratching the inflamed surface of my bottom as she frantically sought to expose me to even greater punishment, and pleasure. "This'll teach you a lesson!" she hissed, her chest heaving, her hands damp and shaking as she roughly adjusted my clothing to give herself the maximum bare target area.

"Yes!" I jeered when she lashed the flexible, two-headed dong across my naked arse with a resounding smack. My plump buttocks trembled, I trembled, as Marianne whaled my behind, raining down blows that blistered me from pink to scarlet.

Then she forced my legs apart and scrubbed my dripping cunt with the two-girl fuck-rod. She alternated between laying a licking on my butt and urgently buffing my pussy. The feeling was incredible and, before I even knew what was happening, my cunny exploded and I was rocked by orgasm. She savaged my bare bottom with stinging wallop after wallop, rubbed my drenched pussy, and a tidal wave of heat churned through my quivering body and consumed me, leaving me devastated in its wake. I came with a pain-induced intensity that I'd never have believed possible, and then lay limp and shattered across Marianne's knees when she halted her furious beating.

"How did that feel?" she asked after a while, lightly stroking my dewy neck and gently rubbing my swollen bum. "I wasn't too hard on you, was I?" She had reverted back to the Marianne of old, the Marianne I'd known exclusively before she picked up that black cock-replacement and pummelled my bottom like a woman possessed.

I sucked some humid air into my tortured lungs and wearily shook my head. She helped me regain my footing, and we both stared in awe at the reflection of my brick-red butt in the mirror above the dresser. "That's gonna leave a mark," I joked sheepishly, tentatively petting my ravaged behind. There were already white ridges forming where she had applied the dildo extra-hard.

I gingerly pulled up my panties and lowered my dress, then gave Marianne a big, heartfelt hug. "Thanks for all your help," I said, tears in my eyes.

"Sometimes a little hurt is the best help a friend can give," she responded, her own eyes glittering.

When Jim finally got home from work later that night, I could hardly wait to show him the visible proof of what I had learned from my good friend Marianne that afternoon. I bared my battered bottom for him as he changed out of his suit and into a T-shirt and jeans.

"Holy shit!" he yelped, bending down to get a closer look at my tender, tortured petoot. "Marianne did that to you?"

"She spanked me silly, yup," I replied.

He pressed a finger against my warm tushy, and shook his head in amazement when the white mark he left behind was quickly swallowed by red. "Christ almighty," he muttered, then straightened up. "What in hell brought all this on?"

"Oh, one thing sort of led to another," I remarked casually. "You know, sometimes girls like to play rough."

"Uh-huh. It looks like it must've hurt – a lot."

I turned around to face him, a mischievous smile spreading across my puffy lips. "It did . . . at first, but once I got into it –

really got into it – it didn't hurt at all; it felt good. Would you like me to demonstrate?"

He retreated a few steps when I drew one of Marianne's yardsticks out from under our bed and advanced on him. "Hey, wait a minute, Kate! What'd you think you're going to do with that?" he babbled.

"Naughty boy!" I said fiercely. "Don't you know that you're not supposed to talk back?" After Marianne had helped me ice down my flaming bum, she'd taught me how to use her various instruments of obedience – for maximum enjoyment.

Jim laughed nervously. "C'mon, Kate, there's no way in hell I'm going to let you –"

"You come on, Jim!" I responded angrily, then moderated my voice. "Do you want to spice up our sex life, or not?"

He mulled that over for a moment, watching me warily as I slid the long, hard, wooden ruler back and forth in my hands. Then he abruptly unbuckled and unzipped his pants, let them fall at his feet. "I've been a bad boy," he said with equal parts contrition and inquiry.

"That's better. Your underpants, too." I smacked the measuring stick across my hand.

He stepped out of his jeans and tugged down his Jockeys, never taking his eyes off of me and my spanking device. His thick cock sprung out, already partially inflated. I ordered him to bend over and place his hands on the edge of the bed, and he quickly complied. His big, bare arse presented an excellent target for my erotic anger. He gripped the bedcovers and spread his legs, then had the audacity to wiggle his bum at me.

I smacked his pale arse lightly with the yardstick, giving him a taste. "Don't get cheeky with me, mister," I intoned, getting in position on the left side of his exposed bottom.

"Sorry," he mumbled.

"What?"

"I'm sorry!"

I swatted his round butt, harder this time, and an inch-wide line of red flashed across his taut buttocks and then winked out. I hit him again, and again and again, the three-foot ruler making a cracking sound as I whacked it against my husband's ass. He moaned, and began tugging on his now fully engorged cock as he clung to the bed with one hand. He thrust his bottom even higher into the air, begging me to hammer him all the more.

I walloped his jiggling buns repeatedly as he fisted his cock and groaned with a mixture of pain and pleasure. The yardstick whistled through the air and crashed into his derriere over and over, his cute caboose flushing as red as my face. His cries got more and more urgent, telling me that he was close to coming – too close, too soon, in my opinion. "You're not going to get off that easy!" I yelled at him, and halted my sensual ass abuse. An idea had occurred to me – an extremely nasty, dirty idea.

He twisted his head around and dropped his rock-hard erection, gingerly touched his overheated backside. "Please, Kate," he whined. "I was almost there."

"Oh, you'll get there," I assured him. "But you're going to have a little more help." I tugged open the bottom drawer of my bedstand, rummaged around, and plucked out the eight-inch red dildo that I'd been relying on far too often lately.

Jim stared unbelievingly at me as I slowly and sexily tongued and sucked the big, plastic faux-cock, getting it all nice and wet. Then he squealed with alarm when I suddenly shoved the bulbous head of the spit-slick pussy-pleaser hard against his clenched pucker. "It's not going to fit, Kate!" he shrieked.

I thumped his ass with the yardstick. "I warned you about talking back," I sternly warned him again, then laid another hiding on his cooling posterior with the wooden sex toy. Once his ass was violently ablaze again, I retrieved the container of lube Marianne had generously given me, and sprayed some of it on my old faithful, and Jim's starfish.

"You're such a baby," I said contemptuously as he whimpered. Then I prodded the head of the slippery dildo into his arsehole.

He desperately tried to reach back and spread his twitching, tenderized pillows as I relentlessly jammed the unbending cock into him. Inch by hardened inch I slowly sank the dildo into his virgin anus, until all but the base was securely lodged in his chute. I wiggled it around, and he grunted and buried his face in the bedspread.

'Hold it in your arse!" I commanded, and let go of the preformed prick and took a step back. I whipped the yardstick around in the air a couple of times to limber up my arm again, refresh Jim's memory, and then slashed it across his beet-red butt cheeks, started flogging him all over again.

"Fuck, yeah!" he screamed, grabbing his enraged dick and pumping it.

I smacked the arse-mounted dildo and his bum at the same time, sending shivers throughout his charged body. He frantically jacked his meat, his hand a blur, his legs shaking as I spanked and spanked his violated arse. Then he bellowed my name and jerked thick ropes of semen out of his pulsating cock.

I kept right on smacking his inflamed, dildo-stuffed arse with my borrowed tree chunk, as he sprayed a huge load of sperm onto our carpet and bed. He was punished for that, as well.

. . My fantasy friend, Marianne, certainly gave me some good advice that day – and one heck of a help-yourself orgasm as I dreamed about her giving me that advice, my passing that advice onto Jim – but when I actually worked up the nerve to discuss the possibility of spanking with Jim for real, he simply laughed it off. Then he gave me his standard, two-minute, missionary position sexing. That's led me to conclude that maybe it's about time I made myself up a sexually open, good-looking, male friend. I'm sure Marianne knows someone.

Encore Performance

Autumn (Porterville, USA)

"All the world's a stage . . ." I prefer to think of it as a movie. How ideal it would be to create my own reality – to leave the imperfect scenes of my life on the cutting room floor, to be the star in my unfulfilled fantasies, to direct the actions of co-stars of my own acquaintance and choosing engaged with me in the pursuit of my innermost desires.

It's my personal escape, my frequent fantasies unbound and uncensored by the harsh reality of my entrapment in this suburban ulcer buried in the agricultural belly of California.

So let the curtain rise and let's light up the silver screen with the projection of a little X-rated version of my "reel life" . . .

My Friday nights had become a social desert, with not even a mirage of a sexual oasis in sight. I had been restless, so restless, with the need to get out and not have to go deaf listening to my thoughts echo throughout the emptiness between these walls. I swigged the last mouthful of wine from my glass – cold wine, chilly as the blood coursing through my veins towards the reheating furnace of my heart – and turned out the lights, locking solitude behind the door as I turned the key.

Downtown, downtown, the drumming in my blood urged me on a four-block stroll to the brick sidewalks and jasmine-trellised walls of the downtown cafes and bars. It was still early in the summer here in central California, hot days melting into balmy nights. I wandered along the pathways, glancing in through plate-glass windows at the lovers holding hands at candlelit tables as they laughed and kissed. I turned away and kept walking westward toward the blazing sunset, its yolk-golden eye winking goodnight to tangerine-and-sloe-gin clouds. Music beckoned from the little bistro on the next block. As I neared, the trumpets sassed me – *are those tears we see, wah-wah-wah* – brassy throats muffled with their mutes; and the lone saxophone wrapped its sensual tongue around me and lured me into its moody melody. *Come here, baby, you got the blues, you come to the right place . . . them blues, they come to life in this joint . . .*

I found a small table off to the side and ordered a Merlot from my favourite waitress. Her name's Thomasina, but she goes by "Tommi". She's a cute little thing, tight arse, big breasts that haven't had the time yet to go anywhere but forward. This particular night, they strained against her thin shirt, some flimsy knitted material, white with thin red horizontal stripes that magnified those magnificent knockers. Tommi has short hair, dyed red with purply feathers of colour at the ends, and wide, green cat-eyes dripping with dark eyelashes. She lines her eyes with kohl green eyeliner and brushes the lids tin-can rust. She leaned over to deliver my drink and smiled slyly at me as she noticed me watching her cleavage.

"Enjoy," she whispered in my ear, the heat and puff of breath sending a shiver through me. I watched her arse undulate beneath her black miniskirt, admiring the firmness and musculature of her calves – she's a hiker, a real mountain girl, and she has the legs to prove it.

The crowd was small for a Friday, all of us drawn in by the pulse of the ensemble resurrecting Charlie Parker and Dinah Washington up on the stage. The lights were low and there was a light haze settling throughout the room. How that room could always be smoky with a "no smoking" ordinance is beyond me, it must be the spirits of the old jazz and blues musicians flowing in with the music.

By my second glass of wine, I was feeling easy and loose, the sax's wail crying a river into my body, the notes tapping on the nerves of my thighs and my pussy. I surreptitiously slipped a couple of fingers under the hem of my short skirt – I was wet down there and I could feel a thrumming between my nether lips. My nipples, long-neglected by pursed lips, were swelling against the silky blouse I was wearing.

Tommi came up behind me and ran a hand lightly across my shoulder, then leaned over me and whispered again. "I'm on a half-hour break. Why don't you come join me?"

I followed her as she manoeuvred across the dance floor where couples were engaged in the tango of foreplay to the groaning of the saxophone. She removed a key from the pocket of her waitress apron and unlocked a door marked "Private" located just beyond the restrooms. There was a steep claustrophobic staircase and she motioned for me to follow her upwards. I watched the muscles ripple across her calves and the back of her thighs and felt something drip down the inside of one of my own thighs.

At the top of the stairs, we turned left and she unlocked a door with "2B" in carved wooden figures in the centre. "Home, sweet home," Tommi said, untying her apron and tossing it over the back of a cane-backed chair.

"You live here?" I asked, scrutinizing her pocket-sized living quarters.

"Yep, it's convenient and cheap," she answered as she wandered around the apartment while she lit candles on the counters and bookcases. The sweet smell of gardenias filled the room. A flamingo flaming in pink neon stood guard in the one window I could see.

Tommi turned to me and those green eyes swallowed up my body, running from my nipples fighting the irritating tightness of my pink silk blouse, down my long waist, down to where my clasping grey pinstripe skirt halted mid-thigh. I'm taller than she, maybe three or four inches, and older by a good ten years. I kicked off my shoes, dusky pink stiletto heels that match my blouse.

She came to me, and brushed a thumb across the nub of one nipple that protruded through the silk. I grunted and moaned softly as she continued with the other hand, then cupped my breasts – heavy breasts, but not as endowed as hers – and I felt that drip continuing down my thigh. She unbuttoned my blouse and unclasped the frail bra that imprisoned my breasts, letting my blouse fall to the carpet. She leaned forward and tongued my nipples, her breath warm, her tongue warm, her hands warm against my skin.

I fondled her tits through her shirt, tugging at the fabric until she pulled back and skimmed the shirt over her head. She wasn't wearing a bra, but those huge globes jutted forward even without artificial support. Tommi's so young and so athletic. Her smooth tanned skin was beading up with droplets of perspiration. I hadn't noticed before how warm it was in there, even with the small window air conditioner running.

Tommi undid the two buttons at the side of her skirt and let it pool to her feet. She was wearing a thong, red, shimmery, with some design of roses embroidered on the fabric. The springy pubic hair peeking out from the front triangle was dark and shiny. She came to me again, sucking my tits harder, her hands gliding down my back to the zipper of my skirt. Slowly, she lowered the zipper, the metal snickering down over the teeth. I preferred a garter belt that night, deep pink and satin, with silky pink stockings. She pushed me onto the bed and gazed down intently as I raised one leg at a time and slicked my stockings down my smooth legs. I, too, stay in shape, dancing and roller blading to fend off the agents of time.

"Let me touch you," she said quietly, the candlelight flickering shadows along her little body.

I lay back on the bed, such a small bed, but with just enough room for the two of us. She knelt between my legs and ran her finger up the inside of my thigh, first one, then the other, from the back of my knee to just where my pubes start. My sensitive skin shuddered at the sensation and a nerve jumped between my labia. Her finger wandered further upward and she played with my lower lips, squeezing and pulling the flesh until we both felt it swelling and thickening. She slipped her finger inside my pussy, inside the hot flesh, inside the steaming folds. My eyes closed as she played with one nipple with her free hand, rolling the nub between thumb and fingers. I sighed as she inserted another finger and explored my crevice.

I reached for her, my hands touching her beautiful tits, feeling their firmness, their softness, rose-petal soft. I touched her waist, her hips, and undid the strings of her thong. She withdrew her fingers and put them to her lips. Her tongue snaked out, a tongue imbedded with a single red tongue ring, and she licked my wetness from her fingertips.

"Popcorn," she whispered. "You taste like hot, buttered popcorn, sweet and salty all at the same time." She straddled my waist and leaned down to share what was on her tongue with my own. Her tongue probed between my lips and I answered with my own exploration of that pink, studded organ, the two of us encircling and enwrapping tongues.

My hands rested on her hips, supporting her as she leaned in. My fingers took off on a journey of their own, travelling between the tight cheeks of her arse until I reached her tiny puckerhole. I dipped in a finger and she hissed with pleasure. I pushed in further and could feel her sucking me in with her sphincter muscles. She pushed herself up above me, her arms straight, her head bent back as she welcomed my probing fingers.

Her head fell forward and those cat eyes gazed into mine, then closed again. She lowered herself down my sweating body, kissing my breasts as she descended, kissing my navel, kissing my bikini line. She dipped her tongue into my pussy, quickly, like a little cat lapping at its water bowl. Then Tommi settled into her desire, into my desire, her tongue pushing deep into my swollen crevice. I felt the stud from her tongue ring rub against my clit and the little bud swelled at the contact. Tommi knew this, that's why she wears the pearl-like orb. She continued rubbing it against my clit, just grazing it, drawing out the nectars of my inner flesh.

Her hands were clenched around my hips, holding them in place as I tried to arch against her mouth. I moaned, I muttered. "Fuck me, fuck me, you red-haired puss, suck it out me," is what I was saying, but mostly in my head. What came out of my mouth were the unintelligible words of rapture, whispered, moaned, grunted, cried out.

She flicked harder now against my clit, and I could feel the gears shift inside my body, I could feel the build-up starting, the line growing taut. The line snapped and whipped as Tommi shoved her thumb up my arse and pressed against the thin wall separating the two orifices. I thrashed on the narrow bed, my head whipping my long hair from side to side as I came inside Tommi's talented mouth. Without breaking the tempo, we managed to switch positions, and I became the one sliding down Tommi's juicy, compact body.

I filled my mouth with her breast, circling around the nipple with my tongue. Her nipples are large and chewy, and I giggled, thinking of red liquorice whips as I nibbled on her. As I slid south, I noticed that she had a small rose tattooed just above her pubic hair. I kissed it, kissed the rose, kissed the soft petals of her pussy. I liked the fact that she doesn't shave her mons like so many of the younger girls. Why look like a child when you are all *woman*?

As I played with her labia, I discovered that she was pierced down there as well. I had heard about the benefits of having labial rings. I pulled with the tip of my tongue at the two she wears and she cried out, not in pain, but in ecstasy. I fluttered my tongue across them, across the opening into her tight little pussy and her hips rose to meet my mouth.

I felt Tommi straining above me and heard a drawer slap shut. "Here," she breathed heavily, shoving something at me with one hand while she raked my hair with the other hand. "Put it in my arse."

It was a dildo, short and thin, one of the expensive ones that has the texture and colour of the real thing. I put it in my mouth and sucked at it, then slipped it inside my soaked pussy, lubricating the surface of the instrument of pleasure. I poked and prodded at her little butthole with the dildo, slowly making headway as she sucked it inside her.

I returned to my investigation of her pussy, lapping at the lips, enjoying the taste of her juices as they ran over my lips and chin, all the while working her slender little joystick inside her back hole. Tommi was a noisy gal, mewing and crying out as she bucked on the bed. I hoped the band was still performing or the bistro patrons would be getting a different type of entertainment in a minute. And it was a minute, a New York minute, quick as the little red-haired fox she resembles. Tommi exploding in orgasm. Her thighs shook and clenched about my head, and she rammed her pubic mound against my mouth as she drenched it with her inner ambrosia.

The storm subsided and we lay there on the bed, our skin cooling in the flow of the air conditioner. We heard the distant rumble of thunder and the pattering of rain on the protruding shell of the air conditioner – another rare summer storm.

Tommi was the first to rise, gathering up clothing and putting herself in order to finish her shift downstairs. I couldn't find one of my stockings, so I gave up on wearing any undergarments whatsoever and pulled on my skirt and blouse. I bent over and ran my hands through my hair until I'd cleared out most of the tangles.

Tommi kissed me gently on the lips as she passed on her way to retrieve her apron. She smiled. "Thank you. I always wondered what you were like, seeing you in here on Friday nights, all by yourself."

"Popcorn, remember. A full box of hot, buttered popcorn," I answered, slipping into my shoes.

Tommi laughed and applied a thin layer of lipstick as she contemplated herself in the mirror hung over her dresser.

There was a gentle tap at the door. "Tommi, girl, you in there, baby?" A man's voice, soft and inquiring. The knob turned and a man's curly-haired head appeared around the door. "Oh, sorry, baby, didn't know you had company. Your break's over and I was just wondering if you were okay."

"I'm fine. Just fine," Tommi emphasized with a smile as she looked at me. "Come on in, Boone. This is my friend, Autumn," she introduced me.

The man and I shook hands and I felt something surge between the two of us. I tried not to react, but Tommi had already noticed. She smiled again. "Boone owns this place. He lets me stay here for minimal rent. We're really *close*," she added.

"Nice to meet you." He finally withdrew his hand which was powerful and sinewy, yet surprisingly gentle in his touch. He coolly assessed me with blue eyes the same ice-blue hue as that of a Siberian husky. I met his gaze with my own assessment of his qualities.

He ran a hand through his deep-red curls. Boone is my age, with a spattering of freckles across his cheeks, but his skin is bronzed, not the pale cream I usually associate with red hair. "Tommi, I'm heading over to the old theatre for the late showing. I think they've got something with Bogart and Bacall. Can you lock up tonight?"

I could already see the gears turning in Tommi's little head. "Sure, Boone. In fact, I think Autumn likes the old movies.

Maybe you two should go together. Nothing like a little popcorn on a Friday night, right, Autumn?" She grinned a devious imp's smile.

"Hey, that would be great," Boone jumped in without waiting for my reply. As though I would have answered anything but "yes". I could feel something quivering between my thighs and I didn't think it was from the previous half-hour's gymnastics.

Tommi scampered down the steps ahead of us as Boone urged me ahead of him with a gentle nudge of his warm hand in the small of my back.

We walked out into the humid evening air, the jasmine's scent thick in the darkness. The thundershower had passed, but an occasional sprinkle drizzled down on us as we walked the four blocks to the old theatre which shows the classics every Friday and Saturday night. We spoke of our occupations, how we had come to know our mutual friend, Tommi, of how talented the band was this evening. Moths, some with wing-spans as wide as Boone's hand, knocked against the lights flaring at the top of the old-fashioned lampposts.

"Two, please," Boone said pleasantly with a charming smile to the ticket girl. "My treat," he waved off my offer to pay my own way.

"So, do you want some popcorn?" he asked, remembering Tommi's earlier comment.

"Um, not really. Actually, I feel like some liquorice whips," I said.

"Hmmm, a woman who likes whips. My kind of woman," Boone growled, then flashed that smile at me. I felt something contract in my loins and my skin flushed. He handed me the box of liquorice whips and, as his hand brushed mine, I felt that familiar fluid sliding down the inside of my thigh.

We headed into the darkness of the theatre, his warm hand pressed to my back, this time just a little lower, as he guided me to the back row of seats. There were only about two dozen patrons there, most of them sitting towards the front. Real film aficionados, I guessed. The storm had come back again, a thunderclap rattling the old building. "Looks like it's going to be a wet evening," Boone commented in a low voice as we settled into our seats.

The lights in the theatre went down, and the film reel started unwinding its tale of murder and love on the rocks with a twist, with Bacall giving Bogie a good look at those half-mast eyes, her husky voice and no-holds-barred attitude reeling the tough man in.

I'd opened my box of liquorice whips and took one into my mouth, savouring the red sweetness, remembering the chewiness of Tommi's erect nipples. I could see Boone from the corner of my eye, his head turned just slightly, pretending to pay attention to the movie. He was watching me intently, his ice-eyes nearly glowing in the reflection on the silver screen, watching me tongue my candy whip, watching me suck on it.

There was a squeak as he shifted in his seat and draped his forearm over the wooden armrest between us. He lowered his hand, its warmth resting on my naked thigh. He slid his fingers higher, exploring my skin, feeling for the panties that weren't there. I spread my thighs apart as his fingers reached my muff. He inserted one digit into my already damp slit and slicked it around inside me. He pulled out his finger and tasted what clung to his skin.

"Sweet and salty," he whispered into my ear as he leaned over the seat.

"A good night for popcorn," I whispered back, and he chuckled as he realized the joke.

It was my turn to play. I placed my hand in his crotch and felt a thick bulge beneath his zipper. I unzipped him, the metallic rasping noise well-covered by the swelling violins on-screen. He wasn't wearing anything, no briefs, no boxers, no anything. Just a handful – well, a little more than a handful – of heated, pulsing flesh that jumped at my touch in excited greeting. I ran my fingertips gently over the plum-shaped head, down his veined shaft, down to his heavy balls. "Feels like a full load in there," I whispered into his ear.

He slipped down a little in his seat and I stroked him harder, keeping an eye out for an usher. Boone sat up suddenly and I withdrew my hand, startled. He zipped himself up and grabbed my hand, pulling me to my feet. He drew me to the rear of the theatre, behind the scarlet velvet curtains draped along the back wall.

"What are you doing?" I whispered ferociously. It was dark and dusty back there, and I had a sudden mental view of big, fat spiders hanging at the end of their webs, just waiting for a couple of tasty morsels such as ourselves.

"Secret passage," he whispered. He was feeling along the wall with his hands, and I heard his hand make contact with wood, then the rattling of a knob. Boone swore. There was the jingling of keys, then the sound of a key slipping inside a lock, turning, and the snap as the tumblers ceded to the key.

Boone pulled me inside the door and closed it behind us. It was pitch-black in there, and I was starting to wish I hadn't stayed up and watched all those midnight monster flicks as a child. There was the sound of a lighter igniting and a small flame lit up the tiny room. Boone held his lighter aloft with a smirk of triumph on his freckled, bronzed face.

"Where are we?" I asked *sotto voce*, looking around me at the empty wooden shelves, barren wooden desk, and plaid cloth couch, its two seat cushions looking a bit dusty, but none the worse for wear.

"This is the old storage room. They used to keep special stuff that the owners managed to purchase from the studios back here. The former owner was quite a collector. We used to come here and smoke and grab a beer or sometimes a thermos cup of coffee and something stronger when I was a teenager."

"Did you used to work here?"

"Yeah. Long time ago. My dad owned the place and made sure I was gainfully employed as usher, janitor, ticket-taker, you name it, to earn my keep."

"And you still have the key to the door?" I shook my head in amazement as I looked around at the room.

"Well, I have a skeleton key to some of the doors in my bistro. Dad owned both places and I remembered while we were sitting out there that he used the same locksmith for both joints. It figures that the key would fit some of the doors here." Boone rummaged through the desk drawers.

"Hah, here we go," he exclaimed, holding up a couple of stocky red candles with a waterfall's worth of drippings frozen along the sides. "We used to smoke some stronger stuff than cigarettes back here, so we had to have something to cover the

smell." He lowered the lighter to the wicks, and after a protesting dust-choked crackle and spit, the candles lit up with a rosy
glow. He placed them on the desk and turned to the couch.
Boone picked up the cushions and slapped them together,
knocking off the gathered dust of the past, and replaced them.

"Come here, Miss No-Panties," Boone ordered, plopping
down on the couch and crooking an index finger at me.

"Who, me?" I asked innocently. I sashayed to the couch and
arranged myself on the cushion next to him.

Boone put an arm around my shoulders and drew me to him.
He kissed me softly on the lips, mouth closed. He touched my
breast through my blouse, then began to unbutton me. I felt
like I was eighteen again, the thrill of a boy's hand on my breast
and his lips on mine making me tingle down below. He broke
the kiss for a second, ridding me of my blouse. His lips
returned to mine, pressed harder this time, more urgent.
Our lips parted, and I tasted the minty sweetness of his breath
as his tongue reached in and snaked around mine. I curled up,
kicking off my shoes; I heard his loafers hit the floor at about
the same time.

I pulled away and unbuckled his belt, unzipped him, and
tugged at his pants. He raised his hips and I yanked his pants
off. I hunched down on the couch, backing up until my arse hit
one of the cushioned arms. I kissed him on the hip, on his flat,
lightly furred belly, on the head of his swollen cock. He played
with one of my breasts while he urged my head down onto his
phallus. I licked the shaft, licked his balls, and took them into
my mouth.

"Oh, yeah, girl, don't stop that," he hissed. He pinched my
nipples; the sensation walked the tightrope between pain and
pleasure.

I rolled my tongue around his balls, feeling how packed they
were. Yes, it was certainly going to be a wet night. I moved on
to the shaft of his cock, thick, solid, veined with throbbing
channels of heated blood. The skin was marble-smooth. I
lowered my mouth onto him, taking his length into my mouth
until the tip of his dick entered my throat. He shoved it deeper
into me, wrapping his fingers in my hair. My tongue glided up
and down the shaft, my lips suctioning him in, savouring his

humid flesh. He was starting to exude the fluids building up in those swollen balls at the base of his cock.

"Not yet," I heard him whisper breathlessly. He took his dick in his hand and pulled it from my mouth, rubbing the head against my lips and cheeks. I flicked out my tongue and tasted the tiny droplets of come leaking from the tip.

"Turn around," Boone directed me. "I want you from the rear."

I complied, curling up into a tight ball, displaying my arse to him. I was still clad in my short skirt, and Boone shoved it up until it bunched around my hips. He still wore his shirt, but the buttons had been undone, and it flailed on either side of me like wings as he mounted me. He drove his cock into my pussy slowly, then withdrew it. He did this several times, teasing me with his instrument.

"Give it to me, Boone," I begged him, wanting his length inside my valley of wet, swollen, pink flesh.

He relented, ramming the entire shaft into me up to his root. He filled me completely this way, from the rear. He reached around my hips and played with my pussy lips, played with my clit as he rocked within me. God, it felt so good, the pressure of his fingertip against my swelling bud. My wetness lubricated his shaft and the sucking sound of him riding my inner shell filled this tiny room. I arched my shoulders as he drove into me and pumped my ass back into his crotch.

He slapped my arse cheeks, softly at first, testing the waters and my reaction. I gasped, but with pleasure at the brisk *crack* of his hand contacting my white flesh. Realizing I welcomed the touch, he grew bolder, spanking my arse harder and harder until the flesh burned red and heated, almost unbearable, but *just* bearable. His breath was loud as he flicked his tongue into my ear. It drove me fucking wild and the combination of his tongue and his finger tips and his punishing palm bringing me to orgasm. I mewed and cried and bucked, crazed with the stimulation and friction against my sensitive sensual spots. Explosions of black and red and brilliant white fireworks filled my sight as he slammed into me. He shuddered and shook, thighs trembling against my arse cheeks.

He came, the white froth of his heated cauldron a shotgun

blast into my pussy, overflowing its small encasement, dripping down my thighs and flowing up into the crack of my ass. Boone cried out, a teeth-clenched rasping howl of ecstasy. His ramming eased back to short, stabbing pokes into my hole as the last of his jettisoned spume escaped his cock.

Finally there was no sound but the harsh, oxygen-deprived gasping of our combined breath. Boone withdrew his cock from me and sat on the couch, pulling me into his arms. He kissed my lips gently and smoothed back a lock of my hair that fell over my perspiring brow.

The candles were guttering – had we been there that long? We pulled on our clothing, racing the failing light of the dying candles. They died out almost simultaneously, and once again I heard the rasp of the lighter as Boone flicked the starter. He relocked the door behind us and we cautiously retraced our steps back along the curtain and out into the theatre. The music was swelling as the credits rolled and the last of the patrons were already filing out the exit.

"Come on, let's take the back way," Boone said, heading for one of the exits that led us out into a back alleyway.

It was raining again, a gentle drizzle that made my silk blouse cling to me. Boone looked down approvingly as the fabric stuck to my breasts and my nipples extruded through the thin cloth. We ducked under awnings and into doorways as we headed back to the bistro.

"Why don't you come on in for a nightcap?" Boone asked hopefully as we arrived at the bistro. The lights were out; Tommi had closed up for the night, but her flamingo stood gaudy guard in the window above us.

"Not tonight," I answered, kissing him briefly on the cheek. "Let me take a rain check on that invitation," I added.

He grinned that perfect-toothed smile and waggled his fingers in farewell as I headed down the emptying streets to my home.

For now, the curtain has come down and my characters are silent. But all I have to do is change reels, flick that sensitive pink switch, and another mental manuscript flickers to life within me.

Spanking Fantasy

Jenny (Lumberton, USA)

I've always dreamed of getting spanked by a lover. I don't doubt I'd hate it if it happened in real life, but in my dreams . . .

As we sit together after dinner one evening, my lover looks up from reading and smiles at me. "I love you, Jenny," he says. "You are close to perfect, but . . ."

Hell! The eternal "but"! "But what?" I ask.

"You're undisciplined and need a good spanking!"

My mouth goes dry. My stomach clenches. My heart races. I look him in the eye. Rather lovely eyes, as it happens. "I don't think so!"

"That comment, my dear, proves my point!" He gets up and crosses the carpet to stand in front of me, his knees almost touching mine. "You are in dire need of discipline. An over-the-knee spanking is what you need!"

"You have to be kidding!"

He isn't and I make the mistake of jumping to my feet. His hand closes around my wrist. "Jenny," he says, his voice soft, with that little tinge of anticipation that always sets my heart racing. Works the same now, but not in anticipation of a nice bout in bed! "You know I don't kid around. You need a little attitude adjustment, and as your lover it's my job to see it comes about. Don't argue with me, or you'll get double!"

I'm scared, angry, indignant, astounded – and turned on! Against every commonsense notion, I nod, accepting his right to punish me. Why? I don't know! Curiosity perhaps, or secret excitement that an unrevealed fantasy is about to come true.

"Follow me!" he says and marches out the door. Towards our bedroom.

I can't believe I'm following him meekly, but I am. My mind too caught up in arousal, fear and anticipation to argue. My mouth too dry and my throat too tight to speak, even if I wanted to. He's obviously planned this ahead of time. One of the mahogany dining room chairs stands in the middle of the bedroom carpet.

"Come on!" he says, his voice stern as he sits down on the needlepoint cushion and looks across to where I hesitate in the doorway. "You've imagined this happening to you, haven't you?" I nod, mute. "We both know it's exactly what you need. Don't keep me waiting!" He pats his knee invitingly. Only it doesn't invite. It scares. But yes, it's true, I have always wondered what this would be like. Must have told him sometime when I'd had too much wine. Why was I hesitating? He was right, I had fantasized about getting spanked, but the looming reality fills me with dread.

Slowly I put one foot in front of the other and approach him. When I get within touching distance, he grabs my wrist and pulls me close. I swallow. Twice. Unable to take my eyes away from his. I bite my lip until it hurts, thinking I'm perhaps dreaming and it will wake me, but I'm not dreaming. He reaches up his other hand to stroke my cheek and lip. "Don't bite your lip like that, Jenny, you'll hurt yourself."

"And you won't hurt me?"

He smiles. "Oh! Yes! You'll be crying and begging me to stop."

At that I pull back but his grip is tight and he yanks me towards him. "Better not resist, Jenny, or I'll add extra."

"You keep threatening to add extra!"

"And I mean it. You're getting a thorough spanking, whether you like it or not." By now, I'm convinced I won't like it. "It's up to you how long it will be. Each argument, each effort at resistance adds another six spanks."

If I had any sense, I'd be running, but he's gripping both my wrists and pulls me until I stand between his open thighs. "I'm scared," I say. It comes out as a hoarse whisper.

"I know, darling." His voice is soft and warm as a caress.

"Of course you are. You're wondering how hard I'm going to spank, how long it will last, and if it's going to hurt as much as you fear. You won't have long to worry. You'll soon find out. Anticipation is all part of it. One of your worries I will answer: It's going to be on your bare bottom."

Now I really do panic and wrench an arm from his grasp and try to run, but quick as a whip, he grabs me by the waist, hauls me back and before I know what has happened, I'm face down over his knee, arms flailing and legs kicking. He lets me struggle until I realize it's useless. He's so much stronger than I am and has me at a total disadvantage. I shudder as I realize how completely helpless I am and how inevitable my spanking.

To think I used to get wet fantasizing about this! But I am wet. Already.

"Stop fighting me!" he orders, smoothing his hands over my back and down my waist to stroke my admittedly ample butt. "Relax." I almost laugh at that but it's hard to laugh doubled over, my nose just inches from the Berber carpet. "If you relax and accept the inevitable, it will go much more easily. If you resist and tighten your muscles, it will hurt more. You decide."

Great choices! But I believe him and make a conscious effort to relax. It's not easy and I don't do a very good job. Even if I could relax my muscles, my mind is whirling, my stomach churning against his strong thigh, my heart racing and I don't want to think what my cunt is doing.

I give a big sigh, feeling my boobs rise and fall against his legs, and wonder why I hadn't gone out shopping after dinner. I could be happily strolling the mall now, instead of face to the carpet, waiting for a whack on my posterior.

"Good girl," he says and kisses me on the back of my neck. The touch of his lips sends my clit throbbing. I'm not sure I can stand any more. But what choice do I have? He's literally got me where he wants me.

"Stay still, just like this," he tells me. "Don't try to resist me. It won't work and will just earn you more and harder punishment. Now . . ." he pauses. His hand moves from my butt. His fingers slip inside the waist band of my skirt and before I realize what he's doing, he pulls it down my legs until it falls off my ankles. Damn elastic waists! Why hadn't I worn blue jeans? That would have slowed him down. At least I'm wearing tummy flattening panties. They're a bitch to yank on in the morning. They won't come off so easily. He strokes my butt. Nothing new in that – he's always liked my butt. Once told me I'd the loveliest arse he'd ever seen.

Why wasn't I warned?

His hand caresses the back of my thighs and up again. I relax a little as he strokes my ass. Maybe he's seen all the spandex and has decided to leave them on. No such luck! With a shift of his leg, bouncing me up a few inches, and a quick yank, they're off and down. He pulls again and they're at my knees. Tight-fitting as they are, they're as good as shackles. I can't move my legs at all. Just what he wants no doubt.

At that I give up and sag against his strong thighs.

He's right. I have longed to know how this feels. Too bad, now it's happening, I'm ready to change my mind!

He strokes my bare butt. The calluses on the tips of his fingers brushing my skin. I like this. I've always enjoyed having my ass admired. I love the feel of his hand caressing me.

Maybe this won't be too bad.

My shoulders relax, and so does my ass.

"Lovely!" he whispers. Whether he's pleased I'm not re-sisting, or admiring my ass, who knows? Who cares? I'm more concerned about the first slap and when it's going to land. How hard will it sting? Will he make me yelp? No! That I won't do! Not at any price!

"How does that feel?" he asks as his fingertips trace gentle cycles over my cheeks.

"Nice," I concede.

"Good," he whispers. "Get ready. I'm about to start. Remember you're forbidden to move."

I can't help it. My entire body tenses. After what seems an age, the first spank lands. It's barely a touch: a little love pat, followed by another. I smile. Why was I so damn worked up? This is easy! Nice in fact. Just gentle love pats all over my butt. I relax. He's moved to my thighs. I feel the slaps, yes, but they don't hurt. I got all in a stew and it's nothing to be scared about. Heck, he's given me harder slaps on my rump in play!

He can keep this up as long as he wants. I almost tell him so, but his hand eases between my legs and he finds my wet pussy.

"Ah! Hah!" He sounds so darn pleased. I want to kick him. Fat chance of that with my knees shackled with my spandex panties! "All those protests and this is turning you on!"

Can't deny it. Damn well don't want to agree. So I keep quiet. Concentrating on the carpet, the warmth in my ass and legs and the ever-growing smell of my arousal.

Two, three more pats on my ass. "Did that hurt?"

"No," I reply, "not at all."

"This will." Before my mind processes his words, his hand comes down. Hard. With the horrid splat of flesh on flesh. I yell, rearing up and struggling to move away.

It does me no good. A hand between my shoulder blades forces me back down and he grabs my flailing arm and bends it up behind me in a chicken wing. Illegal wrestling moves must be allowed when spanking.

"Let go of me!" I tell him and I half turn to scowl at him.

"Not until you promise not to resist me."

"That hurt!"

"Of course it did." He sounds irritated. "This is punishment, Jenny. You must expect it to hurt. That was just the first of many you deserve, and I intend to see you get them all."

"The first ones didn't hurt."

"They were just to warm you up for the punishment proper."

Friggin' hell!

Silence for several, long seconds. "Well, Jenny?" he barks at me, like a drill sergeant in the movies. "Are you going to promise not to fight me? I'm waiting."

"What if I refuse?"

Silence and a long sigh. "You have two choices. Either lie still on my knee and accept your punishment without resisting. A punishment you know you've longed for and justly deserve. Or . . ." he pauses, hand on my warmed over ass, as I wait to hear the alternative that I just know will be worse. "If you resist the spanking, I will bend you over the foot of the bed, tie your hands down, and give it to you with my belt."

Sheesh! Why had I ever thought this would be fun? Even

more to the damn point, why were my pussy lips wet with arousal? No point in trying to think that one out. I most certainly did not want to feel his belt on my arse. His hand was bad enough.

"I won't fight you," I reply and my body sort of sags against his legs. I want this, I have to admit. But I'm dreading it. How many more like that last one will I get? Can't be too many. It has to hurt his hand too.

"Good."

Takes me only moments to regret that promise, but what's my alternative? His belt? I shudder under the onslaught and accept each punishing slap as my arse burns and throbs.

At first, I count. Four slaps and a pause. To let his hand rest more likely than to ease my sore ass. Four more. Another pause. Four more – harder this time, I swear. I give up counting. It takes all I have not to scream, but I don't. Tears come first, spilling hot down my cheeks onto the carpet.

I'm hurting. Bad. Every inch of my butt stings and smarts and it gets worse with each hard slap. I let out a yelp here and there, unable to hold it all back and my tears run faster as I sob. I lose track of time and place. I'm aware of nothing but the building pain in my ass and the increasing throb in my clit. Through my tears, I smell my arousal. This is crazy, insane and . . .

He stops.

It takes me a few sobs and gasps to realize he's no longer spanking. I'm just lying there, hurting, arse burning, pulse throbbing in my ears, eyes sore from crying. Through the morass of sensation and emotion, his lovely voice comes clear.

"It's over, Jenny."

As he helps me to my feet, and holds me close, I know that's not true. My arse might hurt but my entire body pulses with arousal.

I look up into his eyes. "I need . . ." I begin, unsure what I really do need.

"I know." He lifts my chin with his hand – the hand that moments earlier was punishing and now caresses. Holding my face between his hands, he brings his lips to mine. A slow, lingering kiss, tongue on tongue and filling my mouth with his presence.

Now I know exactly what I need! My hips rock of their own volition and I feel his erection under his jeans.

"Please . . ." I begin, too tired, too sore, too aroused, to talk straight.

No problem. He knows. He picks me up and lays me on my side on the bed. I shut my eyes a minute, absorbing the warring and confusing sensations in my body. The mattress shifts. He's lying spooned behind me. I feel bare legs against mine. He's shucked his clothes. I sigh and lean back into him, pressing my still-sore arse against his glorious erection.

This is what I need! He slips into me sideways and lies still. His cock pressed deep in my cunt. Filling me. His warm belly against my burning arse. His hand cups my breast, as his fingers brush my nipple and I feel it down to my cunt. I thought I was aroused before. Now I'm about to go into orbit. I shift, pressing him deeper into me. He starts moving, gently as if aware how sore I still am. But the pain fades into the background as my arousal builds and peaks.

I'm whimpering with pleasure, groaning with need. His hand eases down my belly and plays my bush, parting my pussy lips. I rock again, pressing his wonderful finger against my clit. He's in me, around me, touching the very heat of my need, and as gentle circles of his fingertip pull me higher, I close my eyes and give myself over to sensation. Another groan echoes in my ears, and another and, with a scream, I come in a mind-numbing climax that goes on and on and on . . .

I'm a sweaty, useless heap of satisfied woman.

My heart resumes normal pace, my breathing slows, I turn to him, careful to rest on my hip as my ass still hurts but the pain is fading to a warm glow.

"That was incredible," I manage between gasps.

He smirks, like a man who knows he's done a damn fine job. "I knew what you needed, didn't I?"

I'm too tired, too weak, and too fulfilled to argue. I smile back and snuggle to sleep in his arms.

I'll save the argument for another day . . . When I'm ready for a repeat performance.

Thursdays at McKinney's

Janet (St Paul, USA)

I hadn't always wondered what it would be like to be with another girl. No sir, I thought I was a straight arrow, got me a boyfriend and everything. And it's not like there were a lot of dykes hanging out at McKinney's. That's the bar where I used to work, waitressing or bartending, depending on the night, to put myself through school. I got nothing against dykes, mind you. I just never gave a lot of thought to them one way or the other.

Not that I had much inspiration, at least not until I got a look at the couple that started coming in every Thursday night. But those two, the brunette and her buddy, something about them was enough to make me reconsider. I mean it wasn't like they were the prettiest girls at the bar or anything so I really don't know what the deal was. But I watched them plenty to try and figure it out, let me tell you. The brunette was big and curvy, with a kind of pretty face and really long brown hair. Her buddy was nothing special to look at. She had sort of shaggy blonde hair and glasses, the expensive wire-rim kind. She always wore pants and looked like she worked out or something.

I don't know how I figured out they were together that way. I mean they could have been just pals, you know? But there was something in the way they looked at each other, the way that they would touch sometimes, just a little. But enough to make me think about what was going on the rest of the time.

I liked to watch the blonde's hands. They were big hands for a woman, all long fingers with short nails. She had this way of moving them around when she talked, like they were an extra mouth or something, backing up everything she said. After a while I started to wonder what they would feel like inside me. Scared the crap out of me the first time it happened. That was when I knew something was up, and it didn't much matter if it was Johnny or not.

Johnny's the boyfriend I was talking about before, only now he's my fiance. He's got fantasies of his own, especially that girl-on-girl stuff. Yeah, he really likes that. Every once in a while he'll show up at my place with a couple of videos. There's always one of those in the stack. Guess he figures if I watch enough porn, I'd break down and bring one of my girlfriends over and put on a show for him. Fat chance. I mean he always denies it but I know how hot he gets after he watches them. One night I even gave him a lap dance and I am still not sure if it was me or the plastic babes on the tube that got him off.

So when it came to the whole girl-on-girl thing, I guess I just figured that those kind of girls were the only option. You know how it is, they look fake and they act fake so there was nothing about watching them that really grabbed me. Plus, no way was I letting somebody with nails that long put them inside me, even if it was just in my imagination. Gives me the shivers just thinking about it.

These two weren't like that, or at least they didn't look that way to me. The brunette now, she did have kind of long red nails, the kind that came out of a shop where they did them up right, not scary long. They looked nice when she touched the blonde's arm with them. She did that a lot, just resting her hand near the other one's arm, then moving over to grab it or brush against her hand or whatever. Then she'd kind of pull back, play with her hair a little and just give her girlfriend this smile that said there was a lot more going on than met the eye at McKinney's.

At first, they freaked me out. I mean, what could two women really do in bed? I knew about dildos and stuff from all those videos that Johnny showed me but it just didn't seem like they could substitute for the real thing. Besides in the movies, a guy always showed up so that took care of wanting something other than plastic inside you. A guy always shows up in the kind of videos Johnny likes. What a surprise.

But I was worried about other stuff too. What if they decided to hit on me? How would I handle it? It wouldn't be like the guys doing it; I was used to laughing that off. I didn't even want to go into the ladies room when one of them was in there, not at first anyway. What if they went after me? They might be more persistent than the guys, might not take no for an answer. The thought got me a little hot even when it scared me most, I gotta admit.

I started watching them every chance I got, especially on slow Thursdays, just to see what they'd do. I mean I was kinda sly about it, wiping down tables, watching the TV over their heads and that kind of thing, not standing there with my mouth open like some yahoo. I didn't want to drive them off, not even when they scared me. But I started hoping that I could see them kiss, maybe watch the blonde slip her hand under the brunette's skirt and feel her up. We get plenty of that with straight couples so, I figured, why not with them too?

I started thinking about what the brunette's boobs would feel like in my hand, maybe with the nipples getting harder when I squeezed. I tried to imagine sucking on them, taking as much as I could into my mouth. In my head, I could see her head thrown back, her eyes closed when I did it, just like I imagined they would be with the blonde. Then I got grossed out and I stopped watching them for a while.

But my gross outs didn't last long. Soon, I started picturing them watching when I was with Johnny. Maybe they'd be naked, maybe kissing. Sometimes I pretend that Johnny was doing me while we watch them. The blonde is always going down on her girl then, sticking her hand up inside her while her tongue got busy. Johnny usually didn't want to do that so I got off imagining the brunette's face, picturing how I'd feel if it was me. But I didn't imagine one of them going down on me, not back then. That took a while.

I started thinking about what would turn them on about watching us and realized there wasn't a whole lot. We usually just did it the normal way, nothing fancy. I mean it was hot for me and all, just not as hot as I thought it could be. The night I figured that out I flipped Johnny on his back and rode his dick for a change. It angled up inside me and felt really good, especially when I kept playing with myself the whole time, rubbing myself off, making him play with my titties. We both came and damn, that was hot! And in my mind, those two were watching and getting all hot over it too. That just made it all that much better.

I didn't have the fantasy about the ladies room at first, I guess because it freaked me out to even think about the two of them in there together, let alone being in there with me. First I started thinking about teasing them a little when I waited on their table, maybe wearing a shorter skirt or unbuttoning an extra button on my blouse. Maybe leaning across the table when I dropped off their drinks and letting them catch a peek at my tits in a nice lace bra. It wouldn't go any further than that, no sir. Just a quick look at what they wouldn't be getting when they got home.

Then one time, they went into the ladies room together. Now, I don't know for sure what they got into in there, but I'm betting it was each other. I mean they were in there longer than any business usually takes and it was a slow night so they weren't likely to be interrupted. After they left, I went in there on my break and started to think about what it would be like to be hidden in one of the stalls when they were going at it. I'd be in there with my feet tucked up so they couldn't see them, just listening. They'd be in the next stall kissing and then the brunette would moan. I'd hear them whispering to each other as they pulled their shirts up.

I could just about see their breasts rubbing together. Then the blonde would lean down and take one of those big round ones in her mouth. She'd get her thigh between her girlfriend's legs and just shove against her crotch. I imagined the brunette's eyes half closed, listened to her pant in my mind until I stuck a hand between my legs. I was getting wet through my jeans. So I unbuttoned them and sat on the stool. Once I got my fingers busy, I came right away, barely had to touch my clit.

I started doing that a lot on Thursday nights if it was slow enough. If it was busy, I just worked behind the bar or worked the tables with my panties riding up between my wet lips. I really had to watch the nipples or the other customers would go nuts. So I always tried to get a "smoke break" those nights so I could take care of business.

After a couple of weeks, though, it wasn't enough to keep getting me off. Not every time any way. I needed something more for that. I mean, don't get me wrong. I love Johnny and we've been together for a couple of years now, but sometimes a girl needs more than that. I was glad I didn't know the blonde and her girlfriend. It would've ruined everything. Or at least made it a lot harder. This way, it was just in my head so I wasn't cheating or anything like that.

So I started upping the ante in my head during break times. First I was listening to them. Then their stall door was open and I'd be watching them. Or the brunette was up on the countertop with her legs spread and the blonde was going down on her. I'd be watching through the crack in the door, my hand between my legs. After a while, they knew I was watching and it just made it hotter. The brunette'd blow me kisses. Or she'd pull up her shirt and pinch her nipples, just to watch me squirm. It'd make her squirm too, which was almost as much fun. I was their little secret and they'd put on a show for me almost every week, with no one any the wiser.

Then I started wondering what it would be like to be in there with them whenever I got bored at work. Well, okay, I got bored at school, too. I like actuarial science and all but it gets pretty slow. So I started really building on the bathroom game. In the best version of it, the last one I had before the bar closed, I worked my way out of the stall and walked over to them when they were kissing. The brunette was up on the countertop next to the sink, her panties off and her skirt yanked up so she could wrap her legs around the blonde.

In my fantasy, it takes a minute before they realize that I'm there with them. Then the blonde turns around and kisses me instead, stepping away from the brunette to wrap her arms around me. It's a long wet kiss and her tongue feels thick and solid against mine. You can tell that she knows what she's doing. I can almost feel her hands pull up my skirt and I'm getting wetter by the second.

The brunette's standing behind me now, kissing the back of my neck while she reaches around to start unbuttoning my shirt. I can feel those long red nails brush my nipples, feel her round tits against my back. The blonde's gotten under my skirt now and I can feel her yank my panties down. I kick them away from my ankles like I've done this before, opening my eyes to watch the bathroom door. I'm almost hoping that someone walks in as the brunette gets my shirt open and the blonde leans down to run her tongue along the top of my bra. She sticks it down into my cleavage as I lean back against her friend and kiss her.

The brunette's got a whole different flavour, all smoke and perfume mixed together and now she's undoing my bra while I suck on her tongue. The blonde's got her mouth on my tit now, practically taking the whole thing in and I'm moaning even before she lets me feel her teeth on my nipple. I lean against the brunette even more and reach back to slide my hand up her skirt. Her thighs are slick and wet and I run a finger along them until I get to her crotch. Then I stick a finger inside her, just to see what it would feel like. I can feel a moan come up from inside her and she's wet and hot against my fingers. Just then the blonde switches to my other tit and her buddy pulls up my skirt.

Those long red nails that scared me so much at first are on their way up my thigh and I just wrap my free arm around the blonde's shoulders and groan. No way am I stopping this now. The brunette's fingers reach up inside me, those nails grazing my clit until I've got goosebumps all over just thinking about it. The blonde reaches up and turns my face around as she stands up and just looks at me. No one says a word because we all know what we want. The brunette's fingers find my magic spot and start rubbing while her girlfriend sticks a hand down her own pants and starts rubbing herself off. The other hand clamps down on my boob and starts working it between her fingers, pinching my nipple until I think I'm going to fall over.

I look away, just for a minute and watch us in the mirror. The brunette's still nuzzling my neck through my hair, her eyes half closed. I can feel her pant against my skin. I'm wearing nothing but my skirt now and the blonde's still wearing all her clothes. That always turns me on even more somehow, like I'm really getting away with something. She

grabs my chin and turns me back to face her. Then she kisses
me again just as I come, my legs shaking so hard that they both
have to hold me up. I can taste pussy juice in the blonde's
mouth now, all sweet and sour rolled up together and it gets me
even hotter.

I'm still shaking when they boost me up on the counter and
spread my legs. They hold them open and make me watch
while they kiss and the brunette sticks her hand down the other
one's pants. I reach down between my own legs and the blonde
reaches out and slaps my hand away. I know I'm just supposed
to watch but I'm so hot and empty I can't help it. I try again
and this time the blonde turns around and sticks three fingers
inside me. I hump them, groaning the whole time and playing
with my own tits. I'm hoping that I'll be hot enough to distract
both of them again and, 'cause it's my fantasy, I am. The
blonde leans over and kisses me while she works all five fingers
inside me. I spread as wide as I can, getting wetter while I
watch the brunette work her hand inside her girlfriend's pants.

That's when the blonde balls her fingers up inside me and
damn near punches her way to my G-spot. I close around her
hand like a big glove and I howl. Then I hear the door open
behind us. Sometimes I make it the manager who walks in,
sometimes just any customer. I can never make up my mind if
they join us while I'm thrashing around or if they just watch.
Either way I put on quite a show. The blonde's way into me,
driving into me until I can't see straight, leaning down to
tongue my clit, then my tits and I come hard, making sounds
that Johnny's never heard out of my lips.

It gets me every time, just imagining how it could have been.
Sometimes I wish I had the guts to talk to them when they
were still coming in on Thursday nights, other times I think
it's just as well that I was too chicken shit. McKinney's closed
eventually and I never saw them again. I mean, you can't have
too many slow Thursdays and still stay open. I hear it's turned
into a fern bar.

I work at an insurance company now and there's no one
around like that couple, no one who I want to think about that
way at least. It's not like I'm attracted to just any girl after all,
just sometimes at lunch or when I'm taking the bus home.

Then there'll be something about someone that'll remind me of them and I'll get all hot and wet thinking about it, just like on a Thursday night.

But I still got Johnny and it's gotten a little wilder between us now, especially since I started suggesting stuff. I still can't get him to do it in a bar bathroom but I'm working on it. I'm hoping it'll be even better in real life.

My Initiation

Deva (Brisbane, Australia)

My best friend Rita had met a new guy and couldn't stop talking about him. Said he was wild and uninhibited. Loved sex and role-playing. At first I thought she was exaggerating but after having met him I knew that all she said had to have been true. His name was Marcus and the guy was fucking gorgeous. I must admit I was very envious.

I was also a bit put out with all the attention she was giving him. We've shared an apartment for nearly five years. Both of us are bisexual and we've always enjoyed each other's bodies as well as company. Now that she was always seeing Marcus she had no time for me.

Anyway, I was lying on my bed, and to be honest I was just thinking about Marcus, when Rita startled me at my door. I felt guilty, as though I'd actually done something with him and my face flushed scarlet.

"Staying in tonight, are you?" I asked hopefully, noting she was only wearing skimpy underwear under her half-opened robe.

"No. I'll be leaving shortly," she said.

"So what's up?"

"Well, I've got a proposition to put to you," she said, a cheeky smile causing her luscious lips to quiver.

"What do you mean?" I asked.

"Well, you know how Marcus likes to experiment with different scenarios and stuff?" she prompted.

"Yeah."

"Well, I was just wondering . . . you know . . . if you're not doing anything tonight . . ." she stammered.

"Yeah." My interest was definitely piqued.

"Well, we've been trying out this new game . . . and Marcus has a two-way mirror in another room . . . and, like, he won't know you're there . . . he won't be able to see you or anything . . . and I was just wondering if you'd like to watch us . . . you know . . . having sex?"

"You're kidding?" I practically choked on the words.

God, would I? Who wouldn't?

"You don't have to . . . it's just that since I've met him . . . well, *we* haven't had much time together . . . I hardly ever see you now . . . and I don't know . . . I just thought you might be interested."

"You mean, while the two of you are having sex, I'll be in a room on my own watching?" I asked, my pussy throbbing at the thought of it.

"Yeah." She smiled. "It'll be wild. He won't know you're there, but I will. It would really turn me on," she said, coming closer to me, so close that I could feel her breath on my neck when she sat down on my bed beside me.

I hadn't had good sex for ages. Whenever we felt randy we'd just, you know, get each other off, better than masturbating on your own. Anyway it had been a while because she'd been so busy with Marcus. I wanted to say no, pretend I was going out, but when her hand stole its way up my thigh, the word no fell from my lips. I wanted to go and see what Marcus was really like, you know, buck naked and performing, but something inside niggled at me.

"I don't think so," I said. "It would be too weird," I gasped as her fingers gently pushed my thighs apart.

"No, it wouldn't. You know you'd love to watch. How many times have we talked about it? It's everyone's fantasy," she continued, her teeth now gently nipping the flesh of my neck.

"Yeah, I know. But fantasies are exactly that. Thoughts you keep in your head. This would be different. I don't think I could do it," I said.

Her lips were brushing over the swell of my breast as she spoke, hardening my nipples.

"Sure you could," she insisted. "I could show you around his apartment and you could see all his kinky stuff that I've been telling you about. What do you say?" she asked, her fingers roaming inside the crotch of my panties.

"I think you should stay here tonight with me," I said, grabbing her hand and holding it in between my thighs where I squeezed tightly.

She pushed me back down on the bed, dropping the robe off her shoulders before her hand slipped inside my panties. I grabbed her breasts, freeing them from her bra. I opened my legs wider, allowing her fingers to roam around my lips, while I squeezed her nipples between my fingers, knowing how much she liked it.

"Hmm, I'd say you really like that idea, judging by how wet your pussy is," she laughed, beginning to finger me.

"I've missed you," I said, kissing her mouth. "I've missed you a lot."

Her swaying breast fell into the palm of my hand as I groped for it, enjoying the heaviness, the weight of her flesh.

"Me, too," she whispered. "It's been too long."

Extracting her fingers, she smeared my silky juices over my clit, rubbing, as only another woman knew how. I held her hand there, enjoying the sensation, and then her mobile phone rang.

"Shit," she said.

"Don't get it," I begged, on the verge of coming.

"I have to. It might be Marcus," she said, leaving me as she rushed from the room. I quickly pulled off my panties and threw them on the floor; pulling back the hood from my clit, I rubbed frantically. I needed an orgasm desperately.

Coming back into my bedroom with the phone to her ear, she eyed me from the doorway. I knew how much Rita loved to watch me masturbating so I put on a show for her, one I wanted her to remember, rubbing myself, lifting up my arse, begging her to come back and finish her job.

She came closer to the bed, still talking on the phone and lowered herself to the floor on her knees between my legs. Her face was just inches away from my pussy. I watched her tongue snake out to lick me. My pussy ached for her.

With her fingers on her lips indicating for me to be quiet, I held back, falling onto the pillows, with my finger poised on my pulsating nub while she spoke.

"No, that's fine, honey," she said. "Sure, I'll be there in an hour . . . what . . . yeah, I'll hang on."

She lay her head between my open thighs, pushing the end of the phone inside my pussy, while her tongue licked crazily at my clit. I was so turned on. I arched upwards, moaning, but a quick smack on my thigh reminded me I was supposed to be quiet. Crushing my own breasts, I stifled a scream as my first orgasm escaped me.

Rita was pushing the phone in and out of my pussy and I bucked into it, wanting her tongue in my pussy not the phone. I grabbed the pillow and covered my face, trying to muffle my moans, while coming again.

"Yeah, I'm still here," she giggled, removing the phone and rising, looking down at my gaping pussy. "Oh, I'd love that . . . yeah, sure . . . I'll have everything ready. I love you," she said before disconnecting the call.

"You fucking horny little bitch," she said, as she devoured me. "I've missed your gorgeous pussy."

I grabbed the back of her head with both hands pulling her into me as her teeth grazed my clit.

"Get your G-string off," I demanded. "Bring your pussy up here so I can give you a good tonguing."

"I can't," she mumbled.

"Just for a few minutes," I begged.

She pulled back smiling. "I have to go. Change of plans. Marcus is coming home early and he wants me to be ready when he gets home, so come on, cover that hot pussy and let's get going."

"I can't," I said.

"You sure?" she asked, her eyes fixed on my open thighs, her tongue licking her finger as she eyed my breasts before rubbing her saliva over the nipple and giving it a squeeze.

I was still in two minds about going. I really wanted to, wanted to go and watch but thinking about fantasies and acting upon them can sometimes be disastrous. I needed more time to make a decision.

I shook my head.

"You'll be sorry," she said, picking up her bra and robe, before sauntering to the door.

She looked back over her shoulder at me, arching her eyebrow. Her naked back tapering down into her sexy arse tempting me, so I looked away, disappointed at having had our time cut and not wanting to change my mind.

As soon as she left, I lay there hugging myself, wishing I'd said yes. The thought of witnessing some live sex had certainly been something we'd talked about. What was the matter with me? Why had I said no?

Pulling on a robe, I made my way into Rita's bedroom. I stood there in the middle of her room, imagining the two of them buck naked on her bed. I visualized what they'd look like, how I'd join in, what they'd do to me.

I moved over to her bed, dropping the robe as I did and lay down on my back. Grabbing the doona, I pulled it between my legs, inhaling her scent, the faint lingering of her perfume reminding me of other times I'd spent in here with her.

I rose, carefully opening drawers, snooping around for something but not knowing what it was that I wanted. Underneath her bed I found a photo album. I flipped the pages over, shocked to see, page after page of her tied up and being whipped. Red welts covered her body and there were some close ups of her pussy, all swollen, glistening with her juices.

This side of Rita surprised me. We'd done a bit of experimenting ourselves but never actually spanked each other. We'd tied each other up for fun, had rough sex, but had never actually physically inflicted any pain on each other.

I lay back on her bed, holding the photo album close to my chest, imagining I was with her now, exploring Marcus's apartment before he came home, just like she'd said we could.

"Pretty cool, isn't it?" Rita would say after giving me a quick tour.

"Wow, check out the waterbed. It's huge," I'd comment as I entered his bedroom.

"And so much fun, I can tell you. Listen, he'll be here soon, so I'll take you into his hidden room," she'd say, pulling open mirrored wardrobe doors.

I'd be eager and happy to hide in there, in a cupboard that had a hidden panel where the clothes slid across to open to a walk in room. There'd be an armchair in there and on the wall would be racks with dildos, whips, handcuffs and things I've never seen before. There'd even be a video camera; a camera where I could record the events as they unfolded and take home with me to watch when I was feeling frustrated.

"Just make yourself comfortable in the chair and when he comes home you'll be able to hear and see everything. Just be quiet, okay?" she'd whisper.

"Sure," I'd say, watching her as she'd quickly open drawers to remove whatever she needed. I'd stay there while she slid the door back, closing me in, giving me nowhere else to go, ensuring I'd see it all.

I'd watch as she'd touch up her face, perfume her neck, slather her lips with gloss before changing into a skirt and skimpy blouse and then she'd sit demurely on his bed to wait. I'd wondered what he would do if he discovered that I was hiding in his secret room. I found myself holding my breath, my heart pounding as I continued to play out this fantasy in my mind.

I squirmed on the bed, luxuriating in my nakedness. I grabbed a pillow and hugged it to me. It was thick and soft. I pushed it down between my thighs, squeezing them together, enjoying the sensation of it as I thrust my pelvis into it.

I lay on my side, my hand stealing its way down to cup my pussy, but it wasn't enough so I stared up at the ceiling imagining Marcus above me, looking down at me, admiring my body, tweaking a nipple before his mouth covered it and sucked it in between his hot lips.

I flipped through the album but all the photos were of Rita. I wanted a visual of Marcus, something to focus on so I wiggled over the side on my belly on my stomach, my pussy creaming her doona as I did. I looked down under the bed and found a box. Inside the box were photos of Marcus, nude photos of him lying in every position imaginable, his thick cock lying like a salami on his open thigh. His cock was huge, just like she'd told me.

Some of the photos were of Rita sucking his cock, close ups of her mouth swallowing him, her lips stretched to accommodate its girth. Some photos had only his eyes and nose peeking over her hairy bush as his mouth must have been working its magic on her pussy.

I imagined him nuzzling between my thighs, licking and sucking while his strong hands groped for my breasts and squeezed hard. I held onto a photo in one hand while the other slipped between my folds, enjoying the wetness as I gently rubbed my clit before dropping the photo to really give it a good working over.

I climaxed, seeing Marcus in my mind, his eyes boring into mine, more handsome than his photos. I'd only seen him once before, when I was running late and they were walking to his car. Rita had introduced us quickly. There was something animalistic about him. I think it was the way he walked. He was confident with himself and his sexuality oozed out of every pore. He was tall with a great body. He'd been wearing a tight shirt, his torso magnificent, rippling with muscles that diminished down to a nice arse and strong legs.

I closed my eyes tight, imagining I was locked in the closet in his room. He'd enter and walk straight over to Rita.

"Hello, Rita," he'd say.

She'd say nothing. Just sit there, with her head bowed down as though she didn't even know that he was there.

"Rita, I said hello. Didn't you hear me?" he'd ask.

She'd look up coyly, a slight smile on her pretty face.

"Well?" he'd ask.

She'd continue to stare at him, challenging him while I'd be sitting quietly perched on the armchair observing all.

"It's rude, you know, not to acknowledge someone when they speak to you. Did you know that?" he'd say.

Still she'd say nothing, eyeing him defiantly, as though daring him to be angry with her. He'd undo his tie and throw it on the dressing table, taking a few steps towards her while rolling up his sleeves. With his feet slightly apart, he'd place his hands on his hips and continue to stare at her.

I could see it all vividly in my mind so I kept my eyes shut tighter and breathed in deeply, desperate not to loose the momentum.

"You're being a naughty girl," he'd say, undoing his buttons to expose a hairy chest.

"I'm not!" she'd pout.

"Oh, so you've found your voice. You're being a very naughty girl, Rita. Come here so I can punish you. Come on," he'd demand, as he'd sit on his chair behind his desk.

She'd stay on the bed.

"Do you like being a bad girl?"

I wanted to be a bad girl.

"No."

"Then why haven't you come over here, like I asked?"

"Because," she'd say, looking up at him through dark lashes.

"Come now!" he'd demand, his voice rising with authority.

She'd rise and walk slowly and seductively towards him.

His desk would be close to the mirror. The chair directly in front of where I would be sitting, as I poised on the edge eager to see what would happen next. He'd push backwards and the chair would roll even further towards me. He'd swivel it out on an angle and pull her closer to him by the hips between his outspread legs. Then he'd sit there with his arms crossed staring at her for a few moments.

"I don't know what I'm going to do with you," he'd say.

She'd suck on a finger before pulling down her bottom lip. She looks sexy doing that and I'd wonder if she was thinking about me, as her eyes would sweep across the mirror.

"You've been a bad girl and now I have to punish you. I want you to bend over my knee," he'd say.

Giggling, she'd do as he asked. Pulling up her skirt, he'd run his hands over her panties and begin to spank her with light smacks. When she doesn't respond, he'll spank her harder.

"Oww," she'll whimper.

"That's what happens when you're a naughty girl," Marcus would chuckle.

"I'm not naughty," she'd pout.

"You are. Now be quiet," he'll say as he gives her a harder smack.

"You're hurting me," she'll whine. "Please stop. I promise I'll be good."

Marcus will keep on slapping her, ignoring her pleas.

"I said that's hurting," she'll say more loudly.

"It's supposed to hurt, Rita, and don't raise your voice to me. You've been a naughty girl, and now that you have raised your voice I think I'll need to punish you some more," he'll say.

I'll have a perfect view of her arse. I can feel my own pussy begin to throb, as I think about him slowly peeling down her panties. Her cheeks will be red and in this position I'll be able to just see her pussy lips glistening with her juices as she squirms over his lap.

He'll rub his palm over both cheeks, a finger slipping down her crack and she'll move her hands back to her panties, trying to pull them up, to cover herself. He'll smack them away. She'll try to get up, her legs opening wider as she does, but he'll hold her down.

"Oww!" she'll cry.

"You shouldn't have put your hands there. You know I don't like it when you disobey me. Now I'll have to spank you with the ruler."

I allow my legs to fall open, slipping a finger inside. Oh, nice and wet, very wet. I slap at my pussy, enjoying the sharp stings as they hit my pussy lips, my clit and the soft flesh inside my thigh. I push my fingers inside me, squeezing my thighs shut as I try to conjure up more of this fantasy.

With Rita still balanced on his knee he'll withdraw a ruler from one of the drawers. It will give me the opportunity to admire his handsome face. Chiselled features with a short crew cut. He looks like a model with his tanned skin and brilliant blue eyes. I'll push my body up close to the glass, pretending it's not there, that I'm pushing myself into him. He'll quickly glance over at the mirror and I'll pull back, startled, as though he's stared straight through me.

I'll wonder if Rita has somehow told him that I'm watching from behind the mirror.

Rita's arse will become even redder as he hits her with the ruler. He'll expertly slip her panties down to her ankles, slide them off one leg to leave them dangling on the other. With his free hand he'll push her legs apart, give himself, and me, a nice view of her pussy, as I'm perched back on the chair close to the mirror.

She'll try to pull her legs back together but he'll knock them apart again before running his hand over her.

"I don't think you should have taken my panties down," she'll say in a silly girlish voice.

"Why not? I know you like it when I touch you. You like me touching your pussy like this, don't you?" he'll ask as he gropes between her legs.

"No, I don't," she'll giggle.

"And what about this?" he'll ask as a finger slips down over her slit.

"I don't like that either," she'll pout.

"Telling fibs now, are you? I don't like girls who don't tell me the truth. Girls who don't tell the truth deserve to be punished, don't they?"

"Yes," she'll whisper, fidgeting on his knee.

"If you don't keep still I'll have to tie you up and spank you, you know that don't you?"

"Yes."

"Well?"

"I'll keep still," she'll say.

"Good, now you're showing me you can be a good girl. I won't tie you up this time, but I still have to finish with you."

Marcus will alternate the spanking, give her one stroke with the ruler, then rub his hand over her arse and give her a sharp slap. Occasionally he'll touch her pussy and I'll watch as she pushes her arse up seductively, obviously wanting more.

She's such a slut, probably why I love her so much.

I want to go in there and give her a spanking myself. With him holding her like that over his lap, her gorgeous arse beckoning for me to join the party. I'll wait, though, not go in, as he doesn't know I'm there and that would spoil our plan.

"Ow," she'll squeal in pain. "Stop it. You're hurting. That's too hard."

"Shut up!" he'll command, hitting her hard on the pussy. "Quiet, or I'll do it again."

Rita now stops complaining and starts moaning, making whimpering noises. The smack on her pussy had made her open her legs wider for him. I open mine too, allowing my hand to roam over my pussy noting how wet I am. This is definitely turning me on.

Marcus's hand cups her pussy. She wiggles on his knee,

opening her legs wider. I watch as he slips a finger into her hot pussy and then smears her juices over her hole. He opens up her cheeks, teasing her as he probes her hole, just inching in slightly.

My cheeks clench together as I imagine his finger probing mine.

"I think you like this, Rita," Marcus says, chuckling. "Do you think I need to punish you some more?"

"Yes," she says.

"Come, stand up for me," he'll say, smoothing her skirt over her naked arse. "That's a good girl. Turn around and face me. That's good. Now take off your skirt."

Rita has a sly smile on her face as she takes off her skirt. It drops to the floor and she kicks up her other leg, discarding her panties and stands in front of him. Pulling her by the hips, he turns her around. He caresses her, lowering his head to kiss her red-hot cheeks. Then he turns her body back around so she is facing him and I note her flushed cheeks. She stares through the glass and smiles, her eyes shining with happiness and excitement.

I've never seen her look so radiant and alive.

"Hmm, very nice," he'll say, rubbing her stomach, his thumbs pressing into her groin, massaging deep, nearly touching her lips. "Take off your shirt."

She undoes each button, teasing him as she does, pouting her lips and looking at him through her dark lashes. Her blouse drops to the floor and she stands there in only a white bra. His hands reach out behind her back, unclasp her bra and discard it on the floor.

Flicking her hair back off her face, she runs her hands over her breasts, down her stomach until she's touching her pussy. She separates the lips and slips her fingers inside. She leans back against the desk, opening her legs.

He kneels down running his tongue over her pussy giving her a long lick.

"Oh, you're a good girl now, aren't you?" Marcus will say. He'll stand, fondle her breasts and suckle at her nipples. "You like being a good girl. Don't you?"

She is now only wearing her high-heeled shoes and looking very sexy as she wiggles back further on the desk. She lifts a leg and places it over his shoulder, her heel digging into his back, pulling him in closer.

"Yes," she'll purr. "I'm very good when I want to be."

"Hmm, I know," he'll say, his fingers seeking out her nipples. "But there's just one more thing I have to do."

"What's that?" she'll murmur.

"Lean over the desk."

She doesn't hesitate. She practically pushes him into the glass, turns around and leans into the desk with her arse twitching in the air. Her feet are slightly apart and she lowers herself to lie flat, her breasts squashed against his papers.

Marcus runs his hands over her back, down over her gorgeous plump cheeks, onto her hips where he gives them a quick slap and then out of his drawer he'll produce a switch. Gently, he'll begin to whip her as Rita moans sexily with every lashing he administers.

I'll pull my panties to one side and finger myself on the armchair, my legs wide open, hanging off the arms. I'd smear my clit with my juices, enjoy my fingers as they roamed amongst my folds and then back to my clit where I rubbed gently, just as I'm doing now.

"That's one hot pussy," he'll say to Rita as he slips in his finger. "Oh, yeah, really juicy. You are enjoying it."

"Oh yeah, baby, I am," she'll say.

I'll watch as he falls to his knees, lowering his head to lick the welts. He'll run his tongue over them, then her hole, stopping just before he reaches her pussy. She'll rise up on her elbows, pull at her breasts, and tease the nipples to make them erect. She'll push her arse into Marcus's face, lifting it higher, trying to get him to put his tongue inside her.

"That's one hot arse," he'll laugh as he pinches each cheek. "Here, stand up."

He helps her up on the desk. She kneels on it; bends over so her pussy is level with his face. He smacks her thighs with his hand, and as her legs open wider he smacks her pussy as well. She squeals with delight. He alternates between smacking her and giving her pussy a long lick, from her clit all the way up to her hole. It is driving her wild. She gyrates her pussy into his face, smothering him, encouraging him for more.

It drives me wild too. I can see myself standing and quickly pulling my panties off, repositioning myself on the chair. I grab at my breast roughly while rubbing my clit. I look sexy, wild and uninhibited as I masturbate madly.

With his free hand he undoes his trousers and they fall to his ankles. He stands there with a massive hard on, his cock only inches from me. I can see the knobbly veins in his shaft as the skin stretches tightly over it. I want it, want it in my mouth, in my pussy, my hole. I watch as he covers her pussy with his mouth nuzzling and sucking while removing his shirt. Now they are both naked, his arse tight, right in front of me, the cheeks clenching and tightening as he pulls her closer into him.

I'll be rubbing my clit; enjoying a wonderful orgasm as it dribbles out of me, just like I am now. I'll finger myself, focus my attention back on my clit as I rub madly but it won't be enough. I can't get enough. Can't reach the high I want. I need to be fucked and I'll wish that Marcus could be the one to feed my hungry pussy.

He is teasing her with his cock and she's trying desperately to grab it and put it inside her.

"I want your pussy wetter," he'll demand. "I'll keep spanking you until your juices are dripping on the desk. Do you hear me?"

"Oh, yes, yes," she'll say eagerly.

He'll slap at her thighs while his cock rubs between her legs. He loves to tease her. Then he'll grab her hips firmly to pull her hard towards him, plunging his cock straight into her pussy; the force of it throws her forward on the desk. He thrust in deeper and harder, causing her to scream and cry out for more. He is holding her tightly, pounding into her ferociously.

"Oh, God, yes," she'll scream. "Fuck me harder."

She's holding onto the edges of the desk as he pummels her. Pencils and papers are flying off the desk.

"Quickly," he'll command. "Turn around and sit on the desk with your legs open for me."

She does as he asks. From my position I can see her pussy perfectly. With her legs spread he stands back and pulls at his cock, making it even bigger. She is whimpering, begging for it, her head hanging off the edge of the desk. He thrusts his cock into her open mouth and she gobbles it deep down into her throat, sucking him madly.

"Oh yes, that's great. You're dripping now. I can see your pussy in the mirror. Good girl. I knew you'd be good. Knew you'd do as you're told. Now you'll get your reward," he'll say, withdrawing from her.

"Oh, yes, Marcus, please. For God's sake, give it to me."

He pushes his massive cock into her while she screams to be fucked harder. I wouldn't be able to stand it any more and I'd look about the room for something to relieve my frustration. I spy a big, black dildo and reach over to grab it. I hoist up my dress and plunge the black beauty straight into me. Oh, it is heavenly. Over and over I push it in and out. Pulling it out, I can see my juices bring it to life, making it seem real.

I'll have my eyes closed on the brink of another orgasm when I hear the creak of a floorboard. He'll be standing next to me, his massive cock only inches from my mouth. I'll grab his shiny, thick, wet shaft and suck his cock deep into my throat. My other hand will still be pumping the dildo in and out and as I gobble his cock. All thoughts about him being Rita's boyfriend will leave me. I will be interested in only one thing and that's getting fucked.

He'll withdraw from me and grab me by the arm, pull me out of the chair. The dildo will fall to the floor. He'll drag me into his bedroom and stand me in front of Rita.

"Lick her pussy," he'll demand of me.

I'll look shyly towards Rita, knowing that this is what we both want. Like a hungry dog I'll attack her, feed off her juices as Marcus lifts my dress, opens my legs, pulls my hips back and plunges that fucking beautiful cock of his straight up my pussy. I'll grab hold of Rita's hips tightly, licking and sucking as he bucks into me. Delirious with passion I'll come all over his cock as Rita bucks into my mouth, her sweet juices filling me as she too orgasms.

This fantasy has me masturbating madly as I imagine what else we could do.

On shaking legs I'll practically fall as Marcus withdraws that wonderful cock from me. He'll strip me out of my dress and underwear and, after helping Rita from the desk, he'll order me to lie upon it. Apprehensive and nervous about my first caning I'll lay there panting as they tie my arms and legs to the desk. I'll be hanging over it, my arse and pussy naked, vulnerable, unable to protest even if I wanted to. But I don't. I want to be spanked, whipped, smacked. I want what Rita had and more.

The first slap will be on my thigh. Then another and another and slowly they'll work their way up to my cheeks where the slaps will become smacks and the stinging pain becomes pleasure. They'll produce a swish and use it over my back, the inside of my torso, my cheeks and thighs. It will be wonderful. It will be absolute and utter pleasure being at the disposal of someone else's hand. I'll love being submissive; to be told what to do and how to do it. I'll love it all.

Then light fingers will run up inside my thighs and caress my back. It will only be a small whip and as Marcus slaps my pussy with it I'll know that this is something that I'll always want, always want to participate in. The tiny red-hot stings will be like an electrical surge all over my flesh, igniting a fire in me, making me wild with passion.

"Oh, for God's suck, fuck me, please," I'll beg. "Fuck me."

"Do you think you've been punished enough for spying on me?" Marcus will ask.

"Yes," I'll whimper.

"Do you think you've learned a lesson?" he'll ask.

"Oh, yes," I'll whisper, barely able to talk.

"Do you think you'd like my cock inside your hot pussy?"

"Oh, fuck, yes. Please fuck me," I'll beg.

I want him more than anything, but part of me wants them to flip me over. To lash at my breasts, to make my nipples harder, to excite me even more.

"Rita, do you think I should fuck her? Do you think we've shown her how much pleasure you can receive even when you're naughty?"

"I think we've given her enough for her first taste and, knowing Deva, I'm sure she'll be back for more," Rita will say as she unties my arms, then my legs.

I'll stand on shaking legs, desperate to have Marcus fuck me. He'll lift me in his strong arms and place me in the centre of his bed. Rita will lie beside me, stroking my breasts, lightly touching my arms, while Marcus will stand at the end of the bed watching us.

"Please," I'll beg, "I can't stand it any longer. Please fuck me."

I can hear something pulling at me, digging into my subconscious. I want to continue on with this fantasy. I want to imagine Marcus fucking me like the stallion that he is. I want to feel his hard cock deep inside me, I want him pounding in me, fucking me mercilessly, but something is bugging me, stopping me for continuing, my stream of consciousness has been broken.

It's the phone. The fucking phone is ringing. I leave it to ring out but whoever it is rings back. I can't get back into my fantasy. I jump out of bed angrily, rush into the kitchen and snatch the phone off the hook.

"Yes," I scream into it.

"Julie, is that you?" a voice asks.

"No, it's fucking not," I scream as I slam the receiver back down.

I run to get back to my fantasy, my wild dreams of lust, but first I take the receiver off the hook. I don't want any other interruptions.

I jump back into bed. Get into the same position. I close my eyes and conjure up where I'd left off but I can't seem to get it back, can't seem to get the momentum going again. Frustrated and angry, I pick up my robe and slink back into my room. I promise myself if Rita brings it up again, I'll be saying yes. This fantasy needs to be fulfilled and the sooner it is the better I'll like it.

Say It

Flora (Garden City, USA)

I'm shaking as I walk into the room because I don't know how to keep myself steady. If he gave me a cigarette, told me to light it, I'm not sure I could control the trembling in my hands enough to make such a simple thing happen.

He's sitting in a chair by the window. The only light is one of the lamps by the bed and a tiny strip of it where the curtains don't close quite perfectly. If there was more light, I might see my toybag beside his chair, might recognize it amidst the shadows. "Pack a bag for me," he'd said. And so I did, left it for you.

"Stop there," he tells me as the door slams closed; even though I expected the sound, I jump. I've only taken three steps into the room. "Stand still."

Every instinct in me screams, "No." It's built-in defiance that makes me want to provoke, ask, "Why should I?", makes me want him to give me a damn good reason to do so. It's the control freak in me that makes me want to take another step and another, just because he told me to stand still.

Somehow I make myself stop, though. My ankles wobble a little in my boots and I try to stand still. I'm sure he can see me trembling, though and I wonder, briefly, if that's going to count against me.

He just sits there, looks at me, watches me, silent, that smug expression on his face, that satisfied smile. The muscles in my neck and jaw tense and my lips press together; I hardly realize I'm doing it. This silence, this lack of movement drives me crazy. I want to do something. Want him to do something.

Want anything but to be standing there, uncertain and trembling, but he's not in a hurry.

I imagine it's a game: which of us will move first. Will I give in to the white-hot defiance inside of me, or will I somehow manage to contain it, control it, leaving him to make the first move?

I don't know how long I stand there; he unplugged the clock, denying me that red glow and the little bit of certainty that comes with knowing. In that unknown time, I manage not to demand, "Well?" or "Are you just going to sit there?" or "Now what?" my lips twitching unconsciously every time I come close to opening my mouth. I think he can tell how much this frustrates me, how maddening it is.

Finally, he says, "Strip. Slowly."

Slowly. And I wonder if he wants a strip tease, or if he just wants me to take my time, forcing me into a longer wait to find out what happens next. He remains sitting there, his expression unchanging, still that smug amusement and I want so much to touch his cheek, kiss him, be close enough that I can't see the expression. Nip at his mouth, drag my tongue over his lips, press it between them.

I peel off one glove, material sliding against my forearm, wrist, fingers. I drop it to the floor beside me. Out the corner of my eye, I catch sight of my reflection in the mirrored closet door, mocking me with the same movement. I unfasten bracelets, metal beads unwinding slowly then falling to the floor with the scraping and clinking of metal-against-metal, muffled in the end by carpet and the first glove. Then the other glove. My hands still shake and I think, perhaps it is a blessing he told me to strip slowly.

I unfasten my necklace, drop it beside my bracelets.

As I strip he tells me, "You are allowed to say, 'Yes, sir,' and, 'No, sir.' Nothing more. Unless you need to use your safeword. You understand?"

I swallow, draw a shallow breath. I know what he wants to hear, what I should say.

"Well?" he asks me, one eyebrow raising.

And my lips part. For a moment, the only thing that passes them is my breath and then not even that. I don't know if I can say it. He waits, watching me in silence, judging my reluctance or defiance, until I whisper, "Yes, sir." I'm not certain I've said it loud enough for him to hear, but he says, "Good girl." I remember to breathe.

"Tell me your safe-word, Flora." I love the sound of my name on his lips.

My hands falter on the laces of my corset. I swallow, press my lips together, then say it – Red – though he already knows; we've talked about this before. He nods and I loosen the laces further.

"Slowly," he reminds me when my hand comes to the zipper at the front of my corset.

Slowly. I take hold of the zipper, pull it down a tiny bit at a time, trying to remind myself to breathe as I do. Eventually, the zipper is all the way down, the air cool against my leather-warmed skin. I shrug my shoulders and the straps slide down. I catch them, then drop the corset to the floor. My skirt slips down over my hips, puddles at the floor around my boots. I've nothing on underneath.

Self-conscious and exposed, I bend to the laces on my boots and before I untie the knot holding them he says, "Leave those on." I close my eyes, whisper, "Yes, sir."

"Crawl to me," he says and my eyelids fly open again, eyes wide with panic. He still has not moved more than to tilt his head to the side. His hands rest on the arms of the chair, long fingers relaxed. "Slowly."

I feel the blush heating my skin, my breath catching each time I inhale. Crawl to him. Submission without pain and I don't know if I can do this thing he is telling me to do. Does he see the struggle as I stand there? Is it written on my face? In the way I tremble? And when I've nearly decided I cannot do this, I find that I'm closing my eyes tightly, bowing my head and sinking to my knees. I whisper, "Yes, sir." The carpet is smooth and rough at the same time. Flat, but ragged against my palms and my knees; I focus on that rather than the sharp uncertainty in the back of my head, rather than the fear.

The room is forever-wide, though it's no bigger than any other hotel room I've ever stayed in. The trek across the room on my hands and knees takes a painfully long time and the only sound is the toes of my boots scraping carpet and the pounding of my heart, pulse hammering in my ears. My back arches each time I drag one leg forward and put a hand out in front of me and I can't look at him, if I do, I might stop, might gather up my clothes and run. I look, instead, at the floor, at the pattern in the carpet, at the chipped polish on my nails. I should've fixed that before I got here; a distracted inane thought flitting into my head and out just as quickly.

Crawl to him. It sounds like such a simple order. Such a simple thing to do. And I don't know if it's defiance or fear screaming in the back of my head, telling me to stop right there, not move another inch. But I keep crawling. Long slow dragging movements, my breasts swaying, a reminder that I'm naked, in case I might have forgotten somehow.

He stretches one foot out in front of me and when I'm close enough, he tells me again, "Stop."

I'm breathing raggedly, as if I've just run a mile rather than crawled the length of the room. He rubs his boot against my forearm, brushes the toe of it against my nipple and I shiver. When he puts his foot back on the floor, he tells me, "Kiss it," and a whimper catches in my throat.

Perhaps he's taking some small amount of pity on me as he leans forward, strokes my hair. But as his fingers tighten and tug, I shiver, go limp. He forces me to look up, to look at him. There is no pity in his expression. "Kiss it," he tells me and he lets go of my hair. Arms trembling, I lower my face to his boot, close my eyes partway and brush my lips against the leather. "Like you mean it," he tells me.

Another whimper from me, the sound almost like a kittenish mewl. I'm lightheaded from forgetting to breathe, from those short little ragged breaths when I remember to take them, from the racing of my heart, from *this*. I kiss his boot again, lips and tongue both playing against the leather now, moving from the toe, along the top, over to his ankle, back around to the toe. I wait eagerly for a, "Good girl," some indication that I'm doing the right thing, but he leaves me wondering. He draws that foot back and puts the other one forward. When I give it the same treatment, that's when I hear, "Good girl." He tilts his foot up, presents the sole of his boot. My eyes close again and I kiss along the sole, play my tongue over it, over the roughness of the treads.

"I can smell you, Flora." And I lower my face to the carpet, certain it is bright red because it feels suddenly like it is on fire. I want to deny it, but I can smell myself. I whisper, "Yes, sir," against the floor and the carpet gets warm against my face.

He chuckles. "That embarrasses you." Not a question, but I nod, whisper, "Yes, sir." I can hear the smile in his voice when he says, "Good."

I want to hide, then. Want to melt into the carpet to escape that embarrassment, his amusement over it, but he's not going to let me. His hand is back in my hair, tugging me up so I have to look at him again. I keep my eyes closed, but he tells me to open them. I never imagined it might take so much energy, so much effort, to open my eyes, to keep my gaze from lowering. "Look at me," he says and I realize my gaze has wandered again: the upholstery of the chair, his thigh, anywhere but looking him in the eye.

I look at his mouth, his parted lips. I want to kiss them and he knows it.

He stands up slowly and I've got to raise up only onto my knees as he does. That movement leaves me unbalanced; he's so close. My chest presses against his legs and my face is against his crotch. He still holds my head so I have to look up at him, my neck aching a little, my back arched. His jeans are rough against my breasts and nipples and as he moves, the denim drags against me. My breath catches and I try not to moan. I fail in that attempt and his smile widens. "I want you to sit on your heels, Flora. With your knees spread and your palms against your thighs." His grip in my hair loosens so I can lower myself. My boot-heels are hard and uncomfortable to sit against. My hands tremble against my thighs.

He sits down again and looks at me. "No matter what I do, you will not look away. You can blink, but you will *not* close your eyes for longer than that. You will watch this, Flora."

A shiver runs through me and I whimper.

He reaches over the arm of the chair to the bag on the floor and when his hand comes back into my line of sight, he's holding a little clear bag full of black plastic clips, some of them small and flat, others like clothespins. Those aren't mine, weren't in the bag I packed. My gaze darts from the bag to his face, then back. He bounces the bag and the clips rattle softly. My fingers curl against my thighs, nails pressing into skin, then I force them to relax again.

"Hold still." He leans forward, lifts my right breast and drags his thumb over my nipple.

It's reflex, I can't help it, I close my eyes and tilt my head back. His hand comes down in a sharp stinging swat against the top of my breast and I open my eyes wide. "Eyes *open*," he says, watching my face.

"Yes, sir," I whisper, those two words trembling on my lips.

I've never realized how often I close my eyes in response to pleasure, in response to pain. Never until that moment. He pinches up the skin of my breast, closes one of the flat clips against it. I suck in a sharp breath and catch myself just before I close my eyes. He pinches up more skin, lines another clip beneath the first, like a black sunray in a child's drawing. One clip after another, five of them in line pointing toward my nipple.

He starts another line of them a little to the right of the first, then another to the left of it. My breast feels hot and stinging and my fingernails dig into my thighs as I try to keep my eyes open.

Five lines on my breast and he touches his fingertip to my parted lips. My tongue darts out over it and he presses his finger into my mouth. I suckle it, tongue sliding over it, tongue ring dragging against it while he strokes it in and out. He pulls it away from my mouth and circles that wet fingertip over my nipple. A soft "ohh" falls from my lips and he takes his finger away, takes out one of the black clothespins. I watch. I watch though I know what's coming, though I want to close my eyes, though I want to look away. He opens it and lets it snap closed; it hasn't been sprung. I flinch at the sound. He opens it again and lets it close more slowly around my nipple.

My nails drag over my thighs and I whimper. Eyes close because I just cannot keep them open. His hand comes down over the top of my other breast. "Open your eyes, Flora."

I pant raggedly, every breath making the clips on my breast

shift. I whimper. It is such a struggle to open my eyes again and it's nearly impossible for me to focus once I do.

He shifts, puts one foot between my knees. His foot shifts as he gives my left breast the same treatment, the side of his foot rubbing against my inner thigh, then the toe of his boot dragging against my labia. I gasp and he pinches my nipple, says, "Shush," reminds me to hold still. I whisper a ragged, "Yes, sir," and he continues with the clips, another half-sun on my left breast, then that last clothespin on my nipple.

I give a little whimpered moan and close my eyes, that damnable reflex. He takes hold of both clothespins and tugs, once for each word as he says, "Open . . . your . . . eyes."

My lips are parted and I'm panting. Somehow I manage to open my eyes again, look up at him. I'm trembling and my nails are digging even harder against my thighs. His boot continues to press between my thighs and my hips arch slightly. He tugs the clothespins again. "Stay still."

I whimper, "Yes, sir."

I think I may very well come with the toe of his boot grinding against my clit and pressing against the barbells piercing my inner labia, my nipples throbbing in the grip of those clothespins. I blush again, hotly. He's not going to let me come so easily, though.

He lets go of the clothespins, lowers his foot and I give a little mewl of frustration, nearly closing my eyes as I do. He tsks softly, looking at his boot. "Clean that up, Flora." The throb and heat of the clips against my breast drown out the urge to say, "I can't," or, "I won't." I've got to lower myself – breasts brushing the carpet, clothespins and clips tugging – so I can lick his boot. The mingled taste of myself and leather makes me dizzy with desire. Every instinct inside of me screams that I should close my eyes as I savour that taste, but I manage to keep them open.

He stands, pulls me up by my hair again as he does. I fix my gaze on his mouth. "You're going to unfasten my belt now. And my jeans. But your hands are going to stay against your thighs."

"Yes, sir," I whisper, my breath warming the crotch of his jeans. I rub my cheek against his thigh, lick and kiss along the fly of his jeans, up to his belt buckle. I nuzzle at it, catch the end of his belt between my teeth, tug. But it's not quite that easy. His shirt brushes against my cheek, against my hair, while I struggle with his belt, giving tiny little whimpers of frustration. Once he unbuttons his shirt, he strokes my hair, trails fingertips over my ear, down my neck. Eventually I get his belt undone, nose it out of the way. It slaps back against my cheek and he takes pity on me, holds it away from my face. I catch his jeans between my teeth. The button is stubborn, but I manage it. The metal of the zipper-pull makes my teeth ache as I tug it downward, inhaling the scent of him as I do.

"Good girl," he says, stroking my hair once more. Then he steps away, takes off his boots and his clothes. I watch him, want to touch him, taste his skin. He's too far away and I whimper again, not realizing I have.

He laughs softly. "Do you want something?" and I blush, glance down at the carpet. "Look at me," he reminds me and I look up slowly. He's a step closer now. "Do you want something?"

I nod slowly, whisper, "Yes, sir."

He takes another step closer. I could reach out and touch him and my hands tremble with the effort to keep them against my thighs. "What?"

I want to taste your cock. I want your mouth against my cunt. I want to feel you inside of me. I open my mouth but can't make the words come out. My throat closes around them and I whimper, flushed and embarrassed.

He presses his lips together and shakes his head slowly and the fear that I've disappointed him burns in my belly. If I could say the words, I would, but I can't. "If you can't tell me what you want, you can't have it."

I whimper again. He strokes my hair. "Come here." He walks to the bed, pats it and I crawl over, climb onto the bed beside him, gasping and whimpering as the clips tug at my breasts. "On all fours," he tells me and he arranges me so my legs are spread, my hands are out in front of me and my back arched so the ends of the clothespins drag against the bed when I move. Or when he does.

"Now we're going to play a game. Twenty questions. I will

ask you a question that requires something more than 'Yes, sir' or 'No, sir'; you will give me an answer. Every question you answer right gives you a point. I will ask three times. Every wrong answer, I get a point." He trails his fingertips down my spine, along the crack of my ass. He draws his hand away then brings it down sharply against my arse. "And I'm going to do that every time you don't answer." My ass still stings. "Do you understand?"

I nod. "Yes, sir." I can still feel the hot shape of his hand on my skin.

"If you win, I'll take these off." He drags his fingers over the clips on my breast and I whimper, shudder. "If I win, I'll add more." His hand strokes down my arse, brushes between my thighs, teasing touch in the place he intends to add them. There's the incentive to win, then.

"I'll make the first question easy." He holds a red satin handkerchief in front of my face. "What colour is it?" and he's toying with me. I either answer the question and this ends, or I don't and he swats my ass again. I bite my lip and his hand comes down, sharp and stinging. "What colour is it, Flora?"

I squeeze my eyes closed tightly.

"You want to tell me, don't you?" he whispers against my ear.

"Yes, sir." Which is truth as much as it is a lie. I want to answer the question. I don't want this to end.

"So what colour is it?"

I keep my mouth shut, lips pressed together tightly. His hand comes down against my ass again, harder this time and I yelp, muscles tensing.

"That's three points for me," he says and I hear the smile in his voice.

It goes on like this. Sometimes he takes pity on me and asks me a question I can answer, a question I will answer. At some point, he's traded swats with his hand for stinging strokes of the rubber slapper and the shape of the fire and ache is different. I'm whimpering and mewling, arching, struggling. My fingers grip the bed tightly and my arms tremble as the questions continue. He trades questions I can answer with questions like, "What colour is a fire truck?" and "What colour are strawberries?" Questions I refuse to answer because I don't want this to end. He teases me after each of those, asks me, "Are you trying to lose?" and I shake my head, whisper, "No, sir," and wish that those questions counted in the twenty he's threatened me with, but they don't.

Eventually, he gets back to the question he asked before the game started. "What do you want, Flora?"

My arse and the backs of my thighs are hot and stinging. If I concentrate, I can picture the shape of the welts from the slapper. One there, one there, another there at a little bit more of an angle, one that caught the sensitive place where the back of my thigh and arse meet.

What do I want? *I want so much. I want this to stop, I want it to continue. I want you to let me suck you, want you to fuck me. I want to come, I want to be denied the same thing.* I want to be able to say this. I open my mouth, breath a ragged, "I . . ." and again the words get caught in my throat.

"You?" And he waits a moment to see if I'll say more. When I can only whimper, he brings the slapper down again. Harder this time, over one of the fresh welts and I arch, clench my jaw tightly to keep back a scream that is pain and frustration and desire braided together. My fingers ache from how tightly I'm gripping the sheets.

"What do you want, Flora?" His breath is hot against my ear and he nips my earlobe.

I want to tell him. "Please," I whimper. "Please, I . . ." I can beg, but I can't seem to beg for what I want.

"Tell me what you want, Flora."

I pull at the sheets, nearly sob and he sighs, brings the slapper down in the same place again and I bury my face against the bed, eyes closed, shivering and panting.

"What do you want, Flora?" And this is my last chance. I don't know what happens if I don't say it, but it doesn't matter because the words start pouring out, surrounded by "please" and "sir". I'm begging him to let me suck him, to fuck me and hurt me and kiss me. Please, kiss me. "Please, kitten," And he takes hold of my hair, makes me look up from the bed. "No," he says. "I'm not your kitten tonight." And I whimper, almost incoherent with want and ache. "I'm sorry, sir."

He strokes his hand over my arse and I flinch, pull at the sheets. Somewhere in the part of my mind that's still clinging to the world, I know I'm going to be bruised tomorrow. "Forty-four to six," he tells me. "I won." He drags his fingers down between my legs, long slow teasing touch, and I mewl, arch, sheets tugging at the clothespins on my nipples.

There's the same plastic rattling sound from before. It hardly registers in my head because, at the same time, he presses a finger into me. I go still, afraid I'm imagining it, afraid if I move he'll stop. "Please," I whimper. He curls his finger inside of me and drags it slowly out, tells me, "Not yet," then he catches my outer labia, pinches it and closes a clothespin onto it. I bite at the sheets and squirm. He swats my arse and tells me to stay still, but it's so hard.

Three clothespins on each labia and he tells me to roll over, knowing I'm going to have to put my legs together at least a little bit to do so. I'm panting as I roll over and he rubs his finger against my lips, wetting them, then lets me suckle the tip of it.

"You can't have *everything* you want, you know." He tells me this as he strokes his fingertip against the roof of my mouth and my breath catches at that touch. At his words. And my eyes are closing again. For a moment I struggle to keep them open, but he keeps stroking his finger against the roof of my mouth and I give in, close my eyes. Then open them and nearly scream when he starts pulling the clips on my right breast. They drag and snap off and I arch my back. He slides his finger out of my mouth and plays it against my trapped nipple before tugging the clothespin off and once again I'm gripping the sheets painfully tight, trying not to scream.

Then the other breast and both nipples ache again as blood rushes back into them. "Such a good girl," he says, stroking my nipples softly, cupping my breasts, kissing one and then the other.

His hands move down between my legs again. "Tell me if you're going to come, Flora." His fingers play against my clit, against the two barbells piercing my inner labia. Every movement of his hand makes the clothespins bounce, makes me gasp.

As I get close, I whimper, "I . . . I'm going to . . ." and he shakes his head. "Not yet," he says as his fingers leave my clit and he yanks one clothespin off my labia. My whole back arches and I forget to breathe. He reminds me, tells me to take a slow deep breath. Let it out. And when I'm breathing normally again, his fingers go back to work.

Six clothespins, six reminders to breathe. And then he's on top of me, pressing into me. "Open your eyes, Flora." I cling to him as he makes love to me, lightheaded, breathless, eyes half open, lips parted. "Please," I beg raggedly.

"Please what, Flora? What do you want?"

"Please let me come," I whisper, arching against him.

"Good girl." And his thumb nestles against my clit, rubbing it as he presses into me. I close my eyes tightly, nails dragging down his back as I orgasm. And even in this he won't let me off so easily, his thumb still circling and stroking until I come again and he's not far behind this one.

I curl up against him, sobbing with the intensity of my release, tears rolling down my cheeks. He holds me, whispers soothing words and the words aren't nearly as important as the sound of his voice and the warmth of his skin against mine.

"You can't have everything you want, not all in one night. And you can't have anything at all if you can't say it." He strokes my hair and kisses my forehead.

"Will you kiss me?" I ask breathlessly, forgetting myself, hazy with pleasure and pain.

He kisses me, lips tender and hungry against mine, and I think even time stops then and it starts again when he draws back.

"Thank you, sir."

"You're welcome, Flora."

I'm exhausted and aching, but content as he holds me anchored to the world by nothing more than his arms around me and the beating of his heart.

The Confession

Justine (London, UK)

We are at a party. The room is full of people elegantly dressed. I look up and he is standing there, a little in the distance, watching me. In his face is blind abstraction, a mixture of pregnant desire and embarrassed self consciousness, his face detained by an emotion that his mind has not yet named. He is tall, always tall, and his eyes are blue, bright cornflower blue. There is something distinguished about him, the drape of his clothes, the length of his neck; always height and length and, above all, elegance in his demeanour, yet not perfection. It is his desire for elegance that pleases me, that focuses my response to his desire. Once registered, I enjoy the minor imperfections; the energetic curl of hair that will not be combed into submission, the disproportionate scale of his slender hands to their thickened wrists, the lopsided charm of a smile that begs to complete itself in happiness.

At first, I look away. But I can still feel the warmth of his stare on my cheek. My eyes steal back to his. I witness confusion. He barely sees me. It is only desire that he is registering. Briefly, I have become a hieroglyph for his private emotion. Only when I get up to move does the self absorption of his desire shutter, falling through his eyes like a pack of playing cards. Then, suddenly, his desire becomes twofold, both actual and imagined. A strange pragmatism intervenes. His feet paw the carpet like a horse. He does not know how to cope with the distance between us. We are in a room filled with people, and yet we might as well be alone.

We know each other, but distantly. We have never made love. As well as liking, there is a fat seam of anger between us.

As I turn my gaze openly to his, he scans my face for evidence of desire. My longing for him is less raw than his for me. It manifests itself as receptivity, trust. He threads his way through the crowd to reach me. He is wearing a long, loose overcoat; in its touch, cashmere. His head and neck rise from its cape of darkness, like a piece of intricate jewellery. His eyes never desert mine; they crease greedily, giddily into a smile. He takes my hand in his and I feel the supple strength, the firm possessive reassurance of his hand in mine. I lean towards him, like an arabesque, my body open to and anticipating every nuance of his. He kisses me on my cheek, then throws back his body full height to again devour me with his eyes; as he does so, he runs both his hands up and down my outstretched arm, kneading my flesh into an expectation, a promise of intimacy. Eyes still locked, we unconsciously manoeuvre ourselves, almost unnoticed, to the edge of the crowd, where gold-framed mirrors alternate with brocade curtains as heavy and as unwieldy as carpets. I catch sight of myself in one of the mirrors; the image startles me. I look like a woman in love; my eyes dance to the blue tune in his. My mouth is wreathed in smiles.

Someone detaches himself from the crowd to approach us, but finds himself repelled by the intensity of our exchange and retreats again, like a leaf, carelessly fallen. I lose my balance slightly, tangling briefly with the curtain. The dull red brocade emits a smell of accumulated dust. His hand moves swiftly to steady me. As he does so, he pulls me towards him and, briefly, I vanish into the ample embrace of his overcoat. As I raise my eyes to his, he rests his forehead against mine. It is a moment of the purest intimacy. My hands are still held in his; his fingers continue to explore my flesh with the press of his energetic fingers. He smiles a shower of cornflower blue into my eyes, then bends his cheek close to mine, to whisper in my ear, grazing the stubble of his chin against the long sweep of my hair, in order that I should hear better.

"I just want to touch you," he whispers. "Nothing else. I just want to know the truth of you."

I stand before him, docile, only half understanding. With one fierce movement, he persuades my hand against the small of my back. The wings of his dark coat protect us. Unseen by the crowd, he lifts the hem of my skirt an inch or two. I look up. The dancing lights of a chandelier dazzle my eyes. Beyond the smooth hose at my knees and thighs are stocking tops secured by broad band ribbons of black silk, stretching, yearning for my knees as they secure the black gossamer nylons to the opulent line of my thighs. His fingers feel persistent, determined against my flesh, with the authority and sureness of touch that only true desire can bring.

"How warm you feel," he whispers in my ear.

He teases my bare skin, butter-smooth soft suddenly at the point where it meets the tautly strained stocking tops, edged with a flirtation of red that he still cannot see. He sweeps his hand under the elastic straps of the suspenders, weighing and assessing desirously the roundness of my thighs. And then the urgent fingers grow fingertip hesitant, stroking gently, deliciously along the edges of the lacy confection of my panties. My step falters. I fall backwards from the exquisite fire of his touch, my body too arched to his to maintain balance. The grip of his hand in the small of my back increases.

"Stand a little more astride," he whispers in my hair.

But still I stumble. I clutch at the swags of heavy curtaining to stabilize myself. In disturbing their heavy drape, I unwittingly expose the point where two curtains divide. Unintentionally, as we trip against the heavy drapes, we are swallowed up by them. Like a conjuror's trick, they close seamlessly behind us, muffling the hectic buzz of conversation.

For a few moments we stand stock still. His hand still grips mine against the small of my back. The other reaches out, like a support, against the tall window frame, beneath whose ledge is an old-fashioned radiator, as bulky as ribbed knitting. Beyond the window is a twilit view of formal gardens, laid out in box parterres, with anonymous statuary illuminated from below. The effect is strangely Christmas-like.

We do not speak. But his eyes scan mine greedily for confirmation. He undoes the top button of my jacket. Gently, his fingers prise the lace covering one of my nipples, exposing it to view. Its smooth pink aureola crinkles into raspberry responsivess. He edges me backwards, until I am leaning against the ribbed radiator. Now, holding both my hands in his, we pause reflectively. He gazes out of the window beyond me and I turn my head to join him in his reverie. All between us remains silent. Then, he turns the full beacon of his handsome face on mine. Beyond his beauty and goodwill is another emotion fighting with itself. A compelling, almost ugly mask of lust mixes with the affection and goodwill. The mask is like an imperative.

"Won't they see us?" I ask, as though I had heard him speak.

"They will never know," he replies. His eyelids flutter strangely, as once again the blindness of emotion devours him. "I just want to caress you. Nothing else." He pauses. ". . . To know the truth." His handsome head bends fleetingly to kiss my raw nipple. With one hand, he again raises the hem of my skirt. The deep sides of his overcoat still envelop us.

I hear someone say, "I really do think Tom Stoppard's *Arcadia* was a better play than his *Invention of Love*, don't you agree?"

"You are my Arcadia," he murmurs in my ear. His fingers return to their preoccupation with the *frou frou* edges of my panties. My body ricochets against his touch. "I have to know," he intones like a litany. "Just to touch."

The movement up and down the frill of my panties is slow and mesmerizing now, all urgency gone. His fingers lick gently at my senses, like waves. I feel myself lost in some filmic dream sequence. Then, suddenly, the brutality of change. His movements become fleet and fierce and urgent again. Deftly, he lifts the edges of lace. It is like someone crossing a line. He slides the plumped prying pads of his fingertips within me, moistening the flattened hair at my pudenda, exploring the sea of my emotions.

"This is what I so longed to know," he whispers, "the truth of your response to me." The fingers that had kneaded the length of my arm in desire begin a fast pace dance within me, searching and provoking, loving and learning. "It is this that is the invention of love." He smiles. He lifts me until I am sitting, rather than leaning on the broad rough ribbed radiator. The crowd murmurs behind us. He tears the lace confection of my panties free from my outstretched legs and rumples them into his overcoat pocket. Beneath the canopy of my raised skirt, I

am exposed. Emotion and urgency exist like a perfume between us.

Briefly, I feel embarrassed. I hear a familiar voice say, "I
wonder where they are?" Decorously, instinctively, I close my
knees. But his touch is imperious. "Not now, don't withdraw
from me now," he whispers. In one sweeping movement
against the exposure of my lips, he touches me again; the
sensation is joyous, electrifying. I lean back, my arms acting as
flying buttresses to my openness and desire. I throw back my
head on my long neck and half close my eyes. The fast
cleverness of his caresses deliver me close to fulfilment.

Through half open eyes, between the wings of his overcoat, I
see him lower his zip. Beneath his long overcoat, his suit is
equally dark. From out of this cashmere darkness, he draws the
pale bounty of his penis. Through slanted eyes, I witness it
stand tall against its dark setting, like a heavy veined column,
against which a joyous blush of purple has settled.

"Only if you want to," he says. "You decide . . . maybe just
let the tip touch you," he says. "No need to go all the way."

I glance down at this effigy of beauty. Automatically, my
hand reaches to caress it. I feel it throb in my hand like a heart
beat. I look into his eye. "Just the tip," I say.

He stands, his legs between mine, before the ribbed radiator
and lets the tip of himself yearn gently at the inflamed
entrance to myself. Briefly, I am like the lip of a jug, sipping
at him hesitantly. I feel the palpitations of inner heartbeat
shoot with sensations of exquisite pleasure. And then, the
crossing of another line, the urgent need to devour and be
devoured betraying reason. All of me yearns for the strength
of that white veined column. He cups his hands around my
buttocks and lowers me gently, beyond the angry tip, beyond
the gentle lip, onto the stretching width of him, onto the
joyous fulfilling length of him. As I arch forward he clasps me
to him, indissoluble. As I begin to call out in crescendo, he
kisses my mouth to silence, then holds us fast in the mutual
embrace of his overcoat, deliberate, slow. Then, last minute, a
change of pace. I feel him race to catch me up, feel the anger of
his desire, feel the heavens in him spill. Suddenly, nothing else
matters.

"That was the invention of love", he murmurs against my hair.

When, a little later, again soignee and composed, with only the shiny blush of our skin to betray us, we push back the curtain, the room is empty, the party deserted, just a waiter or two disappearing in the distance. We are left alone with our love.

Lessons Learned

Marie (Ann Arbor, USA)

When I was growing up, my best friend was a girl named Josee. We did everything together, up until the time that we started attending college, and were separated. My Dad insisted that I go to his alma mater, the University of Michigan, while Josee's parents couldn't afford to send her there, and our resulting break-up was heart-wrenching.

I haven't seen the girl for three long years now, but I often think of her, and what might've been – maybe still could be. You see, I've always had an enormous crush on Josee, but I've always been too afraid to do anything about it. Number one, I didn't want to ruin our wonderful friendship; and number two, my parents would've killed me if they ever suspected I might be lezzy – which I don't think I am.

So, now, whenever I'm forced to help myself to some sexual satisfaction, I fantasize about Josee. I dream about what it would be like to have the courage to express my true feelings, and how I'd go about expressing them . . .

I finally hooked up with Josee at the college she was attending. After she gave me a tour of the campus, we headed back to her dorm room to get ready for dinner – my treat. Josee hadn't changed any since I'd seen her last; she was still the same sleek, dark beauty she'd always been. Her breasts were high and firm – not too big, not too small – and her skin was smooth and pale, her delicate face framed by shoulder-length coal-black hair. She was shy and a little awkward, but she had a warm smile and look that said "still waters run deep".

"So, what do you think, Marie? You going to transfer?" she

asked, unlocking the door to her dorm room and letting me inside.

"Well, I don't know," I said, playing it coy. "What's the after-class atmosphere like around here? You know, the party scene?"

She blushed, put her keys down on a small wooden desk, and then perched on the edge of one of the two beds in the tiny room. "I thought you said you were finally going to get serious about your studies?"

I sat on the other bed, facing her. I studied her dark eyes, her full, red lips. She had a pair of faded blue jeans on and a white T-shirt, and I could smell the sweet body spray that she was wearing. "Oh, I intend to get serious," I told her.

There followed a long and awkward silence during which I stared openly at her, at her face and body, the burning lust in my eyes sending out flaming tendrils that desperately sought to spark her own desire. An easy-going, big-breasted blonde like myself had no trouble attracting the guys, but it was girl-love I was after now – with my best girl.

I shifted positions, sat down next to her, and placed my left hand on her leg, up around her thigh. Upon contact with her hot, hard body, my nipples instantly grew erect under my thin halter top, and my pussy was consumed with so much heat and moisture that I thought I'd soak my cut-off jeans. "You must get lonely without me around?" I whispered, my voice breaking. I blatantly squeezed her leg, then let my hand drift higher, up around her hip.

She turned beet-red. She glanced at my hand, swallowed hard, and croaked, "It's, uh, not so bad. I . . . have a roommate. She's supposed to be –"

I halted her foolish prattle by moving my bold hand over the top of her crotch. I began rubbing her there, softly yet urgently rubbing her. I'd waited so long, masturbated so many times to the mental image of her and I ravaging each other with the pent-up fury of secret lovers, and I was determined to make up for lost time.

I said, "Your roommate doesn't do this, I bet," breathing into her innocent face, reaching out with my right hand and touching her neck with my fingers. I caressed the delicate, ivory skin on the side of her throat, then my fingers wandered across her shoulder, down her back, and up and under her T-shirt. I kept rubbing her pussy through the thin fabric of her jeans, as I pulled her shirt out of her pants and slid my hand underneath and began stroking her bare skin.

"Marie, I'm . . . not sure . . ."

Her words caught in her throat when I popped open her bra and bent closer to kiss her on the cheek. I pressed home my advantage by pushing her down onto the bed, until she was flat on her back and I was on top of her. "I've wanted this for so long," I murmured, grasping her shoulders and kissing her gently on her soft, soft lips.

"Oh," she exclaimed, startled by my overpowering craving for her.

I peeled off my top, exposing my large, heavy breasts to her wonder-struck eyes. My nipples are thick and long – chocolate-brown compared to the rest of my sun-burnished upper body. I kissed her again, but this time I lingered. I pressed my lips hard against hers, covered her mouth with mine, began to consume her. My tongue darted out and painted her pouty lips with hot saliva.

She mumbled something about slowing down, but I swallowed her protests. I attacked her mouth, ploughing my tongue up against her teeth, forcing my way inside. I hungrily explored the soft, moist interior of her mouth, swirling my tongue around, trying to engage her own tongue, my damp hands gripping the sides of her head, my fingers buried in the shimmering black curtain of her hair. I devoured her sweet goodness, kissing hard and long and openly, waiting impatiently, desperately for her to respond, until, finally, I felt her hands cover my bare breasts! She gently caressed and squeezed my big tits. My body flooded with pure, blinding joy and my head spun.

I gazed into her half-frightened, half-lusty eyes. "I'm going to make love to you, Josee," I said.

"Please," she murmured.

I kissed her, and this time my yearning tongue was met by her tongue. We slapped our tongues against one another, and I moaned into her open mouth when she pulled on my rock-hard nipples. My body tingled with the sensual sensation of her eager, shaking hands. Her tongue snaked out and I caught it between my teeth. I sucked on her tongue, sucked up and down its slippery length as if it was a hardened cock. Then I kissed her neck, licked her neck, bit her neck, kissed and licked behind her delicate ears.

Her super-heated body fired my raging desire into an inferno. "Take off your clothes," I moaned into her ear, then swirled my thick tongue around the inside of it.

"Yes," she anxiously agreed. "Yes."

I released my sexual convert, and she scrambled up off the bed and tore off her T-shirt and pulled down her jeans. She fumbled her shoes away and stepped out of her jeans and stood in front of me, naked except for her girlish, white, cotton panties. Her overwrought body trembled as my eyes drank in her sculptured, porcelain beauty. Her breasts were beautifully shaped, milky globes peaked by inch-long, impossibly pink nipples. Her stomach was flat and hard, her waist narrow, her hips round and firm.

She smiled nervously and reached for her panties, but my hands shot out and stopped her. "Let me," I said, licking my swollen lips. I stood and slowly stripped off my shoes and shorts and panties. Her eyes flashed fire as she beheld my nude, over-ripe body. I cupped my huge, bronze breasts and spread my legs, and she stared in awe at my shaved, glistening pussy. My pink folds were wet and raw with want.

"Fuck me, Marie!" she hissed, unable to control herself any longer.

I knelt down in front of her, as Roman she-warriors once knelt down before the goddess Venus, and I groped the full roundness of her firm buttocks. I squeezed her taut arse cheeks, fondling their splendid shape with my worshipping hands. Then I grasped the sides of her panties and tugged them down, left them puddled at her feet. She lifted her long, slender legs and stepped out of the discarded undergarment, and I gazed hungrily at her slickened slit. She, too, was shaved for maximum pleasure, except for a small tuft of soft, black fur that crowned her juicy pussy.

I lashed out my tongue and slashed at her cunny. She

shuddered with the impact. I teased her pussy with my tongue, then lifted her right leg off the floor and placed her foot on the bed. Now I had unrestricted access to her gaping, glistening cunt. I lapped at her moistened folds ferociously, forced my pointed tongue into and through her plump, pink pussy lips. I spread her wider with my fingers and buried my tongue inside her twat, joyously tasting her hot love-juices for the very first time. I slammed my tongue in and out of her, fucking her with my slimy pleasure tool like it was a swollen cock.

"Yes!" she cried, frantically squeezing and kneading her pert tits, viciously pulling and rolling her engorged nipples, her tawny body quivering with the sexual shockwaves that my talented tongue was generating within her molten pussy.

I lapped at her cunny like a kitten laps at a saucer of warm milk, revelling in the taste of her. Then I ploughed two fingers into her steaming lovebox and began fervently finger-fucking her as I teased her clit with my tongue. My fingers flew in and out of her tight pussy, driving her wild, driving me wild.

"I'm going to come, Marie!" she screamed. Her face was contorted into a grim mask of barely contained ecstasy, and tears of lust trailed down her flaming cheeks and into her open mouth. She let go of her titties and grabbed my head, tore at my hair, desperately clinging to me as her body was inundated with red-hot passion.

I pulled my fingers out of her soaking wet pussy, carefully licked off her juices, and then spread her wide and sucked hard on her clit. I was anxious to have my greedy mouth flooded by her impending orgasm.

"Fuck, yes!" she yelled out, oblivious to the other residents of the thin-walled dorm. Her slim body was jolted by orgasm. Muscles contracted up and down her exquisite torso, and she spasmed over and over, her tits jouncing up and down as she was torn asunder by white-hot ecstasy that centered on her pussy and my mouth.

I frenziedly sucked on her clit, and was quickly drenched with the liquid fruits of my labour of love – an orgasmic release of a tidal wave of fiery girl juice. She came on my face, in my mouth, her hips bucking, her butt cheeks shuddering, her mouth opening and closing with silent screams of total abandon. I drank in as much of her womanly goodness as I could. I swallowed and swallowed her come as she was devastated by multiple orgasms.

"Jesus!" she finally gasped, her tits trembling with the aftershocks of volcanic release, her body sheathed in dewy perspiration.

I licked up and down her pussy, slurping up the last few drops of her tangy come, and then nipped at her clit in a parting salute. I looked up at her and grinned, my lips and chin shiny with her honey. "Now it's my turn," I said.

"Sure," she agreed, sounding exhausted. "Why don't –"

We were suddenly interrupted by the door popping open. We whipped our heads around and stared at the intruder, a young woman. If she was surprised by the spectacular sight of two naked, nubile girls, one kneeling at the drenched pussy of the other, she didn't show it.

"Hi, Taylor," Josee said easily.

I glanced at her in surprise, at the mischievous smile playing across her puffy lips.

"Hi, Josee," the girl called Taylor replied, closing the door securely behind her. "Looks like your plan worked, after all."

Josee shrugged her shoulders, smoothed my hair down. "Well, actually, it turned out that Marie had a plan of her own. I just sorta played along."

Taylor advanced into the room as I scrambled to my feet. "Nice to meet you, Marie," she said. "I'm Josee's roommate. She's told me a lot about you." She reached out and shook my hand, which seemed a strange thing to do to a naked woman, but she topped that by kissing her roommate squarely on the lips. They frenched each other familiarly as I gaped in amazement. My shy, innocent Josee obviously wasn't nearly as shy nor innocent as she had led me to believe.

"Are you and Josee . . . lovers?" I asked Taylor in disbelief, when the two girls had finally ceased their tongue-wrestling.

"Every chance we get," the young woman replied, laughing. "Right, Jo?"

Josee nodded. "But we've never had a threesome before. You up for it, Marie?"

"Oh, I think she's up for it, all right," Taylor replied for me, reaching out to fondle my swollen nipples – the exclamation points on my mounting excitement.

I looked at Josee, and she grinned back at me and fingered her pussy. "Uh, I–I . . ." I stuttered, then gave up as my body was suffused with the erotic heat of Taylor's tit-groping. She really knew her way around a girl's mams.

"Mmm," I moaned, as Taylor squeezed my big tits together and rolled my nipples. I regarded her through lowered eyelids and saw that she was built along the same lines that I was – big and curvaceous. She had long, wavy, auburn hair, and her large eyes were warm and brown, her chest huge and heaving. She was barely wearing a red tube-top and black spandex pants. I closed my eyes for a moment, basking in the warm feel of her hands on my tits, and then, when I reopened my eyes, Taylor was wearing nothing at all. And now Josee was the one fondling my tits, firing my pussy.

"Now, how shall we do this?" Taylor pondered, bouncing a finger on her puckered lips. "Oh, I know. Josee can eat out Marie's pussy, while Marie gives me a little of what she gave Josee. Sound fair?"

We both nodded. When the positioning had been hastily completed, the erotic entanglement left me lying on my back on one of the beds, Josee's head between my legs, with Taylor balanced just above me, facing the wall, her knees on either side of my face. I quickly grabbed onto Taylor's plump, round buttocks and pulled her soaking snatch down into my mouth.

"Yeah," she moaned. "Do me like you did Josee."

I lapped at Taylor's cunny and massaged her beautiful behind. She tasted as good as Josee, and I couldn't get enough. Meanwhile, Josee was driving me wild by licking my pussy with the polished, frenetic skill of the dedicated muff-diver. I moaned into Taylor's cunt and the girl's body quivered with the vibrations of my voice.

Josee reached up and played with my titties while she kindled my cunt-fire with her tongue. She squeezed my breasts and sucked on my clit, making me dizzy with her sexual skills, and it was all I could do to keep on tongue-lashing Taylor's luscious snatch. I licked up and down her pussy, over and over, then around and into her arse. She jumped when my wet, probing tongue explored her tiny bunghole.

"What a fantastic sight," Josee said, momentarily raising her head from my shiny womanhood to gaze at the sexy scenario of her pretty roommate climbing the wall as I furiously lapped at her pussy and arse.

"Fuck almighty, I'm coming!" Taylor cried out, cutting short the time for introspection.

Josee dipped her talented tongue back into my pussy and redoubled her efforts, trying to bring me off in sync to Taylor's mounting orgasm. I clenched Taylor's butt and drove my tongue deep into the quaking girl's cunny. Josee was sucking hard on my clit, and my head started to spin as my senses were overwhelmed with the smell and taste of Taylor's molten womanhood, and the sensuous sensation of Josee's cunt-licking.

"Here I come!" Taylor shrieked.

Her butt cheeks jumped around in my hands as her perfect body was wracked by a tongue-inspired orgasm. I frantically clung to her pussy with my mouth, drinking down her liquid ecstasy as she came over and over again. Then, before Taylor had ceased her gyrations of joy, my own body blazed with fire and my mind was sent reeling. Josee's cuntwork had pushed me over the edge. I shut my eyes and clung to Taylor's bucking rump as the tingling in my pussy exploded into electric shocks that jolted my body like I'd been plugged into a wall socket. My pussy erupted and I drenched Josee's sweet face with my lovejuices.

"Yeah!" I screamed, shattered by thundering orgasms that detonated inside of me and wasted my body and mind. I gasped for air, found only pussy, and my ecstasy was like nothing I'd ever experienced before.

Taylor dropped down onto my stomach and covered my gaping mouth with her own, swallowing my cries of pleasure, as Josee continued to relentlessly tongue-fuck me and polish my clit with her thumb. I thought I was headed for blackout when a final orgasm, the most powerful yet, tore through my body and into Taylor's sucking mouth. Then I lay shaken and dazed in the afterglow of total fulfillment, my body dappled with sweat, my soul obliterated.

Josee crawled up behind Taylor, encircled the babe's tits with her arms, and the two girlfriends shared my come with each other, swapping it back and forth with their tongues. I watched through a thick, warm haze, my body languid, my brain struggling to regain a foothold on reality.

"Do you think Marie's going to transfer, now?" Josee asked Taylor, as the devious scamp felt up Taylor's big tits and pointed nipples.

They looked at me.

"I don't know," Taylor replied. "I think she still needs some more convincing."

I smiled weakly, willing to learn all I could.

. . . That's just one of my fantasies involving Josee. I've got lots more, which I dream up as needed. And with study break approaching, I'm thinking that maybe it's time for a road trip – to a friendly campus where I can hopefully put some of the lessons I've learned in my head to good, practical use.

Ticket to Ride

Bekka (Birmingham, UK)

Like a lot of people, I have a long dull trip to work, and sometimes I've looked at my fellow travellers and wondered what they did for a living and where they'd come from. Then one year, I ended up doing a lot of shift work, late in the evening and there weren't many people to watch. Particularly on the homeward bound journey. Often there was only one other man. He was good-looking, but very shy as he never said a word to me, but sat with his nose in a book or magazine for the entire trip. I began to fantasize about him, who he was, what he was doing coming home so late every evening. When I realized that these fantasies were becoming sexual, I decided to do something about it. Now I'm not backward in coming forward, but even so, I managed to shock myself as I day-dreamed and wove my cunning plan. Would it work?

So one evening I found myself standing on the metro platform, shivering with a combination of cold and anticipation. A chilly breeze managed to whistle round my bare knees, even under my long coat. I stamped my feet and looked at my watch. The tram should be here soon. This late at night the metro only ran every half hour. I grimaced and bit my lip with nerves. What if he wasn't on this tram? I would have frozen my behind off for nothing. The rails began to sing and I sighed with relief as the tram pulled into the station. At least I could get out of the cold.

Stepping into the deserted carriage, my heart sank. He wasn't there. Then I saw the familiar mop of dark hair, at the far end of the carriage. My heart thumped again, this time with excitement. He was sitting facing forward. That would make everything so much easier. The tram set off and I made my unsteady way towards him

The seat I chose was facing him, with its back to the driver's cab and raised a step up. I carefully climbed the step, a little wobbly in my spike-heeled boots. I paused before I sat down to undo the buttons of my long coat. He barely glanced at me as I took my seat, his nose in his book.

I adjusted my clothing, hitching my short stretchy skirt up higher and allowing my coat to fall open. Now for part one of my action plan. I crossed my legs carelessly. As I did so, I caught his book with my toe and knocked it out of his hands.

"Oh, I'm so sorry."

"That's OK, no harm done." He bent to pick the book up. He sat back in his seat, and his face flushed as he stared at me. He obviously couldn't believe his eyes. I knew he recognized me. We regularly commuted to and from the city on the same bus and tram. But he had never seen me looking as I did tonight.

Normally I dressed for work in modest clothing, with a skirt that falls below my knees and a high-necked blouse. I always wore sensible shoes; after all, I was on my feet all evening. Now I sat across from him with my legs apart, my skirt hitched up, almost to my waist and my naked pussy clearly visible to his amazed eyes. He gulped and looked me in the face. I could feel that my cheeks were hot and flushed, partly with embarrassment, but mostly with excitement. I grinned at him, and he nervously grinned back.

From the look on his face, my next actions almost gave him a heart attack. I took one of my fingers and slid it lingeringly along my pussy lips. I was still wearing my black gloves and the leather-clad finger against my pale skin would have been a shocking contrast. He watched, mesmerized, as I slid my finger up and down my slit.

His cock must have been hard enough to make him uncomfortable as he shifted in his seat. I couldn't help the little gasp that escaped my lips as I stared at his zipper. He glanced up at my face and saw that I was staring at his groin. Tentatively he ran his hand over the hard ridge in his trousers and I moaned with excitement. I opened my legs wider, my eyes riveted to his cock. Almost absentmindedly, I slid two fingers inside myself, then slowly withdrew them, the black leather shining with my juices. It was his turn to groan. He stroked himself harder, pressing firmly through the fabric. I wondered if he was going to come in his pants.

The jerking of the tram brought us back to a sense of time and place as it slowed and came to a halt at the next station. I teasingly removed my fingers from my cunt and slowly brought my legs together. The carriage doors whooshed open, but no-one got on. It seemed like an eternity before the bell rang and the tram moved off again. He looked regretfully up at my face. I could guess what he was thinking. Ours was the next stop, only a minute away. No time for more naughty games. Of course, he was quite wrong.

I stood up slowly, my short knitted skirt stayed where it was, rucked up above my buttocks looking more like a wide belt than an article of clothing. I stepped carefully down from my seat and came to stand in the aisle beside him. I am quite tall and, with my high-heeled boots, my naked pussy was almost at his head height. Teetering precariously as the tram swayed along its tracks, I held a grab rail in one hand and stuffed the other in my coat pocket. I held that side of my coat open, shielding the object of my desire from the driver.

His face at my pussy, he stared at my springy fair curls, now covered with beads of moisture. He must have been able to smell my arousal, and the thought was driving me crazy. He ducked his head and stuck out his tongue, pushing the rigid flesh through my hot damp folds to find the hard nub of my clit. I groaned and thrust my hips towards him; I was *so* close to coming. I almost screamed with frustration as the tram began to slow again as it neared our stop. He pulled back and my cunt felt achingly bereft.

He gently pulled my coat around me and began to do up the buttons. "Our stop, Miss."

I groaned and if I hadn't have been so precariously balanced I would have stamped my feet. I pouted, "My name's Bekka." Both my name and my blonde hair are inherited from my Scandinavian grandmother.

"I'm Sam. Here, let me help you." The tram pulled up and

almost jerked me off my feet. Sam slid his arm round me. "Number thirty-two bus, as usual?"

I nodded and cuddled into the comfort of his arm. My legs were unsteady and I appreciated his support. Fortunately, the bus stop was just across the road from the tram, so we didn't have far to walk.

The night bus was already waiting at the stop, the only other passengers, a couple of teenage boys and an elderly man, already on board.

"Want to sit upstairs?" Sam asked diffidently when he'd paid the driver. I nodded, a small smile beginning to appear. Perhaps the night wasn't over yet.

"Ladies first." Sam stood back to allow me to climb the narrow stairs. Once I was high above him, on the curve of the staircase, Sam grabbed the back of my coat, jerking me to a halt. I held my breath, heart pounding with excitement as he slowly rose up the stairs behind me, sliding his hands under my coat and up my shiny leather boots, over the soft smooth flesh of my thighs until he reached my bottom. He squeezed my buttocks and briefly ran a finger between them, stroking along the crease, and pressing gently on my tight little hole, before he released me.

I quivered and bit my lip, stifling the moan that rose to my lips. On stiff legs, I made my way halfway down the aisle. There was no one else upstairs, so we had our choice of seats.

Sam let me sit down near the window, then slid in next to me. Turning my face to his in one firm hand, he kissed me, his warm tongue thrusting into my mouth. I sighed into his mouth as his fingers nimbly began to unbutton my coat. My coat fell open and he slid his fingers between my pussy lips and stroked my clit. Instant heat flashed through me, pooling in my groin. I moaned and sucked his tongue. Sam thrust his fingers into my sopping wet cunt and I went wild, screaming softly into his mouth as I came in convulsive waves around his hand. It was sheer ecstasy.

My head fell to his shoulder as I gradually came back down to earth. I felt Sam kiss the top of my hair before he gently removed his fingers from inside me. I caught his slippery hand and brought it to my mouth.

"Here, let me." Slowly I sucked each warm, wet finger into my mouth and licked it clean. I took my time about it, savouring the combination of relaxation in my pussy and the tenseness of Sam's body. "There, all done." I replaced his hand on his thigh and snuggled down so my head was in his lap. I could feel the hard ridge in his trousers and I teased him by rubbing my cheek along it.

Sam slid his hands into my hair, unable to resist holding my mouth to his cock. He must have been able to feel my hot breath through the fabric. I wondered if his cock ached as much as my pussy had a few minutes ago. I gripped the hard ridge gently with my mouth and growled softly as I ran my teeth up and down him, nibbling him through the thin material. I felt his hand move towards me, as if in protest as I slowly unzipped his fly, but then I reached inside and touched him, my fingers cool against his heated flesh and any objections instantly disappeared.

I eased his cock out into the cool air and stroked it briefly, my fingertips softly smoothing the moisture that oozed from the tip all over the head. It was a lovely warm, silky piece of flesh, not too big, not too small. I grinned at the thought, feeling like Goldilocks. Sam's cock was just right. I opened my mouth and took him inside. My nose nuzzled his pubic hair. He smelled delicious, a combination of musk and soap and tasted even better. I do so like the taste of pre-come, sweet and salty all at once. Resisting the impulse to bite this delicious lollipop, I pulled slowly away, took a deep breath, and sank my face back down on him.

It was his turn to lose all control. Sam groaned and thrust his hips, and from the shocked sounds he was making, I realized that he had never had all his cock buried inside a woman's mouth. Grabbing my hair, he eased me up and down on his cock. God, it felt so good, sexy and slightly scary, as his cock plunged further and further inside my hot mouth, then finally down inside my tight throat. I swallowed convulsively and the movement triggered his orgasm. Uncaring and unaware of any spectators, Sam shouted and came, his semen flooding my throat.

I came up for air, gasping and flushed, a huge grin of

triumph on my face. It quickly disappeared when I caught sight of a road sign, flashing past the window. "Our stop," I wailed and pressed the bell, "We've missed our stop." Sam stared at me blankly as I pulled my coat together. "Get up, Sam. If we get off here, it won't be too far to walk back."

My handsome conquest shook his head as he came rapidly back to reality. Hastily adjusting his clothes, he stood and staggered down the aisle to the stairs. As we got off the bus, I thought I saw the driver wink at him, before he drove away.

Arm in arm, we walked slowly back up the long road towards our stop. Sam was very quiet, I only hoped he wasn't regretting what had just happened.

"Penny for your thoughts."

Sam opened his mouth and looked amazed by what came out. "I want to fuck you. Here, now."

I giggled, pleased and surprised by his frank honesty, "OK, but not exactly here," and I gestured at the wet pavement. "Come on." I grabbed his hand and dragged him out of the light of the street lamps into the shelter of an unlit shop doorway. I think Sam was beginning to have second thoughts until he felt me catch hold of his hands and place them on my breasts. His breathing quickened as he felt the hard nubs of my nipples, through my sweater. I knew then that I had his undivided attention. I could feel his cock stiffening again as he pushed my knees apart and stood between my legs, our crotches glued together.

He cupped my warm breasts and slid his hands under my jumper.

"It fastens at the front," I murmured in his ear.

I wonder if he realized then, just how much thought I had put into seducing him. I was hardly wearing any clothes, and those that I did have on allowed easy access to my body. Undoing my bra, he pushed my jumper up, and bent his head to my breasts. I moaned as he sucked and nibbled at my nipples, his teeth grazing over the ridged skin. I rubbed my pussy against his hard cock, the fabric of his trousers delightfully rough against my sensitive skin. Slipping a hand between us, I slid his zipper down and released his cock from its bondage. My pussy met it eagerly and he slid easily inside, I was so wet.

Grunting, he thrust into me and I gasped at the power of his strokes. "Beautiful slut," he murmured in my ear and I took it as the compliment that he intended. He thrust harder and faster, taking me higher and higher with each stroke. It was an exquisite journey, which ended far too soon. "I'm coming," he moaned softly in my ear and gave a final couple of thrusts, holding me so tightly that I could hardly breathe.

He withdrew from me. Trembling with a combination of arousal and disappointment, I would have turned away from him and fastened my coat but he stopped me, holding my hands tightly. "Stand still." He slid his hands to my waist and slowly knelt down on the cold stone. Grasping me to him, his hands round the back of my thighs, he buried his face in my pussy. His tongue licked and lapped at me, cleaning away our mingled juices and replacing them with his saliva. My knees shook and moments later as he flicked his tongue over my hard clit I came in waves, my hands threaded into his dark hair, forcing his face into my cunt as hard as I could.

I was shaky on my legs after that, and had to lean against the shop door as Sam tenderly smoothed my skirt back down to cover my buttocks. He rose and gently adjusted my clothing, refastening my bra and pulling my sweater back down. "There," he kissed my closed eyelids, "All nice and tidy."

Wearily, I opened my eyes and smiled back at him. "Thanks." I yawned and he looked worried.

"Come on, not far now. I only live just around the corner. You could stay if you like?"

I liked. Leaning heavily on his arm, I made the last hundred yards in a satiated daze. He lived in a narrow terraced house, but apart from noticing that it was in the middle of the row of houses, I was too tired to take in any more details. He led me upstairs to the bedroom. I remember lying back on the bed as he helped me get my boots off and then no more.

"Miss, Miss. Excuse me, Miss, wake up."

I felt someone shake me and blearily I opened my eyes, confused by my surroundings. I was sitting on the tram, my head leaning against the window. I swallowed to ease my dry mouth and gingerly moved my stiff neck.

I looked at the man hovering nervously beside me. It was Sam. I frowned at him and he flushed. "Sorry to wake you, Miss, but I think that this is your stop."

I nodded stiffly and he removed his hand from my shoulder, the overhead lights glinting on his wedding ring.

"Thank you." As if in a dream, I stepped out of the carriage and onto the wet platform, the cold rain and rising wind blowing away any last vestiges of sleep. Wide awake, I watched as Sam walked away from me towards the car park. Unusually, there was a car waiting for him. Green with envy, I saw him bend to kiss the driver on the cheek. I assume the woman was his wife.

Sighing, I buttoned my coat up tight against the weather and headed in the opposite direction towards the bus station. As I sat on the bus, I tried to remember my dream, but it only came back in vague wisps of memory. All I had to remind me was a feeling of sleepy satisfaction. I blushed as I realized I had come in my sleep. Had I cried out, or made other embarrassing noises? I bit my lip and huddled down into my seat. Tomorrow, I vowed, I would take care to avoid the brown-haired man, that my dream had named Sam.

All About Me

Lee (Arcadia, USA)

What is her name? Peg, Meg? I can't remember. Couldn't be all the beer. I know she's with Carlo, though. I lean around to follow the curve of her arm as it snakes around Carlo's waist and ends on Greg's arse. Lucky bitch.

"Is anyone else hungry? Why don't we get a pizza?" No response. I must be invisible, same as I am at home with Tad. I have drunk myself into a state of invisibility. Now I can openly stare at Carlo and Greg both rubbing themselves against her – Meg, that's her name. Look at them, they love it! Why doesn't Marla care what that slut is doing? I take advantage of my transparent state and pluck someone's nearly full beer from the coffee table.

Okay, I can pout or enjoy this. Pout about the fact that Tad is on his way to Thailand without me, that I am here at a party alone, in my shortest sundress and no one is noticing. Or, enjoy the fact that I am in an apartment on the beach in Venice with a terrific view, lots of beer, and no husband bothering me. I can stand on the couch if I like, take in the sunset and watch my single friends frolic like bunnies in spring.

Well, I wonder, savouring a sip of beer. Who would I pick if I was single, if I had no husband and it was all about me? How about Marla's boyfriend, the blonde, scruffy Greg, with his knobby knees and eighties fashion sense? I glide closer to examine the curly trail of hair descending into his loosely tied paisley shorts. I admire the dreads touching the nape of that spot on his neck that feels so good to lick, and tongue the neck of my bottle.

What about our host, Carlo? I step lithely around Meg and

insinuate myself in the space behind her to appraise Carlo. His thick, black shoulder-length hair sets off his brown eyes and lips pale as seashell against his burnished skin. His age shows only in the deeply etched laugh lines framing his eyes and the mottled grey stubble trailing from his chin. I sniff the vapour of pheromones twining about his chest. Now that I am invisible, I can see hormones and heat. They exude a smoky, reddish glow.

"How about going to that little club around the corner?" Carlo suggests, and I jump back, but he doesn't seem to notice my strange behaviour. "They have a good jazz set after nine," he says, smiling at me. He could just as easily be smiling through me, I think. It's as if they're not seeing me at all.

"No, let's stay in," Marla says, to my relief. After so many beers, I can't imagine navigating the crowds. He shrugs, and turns his smoky eyes back to Meg. Marla huffs a little and walks toward me but, just before we would collide, she says, "Excuse me" and brushes by. So I am not invisible! I am just flying below the sexual radar.

Leave them to it, a fuzzy voice murmurs in my head. I am not getting any tonight, so I may as well go outside and sober up, think about going home. I slip out the apartment door and up the steps to the roof to see the sights of Venice Beach. As I clear the doorway, a cooling mist caresses my swollen face and I follow the wet, briny breeze up the steep attic stairway and ascend to a ceiling of stars.

A seaward Santa Ana gust nudges me toward the edge of the roof. I sway backward, straining to find a flaw in the perfect scattering of starlight above. It's so beautiful; I could just sleep out here if I had a cot. Maybe I could bring a blanket up.

Just one light illuminates a circle of vacant roof, and makes the rest of the area that much darker. I have to duck away from the glare and peer into the far edges to see anything. I am backing around a trashcan when the warm breeze wraps about me, like an arm catching me smoothly around the waist.

I relax into the feel of finely muscled thighs, and grip them instinctively as they pull me back and into their warmth. As I crouch in the shelter of a vast muscle of chest, my feet leave the roof and I am encased in another body – a body all around me with an erection curving against my tailbone. I feel the thinness of surf baggies with nothing underneath, and my dress of sheer rayon is just a whisper between us. A languorous sexuality surges in me, and I reach around lithely and grasp for the firmness. This one is for me.

Two hands brush fleetingly over my chest, the mountain of muscle moves, and I lose my grip but slide firmly over the erection on my way to the ground. I knew from his own forward sway and pulse that he welcomes my touch, and once I can stand on my own, he leaves one hand on my ribcage to keep me close.

"You okay?" I hear a voice whisper. "It's too far to dive from here."

"I'm fine," I say, struggling to take in fresh air and appear composed. He thinks I was going to jump? "I was just looking for a place to sit." He steers me gently further into the puddle of darkness beyond the arc of lighted roof. This is bad. Should I scream? I have to face him, explain calmly that I am not a lunatic and make sure he isn't either. Even though I'm the one who was holding him by the dick.

I turn around and then a gust, like a fist gathering up a handful of my hair. My head tilts back and I open my mouth to scream, but it is smothered by a ravenous kiss. My tongue tastes lips and teeth, then another tongue, tangy as the ocean brine. I relax and suck gently on it and then take it into my throat. This is so easy, to forget everything except this tongue touching mine.

I feel like we are dancing, taking tiny, languorous steps until we discover a tattered chaise and sink down, still entwined. I gasp at the frigid feel of the damp plastic strips under my thighs contrasted with the burning warmth all over the front of me. I open my eyes to a halo of light all about me, and then a dark, featureless mane swims into focus. All about me, I think and giggle as I imagine his swollen lips, his startled eyes wondering at me.

"Who are you?" I sigh, and regret asking immediately. "Never mind," I whisper, and trace a line of shadowy stubble. "It doesn't matter."

I watch raptly as the darkened lips seem to move, but any

sound they make must be blowing away in the warm wind. Or maybe I am just that drunk. I am so drunk. What am I doing? I look at my hand lingering on his chin. My other hand is moving his shirt, moving back down to the bulge in his surf baggies. This is all I want. I feel him nod, as if he is as dumbstruck as I am.

I stroke my hand along the rigid length of him, as confident as an actor in a porno movie. If he doesn't want me to, he can stop me. But instead, he leans in to kiss me again. My sudden relief surprises me a little, and I sigh with pleasure. His dark hair tumbles around us, stroking my neck, and I imagine our bodies merging blonde and black in a private spotlight.

My dress buttons down the front and his hand follows the buttons down as I caress him. Please don't come fast, I beg silently. I want this to last.

I slide my palm down and into his shorts and pull loose the drawstring where the tip of him pokes out. The thought of what I am going to do gives me a thrill, and I murmur, "I want to taste you," as I slide down until my tongue reaches his velvety knob.

He shapes his hands to my breasts, still encased in the filmy rayon. "Suck on me," I hear from somewhere, and so I pull his shorts down and take him fully into my throat.

His shaft pulses around my lips. I feel reckless and nasty. I suck him to the hilt and back, my own jumbo lollipop. "Fuck my mouth." I order and plunge my lips around his throbbing shaft. I hear no answer, just a faint pant of pleasure or surprise.

I want him to pump into me, to fill my mouth and stroke my throat. He rocks his hips and sends his shaft plunging into me. I suck, release and then grip tight with each thrust. He pauses and straightens from the waist and I feel a rush of panic.

"Turn around," the air whispers to me urgently. I spin under him so he can penetrate deeper into my mouth. My dress slides above my knees, open to the navel, and my toes grip the head of the recliner. He kisses my exposed thighs and slides a finger under a corner of my soaked panties. The finger strokes my frothy lips as his cock swells to fill my throat.

I swallow him to the hilt, until I can feel the tip of his cock expand against the skin of my neck. One finger, then another stretches the liquid walls of my vagina. I ease his cock back out, fluttering my tongue along the underside of his ridged and veiny shaft, swirling it around the flare of his head as it bumps the roof of my mouth. His head swells with a sudden surge of blood.

"Don't come yet," I moan and suck him into me again. One hand feels for the bony extension behind his balls and I press there to stem his orgasm while his fingers search for my clit. He gasps, pauses and shudders with restraint, then begins again to pump into my throat. I hold him there on the edge of orgasm, my tongue teasing his shaft and my hands cupping the softness of his scrotal sac, until I feet his balls tighten.

I tickle his balls with one hand and suck in hard one last time as warm semen courses down my open throat. He collapses, kissing my soaked crotch and cradling my arse in both hands.

I whisper, "You have to finish. I have to feel you inside me." He kisses my salty lips, tentative and then insistent. His mouth closes over mine as if to capture my breath, and I shiver with my own answering effort. He pulls back suddenly and I catch an image of a wicked smile, like a teenager copping a feel, and I know he's not finished with me yet.

"Maybe we should go inside?" I suggest.

Somehow I button, arrange, and make my way downstairs to the darkened apartment. Marla and Greg are asleep on one end of the sectional couch, and I hang back in the shadows until I see a pile of blankets left out for me. Have I been gone that long, or did they just pass out? Did I miss an amazing menage a trois? Well, I can compete with that, I giggle to myself.

I arrange the blankets a few feet away on opposite ends of the long sectional and then crawl over to the coffee table and swallow the warm dregs of an abandoned beer. Maybe I should lie down for just a minute. The sound of the stereo startles me awake. All about me, heat and hands invade my blankets, opening my dress again. He's back. Where was he?

"Quiet," I whisper at the formless mass. I smile and wonder what he's up to, whether it's my turn now. My bra drops on the floor and lips nibble at the tip of one breast, just the way I like it, until I feel it swell and harden. He sucks firmly on one tit and rolls the other between his calloused fingers until I groan in ecstasy and bloom again with moisture. "Bite it," I gasp.

I feel my nipple in his teeth and slide a hand down to hook my panties. He pushes them below my knees, and then I hear a delicious sucking sound. Three slick, roughened fingers trace a burning line down my belly. When I open my eyes to the soft green glow bathing my busy blankets, I am sure that it is my own molten desire lighting up the room. I can just make out the tinny strains of "Watermelon Man" and remember the stereo. Did he turn it on to cover up the noise he knew we would be making, I mused. Or did I? I can't remember with that hand circling around my centre but never getting any closer.

Finally, I feel his prickly chin, then his hair caress my belly. His head follows his fingers down my torso and his tongue touches just the tip of my clit. More, I whimper silently and arch upward. But his hands hold my hips down as he moves lower, teasing the burning root with soft licks. I open my hips wide and bring my feet between his shoulder blades, willing his tongue to touch the white-hot centre of my clit again, but he pokes his tongue into my womb and pushes a finger into the smaller opening behind.

"Please," I hiss, grasping my own breasts in each hand and squeezing my nipples between fingers and thumbs. I contract inside against the poking pressure of his finger and finally feel the meat of my throbbing clit against the warmth of his mouth. Now, I know I will come. That's all it takes for the contractions to explode around his fingers and tongue. Just as sudden and violent, he pulls out to replace his mouth with his rigid shaft.

The shock of his entrance makes me contract again harder and I struggle to throw off the blankets tented over us. "I have to see you," I cry, frantic with need and sensation.

"Shh." The sibilance rises as if from inside me. "You want everyone to see you?" Shit, that's right. We aren't alone in the room, this isn't my husband, and I don't even know his name! The blankets billow and a surge of heat escapes and suffuses my face. I see a glint that could be his eyes reflecting the low light from the stereo. He nuzzles between my breasts and rises up onto his hands, pumps once, twice and then slows. I love that feeling, of a turgid cock filling me, motionless but still throbbing from within. When our hips separate again, the tip sucks apart from my own lips with the sound of sloppy kiss. He inches back in halfway, then out, then halfway in again as I buck to receive him. "You'll make me come again," I warn, and feel him slide into me until his balls rest silky and cool on my arse.

"Not yet though," I whisper. "Fuck me hard and I will," and I grip his arse cheeks to pull him deeper. Wouldn't those balls feel even bigger from behind, I think idly and then hear a throaty animal moan. Is that me? Did I say that out loud?

"From behind," echoes in my ears and he must hear it too, because he withdraws just as I roll over onto my knees. I turn my head, aching to see the pussy-slick dick before it plunges back inside. First, he presses it into the cleft between my arse cheeks. His solid warmth pulses against my arsehole and I feel it grow pliant and yielding. Tad never touches me there. I didn't know it could open so much, so easily. He could fuck me in the arse and I think I would like it!

Instead, he slides down until his slick head finds the more familiar entrance. He grips my hip-bones with his hands and plunges in. The instant his head reaches the top of my womb, I come again from deep inside. I hear a satisfied, animal grunt and then his solid middle finger finds my tighter hole and plunges in, impaling me in both places. Nothing could feel better than this – except two cocks? I imagine that his finger is just that, another cock filling me to the hilt.

Make me come hard, I order my phantom lover, and finally peak and ride on a wave of pleasure. He wraps one arm around me and pulls me against him as he drives into me. I feel his balls sway loose, then gather up and tighten. Come now, I urge him, as I watch a fine funk of sweat rise in a golden halo around us. If I hold still against him, let him pound me deep, I know he'll come. He does, pulsing inside me over and over, shooting sperm deep into my belly as he sinks his finger just as deep into my arse one last time.

I lie gasping and listening to the sound of my breath against the rhythm of a blues melody. Time to turn that off. I can't sleep with music playing.

I roll off the couch and crawl over to switch off the stereo.

Just before the light fades, I look over at Marla and Greg, but it's obvious that we haven't disturbed them. We must have been quieter than it seemed inside my head. Beer makes everything sound louder.

I creep back under my blankets, and snuggle over against the spine of the couch. No warm body greets me. Maybe he went to the bathroom. Just as well, there isn't that much room, I think as I drift off to sleep. Even though he is gone, in that last involuntary twitch of limbs and synapses that fire before sleep invades, I can still feel a cocoon of heat all about me.

Jack Kerouac, My Lover

Valerie (Los Angeles, USA)

A Preface, of Sorts

Possessing little money and no job but a few credit cards, I was ready to track Jack Kerouac down the big sexy American highway. I also wanted to fuck his ghost but I'll get to that later. I'd just finished graduate school, all but my thesis, and had managed to convince my professors that – aside from giving me a great chance to see the country – retracing Kerouac's steps across America would yield this last bit of required scholarship. My thesis committee consisted of two men and one woman and I was casually sleeping with all three, so my "convincing" obligated me to do a lot of sucking dick and eating pussy. I didn't mind, of course, which will later become quite obvious; from the beginning, after all, my journey with Jack Kerouac would entail a lot of sex . . .

O! Jack Kerouac! my heart sang to hidden desire and fancy: *my lover!*

Route 66 exists only as a fragment of its former self, so I headed east on Interstate 10. Leaving Los Angeles in a rented Buick, I drove through the backside of the sunset into the empty deserts of Arizona, the endless stretches of land called Texas, the bogs and bayous of the South. The only thing we had less of than money was time: we were re-enacting Jack's cross-country scrambles far more closely than I had ever intended, or wanted. Like Jack (my secret lover) when he complained in *On The Road*, we too were "rushing through the world without a chance to see it."

Moving at this pace, my experience of place transmuted into a kaleidoscopic slide show flashing by at warp speed. I had less than six weeks to hit as many cities, straddling both coasts – legs spread, of course, and pussy wet and willing. The effort left me dazed and uninformed about the deeper histories of my ever-changing surroundings, mottling me in an intense mosaic of sensory impressions.

And, as I said, my pussy was always wet.

New York City in Two Days

Day 1

I A.M.

Let's say I'm on my way to New York. Let's say I'm on the train. Its rhythm keeps rocking me to sleep, and then I wake up, worried about missing my stop – the route is, after all, unfamiliar. Let's say the movement of the train makes me horny and I'm thinking about shoving my hand down my pants and fingering my little cunt. Let's say I'm thinking about Kerouac's declaration that the East is "brown and holy and California is white like washlines." Let's say I'm thinking brown is like a puckering arse and white is like thick gooey semen – I can taste both in my mouth as the train lurches forward. Ah yes: the difference between old and new. Old being decrepit and historic. New meaning clean and vacuous. Brings to mind the TV ads I saw when I was a kid, ads for cleansers. The whole homogenizing kind of television commercials that were so popular back then. I think about fresh-smelling bed sheets (the kind you sniff in a hotel room just before you're about to get fucked by a stranger you met in the bar) and the scroungy apartment that's got old dirty laundry on the floor (underwear stained with come, piss and shit) . . . yet has *all kinds of stuff* there. Like a vibrator in the drawer; a two-headed dildo under the bed; secret butt-plugs under the pillow.

Warm, very warm, air whisks by me. It smells unclean, like it is coming from the bathroom – and that makes my pussy contract as I think about giving Jack Kerouac a blowjob while he sits on the toilet, one hand on my head and the other holding a beer can. *Faces reflect in the train's window like pictures in a frame.* After Jack comes in my mouth, he urinates.

I go into the bathroom. I pee and then I stick my hand between my legs and think of Jack's deep green eyes.

Well, I'm in New York; I'm in Greenwich Village and I'm hitting that moment that I knew I would . . . when I'm beginning to wonder about the sanity of this whole idea of mine. Does it really make any difference to be where Kerouac was? Perhaps my conclusion will simply be that the thing about literature *is*: it takes you to worlds you might not otherwise get to see and explore, and the thing about *On The Road* is that it compelled more people to go to those places and see the world for themselves. Or so I've been led to believe. And that's *exactly* what I'm doing. One of the things I think I'm finding is an understanding of Kerouac's fascination with the open road because he lived in a place where he didn't drive, where he didn't *need* to drive. Being the one behind the wheel, and with the endless stretches of highway – it's a new kind of freedom for him. It's more of an extreme kind of freedom to him, whereas on the west coast we're always behind the wheel and the open road is crowded with traffic –

I want to die in a car crash while being fucked in the backseat –

Yeah, I know that's too much like Ballard's *Crash* –

As for Jack – and Dean Moriarty/Neal Cassady, his pal, his Huckleberry friend . . . just a diversion, an entertaining diversion for my Jack K. Because he ultimately had his suburban home to return to, his mama, and his middle class respectability. Places where Dean could never go. Dean was just a lark for JK.

Cassady had two wives. I bet he was a great fuck.

He looks like a hunk in his pictures.

I would have fucked Neal Cassady – then again, I'm pretty open to fucking any man or woman who is attracted to me and wants to make that quick, lovely physical connection.

Test question: Is the quest an excuse for living however you want to, without regard for anybody else or their feelings?

Times Square, one of the many places that is mentioned again and again throughout the time spent in New York within the pages of *On The Road,* and really it's a terminus. It's a terminus, and so I guess it becomes the landmark of arriving home for Kerouac.

I'm on Bowery Street, venturing into the part of town someone warned me against. "You'll get raped if you're alone." Paranoia seeps in. This state of mind of mine – I came in open, trusting, *willing.* Now I find I'm closing myself off because I've been told that's the "smart" thing to do. "Trust your sixth sense," my waiter at the first cafe told me, but all I could do was look at his crotch and think about sucking his dick. My sixth sense is going all out of control and I feel as if I've dropped acid and walked into some strange parallel universe. Everyone's noticing me, how out of place I appear. Everyone's plotting scams. They all want to gang rape me. I'm testing my limits and finding out what they are. I want them to fuck me, I want to know what that's like, because the whole point of this journey is to experience the extremes –
    I will not be smart –
    But I will follow my true heart.

I had initially harboured hopes of tapping into some wild, crazy mode, a network of irregular characters as adventurous as Moriarty, or as hip to the literary scene as Kerouac – the looseness with which they invaded the homes and lives of the people by whom they passed.

"Of course, all of this is much different from how it was in Kerouac's time," says Todd (he's one of the hallowed two percent of the acting community able to actually earn a living in the theatre scene). "None of the places he hung out at are even around any more," says Todd. He takes me through Times Square late at night and points out how the drug dealing that used to go on there back in the '50s has radiated much further out.

"What about prostitution?" I ask.

"There are always whores," he says.

"Peep show booths?"

"Gone."

"Live sex shows?"

"I doubt they existed."

"Kiddie porn?"

"That's a myth."

"Donkey shows?"

"Only in Mexico."

Todd takes me back to his tiny apartment in the Lower East Side and I let him fuck me on his musty futon. First, I take off my jeans and panties and he eats me out. He comments on how wet and sticky my cunt is. My cunt smells strong, maybe bad. Todd likes the stink, he keeps rubbing his nose into it. "What a nice little pussy," he says. I say it's always dripping and *always* wants to be fucked. "Are you always this quick and easy?" he says. "I've barely known you for two hours," he says.

I shrug.

He says, "Do you want me to wear a condom?"

"It's up to you."

"I'm clean and safe. Are you?"

"Yes," I say.

His dick is curved like a banana. I ask if he wants me to suck it. "I have to fuck you right this minute," he says. He lifts my legs onto his shoulders and he fucks me.

I scream when I come; that curved cock does the trick.

Later, I suck his dick and he shoots off in my mouth.

Phoned one of my professors earlier, complained how the wild literary crowd Kerouac ran with is unavailable to me. That even if it exists today, I'm not tapped into it. He said that the network of Kerouac's time is no longer around. That the literary community of the 21st century is disjointed. He'd given me a long list of writer friends of his before I left. He gave them all advance notice that I was an eager girl and willing to spread my legs and explore the literary possibilities of being a total slut. "Fuck them all," my professor said. "They are lonely men of American letters." Looking at it now, I see what he means: they're scattered all over the country. Many of them don't even know one another.

For instance, last night in Philadelphia, I sat on a living room couch with a writer named Ed, going through the collection of photographs he'd taken over the years. He's got so much passion for photography – a skill and talent. He didn't pursue it as a career because he thought it would prevent him from being the kind of husband and father he wanted to be. He traded away that passion in favour of stability. I asked where his family was now. He said his wife had divorced him and his son and daughter were grown up and had their own families. Ed's fifty-two. He gently placed his hand on the back of my neck and told me to blow him. He didn't ask, he ordered me to. I said: "Okay, take it out." He did and I buried my face into his crotch and satisfied his need.

"How old are you, my dear?" he asked after we had some wine.

"Twenty-seven," I said.

"You're younger than . . ."

"What? Who?"

"Never mind."

"Do you want to screw me?" I asked.

"Very much so," he said.

In bed, I allowed him to do me anally because he said his wife would never let him do that and he was curious what it was like. "I've never done it with anyone," he said. "I feel I've missed out on a lot of things in life."

Kerouac wrote feverishly of something he called IT: "the point of ecstasy" he'd always wanted to reach, a "complete step across chronological time into timeless shadows" where he finds himself "hurrying to a plank where all the angels dove off and flew into the holy void of uncertain emptiness, the potent and inconceivable radiance shining in bright Mind Essence, innumerable lotuslands falling open in the magic mothswarm of heaven."

*   *   *

Ed said into my ear: "Being up your arse is like Heaven."

Capturing life's brightest flame within your hands, yes? George Eliot wrote that:

> The growing good of the world is partly dependent on unhistoric acts; and that things are not so ill with you and me as they might have been, is half owing to the number who lived faithfully a hidden life, and rest in unvisited tombs. (*Middlemarch*)

Maybe Ed found IT, after all.

4 A.M.

Saw a western tonight in New York City. Between fucks: the TV on. The myth that propelled Kerouac down the road. "It's ironic . . . to be in New York, watching a western," I say to Todd – I being a westerner, having driven through those spaces only a week ago.

"Do you want to stay and fuck more?" Todd asks.

I tell him sure, sounds fun.

"If you're *really* into sex, I know some guys who'd love to do you."

"Pimp me out on Times Square," I say, and laugh.

He laughs.

He kisses me.

I turn away.

"You don't like kisses?" he asks.

"Too intimate," I say.

"So what's this?" he says, touching my wet pussy.

"Fucking," I say, "nothing more, nothing less."

Day 2

11 A.M.

St Mark's Bookstore. It overwhelms me. The shelves go up twenty feet into the air, and they're all filled. I see a photograph of Drew Barrymore on the cover of a magazine. She looks like a little girl. It makes me think – that's exactly what women are in our society. What they're supposed to look like, anyway. They're supposed to be little girls. Men like little girls – or women who *look* like little girls. The fantasy thing.

I wonder what Jack fantasized about.

I can see now why New Yorkers are so hooked on their city.

People, before I got here, talked about how Soho and Greenwich Village have grown trendy, gentrified, tourist sights. Yet if I'm seeking the literary community, I am told the Village (the East Village to be precise) is still the place to go.

I gravitate toward a restaurant called Dojo, and wind up sitting between a Czechoslovakian student and Peter – he's a fund-raiser for PBS who recently returned here after a nine-year stint in L.A. (When he was in L.A., we went to bed a couple of times.)

"Allen Ginsberg* used to live in this neighbourhood," the Czech student says to me. "Sometimes you can see his ghost passing by."

Peter says he prefers New Yorkers because they have substance. "L.A. is so pretentious," he says. "People *there* have to find out what hill you live on, what kind of car you drive, before they decide if they want to know you."

"The people in New York are *real*," says Peter.

I write a small poem on a napkin:

> I am in "brown & holy" East
> I watch
> westerns
> starring Clint Eastwood, leather
> shops of cowboy fringe
> I am silent inside
> & my cunt always
> wants to be filled

---

* This instantly sparks a fantasy of a chance meeting with the old Beat poet – who better to talk to about my reason for being here? But when I offer him sex he reminds me that he's gay. "If only you were a young boy," says Ginsberg. I tell him we can pretend but he shakes his head and says: "That will never work."

I go with Peter and the Czech student back to Peter's place in the Village. There, the three of us get nasty. They take turns "mouth-fucking" me with their cocks – that's what they call it, that's what Peter says: "Can your mouth take a fucking like you were getting it in your twat?" I said I suppose so. First I'm on my knees and they take turns, holding my head, moving their cocks in and out of my mouth like pistons. Then I lie on Peter's bed and each guy hovers over me and pounds his cock down my throat. It chokes me, there's saliva and pre-come flying everywhere, my mascara is smudged and runny – I find this all very sexy and as they mouth-fuck I play with my clit and I reach orgasm over and over again. I could be satisfied just with this but then Peter and the Czech student fuck my pussy, then I find myself on top the student and Peter is sliding into my arsehole. I close my eyes and imagine that I am being fucked by Jack and Neal, Sal and Dean: we're in a motel someplace, somewhere on the road, and I let them do anything they want to me, like I allow Peter and the Czech do what they desire to my body.

Kerouac "yearned to see the country," a feverish desire spawned by westerns, the mythic cowboy heading into the sunset. In *On The Road*, he departs from New York numerous times. But he always returns.

> I never want to work again
> but sit @ cafe tables watching
> catching conversations, smiles,
> glances, voices, radios, silent
> billboards & rolling-by garbage
> trucks
> have sex with strangers
> fuck & fuck & suck & fuck

How far we can go and still be inside our own borders – to the end of the road, the end of the rainbow? A pot of gold, of sorts, waiting in sunny California – a fool's gold, you know –

My lover, Jack Kerouac, gave me an excuse to run away from home at a time I was long past the age for getting away with it. I longed to travel across the country, to hunt and gather the sights and sounds and places and faces of America, to somehow piece everything into some all-encompassing piebald quilt. Let's say I also wanted to fuck my way across America because it sounded so juicy and fun.

Not Only a Trip Through Space

"To see how Kerouac actually lived in the places they lived is not a bad idea," says a sixty-five-year-old writer that I visit. Another one on the list. He kinda looks like Burroughs, or I pretend he does. He's a self-proclaimed expert on JK's life and words. "You should read every one of these books on Kerouac," he tells me. "It wouldn't take you long and it'll save you a lot of trouble. And you should go in his footsteps. You might even have a publishable book out of it. Did you see the places in Denver? I think you probably could search out most of the places he lived, although in Denver there's been a lot of urban renewal, so-called. They've destroyed lots of that."

"I did talk to the owner of one of the old jazz bars in Denver," I reply. "He said he served Jack Kerouac when he used to come in. He just thought JK was a drunk, and . . . it's kind of interesting to see his perspective of 'why do these people keep coming in here year after year and asking me these questions?' How does it feel to have all these people coming to you, year after year?"

"They're sincerely interested in Jack and that he was a pretty good writer, and there's a whole cult of Kerouac. Because of differences in generations and culture, the social gradations in society as it existed then, when young men were upper-middle-class boys and Kerouac was strictly a working-class kid, and Ginsberg was different because he was . . . well, the child of intellectuals, and his mother was a beautiful mad communist poet in her own right. You can't really understand it without seeing all the social gradations. A guy like Burroughs came from a family that ran the country. A different kind of family. So that's what's very interesting. And Kerouac, his range of going from the dregs of American society to pretty high up in that society."

"That's something I noticed in his biography, that he seems to have had no trouble traversing different –"

"No. And he was always himself. He never tried to change his personality for that. He certainly changed his behaviour to people who sometimes could do him some good. And he had this problem with bisexuality, that complicated his life. And that's in *Jack's Book*. Did you read *Jack's Book*?"

"I did read *Jack's Book* and –"

"There's the episode with Gore Vidal . . ."

"Yeah."

"About Jack sucking Vidal's cock."

"Yeah. 'I blew Gore Vidal!'"

"What did you think of it?"

I shrug, say, "Is it true?"

"I mean, what do you think about sucking cock?"

"I think about it all the time," I say with a smile.

"Are you a cocksucker?" he asks.

"Oh yeah," I reply, "you can call me *that*."

He takes out his dick and says, "So suck on this one here if you're such a cocksucker. Show me how you do it. Show me how good you are."

I lean down and blow him. His penis tastes like loneliness and cigarettes.

I eat his runny come.

"They had a strange attitude toward women, those guys," he says, zipping his pants up. "Of course, Ginsberg made a stab at going straight for a while. But he was primarily homosexual."

"That was pretty radical then," I say, swallowing.

"He was a cocksucker, and it goes without saying he liked fucking other men up the ass."

"Yes, I suppose so."

"What about you?"

"Do I like fucking men in the ass?" I say. "Give me a strap-on and I'll do it." I grin.

He laughs. "Yeah, baby, that might be fun. But you – do you take it in the ass like a gay man?"

"I've been known to."

"Maybe later you'll let me do that to you."

"Maybe," I say, smiling.

"It was radical to be as open about it as Ginsberg was. Kerouac was never really open about it. To that extent. Kerouac was Catholic. He had all kinds of hang-ups. But what can I do for you?"

"What?"

"Sexually."

"You can eat my pussy."

"Love to," he says.

I take my jeans and panties off. I lay back on the couch and he eats my cunt. He's good at it. He slides his thumb into my arsehole. He makes me come twice.

"Thank you," I say, catching my breath, "that was nice."

"Back to Jack," he says.

"Well, I think this has become a cult thing," I say. "I mean, you're seeing people who are coming from a completely different generation, they read *On The Road* –"

"You can't possibly understand Columbia at that time, or San Francisco at that time. They're different places today."

"I realize that. I'm going to these places and, like in Denver, Larimer Street's been completely redeveloped. The people that I talk to are talking about the difference between what Skid Row was like forty years ago and what it's like today."

"There's different people. There were Indians then. The place was filled with Indians."

"Do you feel baffled why a book like *On The Road* still continues to draw people?"

"No, because dissatisfaction with . . . Look, in the forties and fifties and even sixties there was a certain . . . there were certainties about American life. You took it for granted that certain things had absolute value. And you believed in them. *I* did. I thought I was put on this earth to make the world a better place. That was the attitude of most educated young people of that time. That continued right up to Kennedy. 'To those much is given, much is expected.' That was gone forever with the Vietnam War, the corruption in Washington. But these people, the Beats – which is a misleading name – had come to that conclusion a whole generation before. Unless you . . . I don't know how well educated you are," he says, "I don't think very well educated, you're just a little slut really. I mean, have you read Dostoyevsky?"

I feel insulted. I feel embarrassed. I say: "No."

"Yes. See, so you are . . . well, sorry . . . these books had a tremendous influence on Jack. Books like *The Possessed* by Mr Fyodor. These books really affected the way he thought. So on this journey – he was propelled into this journey by a mixture of personal experience and literary experience. *He was a writer*. Have you read his earliest book, you know, *The Town and The City*? You know, you really can't do serious work unless you do the reading. You can't understand *On The Road* unless you read this earlier book."

"I'm afraid I have not."

"You should read it because it's fun, you buy it in paperback from City Lights. I'd like to help you, but I don't know exactly how I can because you – these other people have all come doing full books on Kerouac and this is just a term paper."

"Yeah. And I've had to really work at trying to keep my focus narrow and not let it get too broad –"

"Broad," he says. "That's the word I was looking for. I wanted to say 'girl'. Look, my cock is hard again. Eating your pussy got my blood going. Seeing you sitting there with no pants – your nice brown skin – so smooth and perfect – well, *I want to fuck you now*. Will you let me fuck you now?"

"In the arse?"

"No, we don't have to do that. I want to fuck you like you are a woman I'm in love with."

I lie back on the couch and spread my legs, open my pussy for him. "Dive in," I say.

He licks his lips. "Now there's a sight for an old fart . . ."

He mounts me. He fucks me slowly, kissing my face: my nose, my lips.

I turn away. I won't let him stick his tongue in my mouth.

"What's wrong?" he says. "What is it, little girl?"

"Don't make love to me like I was your wife or girlfriend, which I'm not," I tell him, "just fuck me like the slut you know I am. Okay? *Fuck me like a filthy whore*," I hiss.

He flips me over on my stomach, roughly, and crams his cock straight up me.

"Ouch," I say.

"Hurt?"

"A little."

"Good."

"Fuck me harder."

"All the way up there," he groans.

"Ouch," I say.

"Hurt."

"A little."

"Good." After, we take turns cleaning up in the bathroom. I put my pants back on. He opens two beers and we sit on the couch and continue to talk.

"The trip is not only a trip in space," he says, "but it's also a drop through American society till you hit bottom and you find Neal Cassady and people like that. And people who are in many ways quite destructive, even criminal. This infatuation with the criminal class . . . it's different than just a dropout class of people. I mean, people who did real harm, like Burroughs shot his wife and I consider that not a nice thing, to kill your wife. And these guys were thieves. See, so I don't share the general admiration that Kerouac had for someone like Cassady. There was a guy when they were young – Thomas Wolfe – and Kerouac loved him. I thought Thomas Wolfe was a jerk. A good writer, but he had no self-criticism, like Kerouac. The stuff came pouring out like piss. Thomas Wolfe also had journeys. There's a train ride from North Carolina. His sister married a sort of white trash guy, or a kind of redneck guy. I shouldn't say white trash, I didn't know him. But no one reads Thomas Wolfe today except a certain kind of English major."

"And yet people read Jack Kerouac."

"Yes, but when we were young, Thomas Wolfe was almost as far in the pack as Kerouac is now."

"So the real test will be in the next 40, 50 years?"

"It's not going to be a classic forever. It's not like *Huck Finn*. *Huckleberry Finn* is the greatest American book. The most important analogy to *On The Road* is *Huckleberry Finn*. Have you read that? Good. All right. So the trip on the raft with Tom and Huck – Kerouac thought of Cassady as the kind of Huck

Finn character in the 20th century, and he thought of people like Bob Burford, upper-middle-class Denver boys, as a smart aleck Tom Sawyer. And the difference between their attitude on the raft going down the Mississippi. But that's a false analogy. Because Huck is always good. Huck is always noble and Neal was a rat. And betrayed people. Huck never betrays anyone. Kerouac saw this the way he wanted to, and you dropped through the bottom of respectable society and found yourself in the basement full of fascinating characters. Kerouac made a great contribution with that. You know, it's a good book. It's going to last for a long time. It'll always be read, probably by young people who want to get out of the trap."

"So you basically look at it as a window into a different reality," I say.

"He himself was a disenfranchised French Canadian. Canook. He came from what was the equivalent of a French hillbilly. They were a fossilized group of French in New England and Canada. They didn't even speak correct French. It was a kind of patois. His pronunciation of French was not as good as mine. It was the way he –"

"It was a dialect, wasn't it?"

"Yes, it was a dialect. In *On The Road* he doesn't treat people very kindly. Not even Neal Cassady."

"You don't like Neal Cassady because you think he was immoral?"

"Yes, and a rat. And a pain in the arse. He was a bad type. Bad news. You didn't want him anywhere around."

"That seems to be the general –"

"Well, no! Young people still think he's a saint of sorts."

"They respect, they enjoy the fact that he was a con man . . ."

"Well, you look at the movies today, these anti-heroes. James Dean was sort of the first non-hero hero of movies. It's people who don't share the values of mainstream America at all. And there's a lot of nice young people who are horrified by certain aspects of American society, or established society any place, so they like this. But that book is incorrect in certain ways. Although Kerouac had the social range, he wasn't particularly sensitive to gradations in it. But if you could read the, uh – what was it?"

"*The Town and The City?*"

"Yes. I'm distracted. God, you're pretty." He touches my hair. "Beautiful."

"Thank you."

"I can't believe my luck, getting to have sex with you, and I'm acting like a big jerk . . ."

"It's okay."

"You're nice."

"If you want more sex, you can have it."

"I'm keeping that in mind. Where were we? Oh yes. *The Town and The City*, you'd get some idea of the background for this, and then some of the biographies of Jack. You don't have to read them all. It gets very sad after . . ."

"I was very depressed after I read *Jack's Book*," I say.

"You know, Scott Fitzgerald said a famous thing: 'There are no second acts in American lives.' Well, there was no second act in Jack's life. He became a parody of himself. The drugs and the drink really destroyed him. And he had physical problems. He had nephritus, this vascular disease, from football injuries. He was a superb football player, at a time when football players were smaller than they are now, and he could have gone to Notre Dame. He had a scholarship, an athletic scholarship."

"Did you ever have any understanding about why he had that trouble with alcohol? Was it just that it runs in the family and you get it with each generation?"

"Well, there's a classic Freudian psychoanalytical theory, maybe it's discredited now, that alcoholism is a suppression device for homosexuals. And, whether it's true or not, I thought it might be true in his case. That he had . . . he was very shaky sexually. That's a big key to him, that he got quite girlish, quite coquettish. And, you know, the sense of restless flight with men, sort of a parable of homosexuality. There's a correspondence with *Moby Dick*, sailing over the whole world. This way, you're driving in cars over a continent."

"There's something you're running away from?" I ask, sitting up.

"Yeah. And always coming back to his mother, who was a

powerful character. Very stubborn. She once told me that the nuns – she was raised in a strict Catholic school – she did something that displeased the nuns, they would make her kneel on rice as the punishment. Uncooked rice, so the rice kernels would dig into her bare knees. She said, 'It hurt me a lot, but I never apologized to them.' So, I think . . . when do you have to turn in your paper?"

"My goal is to have my first draft completed by mid-May. I'm just going to see how it works out. I want to approach this in a very open-ended way, without preconceived ideas or expectations."

"Ah yes. That's *very* Kerouackian. Wanting the constantly fresh experience this experience of the frontier or the new places. There's something, the frontier, you come to a place and take what you can from it. You even soil it. And then you move on to a new place. And that's what the pioneers did."

"It seems like an eternal cry, sort of this eternal call of the wild, that final –"

"Jack London is a writer, you know. Kerouac even looked like him. Those young handsome photographs of Jack Kerouac in a sea captain's hat or petty officer's hat. Jack London posed that way too, handsome. That was before Jack London got fat, bloated, drunk. And Jack London, in a very innocent way, was a thief. He used to rob oyster beds in an earlier time. So if you go on with your studies of Kerouac, there's some analogy. So I think if you can capture that . . ."

"My younger sister, who is into a completely different thing, is into this capital I, capital T thing, you know, the IT Jack talks about in the book . . ."

He touches my hair some more and says, "Another influence is Rimbaud and, have you ever heard of the French poet Rimbaud? There's a famous poem called 'The Drunken Boat' in which the poet himself is like a drunken vessel going down this powerful river without a destination, saying good-bye to the ancient parapets of Europe, parapets meaning the old castles and palaces of Europe. And he went to Abyssinia, and he had certain similarities to Kerouac. Bisexuality."

"I thought he was pretty definitely homosexual."

"Yeah, but then he went straight in Abyssinia and had been

homosexual with Verlaine, and violent. He stabbed him. So, yes, you get that wildness which verged on criminality. Kerouac himself was not vicious. Kerouac was basically kind and he always thought people would get along together if he liked them, that all of his friends liked one another. But they couldn't. That's just not the way the world works. Everyone doesn't love everyone else."

"Didn't he get pretty alienated from his friends?" I say, thinking of Christine.

"Yes. In the end, Ginsberg . . . you know, he always had this anti-Semitic side to him and his mother hated Jews so . . . they had this narrow, bigoted French Canadian Catholic outlook. It's hard to imagine the primitiveness of that life."

He reaches over and kisses me.

Fuck it, I let him – a sixty-five-year-old man making out with a twenty-seven-year-old woman –

We kiss for a while but my head is somewhere else.

"Will you, uh," he says, "will you suck my cock again?"

But what I discover, when I open my eyes, is that I'm sucking on a Hebrew Nation all beef hot dog, not on this man's cock. The man doesn't even exist, although I have to admit it would be nice if he did.

Oh well.

I can't masturbate all night with these images in my head, alone in my apartment. I have to get back to writing my thesis concerning image and metaphor in *On the Road*.

If I could just keep to the scholarly writing rather than lapsing into pornographic fancies, I may just graduate this year.

I erase everything I have just written, except for one line:

Route 66 exists only as a fragment of its former self.

A Bit of Discipline

Louise (Leicester, UK)

Now that I'm fifteen years older (though not necessarily any
wiser), I actually find my childhood sexual fantasy even more
exciting than I did at the time. The application of knowledge to
juvenile imagination helps to turn a once quaint notion into
something which sets my heart racing.

But there's possibly more to it than that. As years go by, as
age transforms me into the object of my childhood fantasies,
I'm left with a yearning to experience, once more, the simple
pains and pleasures of naivety. And it's the desire to revert to
that gauche and uncertain being I once was which has fed the
transformation of my old fantasy into the version I have now –
a version I believe may finally be about to come true.

I was a bit of a slow developer, and aged eighteen I was the
oldest virgin in the world, or so it seemed to me. I wasn't shy,
but as soon as conversations took a romantic bent I was
overwhelmed by terror and my frightened mind invented
problems: I wouldn't know what to do, or I'd smell, or I'd
fart – and in the face of such prosaic fears, romance had no
chance to bloom. In its place grew an active imagination and
agile fingers, an outlet for my frustrations and inquisitiveness.

And I was aware, around that time, of something new
entering my thoughts. Previously, my daydreams had revolved
around boys, around cocks and penetration, sperm and copu-
lation; but gradually my fantasies began to change. The first
couple of times I barely even noticed: it was only at the end, as
my fingers flashed myself towards climax, that a solitary,
unconnected image came into my mind and sent me over
the edge into tumult.

The image of a woman.

At first it was Everywoman, a generic lover to take my hand and show me the road. I was rather embarrassed about it, because I came from a small town, and lesbianism was the stuff of sniggering and finger-pointing, not a serious prospect. So I enjoyed my dreams but tried not to let them dominate my fantasy world.

Eventually, though, they did.

And as they did, Everywoman became one woman, a particular person, a woman with whom I could feel myself becoming obsessed. Reserved people don't like to lose control, but increasingly I was finding it difficult to maintain the ambivalence I habitually used as a screen from reality, and that gradual unbinding of my thoughts was truly frightening.

She was a research student called Hilary Wentworth. She was older than me, probably in her early thirties, and to me – a Business Studies fresher – she seemed impossibly sophisticated. She had very short hair – remember this was in the eighties, when hair was long and wild – and she exuded self-confidence and grace. Her mouth was permanently set in a satisfied smile – not smug, just contented. Her eyes were hazel, dark and exotic and deep-set, seemingly etched into her face, glinting above a long, slender, delicate nose.

She was certainly attractive, but what really entranced me was her independence. At a time when I was dowdy and nervous, her positive demeanour was utterly beguiling.

There's no question I developed a crush on her – how could I not, when she embodied everything to which I aspired but couldn't dare? It all started innocently enough, borne of simple admiration and gently developing into a desire to be like her; and from there, inevitably, it took flight into fantasy. I couldn't help myself.

Those early fantasies were simply a product of my circumstance. She was an older woman, confident and worldly wise, while I was quiet and introspective. Naturally, my fantasies revolved around seduction by the older woman. To begin with there was no plot, the fantasy resting purely in the realms of sex. I imagined being taken by her, made to undress, made to play with myself in front of her. I pictured her stripping –

slowly, seductively, making me watch in silence – then sliding on to the bed and beckoning me between her thighs, my face to her pussy, tongue pressed between her lips and then up, up against her clitoris. She would leave me there for minutes, hours, forcing me to lap her, love her, and I would obey her every whim.

Satisfying though such dreams were – and they satisfied me comprehensively, I assure you – I gradually found a need to elaborate on them. I wanted a context within which to set the fantasies to make them seem real, and so I created a utopian existence which revolved around Hilary. Indeed my real world was increasingly dictated by her, too: I would try to pass her in the corridor, timing my walks to coincide with the start or end of the teaching sessions she did to help pay her way. I would be successful every couple of days, and my heart would hammer as I saw her saunter down the corridor towards me, hips swaying, head tossed back confidently. Forcing myself to look up, I would smile and try to look alluring. She must have thought I was a simpleton, but at the time I didn't know what else to do.

And with each failed attempt to make contact, my fantasies became wilder and wilder. It was no longer enough to simply make love to her: increasingly my dreams focused on Hilary dominating me completely, turning me into her plaything. There was one particular fantasy I came back to again and again, refining it slightly each time, but always keeping the basic outline. In fact, fifteen years later I still occasionally revisit its hoary delights.

In it, I enrol on one of her Scottish literature classes. In reality, my Business Studies degree would have precluded such a course, but fantasies can overcome trite reality. I begin the course full of anticipation. She wears tight jeans which show off her backside and a T-shirt which clings to her body, affording a tantalizing view of slightly raised nipples. Needless to say, I spend the lesson ogling her, listening to her sweet, husky voice without taking in any of its meaning. And, thus, I become a poor student.

Exam time and I discredit myself. With an expression mingling reproach, annoyance and indulgence, she returns my exam script, crossed through with red ink.

"Tell me," she says, "what century do you think MacDiarmid lived in?"

"Eighteenth?"

"Hmm, that kind of explains things. Not really good enough, Louise, you're going to have to work much harder if you're going to pass your final."

I ask for a private tutorial to go through my exam paper, and she guides me through each question in turn, pointing out my inadequacies. As she does, I fall more and more under her spell. I stare and dream, glorying in the strictness of her tones . . .

"Are you listening to me?"

"I'm, I'm sorry . . ."

"How the hell do you expect me to help you if you won't help yourself?"

"I know, I'm sorry, I'll try . . ."

"Makes me really angry. I work my bloody guts out here, you know. I've got plenty of my own work to be getting on with." I try to interject but she carries on. "Discipline, that's what you lot need."

As she says those words a frisson of excitement shivers up my spine. I know she means discipline in work, but my mind creates its own interpretation. Clearly, my face gives me away, as she stares at me curiously. I can see a glimmer of understanding in her eyes and I begin to redden with embarrassment. I squirm in my chair.

"Don't you think?" she says, after a weighty pause.

"Yes," I whisper.

The compact is made.

"You need some remedial attention, I think. Come back at eight this evening." I nod and stand, my breath shallow and heart pounding. I turn to leave. "And, Louise, wear something nice – not those boring old jeans." I am too scared to reply.

By eight o'clock I am in a state of panic. In reality, I know I would chicken out, but fantasies are wonderfully liberating things. I knock and follow her instruction to enter.

"Lock the door." I still can't believe what is happening, and every confirmation – such as this instruction – comes as both a relief and a shock. I lock it and turn towards her. "Very nice," she says. I am wearing my only dress, a dark blue, flouncy effort riding just above my knee which I like because it makes my breasts look fuller. Smiling at her flattery, I follow her hand and sit in the seat beside her.

"I can't decide," she says, "whether you were being provocative or just dense in your exam. You must know Mac-Diarmid was twentieth century. Don't you?" I know no such thing, but nod anyway. "So you were being provocative? What for? Were you trying to annoy me? Taunt me?" I make no reply. "It's inexcusable behaviour, anyway. Isn't it?"

"Yes," I murmur.

"Deserves punishment, in fact."

"Yes."

"Discipline. Like I said earlier."

"Yes."

"You agree?"

"Yes."

Her eyes, dark and erotic, gleam with anticipation. "I think we understand one another here, don't we?" I nod. "It's late, there's no one about. I'm free to do whatever I want."

By the time I reached this stage of my fantasy I would generally be squirming in my bed. The point of surrender is the most thrilling part, the moment where I lose and put myself in her hands totally. In my fantasy I nod acquiescence.

"I'm going to spank you," she tells me. I gulp but say nothing. "Stand up. Turn round. Bend over." I follow each instruction in turn, aware of the blood pounding in my head and my heart hammering in my chest. I hear her move and feel her heat as she presses close. Her hand rests on my arse cheek, feeling me through my dress. Slowly, she lifts the dress, peeling it inch by inch up my thighs and backside, exposing me to her gaze. I stop breathing. She bunches my dress over my hips and guides my hand towards it to hold it in place. Walking round, she stands in front of me.

"Look up," she says. I stretch my neck and look into her eyes. "I'm going to take your panties down and spank your bare bottom. Is that okay?" I nod. "Is that okay?" she repeats.

"Yes, it is, thank you."

Walking behind me once more, she rolls her palm over my panties and I feel her fingers – cold and firm – on my flesh as she grips my waistband and tugs the panties over my cheeks and thighs. She is kneeling, her head almost touching my skin, and I shiver as I feel her breath waft over my crack. Pulling, she eases my panties to my feet and makes me step out of them. I am bared in front of her, and I feel an extraordinary mixture of humiliation and excitement. She remains beside me for what seems like minutes, examining my most intimate areas, her breath whispering across my flesh like a silent portent.

Finally, she rises. "Touch your toes," she commands. I grip my fingers around my toes and wait, tensed. She strikes me once, twice, three times in succession, each on the same part of my left buttock. None are particularly hard, but my arse stings all the same. Then she spanks me again, this time on the other cheek, and much, much harder. I yelp in alarm but remain in my position. Five through to ten are increasingly firmer and by now my backside is burning, cheeks alive with pain. She doesn't let up. On to twenty, twenty-five, and I am crying now, my knees buckling. I want her to stop, and yet it is the most thrilling experience imaginable.

Finally she finishes. "Stand up," she tells me. I straighten my back gingerly and run my hands across my arse cheeks. They are burning, and I can feel a swathe of raised marks, parallel lines identifying the progress of her fingers over my once-smooth skin. Hilary wipes tears from my cheek and smiles. "Discipline. Don't you feel much better for that?"

"Yes," I reply.

She observes me curtly. Her eyes narrow, her lips purse, and I can tell she is considering her next course of action. "I'm a very busy person," she says. "I need an assistant – a menial really, someone to do the crap jobs for me, take away my drudgery. You could be that person." I raise an eyebrow. "No pay, of course. You'll do it because I ask it of you. You're not going to refuse me, are you?"

Whenever I reached this point in my fantasy I would have to stop playing with myself or I would come to soon. This is the crux, the point where I submit irrevocably, where I present myself to an older woman to do with as she pleases. In my daydreaming, I always say the next words aloud.

"No. I will never refuse you, thank you."

She smiles and claps her hand. "This calls for a celebration. And what better way to cement a relationship than this?" She unzips her jeans and slides them down, kicking her way clear. Sitting on the sofa at the corner of her office she beckons to me. "Lick, little girl. Lick."

I get down on my knees and position myself before her. Gingerly, almost reverently, I place my hands on her knees and pull forward, towards her. I can smell her, a delicious blend of perfume and pussy, and I nestle my nose against the rasping softness of her cotton panties. She grips my head with her thighs and pulls me closer, pushing my mouth harder against her. I begin to lap, at first feeling nothing but the weave of the fabric, but as it becomes moist with my tongue and her juices, I begin to discern the shape of her lips, feeling them slide apart, open for my tongue. I press forward, forcing the cotton inside her, smelling her musk, sensing her excitement. The constant rubbing begins to hurt my tongue, but I will not stop, not for anything. Finally, she sighs and shifts above me, manoeuvring her panties over her backside. She kicks them off and I am presented with a view of her pussy lips, soaked and puffy, with a glorious crimson passage between them. Once more I lower my mouth on to her and for the first time in my life experience the taste of another woman.

Only now, of course, am I able identify that experience, to know the subtle, silken perfection of a woman's cunt: back then, a virgin, I had to use my imagination, and I wasn't up to the task. This is one way that my favourite fantasy has an extra resonance today: age has its compensations.

Hilary grips my head, forcing me hard against her, my tongue splicing her folds and entering her. I lick upwards, towards her clitoris, anxious to have it in my mouth, to service this glorious woman. I circle it with my tongue, round and round, nibbling gently at its hood, sucking with increasing force. All the while, my hand is on my own pussy, middle finger pressed to my clitoris while my index and fourth fingers slide up and down my lips.

And while I fantasized thus, lying alone in my student flat, I would be doing the same thing, bringing myself to a shuddering climax. I would cry her name, "Hilary, Hilary," as I came, my muscles tensing, thighs jamming together, whirls and whorls of tumult tracking through my body.

I used that fantasy hundreds of times, each time revelling in the control the older woman exerted over me. It never came to anything in reality, although in retrospect I think she may well have been interested. I simply didn't have the nerve to do anything to make it happen. Too nervous, too submissive: I needed someone to tell me.

I did experience lesbian love quite soon, however, while I was in my second year, and it set me on my life's path. Only once did I have an older lover, a woman of forty, but she was too kind to indulge in the sorts of escapades I craved. And so, while happy with my love life, there has always been something missing. While I have adored the loving environments in which I've settled, I've always longed for that edge, that spark of nastiness. I thought it would never happen, indeed had resigned myself to it. As the years slipped by and I was no longer an ingenue, it became evident that my chances of being seduced and abused by an older woman were disappearing.

Until I became the older woman.

I used to wonder, when I was eighteen and in the throes of my Hilary fantasy, what I would be like when I was thirty-five. Would I become Hilary? Would I be the temptress, on the lookout for young virgins to corrupt? I rather hoped so, but it hasn't worked out that way.

I still have the same basic fantasy today, only now I play the role of the older woman. And, of course, dominance isn't really my thing so my fantasies now, like a mirror image of the old ones, involve me being used by a younger woman. *Plus ça change*, I suppose. And the glory is that these fantasies may well soon come true.

I work in an office with four other women. I am in charge. Three of the women have been there for years, but the fourth, Paula, is new, fresh out of college. From the word go she's been trouble. I don't think she has ever intended it, but she is full of self-confidence, almost to the point of bossiness. I like her enormously, but she is difficult to manage. There were just the two of us in the office one Wednesday afternoon, and we were chatting contentedly. She had failed – yet again – to fill in her timesheet and I chastized her good-naturedly: it was important, but not a treasonable offence.

"Discipline," I joked, echoing the words of my fantasy Hilary, "that's what you young people need. A bit of discipline – a proper regime."

"Aye, aye," she retorted, winking extravagantly. "Discipline, huh? Bet you're a one for discipline, Louise." I blushed profusely, an adolescent habit of which I've never been able to cure myself. Paula saw, and immediately realized she had struck closer to the truth than she had realized. "Well!" she continued. "I think you do, as well."

I was mortified. I had long embraced these notions of submissiveness as being part of me, but they were a hidden part, which I had never shared with anyone. Now, they were in danger of unravelling before the titillated gaze of this twenty-something girl. I changed the subject, but I sensed Paula would not let it go.

Indeed she didn't. A week later, when we were alone once more, she broached the subject again. "So tell me, Louise, this discipline thing. How does it work? I guess you're not into heavy stuff. BDSM and the like?" I shook my head, which was a mistake. By denying that, I was implicitly acknowledging that there was an element of discipline to which I *was* partial. Paula seized on the chance. "Not that then, but something milder, I guess."

She walked round the room, as though weighing up her thoughts. "So what we're talking about here is something like, maybe, a little. . ." She paused melodramatically. "*Spanking?*" Again I blushed, but said nothing. "Now," she continued, taking my silence as affirmation, "I would guess you're not the one who administers the spankings. Am I right?"

"I've never done anything like that in my life, Paula," I said as haughtily as I could manage.

Paula was undaunted. "Maybe not, Louise. But I bet you've wanted to. Am I right? Well, am I?" Inside, I was cringing. This was the most excruciating conversation I had ever had. It was my fantasy coming to reality, and as such everything I had ever dreamed of, but it was torture to endure. I gulped and stared into her eyes. She was gloating, relishing her control of the situation. I sensed the power she had and knew, in my heart, that I could only submit to it. "Yes," I whispered, "I have."

She clapped her hands with glee. "Thought so! God, that's kinky, who'd have thought it. Louise, you little minx, you." For the first time, some sexual stirrings began within me. I couldn't stop myself: I wanted to end the conversation, to forbid any mention of it again, but as I observed her face, the casual, fresh-skinned arrogance of her demeanour, I knew I couldn't.

"Well, it's not exactly like that . . ."

She cut me off curtly. "So am I right? You're not the one to do the spanking?"

I had completely lost by now. "No," I replied.

"So you want to be spanked?" She sounded incredulous.

"Yes."

"Jeez. I'm going to have to think about this."

"Please, don't tell anyone," I stammered.

"Relax, Louise baby. Your secret's safe with me." I smiled, and she grinned back. "As long . . ."

"As long?"

"As long. Now then, as long as you behave appropriately, shall we say?"

I went cold. I had known the drift of the conversation; I had known what was happening, but still I think I believed it would blow over and nothing more would be said. It would be something Paula would tease me about, but no more than that. When she spoke those words, though, I knew that she had other ideas. And worse than that, I knew, deep down, that I wanted her to.

That happened last week. I'm going round to Paula's to-night. I'm cooking for her, apparently, because she doesn't like cooking. And washing up afterwards. I think I'm going to be spanked. I think I want it.

No, I know I want it. I've waited eighteen years for it. I'm more scared than I have ever been.

Strategy

Julia (San Francisco, USA)

The cool Scandinavian decor of the boardroom only amplified my raging heat. The five of us at the teak table projected sleek confidence and fashion savvy as we listened raptly to Romaine present her buying strategy for the spring season.

I probably looked calm and collected, too – it came with the retailing territory. Buyers who lost their cool were forever branded as "difficult" or "unprofessional". Screaming at assistants or outside vendors was perfectly acceptable, but I made it a point to maintain my composure even with them. In this so-called "glamorous" profession, appearances were as important as competence and I was careful to preserve mine at all times.

So, as Romaine spoke, others would have considered my relaxed but efficient cross-legged posture and passive facial expression primary indicators of an undisturbed mind. But they would have been seriously misinformed.

I had no idea what Romaine was saying to us at the meeting. All I heard were replays of what she'd confessed to me at lunch.

"It's crazy, I know. Theresa's married, for crissakes! But I can't stop thinking about her."

"And she has two kids," I reminded her between bites of my Nicoise salad.

"She's starting to become the reason I come to work every day!" Romaine continued, oblivious to my comment. Her blue eyes glistened like they had when those panties from the new Parisian vendor not only came in early but sold like hotcakes. "I feel like she's been flirting with me, though, so she must feel something, too. Has she ever mentioned me to you?"

"She's my assistant, Rome, not my buddy. You don't get chatty with *your* assistant, do you?"

"No, I guess not. Still, maybe she gave you some clues? I just don't know what to do here."

Romaine the Rigid, Romaine the Unflappable, Romaine the Lesbian had been bested not by an unanticipated lingerie trend or a vendor who failed to ship on time, but by a crush on a heterosexual, married mother of two. Why Romaine's confession should have affected me so profoundly, I was at a loss to explain. I only knew I felt like the wind had been knocked out of me.

Barbara, the divisional merchandise manager, whom I long suspected had had her limbic brain removed for purposes of workplace efficiency, began the meeting with her usual pedantic inquiries. The woman's warmth was buried somewhere with her empathy, and the only reason anyone showed her any courtesy was because she controlled the purse strings.

"Summarize this past season's trends for me. What have you seen that you expect will carry forward?" Barbara asked.

Past trends. Let's see . . . I'd known Romaine for six years and had confessed my own misguided love interests to her during that time. In her own restrained but caring way, Romaine always listened and imparted advice only when I solicited it. Now that the tables were turned, I wanted to be as careful but supportive as Romaine had always been toward me. So at lunch today, I sympathized, even consoled.

As Barbara shot the usual probing yet predictable questions at Romaine, I grappled with some questions of my own. First and foremost, had anything transpired between me and Romaine that set some sort of tone or precedent for us?

I recalled the buying trip where Romaine took me to the batting cages to teach me how to swing a baseball bat. Though I had been a tomboy in my childhood, once adolescence set in, my ability to crack a bat against an oncoming ball had long slipped into my past. But Romaine played softball often and had never lost the knack. With unfailing patience and a teaching stance that required her arms wrapped around me, she imparted her secrets of slugging. I didn't retain much from the batting lesson, other than the indelible memory of Romaine's warm, womanly curves pressed against my back.

Hadn't Romaine felt that little charge of excitement at our physical closeness? Wasn't my incessantly girlish giggle a signal of some sort? Shouldn't Romaine have noticed that? After all, Romaine was the lesbian. She was the one who should have known how to respond to a potentially sexual situation between women, wasn't she?

And then there was the time, just after Romaine and her long-time girlfriend split up, when I spent the afternoon at her home. The place was enormous – four bedrooms and a kitchen designed for entertaining, which Romaine never did – and now it nearly echoed from the loneliness inside. Romaine was working from home, and I knew it was because she couldn't face the continuing onslaught of questions about the break-up. I swung by to get her signature on some purchase orders. To my surprise, Romaine came to the door in her bathrobe.

The robe, a flannel-backed Natori classic in a luscious sky blue, emphasized her vivid blue eyes and imparted a soft sensuality Romaine never showed at work. Later, as we sat on the sofa in one corner of one room in the excessively large house, the occasional gap in the robe's front wrap mesmerized me. Romaine never wore clothing that revealed any part of her chest, so the robe's opening provided glimpses of skin I had never seen and would likely never see again. Once, and only once, I saw a pale strip of skin that followed the smile of one breast's slope. Thankfully, Romaine had been talking and never heard my quick intake of breath. But the memory of that vision still quickened my pulse to this day.

"What are your customer profiles like this season?" Barbara asked in her traditional monotone.

I knew Romaine's "profile" pretty well, I thought. I had struggled with my own, though. The baseball incident had prompted me to mention it to my therapist the following week.

"Julia, this isn't the first time you've mentioned feelings toward Romaine. Maybe there's something there worth examining," Seamus said, eyes full of mischief. Mischief. From a therapist.

"When you say 'worth examining', you mean that I should consider whether I'm bisexual or a lesbian or something?"

He smiled. "Something. If you're feeling an attraction to another woman, especially one who's not only a friend but also a lesbian, this might be an ideal opportunity to explore a new side of yourself."

"Oh, God. I wouldn't want to explore this stuff with somebody I *know*!" The idea mortified me.

Seamus chuckled. "Oh heavens no!" he teased. "That would be too pleasant!"

Exploring my feelings for Romaine with Romaine herself had never crossed my mind until Seamus forced me to think about it. I had no idea how to seduce a woman. And I had no idea whether my friendship with Romaine would survive a failed attempt at seduction. It was all too risky.

"If Romaine is interested, she can let me know. I wouldn't know how to come on to her," I told Seamus, who, wisely, let the subject drop temporarily. I then steered the discussion back to my woes with the married man I was seeing; safe territory that had been the focus of my therapy sessions for the past three years. Besides, Romaine would never make the first move and it was useless to explain that to Seamus. She'd lamented her shyness to me on more than one occasion, blaming it for her uneventful love life. She considered me an incorrigible flirt with men, so I would offer tips but they sounded silly when I put words to actions that were second nature to me.

"You've just got the knack," Romaine told me. "I don't." It was the only area in which Romaine ever expressed disappointment with herself.

"What are the vendors showing?" Barbara asked. "What's hot?"

Romaine now yielded the floor to her assistant, a mousy girl with a low threshold for stress, who began talking about the intimate apparel she and Romaine had seen in New York last week. Romaine busied herself with her papers, keeping her eyes lowered.

So, what was Theresa showing that made Romaine hot?

My eyes roamed in my assistant's direction, hoping to discover what the woman possessed to discombobulate the eternally practical and unerringly grounded Romaine. Seeing Theresa – a sexy, petite, and delicate Filipina with a real aptitude for both spotting trends and hounding uncooperative vendors – as the object of Romaine's affections was a startling revelation for me. Theresa's desirability was not in question, but Romaine's judgment certainly was.

Romaine once told me lesbians often fantasized about seducing straight women. I had initially felt hopeful about the remark but now felt merely foolish for thinking Romaine considered me seduction-worthy. Apparently, straight and married with children was more of a turn-on than uncomplicated heterosexuality.

Should I have rubbed my desire for men in Romaine's face? Was a confirmed, unflinchingly straight woman what it took to get Romaine's motor running? Had she caught me stealing glimpses of the swell of her breasts in those silk sweaters she favoured? I thought I'd been careful about admiring Romaine's trim, athletic body, but maybe not. Maybe those selfish, stolen glances made me seem less straight to Romaine, and therefore, less desirable. Maybe I had ruined my chances to feel Romaine's thin but sensual lips on mine simply because I longed for it too visibly. But I wasn't even truly aware that I longed for it, so how could it be visible?

But maybe it was something else. Maybe Romaine liked the subservient position Theresa was in as my assistant. Romaine had a strong personality – maybe the whole dominance thing flipped her switches. Theresa would have to do what she told her, unlike me, who was a colleague and an equal.

I assessed Theresa more boldly now while Romaine's assistant droned on. She was so unlike what Romaine had shown interest in previously. Her ex-girlfriend was a dykish, semi-overweight sports enthusiast who probably knew as much about intimate apparel as an eight-year-old boy. Theresa, with her size four frame and smooth black hair, was a walking advertisement for cocktails and luxury. Her skin glowed with a natural, subtle bronze hue and her legs comprised an enviable portion of her height. In contrast, my size twelve body, with breasts that always entered a room before I did, might not be

Romaine's cup of tea. Perhaps something less . . . feminine . . . was what she wanted. But Theresa oozed femininity, despite her lack of pronounced curves.

I wanted to slap myself for objectifying myself and my assistant like any man would have done. What had my jealousy reduced me to?

Jealousy. There it was. The heat between my legs since lunch, the urge to yank Theresa's perfectly conditioned hair from her skull strand by strand, the compulsion to lay Romaine on the boardroom table, kiss her, and finger her until she screamed – all these reactions were the verdant, vile out-growths of an emotion as useless and debilitating as the attraction itself.

"Julia, are you with us? I need your report, too," Barbara said, loud enough to jar me from my silent epiphany.

"Oh, sure. Sorry."

I paused. I'd originally planned for Theresa to present some of the information today, but now I hesitated. Theresa talking meant Romaine looking. Could I stand to witness Romaine's desire for another woman right now? Yes, yes, of course I could – changing plans would look suspicious and disappoint Theresa, who'd been eagerly awaiting her opportunity to impress Barbara.

"Theresa, why don't you go ahead and fill Barbara in on our findings and then I'll close with our strategy."

Theresa's eyes lit up and she smiled with gratitude at me. I squelched the urge to spit at her. I refused to watch Romaine's reaction to the sex kitten's presentation.

Instead, I sat back and tried to think about strategy. As my mind reeled, my posture remained controlled. I slid my hands under the table and picked at my cuticles. Strategy, I realized, was precisely what I'd overlooked where Romaine was concerned. Because I'd ignored this essential element of games-manship, my fate hung before me now like an enticing bra – full of sexual promise but limp and hollow for the moment.

Based on what I knew about myself and Romaine, both separately and together, what could I have done to seal our fate or at least direct the course of our relationship?

Scenarios ran through my head, not exactly in succession

because my brain was so addled with pent-up desire and newly introduced confusion.

Scenario One

I imagined myself sitting Romaine down and confessing my attraction, much the way Romaine had confessed her interest in Theresa today at lunch.

"I don't know how else to say this, Romaine, so I'll just come right out. I'm very attracted to you and suspect that you might feel the same way. I just don't know what to do about it."

Romaine looks at me with pity and a smidgeon of revulsion. *"Oh, Julia. I'm so sorry if I ever did anything to make you think I was interested in you in that way. Anyway, we're friends and, if we fooled around, who knows what would happen? I would never want to lose your friendship."*

So much for confession.

Scenario Two

I'd read a lesbian novel once, a very long time ago, before I even knew Romaine. The women had an interlude that began in the ladies' room. Though it had seemed implausible and contrived at the time, maybe that was how women stole intimate moments together. Maybe I'd been too quick to scoff.

"Oh, no. Look at this stain on my blouse. This will absolutely never come out."

"No, I think it will, Julia. You just have to pretreat it a bit," Romaine says, moistening a paper towel and adding a teeny bit of soap to it. *"Here, let me show you."*

She dabs at the stain sitting smack in the centre of my cleavage. To get better access, Romaine unbuttons the area closest to the stain and slips one hand inside to provide a base for the area to be treated. With Romaine's face so close to mine, I inhale the scent of her lavender-scented shampoo and brush my lips against her hair. In response, Romaine moves her fingers subtly to caress the gentle slope of my breasts. My skin is instantly warmed by Romaine's touch.

Romaine then seeks out my mouth and we melt into a scorching embrace. We are interrupted by Barbara bursting in on us on her way to complete her morning constitutional.

"What are you two up to? You've got a weekly sales report due to me by ten!"

Ladies' rooms are private love shacks only in books. In real life, they needed locks.

Scenario Three

I saw a scene in a porno film once where two women were happily baking in the kitchen. One thing led to another, and well, the pie-crust wasn't the only thing that got the rolling pin treatment.

Romaine giggles as I pour the milk meant for the pie filling down the front of her sweater.

"Well, I can't wear this now!" she exclaims. "It's making me cold because it's so wet!" Her pout is irresistible.

"You'd better take it off, then," I say as I coax her nipples further outward by rubbing them through her drenched sweater. It clings to her as seductively as any bimbo's in a wet T-shirt contest. The little pebbles her nipples form are so adorable, I can't wait to see how they feel in my mouth.

She is uncharacteristically compliant as I peel her sweater from her soaked torso. The slick heft of her pert, round breast in my palm sets my imagination reeling. I impulsively grab a handful of butter and slather it over both her perfect tits. The butter melts easily when it meets the elevated temperature of her skin. As I knead her breasts, they are so slippery, I have trouble keeping them in my palms.

Inspired by another impulse, I reach for the flour and move to sprinkle some on the buttery sheen I've created. But I miscalculate and several cups of the stuff hit her breasts in an enormous powdery plume. We are both stricken with coughing fits and are forced to leave the kitchen for relief. We take separate showers because the mood has been unalterably broken.

Knowing that the only thing Romaine ever made for dinner was reservations destroyed my culinary fantasy as quickly as it was conceived. Anyway, we both adored our wardrobes – neither would be willing to sacrifice any garment to such silly kitchen antics, even for the sake of carnal pleasure.

So, what remained? Should I just "be there for her" when

the day came when Theresa rebuffed Romaine's advances? Was that bastion of female strength, Consolation, the only weapon I had in my seduction strategy arsenal? And what if Theresa didn't object to Romaine's invitation? Then there'd be no need for consoling.

But if Romaine was shy about making the first move, as she'd always been with others, the likelihood of her making a pass at Theresa was slim. My heart skipped a beat at the thought. Perhaps I was blowing all of this out of proportion. Romaine would be intimidated by the very act of flirtation and knew that a straight, married woman with two children was far from a slam dunk proposition.

What was I worrying about?

Did I still need a strategy? Yes, clearly I did, but whether I needed it right now was an equally important question. I could wait a while, at least until my feverish brain quelled a bit.

". . . with that, I'll turn things over to Julia," I heard Theresa say.

"Well done, Theresa," Barbara said with unprecedented sincerity.

"Yes, that was just great," Romaine beamed at my exotic assistant.

Good lord. What on earth could Theresa have said to make both these hardened retailers so effusive with their praise? I'd never gotten a "well done" from Barbara in all the years I'd worked for the old crone.

I attempted an expression that approximated pride in my little vixen of an assistant and proceeded to disclose Robes and Loungewear's buying strategy for the coming season. The words came easily; this wasn't rocket science and I'd been doing it for years. The disconnect between my words and my thoughts today didn't concern me nearly as much as the disconnect between me and Romaine.

"I love Theresa's idea for joint merchandising," Barbara said to the room at large at the close of the meeting. "You're sharing several vendors this season and we could save some money if you coordinated marketing efforts."

"I can't believe we never thought to do that before," Romaine said, smiling.

"Thanks. It just seemed to make sense," Theresa said. "Would you like to meet sometime this week, Romaine, to see what we can work out?"

I watched open-jawed as Romaine eagerly agreed to Theresa's suggestion. I stared as they walked out the door together.

"That Theresa is a real gem, Julia," Barbara observed. "She can make you think you always wanted something you never even considered. And then she knows how to implement her idea the moment she gets buy-in. A natural strategist."

All this time, I could have been taking strategy lessons from my very own assistant. Now, all that appeared to be left to me was emulation and imitation. I had let too many opportunities pass and, as I'd learned from my buying experience, once a trend had passed, it was gone until someone revived it again twenty years later. I wasn't big on retro, neither in fashion nor affairs of the heart.

While I was focused on appearances, Theresa dealt with realities, strategizing to get what she wanted, which just happened to be the very same thing that I wanted: Romaine. I thought I was preserving some sort of professional image and had blamed my lack of action on everything from Romaine's shyness to her rigidity. With the right strategy, I could have countered that shyness. But I didn't and now it was too late.

"Yes," I said to Barbara. "She's wonderful, isn't she?" I was the epitome of composure as I left the meeting, fighting back tears that only I would ever know about.

Only For My Husband

Rebecca (Sydney, Australia)

My husband John is the greatest guy, so for his fiftieth birthday I want to do something really special. We've got plenty of money so whatever I decide on I know we can afford it. The problem is that he has everything. Everything materialistic of course.

This birthday I want to plan something he'll never forget. My dilemma is, what? He's been skydiving, raced fast cars, explored the jungles of Africa, climbed mountains, seen the Pyramids – we've both done it all.

We're lucky too that we have a great sex life and are both faithful to each other, although I know one of John's fantasies has always been to have a threesome. To be honest it's one of mine too. I would have loved to have participated long ago but never told John, didn't want him to think I wasn't satisfied with him.

Sitting here thinking about it, I've decided that I *will* organize one for him. I'll make out my participation is only for *his* pleasure. Excited at the thought of it, I'm pleased I've finally made the decision. The problem now is, how to go about it?

I have a good friend, Melissa. She's someone I can trust. After all, this isn't the sort of thing you broadcast to just anyone, now, is it? I mean, how would it look?

I decided to pay her a visit.

"You're not asking me, are you?" she asked coyly, her eyebrows arched questioningly.

"Oh, no," I quickly answered. "I just thought you might know how I'd go about finding someone. I couldn't possibly do it with someone we know. I'd never be able to look at them in the same way again."

"What about a brothel?" she suggested.

"Hmm, no I don't think so."

"What about cruising the streets until you see someone who turns you on?" she prompted.

"You've got to be kidding. God knows what we might pick up," I said shuddering. The thought of sexually transmitted diseases left a chill in me.

"What about a stripper? Yeah, you could hire some strippers, see what you think," she said excitedly.

"Hey yeah, that's a good idea," I said. "How?"

"Easy," she laughed. "Let's look through the advertisements."

We spent an hour poring over them and finally decided on three.

"Where do you think we should do it?" I asked.

"Not at home," she said. "Too dangerous. What about a hotel room? Some expensive place in the city."

"You think so?" I asked.

"Yes, it's neutral ground. It'll be perfect. Leave it all to me."

She booked us into the flashiest hotel for the following week and hired the girls at one-hour intervals. That way, she said, we could check them out, discuss together what we thought when they'd gone, before deciding on the right one. The difficulty would be asking them if they were into that sort of thing, but I thought if I never asked, I'd never know.

"You have to come with me," I told Melissa.

"No way," she said.

"I can't do this alone. It was your idea," I pleaded.

"Oh, all right," she said a little too quickly," but I'll deny it if you ever tell anyone."

The following week we both dressed to the nines and booked into the hotel. I rang the three agencies and gave them my room number and confirmed the times. Melissa and I sat there drinking champagne and nibbling on finger food while we waited.

"Nervous?" she asked me.

"You bet," I said as the doorbell rang.

A gorgeous blonde stood in the doorway.

"Vanessa?" she purred.

"Yes," I answered. "Please come in."

I sat back on the couch with Melissa and watched her go through her routine. She was dressed very provocatively, and her CD was a sexy Latin number. She had a great figure, but unfortunately had silicone tits. I knew John hated them so after she finished I thanked her and she left.

I sculled down my drink and popped the cork on another bottle.

"That was so nerve-wracking," I told Melissa.

"I know," she said, downing her drink too. "Half the time I didn't know where to look."

The doorbell rang again.

This time it was a sexy redhead. She was dressed as a police officer. We laughed as she stumbled in the routine when taking off her trousers. When she was down to her G-string she picked up the baton and surprised us by smacking her thigh with it.

Then she had it working up the inside of her leg, but before it reached her pussy she closed her thighs tight. She pushed it in and out, rubbing hard against her slit, moaning while massaging one of her breasts.

I clenched my own thighs together but that made things worse as my thighs caused a delightful tremor to ripple through me as my clit was squeezed between my outer lips. This was turning me on. Colour flushed my cheeks. I wondered what Melissa would think if she knew.

The stripper then pulled her panties forward and pushed the baton down in between her folds and over her slit. She allowed the baton to slip in and out easily and with her panties so far down we could see that she was a definite redhead. When she lay down on the floor with her legs spread and began to insert the baton, I told her, thank you very much and she left.

"Phew, I don't know if I can go through with the third one," I said, fanning myself with a cushion. I'd clearly had too much to drink.

"Why?" Melissa giggled.

"I don't know. It's different to how I thought it would be," I said.

"Is it turning you on?" she asked.

"Er . . . not really . . . well, maybe just a little bit," I laughed.

"Well, it's really turning me on so just relax and enjoy it. Here, have another drink," she said, her speech slightly slurred.

The phone rang and she leaned over to pick it up. I felt a distinct throbbing in my pussy as my eyes fixed themselves on her arse. The thought of seeing her naked was becoming more and more appealing. When she stopped talking on the phone I didn't even notice.

"Are you listening to me?" she asked, shaking a shoulder.

"What?"

"What's the matter with you?"

"I think . . . I'm not sure . . . I've had too much to drink," I giggled.

"Well, that was the agency of the next stripper on the phone. The woman's running nearly an hour late."

"You're kidding," I slurred; my eyelids were feeling very heavy.

"Hey, I think you better lie down for a while," she said, hopping off the couch to make more room for me.

She pulled my shoes off my feet and lay me down, fluffing up a cushion to prop behind my head. Her mobile phone rang and she left me there while she answered it in the bedroom. The thought of her naked in the bedroom brought a smile to my lips.

I really would love to see her naked.

When the doorbell rang again, I sat up and downed the contents of my glass, noticing I was a bit more than tiddly as I staggered to the door.

Whoa, this woman was gorgeous. And black. She sauntered into the room dressed in a skin tight leather dress. It was black and so were her high-heeled stilettos. She had long black hair that hung down to the back of her waist and wore very little make-up except for her red painted lips. She was stunning.

"Where's the party?" she asked.

"Oh, it's private," I said. "We just want you to strip for us. I

want something special for my husband's birthday and I want
to make sure you're exactly what he'd like."

"Oh, he'll like me – don't you worry about that," she
laughed. "Mind if I have a drink?"

"Er, no," I said, a bit taken aback as she already began to
pour out a drink.

She sat in the chair opposite us, crossing her long legs. I
glimpsed white underwear and looked to Melissa to see how
she was reacting.

"Do you do private affairs?" Melissa asked boldly.

"What do you mean?" she purred.

"Do you become involved with the clients?"

"Only if I like them," she said.

"Well, to tell you the truth," I said, "I'm looking for
someone to participate in a threesome with myself and my
husband."

Her eyebrows lifted just a fraction.

"You ever done this before?" she asked.

"No, can you tell?" I laughed.

"Hmm, yes. I'll tell you what I'll do. It's no good just
thinking about hiring me on the day and then getting all
awkward when it comes time to get down to it," she said
moving out of her chair like a panther and coming towards me.

She sat in between the two of us; her attention focused on
me.

"You like what you see so far?" she asked.

"Well, yes," I said, nervous as my stomach dropped.

Like a snake about to strike, her head very gently swayed
until she closed in on my mouth. Her full lips were soft and her
scent intoxicated my senses. The alcohol had me uninhibited
compared to how I usually acted, so I kissed her back, my lips
parting hers.

Her tongue touched the top of my lip and like a shiver of heat
I boldly thrust mine into her mouth, kissing her more passionately than I'd kissed John in a long time.

"Very nice," she whispered against my mouth. "Very nice
indeed."

Now her hand was at the back of my neck where she held me
firmly while her other hand found my breast. Tightening her

grip, her fingers opened the buttons on my blouse and slipped inside. Then her hot mouth trailed its way down into my bra.

My pussy began to pulsate.

I could barely breathe, I was so turned on. She released her hold on my neck and with her hand now on my waist she helped me to stand. We stood there looking into each other's eyes as she slipped my blouse off and discarded it on to the floor.

Her hand was at the back of my bra and with a quick flick of her fingers that too fell to the floor. She was back at my mouth; her tongue flickering around while her hands roamed my body. Somehow she unzipped my skirt and suddenly I was left in only my G-string and high heels.

She fell to her knees and her tongue tantalized my navel while her fingers explored the edge of the crotch of my satin panties. With her fingers tugging at the flimsy material, she ripped them from my body. I stood there quivering before her, forgetting all about Melissa, not knowing or caring where she'd gone.

Laying me on the couch, she opened my legs so she could inspect my pussy. Her breath was hot on my quivering lips as she opened the folds to locate my clit. Then her amazing mouth was all over me, her tongue searching to flicker over my clit. I grabbed my own breasts and squeezed them, my head falling back and my eyes closed in ecstasy.

I could feel myself peaking as my body began to spasm and my back arched away from the couch. She looked up at me as I peered down into her dark face with half-closed eyes and, with her mouth latched on to me, a wonderful orgasm broke free.

As I fell back on to the couch, she rose and pulled her dress over her head. She stood there before me in brilliant white underwear, her tanned ebony skin shimmering and my eyes opened wide as her fingers fumbled behind her before she dropped her lacy bra to the floor.

Her breasts fell free, swaying, her nipples dark and protruding, shiny nipple rings glinting at me. Her hands cupped each breast and she squeezed each nipple between her fingers, moaning lightly as she smiled down at me. Then she was tugging at the rings, stretching the nipples forward, her tongue sliding over her top lip as she eyed me watching her.

I lay there, my legs splayed open for her, my wetness apparent for her to see. My pussy began to throb, sending a pulse through the whole of my body as she inched her panties down and stepped out of them. Her body was void of all hair, her pussy naked, lips poking out, begging for a licking.

I lifted my hands toward her and she lay between my legs, her tongue lightly darting over my trembling pussy. I grabbed her head, pulled her closer into me as my legs locked around her head. She attacked my pussy, devouring it while I ground my pelvis up to her.

She rolled me off the couch and on to the floor, disengaging my hands and moving her body so her pussy was over my face. I looked up into the only other pussy, apart from my own, that I've ever made contact with and inhaled her beautiful scent.

Grabbing her hips, I pulled her down to me and tentatively licked her outer lips. Her skin was smooth and as my tongue slipped and darted about her pussy I was overwhelmed with passion. I smothered myself into her, licking, sucking, and slobbering all over her. I was wild with raw emotions and wondered why I'd never done this before.

Suddenly strong hands tore her away from me and a huge cock was dropped into my open mouth. I looked up, shocked for a moment and then latched on harder and sucked deep into my mouth. This was something I knew, something I loved. This cock was John's.

How he was here and why I didn't care. For the moment all I wanted to do was enjoy this wonderful experience. Then, this woman, whose name I didn't even know, was kissing John. Her black hands roaming over his body, her fingers only inches from my mouth as her red painted nails dug into John's pubic hair.

But a mouth was still latched on to my pussy. I lifted my head a fraction, John's cock still full in my mouth, and saw Melissa attacking my pussy, her eyes glinting up at me with mischief. How was this possible? They had obviously planned this all along. I had no time to ponder this question as the three of them ravished my body.

"Move, both of you," John commanded after what seemed like an eternity.

He lifted me to the bed and lay me down on it. The two girls sat on either side; their nakedness seeming somehow normal as John positioned himself between my thighs. He began to fuck me slowly, with deep long strokes, just how I liked it, while the two women caressed a breast each, Melissa taking my nipple into her mouth and sucking it between her teeth where she stretched it out before biting hard on the tip of it.

The pain was exquisite.

John picked up his tempo, lifting my knees to rest against his hairy chest, while he gave me a playful slap on the arse. Holding me tight, he rolled us over so I now straddled him. Hungry for him, I began to hump him wildly. He grabbed my breasts dragging me forward while he pulled a nipple into his mouth.

Hands were at my cheeks, pulling them apart. Then a tongue was rimming me before I felt something firm but soft probing my hole. I looked over my shoulder to see the black woman, wearing a black dildo, crouched over me trying to insert it.

I was bursting with desire. My biggest fantasies was to be fucked by two men at the same time – one up the arse, the other in my pussy. I'd always visualized John watching, sauntering over to me to drop his massive cock into my mouth while the two guys had their way with me.

I came immediately, just thinking about it, shuddering against John. He would have probably guessed what I was thinking and he began to pump me harder as the dildo hit its mark.

Now Melissa was kissing John right in front of me. I can't tell you what a turn on it was to be naked with these two women and my husband. To watch them kiss and fondle him was one thing, but I wanted to watch him fuck them. Spurred on, I pushed back into the dildo, grinding my pussy into John's pelvis, coming like never before.

I collapsed on to John's chest, pushing Melissa away while the dildo disengaged itself from me. I kissed him hard on the mouth, my tongue exploring his mouth, my passion animalistic.

"Fuck one of them," I demanded.

"All in good time, my dear," John said, smoothing my wet hair away from my face.

"Fuck one now before I go insane," I screamed.

"Your wish is my command," he said, and the black woman jumped right on.

You can't imagine how wonderful it was to lie there next to him humping this gorgeous woman. I opened my legs, found my clit and rubbed madly coming over and over again.

I felt like a fucking nymphomaniac.

Melissa threw herself between my open thighs, taking over, rubbing my clit and fingering me with her other hand. I turned my head towards John and he to me and whispered how much I loved him.

We kissed while the two women were attacking our bodies in unashamedly wanton sex. Our bodies slick with perspiration, we fucked, sucked and licked each other all afternoon.

After paying off the black woman, John settled down between Melissa and I, the three of us sipping a bottle of expensive Champagne.

"How . . .?" I asked.

"Easy," Melissa said.

"What?" I asked, dumbfounded but pleased to have had this experience.

"It was easy," she said. "John had approached me in the same way as you had. He wanted to surprise *you* with a threesome so when I told him what you had planned we decided to use this to our advantage."

"And what a surprise it turned out to be, wouldn't you say?" he asked me.

"I can't believe you managed to do all this. When did you organize it with the black woman?" I asked.

"I didn't," he laughed.

"What? What do you mean?" I asked, confused.

"She wasn't part of the surprise, although I must say she certainly made the fantasy a mind-blowing one," he said.

"What . . ." I looked from one to the other.

"None of that was supposed to happen. We'd planned that

I'd ply you with alcohol, just for you to drop your inhibitions, and after she left I'd make a move on you. We were counting on your responding and then John, who was already here in the bedroom, would come in and join the party," she explained.

"You were here the whole time?" I asked, shocked.

"Yep. I was watching you and the other girls. I must say the redhead certainly had me going with that baton. Took all my willpower to stay quiet in here," he laughed.

"And you really had no idea about the black girl?" I asked, still not knowing her name.

"None. That was a bonus. She was sensational, wasn't she?" he asked

An arm shaking my shoulder and a voice pulled at my subconscious. I opened my eyes; my head pounding as I looked up into Melissa's worried face.

"I . . . you . . ." I mumbled, wondering what on earth was going on.

A black woman was standing beside her, wearing a skin tight leather dress. Her lips were painted in a bright red gloss and she had stilettos on.

"You okay?" Melissa asked.

"What?" I muttered.

"The third girl's here. Been here for ten minutes. I've been trying to wake you the whole time," she said; concern had wrinkled up her brow.

"Tried to wake me? What are you talking about?" I asked, looking down at my clothed body. The only thing I could see missing were my shoes.

I looked from one to the other.

"Where's John?" I asked.

"John? I don't know. Probably at work. Are you okay? You've been sleeping restlessly for over an hour."

"Asleep? You mean John's not here . . . that . . . you . . . and . . ."

"Do you want me to begin?" the black woman interrupted. "I get paid by the hour, you know."

"Oh, sorry . . . yeah . . . sure," I said, sitting up, smoothing out the creases in my clothes.

"Were you dreaming or something?" Melissa asked.

"Or something's right. Phew, you wouldn't believe it," I whispered.

As I crossed my legs trying to regain my composure I noticed my panties were missing. I wiggled on the couch, pretending I couldn't get comfortable, the satin lining of my skirt cold on my bare arse and hot pussy. My panties were definitely missing. What had happened while I was sleeping?

With the black girl stripping to her raunchy music, I stared at Melissa from the corner of my eye. She caught my stare and winked, causing me to blush with not only embarrassment but also longing. Had she done something while I had been sleeping?

Focusing my attention back on the stripper I decided that whoever said turning fifty was depressing and unexciting, certainly didn't have a friend like her.

Toothin' It

Robin (New Haven, USA)

The Brits have it down pat. Cruising, that is. First they were out doggin' it in the countryside and now they're toothin' it on trains everywhere. Damn, but they've thrown caution to the wind and, living here in today's America with its reawakened Puritanism, I long for a revolt that would get us wild in the streets. Or at least in back alleys. If only we'd motivate ourselves to upgrade our PDAs and cell phones so we can ply each other with requests for anonymous sex!

Sitting here on a Metro North train, nursing my chai tea, I wonder who I'd pick "to tooth". I spy a lot of Gold Coast wealth – women coming home from city shopping, weighed down by Bloomie bags and designer purses, and Wall Street stiffs, their faces drawn serious by five o'clock shadow and by the strangle of red neckties (power ties, they call them). It's not the delightfully democratic mix that you get on AmTrak, but there's a scattering of interesting individuals who liven up the surroundings with their body art and alt-whatever wardrobes.

So who would I pick? Who would I aim my lust at? My gaze wanders until I spot a certain young woman. She's reading Bertolt Brecht so she's likely college-aged. Given the fact that her short spiked hair, conch-embellished earlobes, and tattoos shout "suicide girl", I bet her parents were relieved to see her off to college. I imagine texting her.

"Toothin'?"

"Yes."

"Restroom."

"M or W?"

"W."

"Wow."

There, in the restroom, I kiss her hurriedly, hungrily, and I hike up her shirt to get at her young breasts. I'm not surprised to find them pierced and I get my hands on them before she pulls away from my mouth and mumbles something about me being a lot older than her.

To which I answer, "Don't look a gift horse in the mouth."

She doesn't get it – it's too old a saying for her generation to recognize – but her "huh?" doesn't stop me from caressing her. I dip down to a luscious nipple made tight by my touch and take it in my mouth. As I tongue it, it gets even harder and flicking its little barbell makes her moan.

I push her legs apart, eager to get my hand under that little pleated skirt of hers. It takes seconds to caress my way up to her cleft and – silly me! – I gasp when I find she's wearing a thong. Yes, I gather that most young women do, but I'm old enough to be among the old lady cotton undies crowd. Still, that doesn't keep me from pushing it aside.

Touching her cunt sends a shiver through me. Such sweet lips, so petite. I stroke, I probe, I feel my way about her labia. I find her hole and discover her clit. My touch is light and, as I search, she grows wet.

I pull away from her breast, kiss her again, then remark, "You like this."

"Oh, yes!"

Her voice is breathy, heated by arousal. As I work a finger into her, I ask, "You ever do this before? Anonymously?" Her hole is soft and fleshy and it gives way to my finger. She wraps her arms around me in an embrace so tight, it's like she's hanging on for dear life. "No," she half-whispers. "Never. Especially not on the train."

A cryptic answer, but I'm far more interested in the mystery between her legs than in her words and when I get my thumb anchored over her clit, I forget entirely about what she said. Her cunt clutches my finger when she feels my thumb hit its mark. "Oh!" she gasps, "I like that."

"Then ride my hand, baby," I encourage. "Hard. Make yourself come."

She undulates. Where the clutching is a response to my

thumb, this motion is a whole body response to my invitation. She launches into an exquisitely uninhibited lap dance on my hand.

"That's it," I coach. "Bring yourself off. Do it, baby."

As she rides me, that tight little cunt of hers affords a second finger and it starts to slurp busily. She's really fucking my hand and I press my thumb as hard I can into her clit. I wish I could stroke it and I ache to grope her tits while she's riding me, but the compartment is too small and she's hanging onto me too much. One false move and we'd fall down.

But we don't fall and sweet girlish squeals escape her as she comes. As her cunt squeezes my fingers, I talk dirty to her. "Yeah, that's it. Give it up. Give it to me. Come all over me." And she does, enough to leave my hand sopping wet. When I take it from her, I notice the train's slowing for one of its local stops.

"Wow, thanks," she says as she straightens her skirt and hair.

"I'll leave first," I devise. "Count to ten before you follow me."

I make my way back to my seat, aware that no one has apparently seen the trick we've shared. The train takes on its Stamford passengers and, as people shuffle to their seats, I see her make her way down the aisle among the throng. To my complete surprise, she exclaims, "Dad! You made it!" Girlishly, she plops down in the seat next to an older gentleman. He gives her a hug and she plants a kiss on his cheek.

"Yes," he answers. "And I was almost beginning to think you hadn't left the city yet."

She giggles, letting out an exasperated yet very feminine, "Oh, Daddy!" It was the kind of exclamation girls use to wrap their fathers around their little fingers.

"So how's your semestre going?" he asks.

"Great! You can't imagine all the new people I'm meeting and all the adventures I'm having."

Amazing, but she sees me then, sitting further down train. She lets loose a huge, beaming smile and I realize that, if not for anonymity, I could become just as tangled around her finger as her father, but in a completely different way.

They chat for a time, father and daughter reunited, before he turns to his Wall Street daily and she takes to listening to mp3s. I realized that, mystery solved, doing it on the train was taboo-breaking for her because she's on Daddy's territory. I smile, sit back, and think about the juice that's dried on my hand.

Then it happens to me. I get a message.

"Toothin'?"

"Yeah."

"Figured. Saw you."

"Huh?"

"With the girl."

I pause. Another send comes my way.

"Two cars back, between."

I get up, gathering up my stuff, and make my way through the next two cars, trying to balance myself as the train rumbles and sways. I don't have the sea legs for this, but if getting this much sex is always this easy, I sure could be tempted to commute by train more often.

When I reach the designated area, I find it's too noisy for my solitary ways despite being enclosed. If not for the intriguing invitation, I wouldn't have stopped there. And I find myself alone with a guy, someone I'd consider a "suit", another boring businessman. His button-down appearance, I don't like but his audacious inquiry? That, I find attractive.

"Rough week?" I yell his way. "Want relief?"

He nods. I make my way into his pants and grasp the growing cock that waits me there. I don't take it out; that would put us on the indecent side of the law and, besides, there's something wildly clandestine and covert about doing a hand job inside a guy's pants. I can feel that he's uncut and as I pull back his foreskin and start to stroke him, I sidle up to his ear.

"This is what I did with her."

He shudders slightly.

"Except I had her wet hole."

He moans. Good – he likes dirty chat.

"She rode me hard. She was a whelp of a whore."

Getting into it, he thrusts into my hand. I like that; it tells me what rhythm he needs to get off.

"You wouldn't believe the tits on that girl."

I tease him with my knowledge of her.

"Pierced, pink nipples."

He groans.

"A hole so tight, it could only take two of my fingers."

His cock surges in my hand. He's close. This, I realize, is going to be a quickie.

"And when she came, she left my hand sopping wet."

"Oh, God," he mutters. I don't hear the words distinctly, but I know their intonation well enough to grasp what he said.

"Her juice is still all over my hand – the hand I'm beating you off with."

I don't have to exhort him any further to get my hand wet with his come. The very idea that the hand which touched her is now jerking him off is enough to make him lose it. He turns beet red, utters a quick groan, and starts shooting in his pants, two, three, four squirts of come. I catch some of it on my hand. Pervert that I am, I want both him and her on my hand. I can't imagine two better mementoes to take from these unexpected, unplanned quickies.

When his orgasm fades, I take my hand from his pants, careful to keep his runny come on me.

"I'm taking this with me," I tell him.

He straightens his clothing and runs a hand through his hair. "I wish you could take me with you, too." He tells me this is the first time toothing's ever worked for him. I don't tell him that I'm a novice as well. Instead, I ask him which stop he gets off on, ludicrous pun and all. "Westport," he divulges.

I dig out my PDA and tooth him my email address – as best I can one handed, that is.

"Maybe we'll meet again someday."

It's a promise predicated on a word: maybe. Who knows if he'll have the courage to meet me again. Where we're all brave sexual explorers online, we're just as often absolute cowards in real life. And pressing the flesh successfully once in person doesn't mean you won't chicken out if given repeated opportunities.

Ah, you see? Even in fantasy, reality bleeds in! Still, I imagine what it would be like to have my hand caked with his come and her dried juices. Would both draw tight on my skin? Would the smell of their sexes combine and give a lasting, musky fragrance to my hand? Would I beg off washing it "ever again" and thus promote their bodily fluids to celebrity status? Or would I keep them with me only as long as memories of our meetings stay fresh in my mind?

Yes, it's a lovely fantasy, "toothing" a series of sexual adventures, cruising my way home in more ways than one. I finish my tea and lean back in my seat. I close my eyes and again my imagination wanders.

I imagine I'm home, perhaps reading, perhaps on the laptop, lost in thought and enjoying the peace and quiet I've carved out for myself. But my cell phone lies close and when the opening theme from Dvorak's New World Symphony sounds, I know my lover is calling. To my surprise, it's a brief text message, in shorthand no less: LUVST. No polite, tentative introduction, no hopeful inquiry, but a very clear message, one which means he'll unceremoniously fuck me upon arrival. I set aside what I'm doing, undress, and make myself ready for him. I bend forward over the back of my love seat and spread my legs just enough to await his cock.

I suppose most women would find this scenario terribly sexist or, at the very least, thoroughly unromantic, but I find it absolutely thrilling. Waiting to get fucked is far more delicious than people are willing to admit.

I stand there, anticipating. The exposed nature of this position and its readiness make me wet. I wonder how long it will be before I hear him enter my apartment, before I hear his steps approach my willing body. Then, those most ex- quisite sounds of all: that of his zipper in motion and his gasp of delight when he enters me.

Jump forward: he's there, entering me. When he seats himself fully in me, he hikes me further over the edge of the sofa. My feet are off the floor now, dangling, and he pulls my hands behind my back and tells me to "keep them there". It's a helpless position, but it's one that's highly attractive to him. In this state, I'm totally available to him. I cannot escape what he wants.

He begins to fuck me and he works me as perfectly in this

fantasy as I did the others on the train. He plunders me with an utterly single-minded focus, and that's what I find thrilling – that he's willing to use me to achieve just one simple goal, to come.

Evidently, I'm not yet enticing enough. He takes one hand from my rump and, after licking his thumb, finds my asshole and pushed it into me. This, I don't take too well. It's rough, it hurts. My body tenses against it and I scream into the pillows that accent the love seat. If I could use my hands, I'd brace myself against this intrusion and if my feet were planted on the ground, I'd surely squirm. But I can't. The only part of my body that responds to his thumb is my asshole and it clenches in protest.

Hovering in this awkward position, my legs and arms are ready to give out, but I have no place to anchor myself and my arms must stay pinioned behind me. I struggle with what little strength and freedom of movement I have and again I scream into the pillows. All the while, he reams me. His cock drills me and his thumb tears at me.

It's enough, though. He's pounding me so fast now that I know he's close. One last push of the thumb, one last protest from me, and he's coming. He slams into me, jetting his come, filling me with his liquid heat.

When he pulls out, I don't move. I know he likes to watch his come drip from me. It isn't until I feel his hand on my arm that I know he's satisfied. He helps me up, takes me in his arms, and kisses me with a passion that's mixed with thankfulness.

"You're a treasure," he murmurs between kisses.

"One that only you can claim," I remark as I fall to my knees. I take his spent cock into my mouth and claim it as my own reward. My tongue gently caresses him clean, a gesture that tells him how thankful I am as well.

So there you have it: toothin' for sex in a myriad of ways. Hot, isn't it? So hot that maybe I shouldn't wait for my cell phone contract to expire before I upgrade its services. I'm too impatient to wait for that. It can't come soon enough. Because, quite honestly, neither can I.

Dungeon

Christina (Catford, Canada)

I owe Joan one. She had taken me on that blind date to Nassau and I had suffered that boring jerk of a brother of hers for one week. I could have killed her.

This is payback time. The seven-hour flight back home is going to be my time to myself. I am going to do everything my way in this dream, this show for myself. If life doesn't give me what I want in reality, I'm going to create it in my dream. At least in a dream I can go the whole hog, be as dramatic as I wish. Gothic even.

I will create a building like a castle, battlements and turrets rising, elegant and imposing in a wooded landscape. It will shine like a beacon through the dark and mist. Keep it pretty. I did not order this cold wind lashing against us, chilling us as we run from car to entrance, head down into the wind. In this story, this fantasy, I will fix her, that's if I don't get pneumonia at the same time. Can I get pneumonia in a fantasy?

Once inside we shake off our umbrellas and coats and I look around for some indication as to what I should be doing. Whatever, it is, it has to be fun.

A cold hallway, marble and dark. Unwelcoming. Why had I decided to bring Joan here? Ah, yes; payback. A man comes to us, something out of the Addams Family, Lurch, perhaps? He's just over the top, too theatrical in his formal suit and shining black shoes. He takes our coats and umbrellas and says in a polite, deep voice, "Welcome, Ladies. Welcome to Hill Club. I am sure you will be pleased to visit. You are both the expected guests of Rhona Degeneris." He gives this speech and bows formally.

I grin back at him and nudge Joan with my elbow. "Yes, exactly. Miss Degeneris said that she would make sure we were expected."

I lead her, hand in hand, like two little girls, to explore the club. Inside, the atmosphere is one of an airport or a railway station, rather than Gothic threat. People amble into rooms, leave rooms, mill around in corridors or halls, eating, drinking, and talking. Every costume imaginable dons bodies turning people into a variety of characters from Queen Elizabeth to John Knox. People join others and leave and join and leave.

"You, my dear Christina, are a pain in the neck. Why I let you bully me into coming here." I squint at Joan. It's plain she doesn't want to be here and perhaps she's right. I'm sure that she thinks that there are better ways of spending an evening than watching men doing tribal things.

As if she knows what I'm thinking, she says, "I'd rather manicure my nails or wash my hair."

"Oh, what a spoiled little princess you are. I'm sure that women will be doing . . . oh, stuff . . . Look, it's a new experience. It was nice of Rhona to get us in as guests. An honour. Something different. I mean . . . I've been once before so it's not easy to get me in again as a guest and to get you in too . . ."

"Some fucking honour! Besides, what's so different?"

"Smile, sweetie." I tweak her cheeks and she turns from me sharply.

"This is too, too much."

"Come on . . . it's something different. Try it. Give it a chance. You're so fucking white all the time. WASP. Work, work, work. Let that hair down." I have lusted to bring her here. I know that she would never, but never, set foot inside a place like this.

"You're being a racist bitch and, anyway, this stupid costume! I feel a real fool as a pink angel with the gossamer wings. Why an angel? Why do black women get all the fun? I mean, just look at you. Bo Peep, for God's sake."

"You could have been whatever you wanted. Anything. I mean . . . you could have been an executioner if you like. Or Bo Peep like me. And besides, angels are sharp. You can wear anything."

She shrugs, sighing as if it's the end of the world. "Oh, well, I guess no one would know us with these masks and it's your night out. Birthday Girl had a right to pick whatever you want. I mean . . . if anything is dumber than an angel in pink it has to be a black Bo Peep."

"Be cool. She said that all we have to do is say, 'Red Alert' if we don't like what's going on. That's all. Red Alert."

"Like what? What could be going on to make us say that?"

This woman's an idiot. I should not have got her into this. Boring. Boring. I think I'll have to move onto another fantasy, another dream.

We stand at the top of stone stairs. The air heaves with a strange acid smell. Jasmine? Joss sticks? We step down into an area set out like a dungeon: stone flags on the floor, bare beamed ceilings, barred windows and arched cubicles. In the quiet, a few people sit in the corridor, talking and laughing. This is supposed to be exciting! Two great iron-trimmed doors close off an entrance at one end.

Joan opens one door. We are in a room the size of a movie theatre that must have been the main cellar. A fire at one end, logs crackling, takes some of the damp chill off the air.

A boxing rink, its ropes enclosing a man and a woman, is the attraction here. We move forward round tables and chairs to get a better look and we stand beside a stone pillar. The woman is naked but for a feather mask and gold cuffs on each ankle and on each wrist. The man stands above her, covered from head to toe in black leather. He wears a small waistcoat over this body-suit; it's studded with gold buttons and hung with long gold chains. The woman is tied to the four corners of the rink by gold ropes attached to her cuffs. His cock bulges through the leather, huge, thick, plain in every detail.

I tremble and move closer to Joan to reassure her. Why would anyone humiliate herself that way? It has to be the most degrading thing to lie naked with a fully dressed man standing above her. No woman with any self-respect would do that. Never. A childish spectacle. Kids playing at being grown-up, naughty, naughty.

The woman's breasts rise and fall as she breathes deeply. The bright light turns her hair into a crown of fire. A small tongue slicks lips. Tears glisten in her eyes. The man places his boot on the woman's chest; up and down, up and down, it vibrates with her breathing. The high shine of the boot glistens in the soft light. The sharp spur seems to rotate with each movement. I want to leave. I do not like this sort of thing. What sort of thing? No, I dream of this every day, every minute I can.

The boot is so hard, heavy looking and rough, such a contrast against the fine, fine white skin of the prostrate woman. The full dress of black leather shouts, vulgar, beside the elegant simplicity of the naked woman.

I feel the boot on her chest, the cold leather on her skin. I turn to say something to Joan. She has gone. Charming. Nice to take off like that and not say a word. Where is the bitch? In this vast hall, watching the performance of these two people, I feel acutely alone, out of it, strange, a stranger. I have no place here, a voyeur, a nothing. This is not my scene. What is my scene? Of course, it is.

The man flicks his whip against the woman's thighs so gently, so gently it's hardly more than a breath. Then he takes the whip and turns the handle so it's a stick. He places it at the woman's small pink mouth, slack and shining. She wets it and licks it and sucks it until it dribbles her juice. He spreads the woman's legs wide apart with his boot and places the whip's handle at the entrance of her sex; her pink open lips curl round the knob. Her blonde hair, wet, flattens against her skin.

He pushes the whip handle into her, gently at first and then, with ever-increasing force, it's thrust deep. The woman whimpers. It could be a horse's cock buried in the mare. The turgid swollen sex weeps and glistens.

He plays with the whip for a minute or two and, just as she's screaming for more, he removes and snakes it across her mouth. She licks it clean, mewling and sighing.

He again whips her thighs, so gently at first and then harder, harder until they are red and covered by stripes.

The woman cries in evident pain one moment and at the next moment demands more.

Two people have moved close to me, one on each side. One is Napoleon and the other is an angel. I half turn and smile. Thank God. Now that I have found Joan, I can leave.

I whisper, "It's barbaric. I don't know how I could be watching this disgusting performance." The angel says nothing.

Now the woman screams, "Yes, yes, yes," and pulls on her wristbands. The ankles and wrists are red with the pressure of the cuffs, her thighs rosy and serrated.

Only five or six people seem particularly interested in this performance, while the rest talk, play cards or drink.

"I wish I was outside. Fresh air and sun." At the same time my mind is saying, no, you want to be here watching this woman being tortured, tormented, to see her scream in pain, in agony. I feel so . . . so superior watching, as if I am the queen and the woman on the floor my servant. Yes, my servant. Now my thighs burn. The moisture of passion dribbles down my legs. My body is soaking; it's drowning in its own juices. I want to leave, this has gone far enough. This is wrong. I am a businesswoman, I am professional, I am equal to men, I cannot tolerate this sort of thing.

"Come on . . . let's get the hell out of here." I try to move away but am held by my arms. "Joan? What's happening? It is you?" Is it Joan behind that mask? I feel myself being lifted, lifted high by the two people and the lights dim and the chains click and the woman on the stage is standing up, leaning against the ropes, a patronising smile on her face.

The two remove my costume and tether me just as the other woman had been.

The naked woman says, "Now, my little fairy, it's your turn. I saw your smile, I saw you lick your lips as I was getting it."

I shiver. If only I knew who it is. If the angel isn't Joan then this could be Joan. It could be anyone: the local doctor, the lawyer. God, she has a beautiful body. Why is she being so mean, so evil?

Yes, there's no need to worry. They had assured me that anyone could shout Red Alert at any time. The game would stop at once. I mean . . . I wouldn't have brought Joan to anything actually dangerous, not dangerous.

Cuffs tighten on my wrists and ankles. The ropes binding me to the corners of the rink tense, to poise me between the corners. Mentally I shout Red Alert.

The naked woman holds the whip and plays with it, weighing it in one hand first and then the other.

I should shout Red Alert now and get out of this den of obscenity. I should have known it would end up as something silly when the business with the costumes started. I am a fool. So . . . I made a mistake. I pray it isn't a fatal one. I pull on the ropes and just end up hurting myself.

The woman nudges me with her boot and the man in black leather kneels between my legs and breathes onto my sex. All I can feel is the warm breath. What is he doing? What is he intending to do?

He stands above me, one leg on each side of my body and holds his cock. It sticks out of his costume, thick and pulsing, blue veined and gnarled like an oak. It's the cock of a horse; it has to be up to his waist. He squats and holds it and brings it across my lips. I turn my face away.

"Oh, it's like that, is it? Well, it's time to teach the bitch a lesson." He takes the whip from the woman and sweeps it across my breasts. Then he lifts it and brings it down onto the floor hard, with such a bang I would have jumped off the floor if I could. The room reverberates with the crack of the whip. Tears gather in my eyes and roll down my cheeks. Thank God for the mask and for the privacy of my tears.

The woman slinks between my legs like a cat. She licks up the insides of my thighs and sniffs every inch of my skin. Up and up, she nuzzles. In a heavy dramatic melodramatic voice she says, "I do believe, Master, that we have to show her what true obedience is. We have to . . . train her."

The man nods. He holds the whip to my face. "Smell it, bitch. Smell the sweetness of her juice. Smell her perfume on the leather."

I can't help but smell it. My head is full of that fleshy, rich juice smell of woman. I want that whip between my legs, between my breasts, on my bare backside. I want the handle of that whip up my anus; I ache for it to be thrust deep into my cunt.

The woman takes the whip and I turn from her, trying to blot the whole thing out of my mind. The whip cracks deafening, hard against the mat beside me. Then it's feathered against my breasts, hardly touching, just stroking. Spun and feathered. Gently, it vibrates between my legs. Just a touch. It jerks against my clit. Just a jerk, nothing more and then it's pulled across my mouth.

"Wet it, bitch." I do as I am told.

The woman swings it across my belly then flicks it just hard enough to warm skin. It lashes against my breasts, just missing my nipples. I scream. I squirm. I ache to shout Red Alert, but my body has its own designs. The man kneels over me and strokes my lips with his cock and the woman bites me hard in the inside of my thigh. I imagine small, perfect teeth sinking into the fine flesh just where it joins the forest of thick black hair.

As a reflex, more or less out of myself, I lick the cock and take it into my mouth. The woman bites the other side. Hard. So hard, I scream and I hear myself scream. Yes. Yes. I relax my mouth so the whole of that enormous cock sinks in easily, down, down into my throat. The stink of rubber and cloying perfume possessed by some condoms.

He moves above me. Something clamps onto each nipple in turn. A ratchet-like noise as each clamp is tightened. I can die with the pain. Die with the pain. The man withdraws his cock from my mouth and angles above me, placing it just at my clit. He moves it back and forward. The woman tightens the clamps on my breasts slightly.

"Oh, doesn't she have the most delightful nipples? See how they bloom and explode with the gold. Yes, she does suit gold. Better than silver on her skin, I think."

The man agrees. "We should find more places to ornament her."

"Not today," The woman says. "We should tempt her back. Keep them for some other time."

Yes, right! I do not think that there will ever be another time. I just want to get the hell out of this time.

Pain, and at the same time his flesh at my flesh. My body shouts for more. More. No, it's time to shout. It's time to get the hell out of here. No. Yes.

Now his tongue is licking me so gently, so kindly. The woman tightens up my nipples even more. Indeed they could explode, take wings and fly right off my body. They are as hard as gold or ivory.

The woman is on my face, presenting herself. Tongue, which has its own life, lifts to find the woman's clit, circles it, licks, strokes, tastes the fine taste of fish and honey and vanilla. Yes.

The man whips my thighs. I imagine them bleeding. Pain, and when not pain a burning, yes a burning and a heat, as I had never imagined before.

My tongue is locked into this woman. It's part of the woman's clit and together they are moving to something else – the pain has become distant and, at the same time, it's right in front of me. I am pain and I am that tongue working the woman and the pain.

The man is stroking me and rooting in my bush. He has a finger in me then two fingers and then his cock. The body above me gyrates in rhythm to my tongue and juices drip down my face as the woman grinds into my face. The man's cock fills me so full I have no body left, and at the same time, his finger on my clit and curling and teasing until I can't stand it any more and I scream in agony. I come, pulling on my restraints, curving my body up to meet his. When I shout, I feel the woman above me gyrate and thrust in her own orgasm. I scream Red Alert. Red Alert. Yes. Yes.

The man takes his time finishing. The next thing I know they are standing looking down at me.

I can't breathe. I am numb. The restraints are removed. No one says anything at first. The man dresses me in my fairy outfit. The woman combs my hair and kisses me gently on the cheek.

I feel ashamed. Coward to shout. I still burn with the heat of the whip. I rub my wrists where the cuffs had scuffed the skin.

Once I am dressed and about to leave the stage the man says, "You new?"

"I guess."

"Coming back?"

"I guess."

The pilot announces that we are an hour out of Heathrow.

My hand is welded onto Joan's thigh and pinching her so hard that she digs her elbows into me.

"What? What's wrong?"

"God! Nothing. Nothing at all. In fact, everything is just right. How about you?"

"Oh, what do you expect. Bored. Bored out of my mind."

I can't say that. No, not at all bored.

Come to the Phone

Brittany (Minneapolis, USA)

I may have only turned eighteen just a few months ago, but with my extremely vivid imagination, I'd be willing to bet that I've had more sexual fantasies in my short life than most girls twice, or even three times, my age. I'm horny just about all the time, but since I'm saving myself for my future husband, whoever that may be, I can't act on my hormonal impulses – except in my head, of course.

I've had more straight and lesbian threesomes, foursomes, and orgies, involving everything from anilingus to zoo animals, in my mind, than most porn stars have for real in a twenty-year career. And two of the stars in my X-rated heaven are my best friend, Tracy, and her hottie of a boyfriend, Matt. Mix me and them together, add a dash of phone sex, and you've got the recipe for one of my typical scorching-hot fantasies . . .

Tracy and I were sitting around yakking one night, about – what else? – sex, when she boldly declared that her boyfriend liked to talk dirty to her on the phone. I yelled, "No way!" and dared her to prove it.

She scooped up her cell and punched some buttons, never one to turn down a dare. "Hey, Matt, it's me!" she bubbled into the phone. She was sitting cross-legged on her bed, right next to me, clad in a pair of pink panties and a sleeveless undershirt. Her nipples pressed hard against the thin material of her top, and I spotted a couple of blonde short n' curlies peeking out from the sides of her panties.

"It's me – Tracy!" she yelled, her pretty face turning angry when Matt didn't recognize her voice right away. Her hunky jock of a boyfriend had a reputation for playing the field, and not just on the gridiron. "Yeah, whatever, anyway, I'm home all alone and, well, you know . . ."

She burst out giggling as Matt said something to her – something dirty, no doubt. Then the cute, suntanned blonde with the Jennifer Aniston breasts and Jennifer Lopez butt set the phone down on her bedside table and pressed a button. "Can you hear me now, Matt?" she shouted, grinning at me and winking.

"Loud and clear, babe!" Matt responded, his deep voice sending shivers down my spine – right to my cunny.

"Okay, good. Now make with the dirty talk. And make it real dirty – filthy – or I'll hang up and let Mr V work his magic."

"Not to worry, babe. I'll give you enough good vibrations to get you off."

I pictured the tall, muscular, blue-eyed, black-haired stud in my mind and rubbed my thighs through my pajama bottoms. Tracy ran her own hot, little, brown hands up and down the sides of her body, blatantly cupped her titties and squeezed. I wasn't exactly sure just how far the horny hottie was going to take this, but I was willing to go along for the ride.

"So, what're you gonna do to me, big boy?" Tracy asked, in a Mae West kind of voice.

"Huh? Yeah. Well, first I'm gonna get a good grip on those sopping wet panties of yours, pull them down your long, smooth legs – pull them off and sniff them maybe, before I toss 'em aside and –"

"Slow down!" Tracy squealed. "Let me get them off, will you!" She snatched up the phone and covered it with her hand. "Wanna help out, Brittany?" she asked me.

"What?"

"Yeah! It'll be fun! You do everything that Matt says he's gonna do to me." Her glossy lips broke into a sly smile. "That is, I dare you to do everything that Matt says he's gonna do to me."

I stared into the turned-on teen's baby-blue eyes, my face as red as a stop sign. So this was how far she wanted to take it; she wanted me to get lezzy on her!

"We'll have a great time," she promised. "And a good laugh at Matt's expense." She bit her plush lower lip and batted her long eyelashes at me, pretending like it was all a big joke – which I knew she knew I knew it wasn't; once we'd gone and done the girl-on-girl deed, our friendship could never be the same again.

Tracy and I have been best buds since kindergarten, grown up together, and we even kissed and Frenched and dry-humped when we were in junior high, just fooling around, mind you – simulating what it would feel like to have a boy make love to us; but I'd never known that the girl had the hots for me. I swallowed hard and let my brown eyes roam over her luscious, eighteen-year-old body – her lithe, honey-dipped legs, her small, delicately-arched feet with the sparkly nail polish, her perky tits with the jutting, porn star nipples, her warm, smiling face – and the rising damp between my quivering legs convinced me that it was indeed time to explore a whole new dimension to our friendship.

"Bring it on, girlfriend," I said quietly.

"Yes!" she yelped, fumbling the phone back onto the bedstand. "You still there, Matty-boy?"

"Yeah, what the –?"

"Say again what you're gonna do with my panties." Tracy untangled her dancer's legs and leaned back against the headboard, started caressing my legs with her playful peds.

"I'm, uh, gonna slide your soaking panties down your long legs . . ."

Tracy slapped my leg with one of her feet and gestured excitedly at me, and I scrambled onto my knees, crawled closer, and slid my trembling fingers under the elastic band on her panties, as she gave me a peck of encouragement on the cheek. My arms shook like willow branches in a hurricane, but somehow I managed to pull her panties down, as she lifted her bum off the bed. I slid the teensy underwear off her legs, then stared, transfixed, at her glistening, blonde cunny. Her rosy-red pussy lips were slick with moisture, and she reached down and pulled them apart, showing off her pink.

"Got your panties off yet?" Matt asked.

"Oh, yeah," Tracy murmured, spreading her legs as wide as they'd go.

"Well, anyway, like I said, I'm gonna sniff your panties, smell your hot cunt juices, and then –"

"Wait!" Tracy shrieked, kicking me again.

I awakened from my trance and brought the sexy girl's panties up to my face, my eyes still locked on her juicy, wide-open cunny. I pressed the soft, warm cotton against my nose and took a good, long whiff, smelling Tracy's sweet, secret scent, my brain swimming and my body going all hot and heavy.

"Then I'm gonna toss your panties aside," Matt continued, "and start strokin' that furry, blonde beaver of yours."

Tracy grabbed my right hand and placed it directly over the top of her cunny. "Yes!" she gasped.

I dropped her panties and started rubbing her muff. There was no turning back now – once you've gone as far as stroking a chick's cunny, you've just got to get her off. I fluttered my fingers through her downy fur, rubbed her damp lips, as she gripped my wrist and moaned, squirmed around on the bed. I rubbed her like I'd rubbed myself so many, many times before.

"I'm gonna pull your top off, get you totally naked," Matt went on.

Tracy let go of my wrist and wrestled her undershirt off, so that she was as nude and lewd as Matt wanted her – as I wanted her. Her titties were as sun-kissed brown as the rest of her hot bod, except for two white bikini triangles that framed her cherry-red nipples. I kept on stroking her gash, getting bolder and buffing her clitty with my thumb, while she groped her bare boobs, squeezed and kneaded them, rolled her inch-long nipples between her fingers.

"Got your top off?" Matt asked.

"Yeah . . . it's off," Tracy breathed, her eyes closed, her head lolling back against some propped-up pillows, as I petted her puss, polished her clit.

"Okay, next I'm gonna grab those jugs of yours and play with them awhile – while we French."

I gulped, the temperature in the room suddenly shooting up a hundred degrees or so. I had to keep blinking my eyes to see straight, but I did as I was told. I lifted my slickened hand off Tracy's cunny and wrapped it around one of her boobs, did the same with my other hand, started gently massaging her firm, warm titties.

I watched in amazement as her ever-hard nipples grew even longer, and then she grabbed my head and mashed her velvety lips against my lips. My overheated body was jolted with sexual electricity as she hungrily kissed me, and I fumbled with her titties, plucked at her rigid nipples, until the gorgeous girl drove her tongue through my parted lips and into my mouth.

I almost fainted as Tracy scoured the inside of my gaping mouth with her slashing tongue, slamming it into my tongue. Eventually, though, I responded in kind, holding onto her handful tits for dear life as we slapped our slippery, pink tongues together, wildly Frenched each other.

"Like I said, I'm gonna swipe tongue with you and juggle your knockers around until you're really hot and bothered," Matt droned on, as Tracy and I urgently tongue-wrestled. "Then I'm gonna apply some mouth-action to your tits – lick those wicked nipples of yours, suck on them like a baby sucks on his mama's teat."

I pulled away from Tracy's mouth, bent my dizzy head down to her heaving chest and started tonguing her girlish titties, her succulent nipples.

"Fuck, yeah!" she groaned, clutching at my long, black tresses.

I licked and licked first one of her obscenely swollen nipples, and then the other, lapping at her buds like a kitten laps at a bowl of warm milk. Then I squeezed her right boob so that her nipple shot out impossibly long, and I vacuumed it into my mouth and sucked on it.

"Mmm," she whimpered, her fingers tightening on my hair, pulling me into her chest.

"And after workin' over your rack for a while, I'm gonna stick my face between your boobs and then drag my tongue from there all the way down to your flat belly, into your muff," Matt said, commanding me to do likewise.

I reluctantly disgorged Tracy's spit-slickened left tit, kissed each of her protruding nips goodbye, and then jammed my face in between her titties. I stuck out my tongue and licked at her cleavage, licked my way down her hot, bronze body – all the way down to her navel. I tongued her silver belly-button stud for a moment, then continued my wet, wicked skin-descent, till I tasted fur.

"I'm gonna open up your pussy and shove my tongue deep into your hole," Matt instructed, his voice rising with excitement. "I'm gonna fuckin' fuck your juicy twat with my tongue!"

Music to my burning ears! I slithered onto my belly, positioned my face in between Tracy's golden thighs, and tentatively touched her glistening glory-hole flaps with my twitching fingers. She moaned, mumbled my name, cupped and fondled her damp titties. I pulled her dewy lips apart and stared into her shiny, ultra-pink pink, and then swallowed my apprehension and took the final plunge into all-out girl-love – dove tongue-first into her dripping cunny, spearing her hot-slot with my pink blade.

"Ohmigod!" she bleated.

I pumped my hardened sticker in and out of her cunny, fucking her with my tongue over and over and over, my brain barely comprehending what my mouth was doing. She tasted sweet and tangy at the same time – just like I tasted – and, after tongue-drilling the writhing babe for a goodly amount of time, I licked her slow and hard clear from her butthole to her clitty, revelling in her funky flavour.

"I'm gonna lick your puss, like, a million times," Matt chimed in, catching up to me. "Then I'm gonna shove two fingers into your tight, little twat and fuck you with my digits – while I slurp on your buzzer."

The guy knew what a girl wants; it was no wonder he was so popular at school. I lifted my head and smacked my lips, swallowing some more of Tracy's honey, and then I eased two of my purple-tipped fingers into her squishy poon, started sliding them back and forth in her gripping love tunnel.

"Yeah, fuck me!" she screamed, supposedly to Matt, but really to me.

I pounded my pokers into my best friend's cunny, while I

teased her clitty with my lashing tongue. She thrashed around on the bed like she'd grabbed a downed power line, gripped her titties so hard that I thought her nipples would shoot off and embed themselves in the ceiling. I frantically fucked her coochie with my digits, desperately licked her exposed, swelled-up nub, until she suddenly let loose an ear-piercing scream and her cunny gushed hot girlie juice all over my hand.

Tracy's sweat-sheened body shuddered violently with orgasm, and when I tore my finger-plugs out of her boiling cunny, I was astonished to see that she wasn't just coming, she was squirting!

"You're gonna squirt come all over my face!" Matt hollered, so loud that it sounded like he was right there in the room with us. "And I'm gonna drink it all in!"

I feverishly buffed Tracy's engorged clitty, as the distraught girl shook uncontrollably, her volcanic pussy spraying chick-jizz straight into my face, my open mouth. She erupted like a geyser, almost drowning me in her honey, but I managed to choke down just about all the squirt she could give me. And then, just as quickly as it had started, it was over. I lapped at her smouldering cunny, anxious to get every last sticky drop of her sweet n' sour goodness.

"Tasty, huh, Brittany?" Matt said – and not through the phone.

I jerked my head up from between Tracy's damp, quivering legs, swivelled it around – spotted Matt standing in the open doorway, his cell phone in one hand, his long, hard cock in the other.

"It got kinda boring down in the basement, so I thought I'd see how things were going up here," he commented, grinning from ear to ear, stroking his awesome tool with a practised stroke.

I spun my eyes back to Tracy, and she popped a thin, tired smile, her girlish body still undulating with the aftershocks of her blistering orgasm. "I've wanted to get with you for a long time, Brittany," she confessed. "And I thought, with Matt's help, I could pull it off." She puckered her pouty lips and blew me a kiss. "You were great, baby."

I stared at her in disbelief, and then my jaw unhinged when

she added, "And Matt's been wanting to get busy with you, too, which I've got no problem with – provided you don't?"

"I–I . . . sure!" I blurted. Who wouldn't want to get it on with the best-looking dude in school?

Matt dropped his cell, and his jeans and Jockeys, ripped off his T-shirt, and stood there wearing only a pair of white sports socks and the father of all hard-on's. Then he eagerly jumped onto the bed, joining us two intimate gal-pals.

Matt and Tracy helped me unbutton and pull off my pajama top, skin away my bottoms, until I was as stark, raving naked as they were. Tracy told me to turn around and lie back against her, which I did, and she wrapped her arms around my chest and hugged me tight, her sweaty hands gripping my bronze, medium-sized titties. I closed my eyes and sighed; I could've lain in Tracy's blissful, skin-to-skin embrace forever.

"Be careful, Matt," Tracy warned, shattering my rapture. "Brittany hasn't had much experience with guys."

"Oh, yeah?" Matt said, as his girlfriend, and mine, softly kissed the nape of my neck, ran her warm, wet tongue in behind my ear, caressed my tingling titties.

Matt grabbed my ankles and spread my legs open for business. Then he crawled into the gap, his huge cock pointing arrow-straight at my moist cunny. He gripped his giant dick at the base and steered it into my puffy pussy lips, shot his hips forward and punched the bloated head of his cock into my greasy slit. He grasped my thighs and lifted me up, jammed his monster cock all the way into my coochie.

"Yeah, fuck me! Please fuck me!" I implored the chiselled stud, my head spinning, my cunny electrified. My body burned with the ultra-erotic heat of Tracy's greedy hands on my tremulous titties, her fingers primping my aching nipples, her tongue swirling around inside my ear; and with the fantastic, stuffed-full feeling of Matt's thick meat buried deep inside my conch.

He grunted with pleasure at my wet tightness, started churning his hips, pumping my twat with his studly cock. He vigorously sawed back and forth in my stretched-out sex-hole, and I basked in the sensual sensations of him fucking me, Tracy feeling me up.

It went on and on and on, until Matt torqued the sexual pressure up a couple more notches by redoubling his already frenzied cunt-stroke, and my cunny tingled alarmingly in prelude to certain, mind-blowing orgasm. I cracked my eyes open and stared blindly at Matt, his rock-hard body coated with perspiration as he hammered away at my cunny with his sledge of a cock, his face contorted into a grim mask of lust.

Then my entire lower body suddenly went numb, to such an extent that I could barely feel Matt pumping my puss, barely hear his body slapping against my thighs, was only vaguely aware of Tracy tugging on my titties, tonguing my neck. Then, just as suddenly, my cunny exploded and everything became crystal-clear – I could see and hear and feel every cock-thrust and nipple-pinch and wet kiss with an almost painful clarity – and I was overwhelmed. "I'm coming!" I wailed, my flaming body going inferno.

"Fuck, yeah!" Matt bellowed, frantically slamming me, then ripping his juice-slick dong out of my cunny and spraying thick, white-hot streams of jism down onto my snatch.

My cunny felt painfully empty without Matt's mammoth cock, but Tracy quickly picked up the slack by reaching down and rubbing my clitty. She stroked me faster and faster and faster, till her hand was a blur, till my cunny exploded a second time and another humungous orgasm roared through me. My body arched like a bow stretched taut, and I desperately grabbed Tracy's arms and held on tight, convulsing with ecstasy, coming close to blacking out as multiple orgasms tore me apart, as Matt doused my gushing cunny with his steaming jizz, dyeing my jet-black fur a sticky white.

I quivered with joy for what seemed a sexual eternity, until finally I collapsed back down into Tracy's arms, my sweat-dappled body undulating with deep-down cunny satisfaction. Tracy kissed my neck and shoulders, Matt my lips and tits, and I closed my eyes and revelled in the warm, wet feeling of absolute fulfillment.

. . . And that's just one of the gazillion or so fantasies that serve to bank my raging sexual fires for the time being, till I finally get married. Then some lucky dude's not gonna know what hit him.

The Librarian

Claudia (Victoria, Australia)

"Hi, Sheila, it's just me," I said, bursting through the front door. I was running late for a dinner date with my sister, Christine.

I stopped dead in my tracks as I spied her coming out of the bathroom. I'd never seen her looking so hot. She nervously brushed a few wisps of hair that had escaped from beneath a towel that was twisted into a turban on her head, clearly unnerved that I'd seen what she was wearing.

"I . . . er . . . I didn't expect you home so early," she stuttered.

I couldn't keep my eyes off her stunning figure. She was wearing a red and black teddy underneath her robe. It was open, revealing her amazing body. She had beautiful ebony skin and the red complemented her, turning her into a vibrant vamp.

"I forgot something," I said, still staring at her breasts.

She pulled the robe tight around her body and rushed into her bedroom. I stood there looking after her. In the twelve months we'd shared this apartment, not once had I seen her go out on a date, yet these last five Fridays, whenever I got home, she was never here and didn't arrive back until Sunday morning.

When I'd asked her where she'd been, she just said she'd been out with some old school friends. I suggested she bring them around here one Friday. I said I'd love to meet them but she just ignored me.

I was a snoop by nature and the fact that she had that sexy teddy on didn't fool me. Normally she dressed very conservatively. She was a librarian and, believe me, usually she looked the part. Hair pulled up in a bun, horn-rimmed glasses. She looked and acted like a mouse.

On the weekends prior she would just bum around in tracksuits and sloppy clothes. She always had her nose in a book. I must admit I didn't have much time for her, always busy with my own life. I had no idea she was so horny looking.

She was seeing someone, but who? And why the secrecy?

"See you," she yelled, as she passed my door.

I felt so alone when she left. I lay on my bed thinking about her. Dinner with Christine now seemed such a chore whereas before I was looking forward to it.

"Can we skip dinner?" I asked Christine when she answered her phone.

"Yeah, why?" she said.

"Oh, I just don't feel like it, that's all," I said.

"You okay?" she asked.

"Yeah, it's just that . . . it's . . ."

Christine knew I had a crush on Sheila. She'd already told me to either tell her or get over it.

"It's what?" she pried.

"It's Sheila. She's going out again tonight and I caught her coming out of the bathroom wearing a very sexy teddy," I blurted out.

"So what? Leave the girl alone. You have to get over this obsession you have with her," she said.

"I'm not obsessing. I'm just curious. Don't you think it's strange, her spending all those weekends away and not telling me anything."

"I think you're strange. She doesn't have to tell you anything. You're not her mother. Don't bug her about it. It's her own business. I've got another call. I'll talk to you tomorrow," she said hanging up.

I rolled over burying my face in the pillow. I didn't care what she said. I wanted to know what she was up to. Many thoughts and scenarios rushed through my mind. I lay there thinking hard, wondering where she was and what she was up to.

I imagined that I'd followed her out, watched as she ran down the steps, her long hair trailing after her. She'd hop into a cab and her coat would ride up so I'd be able to see the tops of her stockings. Stockings meant suspenders and suspenders meant no ugly panty hose.

I'd keep my distance as the taxi sped through the quiet streets. It would stop in a seedy part of town where there were old warehouses. I'd cut my lights and idle along, just like in the movies. When she knocks on a door someone wearing a dark robe will answer it.

I can't see what the person looks like as the light from inside the room shadows his face. She slips inside and I'm left to wonder what to do next. I decide to cruise by slowly; my lights still off and park just around the corner of the building.

What would happen next?

Faint music would be coming from inside. There are windows but they are too high for me to see into. Skirting around the back I'd find an old milk crate. I take it with me back to a window and balance carefully on it. I'm able to peer inside, just between the crack of the curtain.

This room is a dining room. A huge wooden table dominates the room with large ornate chairs that could seat about twenty people. Nothing at all mysterious about this room, quite boring actually and then I see someone walk past the room so I'd pull back on instinct, become more interested and grab my crate and go to the other side.

Can't have my fantasy too boring. I'd have to make it more exciting.

This room would be nothing like the other. This one is decked out with what looks like thick and luxurious carpet, with deep mahogany furniture and plush red velvet covers. There is a huge chair, more like a throne, placed at the centre of one of the walls. Small tables and armchairs are scattered about the room.

Large wooden posts are attached to the ceiling at the same end as the throne and there is a crate or cage with wooden bars nearby, an array of whips adorn the wall and in a glass cabinet I spy dildos, vibrators and other interesting toys.

Yes, that gives it a definite intriguing atmosphere.

Voices alert me to the doorway. Sheila is leading the way, wearing a long purple robe. As she walks the gown parts and underneath I see she is still wearing the sexy teddy and definitely stockings and suspenders. Her hair is draped around her like a shawl. Even from this distance I'll be able to see she has her face beautifully made up and as she heads for the throne, others will enter the room. All will be women.

Sheila will be the only one in purple. She'll stand out, look special. Some will have black, some red and two girls will sit at Sheila's feet wearing white tunics, white see-through tunics. I'll peer harder, nearly topple off the crate to see if either of them are wearing underwear.

They won't! Dark nipples will stand out like beacons as the girls cross their legs to sit on the floor. Most of the armchairs will be taken up. Waitresses, dressed only in a short apron and nothing else, their breasts swaying as they walk, will enter as well as two men wearing tight leather pants and no shirts. They'll stand on either side of the girls who are at Sheila's feet, their arms crossed, muscles flexed.

My pussy throbs as I plan which way to go from here.

I'd be intrigued for many reasons. Firstly, that Sheila would be the head of anything as she is normally such a mouse. Secondly, that women would dominate this room. They'd have to be part of some sort of association, which definitely has nothing to do with the library association. Thirdly, naked female waitresses will serve drinks to women who slap them on the arse or pinched their breasts. They'll be so submissive that they show no reaction.

My hand steals down to my pussy and I feel the heat emancipating from there and I smile. This is the randiest I've felt for ages.

I can't hear what is being said, the walls would obviously be sound proofed to keep away nosy people like me and I can't even imagine what they would say anyway. The two men will walk from the room and minutes later come back, both holding the arm of a beautiful young woman who they stand in front of Sheila.

I need to add some drama to this.

Some sort of heated argument will ensue and their body language will be tense. The woman will struggle to move away but the men will hold her firmly in their grasp. Sheila will approach the woman, look her up and down as though she is for sale. One of the girls who had been at her feet will hand her a cushion. Something will be resting on it.

It will be a knife.

Sheila will run the blunt edge of the knife down the side of the girl's face, over her neck and the swell of her breasts. Then down and under her shirt where with one quick upward motion she'll slice off the buttons and the shirt will fall open. The two men will rip it from her arms and discarded it onto the floor.

I really should get into this sort of stuff; it's definitely a turn on.

Now they'll hold her arms more firmly as she begins to struggle. I'll watch, mesmerized, as the knife moves under her bra straps and slices through them. Her bra will fall forward, exposing a luscious pair of breasts. Now Sheila will trace the knife around her nipples before lowering her head to suck one into her mouth.

She'll laugh while the girl struggles against the men. One of the girls in the white tunic will remove the woman's skirt until she is standing in only her panties and cut up bra. Her gorgeous breasts will be heaving as she continues to struggle.

Sheila will place the tip of the blade at the edge of her panties and slowly inch its way down to the crotch. She'll rip her panties off and with a quick slice into the centre of the bra the woman will stand before her naked.

The woman's body is beautiful. She has dark black hair that hangs over her face as she continues to struggle with the men. Her pubic hair is also dark and stands out against her pale white skin. She'll have a perky arse and long muscular legs.

If this fantasy was real I'd want to go in there and throw myself into the woman's pussy. With all those other women in the room watching me I'd let them rip off my clothes and have their way with me. That scenario will be for another fantasy, though.

I'd be so hot watching that I'd carefully slip out of my panties and quickly stuff them into my bag. I'd run my hand over my mound and pussy before sliding a finger into my wet slit. That would feel so good. I'd throw my bag over my back to allow me the use of both hands as I pull back the hood of my clit, smearing some of my juices over it and begin to gently rub it.

My attention will be drawn back to the activities at hand and while fingering myself I'd watch as they lashed her to something on the floor. A waitress is on her knees in front of a woman whose black robe is open, revealing her nakedness underneath. The woman slings one leg over the arm of the chair and the waitress will use a vibrator to stimulate her. Then she'll lower her head; her tongue will flicker out to lick her. The woman will grab the back of her head and draw her in closer, before collapsing back on the chair to enjoy.

While this is going on the two guys will hoist their captive up to what looks like a rack after they have already spreadeagled and tied her to it. They hook the pulley ropes to one of the pillars and then move away.

Sheila will walk around her to admire her body, her fingers trailing over her skin. She'll have a small whip in her hand, and she'll stand in front of the girl, smacking it into the palm of her other hand as though to frighten her. Something is being said but I'll have no idea what. Then she'll lash at the girl's breasts while she begs for her to stop.

This is turning me on. I smear my juices over my clit and rub hard, enjoying the rawness of it all. I'd never been whipped or spanked, well not like that, and I'm finding it quite a turn on, imagining what it would feel like.

Sheila will continue to whip the girl and I will see faint welts rising over her body before she falls to the floor in front of the girl and begins to lick her and I'll be so turned on just by thinking how my mousy flatmate would be into this sort of thing as I balance precariously on the crate.

Her tongue will roam over the girl's body before she stands and retrieves the whip. She'll take the handle and probe it into her pussy and I'll watch, licking my lips, as she inches it in and then begins to fuck her with it. This will all be too much for me and my juices will run down the inside of my thigh.

Now all the women in the black robes rise and come towards the girl on the rack. Their hands will be all over her, pawing at her breasts, fingers in her pussy and her hole, mouths licking every part of her. The men will not move from their position and from what I can see they certainly won't have hard ons. I'll assume them to be gay! How could you not be turned on by that display?

I can't see much; their bodies will block my view. I'd be so turned on that I'd lean my back against the wall and rub my clit harder, bring on a powerful orgasm and secretively hope that someone is watching me. I'd be as horny as hell. I'd want to see my girlfriend Louise but would be hesitant to leave.

An approaching car will make the decision for me. I'd jump from the crate and hide around the back. The car will drive past though, not even slow down. I'd be pretty sure that this is where Sheila has been going every Friday night and know I can always come back every Friday night to watch. I'd need some relief so I run back to my car to visit Louise.

The desire to be fucked and the thought of Louise wearing her big black dildo has me driving like a maniac. I don't tell her what I've witnessed but Louise is wondering why I'm so randy when I practically tear her clothes from her and demanded a good fucking.

The thought of fucking Louise right now nearly has me putting a stop to this fantasy but I want to continue on, to play it out to the end.
We'd spend the night and the next day locked in each other's arms but I make sure I'll be home early Saturday night so I'll be fresh for Sunday morning. I'll confront Sheila about her sexuality and I'll definitely want to see her naked so I'll have to come up with a plan.

I'd be nervous. Butterflies would flutter around my stomach as I bathe and make myself up. I wouldn't be quite sure how to go about it, and by the time Sheila does come home the thought of ravishing her body will be the only thing on my mind.

"Have a nice weekend?" I'd ask as she tries to sneak in.

"Oh, you're up," she'd say, stating the obvious.

"Yeah. Thought I'd get up early and welcome you home," I'd say.

"Why?" she'd ask.

I'd rise from the couch and walk towards her. Her eyes would be open wide, her tongue licking at her beautiful full lips. I'd lift my hand and release the clasp from her hair. It would fall around her shoulders and I'd remove her glasses and place them on the table. Slowly I'd unbutton her coat, slip it down her arms to reveal her sexy teddy that she'd still be wearing.

She'd stand there breathing hard as I soak in her beauty. I'd run my hand down the side of her face and grab the nape of her neck. I'd pull her back by the hair and kiss the hollow of her throat. She'd reward me with a low moan of pleasure.

My tongue will seek out a nipple as I pull her hair back harder. I'd flicker my tongue around draw it into my mouth to suck on as my fingers roam her abdomen; her mound, and then I'd cup her pussy.

She'd grab at me, pull me into her body as her tongue kisses my mouth with such passion. My hands will be all over her, pulling at her stockings, tearing them in the process, while I try to undo her teddy. She'll laugh, push me away from her, and wiggle her way out of it.

She'll stand there before me only in her ripped stockings and stilettos. I'll lay her down on the white couch, her dark skin standing out beautifully against it. I'd run my hands over her body, cup her beautiful breasts, lick at her dark nipples, smother myself into her cleavage before my hands go down further, into her kinky pubic hair and down to her slit.

I'd open her up like a flower, her outer lips will be like soft petals, her scent intoxicating as my nose nuzzles against her clit. Her hands will massage my scalp, pull me closer to her as the tip of my tongue runs over a stud that will be pierced through her clit.

Her long legs will wrap themselves around my head, crushing me while I devour her. I'll pull back to feast my eyes on her while I quickly slip out of my own clothes. I'd lie on top of her in the 69 position, my legs straddling her head.

I quickly remove my clothing so I can touch myself, massage my breasts, finger myself while I think about what I'd do to her if she was really here in my bed with me.

I'd be fascinated by the colour of her dark skin and hair against my own light complexion and blonde hair. My hair would fall over her mound and for a moment the contrast of our colours would hypnotise me. She would pull at my hips, try to drag me down. Her scent will waft up to me, awaken me and I will ground my face into her, allow her juices to smear over my cheeks, lips, chin and mouth.

We'd ravish each other, pleasing, as only women know how. Later we'd lie on the couch locked in each other's arms.

"How did you know?" she'd ask.

"I didn't," I'd lie.

"I didn't want you to know," she'd say.

"Why?" I'd ask.

"Every time I live with a girl, their girlfriends always get jealous and I'm asked to leave. So I decided this time to play it cool, hide who I really was," she'd say.

"I can understand why people would get jealous of you. You're beautiful," I'd whisper into her hair, as I'd hold her tight.

"Come with me," she'd giggle. "I've got something to show you."

She'd lead me into her room and I'd watch her sexy arse sashaying provocatively before me. She'd lay me on her bed and retrieve a box from underneath.

"See anything in there that you like?" she'd ask.

It would be full of dildos and sex toys. Some I've never seen before. I'd pull out a huge black one with a tickler attached. I'd lift my eyebrows indicating I'm interested. She'd laugh and strap it on.

I'd lie back on her bed; my legs open and she'd kneel before me. She'd probe my outer lips, I'd reach up to pull her to me, kiss her hungrily on the mouth. I'd be able to taste myself on her lips and I'd grab her by the arse so the dildo could ram into me. She'd be amazing, having mastered the strokes so that in no time I'd be coming.

Oh, the thought of her and the dildo had me rubbing my clit wildly, my back arching as an orgasm builds up.

Then she'd roll me over, hoist up my hips and have me in the doggy position. This way the dildo would reach into the very depths of me, hitting my G-spot while the tickler tantalized my hole.

She'd be an amazing lover and we'd spend the whole day in bed together. Later, while lying in the bath, I'd want to broach the subject of her weekends away.

"So does this mean your Friday nights will change?" I'd ask.

"I don't see why," she'd say, allowing soapy bubbles to slide over my breasts as her hands caress me.

"I just thought maybe we could spend more time together?" I'd ask.

"We have all week," she'd say evasively.

"Yeah I know," I'd say. "But what if I want to take you out somewhere?"

"We'll talk about it when the time arises," she'd say. "What about Louise?"

"What about her?"

"You'll still see her, won't you?"

"Of course." The thought of a threesome would be uppermost in my mind.

"Good," she'd say "I don't want to spoil what we've got either. Our living together has always been comfortable."

I'd wonder why she wouldn't mention the warehouse and the group she is involved with. I wouldn't care. I'd hope that one day she'd initiate me into their ways. The thought of being tied up and at her mercy would definitely appeal to me. It would appeal to Louise too.

Louise. Still sexually aroused I pull myself away from this fantastic fantasy and decided to ring Louise.

"Hello," she said sleepily.

"Oh, sorry. Did I wake you?" I asked.

"What's wrong?" she wanted to know.

"Just wondering if you'd like some company. Thought we might pull out your box of toys and have some fun tonight."

"Do you know what time it is?"

"No, what?"

"It's four in the morning," she said.

"You're kidding," I said truly surprised.

I didn't realize my fantasy had gone on for so long.

"I'm feeling horny," I said.

"Obviously," she laughed. "Hurry up and get yourself over here, then."

We had the best sex ever that night and from now on I intend to conjure up lots of fantasies, thought I might even write about them, see if I can get them published. Let other people enjoy them as much as I did inventing them.

Three-Way Play

Heather (Dundee, Scotland)

Ever fantasized about your boyfriend or husband having sex with another man, or each other – while you watch? I have, repeatedly. After all, what's more exciting than seeing a beautiful man make love? Seeing two of them make love, to one another, of course; for the same, simple reason that men can't get enough of two gorgeous girls getting it on. And what's good for the gander, is good for the goose, in my humble opinion.

My sexual fantasies are chock full of hunky, naked men cavorting together, with one of those heated fantasies going a little something like this:

I sit down next to Brandon on the couch and say, "Tyler told me that he thinks you're quite the good-looking guy."

Brandon nods, never taking his eyes off the football match on the telly. "Guy's right."

I try again. "I mean, he thinks you've got a hot body. You're a hunk in his eyes." I look at Brandon shyly, hopefully.

"He's got a keen eye, babe," he responds, after cursing out his team's coach for putting on a substitute. "Free weights are the way to go. None of that isometric shit." He chugs his beer and munches some more pork rinds.

I shake my head. Brandon's a great boyfriend, in the physical sense – big and tanned and muscular, with short, blond hair, crystal-clear blue eyes, and an incredible eight-inch cock that can fill my pussy to the G-spot – but he isn't the sharpest knife in the drawer, by any means.

I tuck my hair in behind my ears and lean closer – so he can feel my soft, warm body against his. And, just to ensure myself his football-saturated attention, I slide my hot little hand over the top of the ever-ready bulge in his jeans. "I think that Tyler's attracted to you," I say, raising my eyebrows to encourage understanding.

He slowly peels his eyes off the TV screen and looks at my hand, my face, my eyebrows, and then grabs me by the shoulders and mashes his gob against mine. His thick tongue ploughs through my lips and into my tongue.

I struggle to push him off. "Did you hear what I said!?"

He licks his plush lips. "Yeah, babe. Sure I did. You're attracted to me. Tell me something I don't know." He plays with my tits through the thin fabric of my halter top.

"No! I said that Tyler is attracted to you!"

He softly pinches my aroused nipples, then holds onto them, comprehension beginning to dawn slowly on his handsome face. "Huh?" he asks.

"Yes," I say quickly. "I always thought that Tyler was straight, too. But lately he says that he's become attracted to men – men like you, Brandon."

Brandon shrugs. "Guy's got good taste," he says, then unlatches my nips and turns back to the football match, which is stalled with an injury.

I rub the big guy's cock. "Are you interested in Tyler at all?" I ask gently.

He looks at me when the game goes into half-time and commercials, and cups my tits, his cock hardening under my expert stroking. He bends his head and licks at my jutting nipples, quickly soaking the front of my top with his heavy tongue until my buds poke out at the wet material, straining to get free, and the humidity factor in my pussy climbs off the chart. "You wanna three-way with this Tyler guy? That it?" he asks.

I stare at him, surprised. "Uh, yeah. I mean, maybe . . . if you want to. How did you know?"

He sucks my nipples for a while longer, his hot, hungry mouth setting me on fire. Then the football match comes back on and he ends his boob play. "Babe, c'mon! You told me a three-way was one of your fantasies – 'bout six months ago," he says. "Remember? When I was shaving your pussy? Personally, I'd prefer another chick, but it's your fantasy, so what the fuck. Maybe next time it'll be my fantasy."

I nod. Like I said, not the sharpest knife, but he can really cut to the point with his razor-sharp memory when he wants to.

The next night, Brandon invites Tyler over to our apartment on the pretext that he needs some help decorating the place for my twentieth birthday party. Our plan – my plan – is that Brandon will seduce the sexually confused Tyler in our bedroom while I watch the gaiety unfold from a closet door left slightly ajar, and then join in as the icing on the sexual cake. Brandon isn't bi by nature, but he's the kind of stud who'd plug his dick into anything tight, if it'd get him off. All the better, he says, if it pleases me at the same time, which it will.

So, when Brandon and Tyler finally saunter into the bedroom, I'm already wet and wild with desire. My naked body courses with anticipatory electricity as I watch the two men sit down on the bed. Tyler is smaller and paler than Brandon, but just as strongly built, with deep, brown eyes, shoulder-length black hair, and an outline in the crotch of his jeans that surely can deliver what it promises.

"Anyways," Brandon says, "Heather told me you're attracted to me. Gotta say I'm flattered, mate, although I didn't even know you were gay."

Tyler blushes and looks away. "I – I'm not sure I am," he stammers. "I mean, I've had plenty of girlfriends, you know, but . . . well, I've been looking at some gay porn on the Internet, and . . . well, it's been turning me on, you know?"

Brandon scrunches up his face in an effort to look sympathetic, reflective even. Then he says, "Sure, mate," and drapes his arm over Tyler's wide shoulders in a gesture as wooden as his acting.

"You mean you – you're interested in me . . . that way?" Tyler asks, his face brightening.

Brandon grins like a used car salesman meeting an all-day sucker, flashing his strong, even, white teeth, sealing the deal. "Hey, man, I'm into anything and everything that gets me off, right?" And with that romantic patter out of the way, he kisses Tyler square on the lips.

I gasp and cup my left tit with one hand and squeeze, my other hand already occupied rubbing my swollen clit. This is it. Showtime!

Brandon places his hand alongside Tyler's face and starts kissing him more and more urgently, until he's grinding his lips into Tyler's red, full-bodied mouth. Tyler is initially taken aback by the strength of Brandon's ardour, but he quickly responds in kind, resting his hand on Brandon's muscled thigh and sticking his tongue into Brandon's open mouth. The two super-hunks French each other fiercely, as I frig my pussy faster and faster. What a beautiful, natural sight, I think to myself – two guys swirling their thick, glistening, pink tongues together – if only they'd get rid of their clothes.

As if by telepathic projection, the two he-men begin shedding their shoes and socks and jeans and shirts, and, finally, their shorts. Their inhibitions are already discarded on the floor somewhere, forgotten. When they are both sans clothing, the two Adonis's stand facing each other, nude and lewd and loaded with 'tude. Tyler's thick, muscular body is an ivory contrast to Brandon's rippling, bronze physique, and the package that Tyler normally hides in his denim turns out to be a handsome, nine-inch cock. I've never seen such an awesome specimen – in person, at least.

Brandon lets out a wolf-whistle. "Wow! You're packing some serious wood there, mate."

Tyler smiles. "It's all yours, if you want it."

"Daddy wants," Brandon responds, and grabs Tyler's monster cock and starts stroking. The two well-hung men kiss some more, their tongues slapping against one another, while Brandon eagerly polishes Tyler's rigid pole and Tyler tentatively grips Brandon's heavy rod.

I jam three of my fingers into my molten pussy and start pumping when Brandon drops to his knees in front of Tyler's ultra-long cock. And I vigorously knead my tit and roll my nipple when Brandon grabs the giant dick at its base and flicks his tongue across its mushroomed head.

"Yeah, Brandon," Tyler groans, "suck my cock."

"You got it, mate," Brandon replies matter-of-factly. He slaps his tongue across Tyler's slit, then balances the man's straining, arrow-straight cock on the end of his tongue and bounces it up and down.

After thoroughly tongue-lashing Tyler's cockhead with his slimy pleasure tool, Brandon closes his lips over the puffy purple hood and starts sucking. Tyler's knees buckle as he feels a man sucking his cock for presumably the very first time. More than one fantasy is flowering to reality in that bedroom right now. "God, that feels good, Brandon," Tyler moans, playing with his thick, pink nipples as Brandon mouths his cock-top.

Brandon sucks long and hard on Tyler's hood, playfully popping it in and out of his mouth until it glistens with hot saliva. Then the full-grown boy-toy licks up and down Tyler's long, hard shaft, painting Tyler's raging erection with his spit, slobbering all over the man's pulsating meat – up and down, up and down. He only stops tongue-buffing Tyler's cock when he jams his nose into Tyler's balls, uses his tongue to lick at the groaning man's heavy, furry testicles.

Tyler staggers back a couple of steps as the sheer sexual intensity of Brandon's balling, of the whole oppressively erotic situation, hits him like a ton of bricks. Brandon hangs onto Tyler's cock, however, and scooches forward and sucks on one ball and then the other, then cravenly sucks Tyler's entire sack into his mouth and tugs on it. He stares up at Tyler, his mouth full of man-sack, and Tyler's body trembles with joy.

Brandon can obviously sense that Tyler is already close to orgasm, as I am, because he disgorges the guy's tremendous balls, lets him settle down a bit, and then goes back to work on his mammoth cock. He gobbles down as much of Tyler's incredible length as he can, then bobs his head up and down, sucking on the swollen tool, slowly, slowly at first, then faster and faster and faster.

"Fuck, yeah!" Tyler cries out, desperately gripping Brandon's pumping blond head. He churns his hips in rhythm to Brandon's cock-sucking, jamming his member as far into Brandon's stretched-out mouth and throat as he can. "I'm gonna come!" he screams all too soon, his cock crammed to the balls inside my guy's talented mouth.

Brandon quickly pulls Tyler's soaking wet meat out of his

throat, and picks up with his hand where his mouth left off, winking at me to let me know that I'm going to see the whole show – money-shot and all. My smouldering snatch catches fire as my fingers blur, and a huge orgasm wells up inside my cunt. And just as I'm finger-fucking myself to boy-boy-inspired ecstasy, Tyler's huge cock erupts with an orgasm of his own.

"Jesus!" he shrieks, as Brandon buffs the guy's enraged cock with his hand. White-hot come rockets out of the tip of Tyler's gorgeous dick and splashes onto Brandon's face, into his open mouth.

Brandon jerks thick, steaming ropes of semen out of Tyler's cock and onto his tongue, all over his face, as Tyler and I are ravaged by blistering orgasms. Brandon's face is soon coated with Tyler's sticky, white goo, but he keeps right on pulling on the man-lover's spurting cock, anxious for more. Brandon milks and milks Tyler's cock, until, finally, Tyler's body convulses one final time and his cock spurts a last dollop of come onto Brandon's outstretched tongue. Brandon takes the spent cock into his mouth and sucks on it, as Tyler groans and strokes Brandon's hair.

Multiple orgasms have torn me apart as I watched Tyler face-paint my boyfriend with semen, but I still stumble out of the closet, weak as a kitten, and reveal myself and my need for yet further sexual adventure.

"Hi . . . Heather," Tyler gasps, catching his breath, seemingly not at all surprised to see me or my nudity.

"Hi, babe," Brandon chimes in, standing up and grabbing me in his arms and kissing me, the taste of Tyler's come still thick on his lips and tongue. "I got an idea how you guys can get me off, now," he says.

Tyler grins and nods. "I think I've got the same idea." He reaches under the bed and pulls out a strap-on that I've never seen before. "Think it'll fit Heather?" he asks Brandon.

"Mate, the question is: will it fit me? Right, babe?"

I smile up at him, realizing that I've been had, bad. Brandon has obviously pre-planned his "seduction" of Tyler, with Tyler, well in advance. I'm not complaining, though. Far from it. Instead, I snatch the strap-on out of Tyler's hands and quickly fasten it around my hips and over my cunt. The flesh-coloured imitation cock is almost as long and thick as Tyler's cock, and I wave it threateningly at Brandon. "Let's see if you can take what momma can dish out, big boy."

Brandon laughs and jumps on the bed and assumes the doggy-position, sticking his hard, round, sun-burnished arse in the air and wiggling it, daring me to shove my faux-cock inside of him. He and Tyler have obviously rehearsed their positioning ahead of time (which leads me to briefly, and enviously, wonder just how much "rehearsing" they've been doing together), because Tyler climbs onto the bed, rolls onto his back, and slides his head in between Brandon's muscled legs. The lusty men quickly begin sixty-nining each other as I gape in astonishment.

"If you wanna stay, you gotta play, babe," Brandon says to me, sucking and stroking his cocky friend to a second incredible hardness.

"Yeah, come join the party, Heather," Tyler says in a muffled voice. He smacks Brandon's studly cock against his lips, then sucks it into his mouth and gets a good, steady, wet rhythm going. His cheeks billow in and out with the effort, and Brandon groans.

It's about time I get into the act. I climb onto the bed and position myself such that my plastic man is pointing straight at the pink entrance to Brandon's beautiful bum. He stops blowing his fellow cocksman for a second, and reaches back and spreads his arse cheeks, inviting me to penetrate his pucker.

I glance uncertainly from my humungous, veined cock, to Brandon's tiny, tight starfish. Then I shrug my shoulders, slicken my artificial hard-on with spit, and press the size-large head up against Brandon's size-small opening.

"Fuck me, babe," he grunts. "Fuck me in the arse with your big cock."

I never would've thought I'd ever hear a plea like that from any boyfriend of mine, but his words drive me crazy, and I push my hips forward until the swollen head of my cock penetrates his arsehole. I begin to sink inside him as he moans encouragement, his own cock now buried almost to the balls inside Tyler's mouth. I recklessly push ahead and my cock plunges deeper into his arse, until, in a matter of tense, erotically charged seconds, I have my entire waist-mounted dildo stuffed inside of that boy's golden arse.

"Yeah," he groans, getting it from both ends. He tries to gobble up Tyler's cock, like he did before, but my thrusting hips smack against his bum faster and faster, jolting his body, making cock-sucking all but impossible. So, instead, he polishes Tyler's prick with his hand.

I grab onto Brandon's narrow waist and churn my hips, sliding my cock back and forth in his arse ever faster and more boldly, until I'm banging his pretty petoot like a drum, splitting him in two with my big-headed battering ram. His taut butt cheeks tremble with glee each and every time that I pound his bunghole with my cock, ripple joyously to the beat of my frenzied anal plunging.

And as I'm butt-fucking Brandon, Tyler keeps right on sucking him off, craning his neck so that he can gulp down as much of Brandon's glistening cock as he can, the breath whistling out of his flared nostrils as he mouth-strokes Brandon's meat. Brandon can only hang his head and arch his arse in dizzy disbelief, as he gets pumped from the rear and sucked from the front.

"Oh, man, I'm gonna come," he whimpers. "Babe and mate, I'm gonna come!"

I hang on tight to his sweat-slick hips and hammer away at his arse, my pussy blazing with the friction of the butt-pounding I'm giving my guy. My tits jounce up and down as I relentlessly plunder the stud's anus, my joy-toy diving deep inside his sun-kissed arse.

"I'm coming!" Brandon yells, and then his body spasms over and over in the throes of all-out ecstasy.

If he thinks that his warning is going to make Tyler disgorge his spurting cock, he's thankfully mistaken. Tyler keeps Brandon's dick firmly locked between his lips, buried in his throat, as Brandon sprays load after load of super-heated jizz into Tyler's mouth. Brandon's big, sweat-sheened body jerks in ecstasy each time he blasts another wad of semen up against Tyler's tonsils.

"Fuck almighty!" Brandon hollers, as I plug his arse and Tyler drains his cock.

When Brandon's heaving, brown body is at last still, I slowly slide my cock out of his violated bum and slap it up against his twitching arse cheeks. Tyler hand-jerks himself a few final drops of salty goo from Brandon's slick, softening meat, and captures them on his tongue.

Brandon lifts his head from Tyler's swollen cock and looks back at me. "Hey, babe," he gasps, exhausted and exhilarated, "let us know if you have any more fantasies. Maybe Tyler and I can help you with them, too."

. . . That's just one of the various hotter-than-hell man-on-man-on-woman fantasies that fill my free time, my idle hands. And there really is a good-looking guy named Tyler, only he's about as gay as Sean Connery, as is my beau Brandon, so the chances of the two of them ever getting together, let alone with Mr Connery, are just about nil. Thank God for Technicolor dreams and multi-speed vibrators!

Baltimore

Anya (Toronto, Canada)

I've made most of my living for the last few years as an erotic
model, sometimes porn actress. At times that has led to a
lifestyle that's admittedly pretty decadent, and situations that
are unusual to say the least. People ask me all the time what I
fantasize about – what is it that you like? Is there anything left
that you've yet to experience? Do you still have fantasies at all?
– but what I've found is that it's not what, but who. My
fantasies are inextricably linked to a person, to somebody, and
sometimes, to a particular place. I saw a man in Baltimore . . .
I've tried to recreate the circumstances just as they were, and
the fantasy just as I experienced it, so vividly it's become a
memory all of its own.

Baltimore surprised me, I have to say. I've become that jaded.
Edward's taken me to Las Vegas, New York City, Chicago. For
some reason, I was expecting less of Baltimore. But as we drive
back from spending the day in Annapolis, drive past the baseball
stadium – a re-creation from the golden era of baseball, a thing
of beauty – on the right the inner harbour glitters, and Baltimore
fascinates me. Maybe I've just had more time to myself here, to
explore it on my own, to find its elegant old heart. Edward lives
outside of the city, somewhere in the suburbs. At night, see, he's
got to go home to his wife.

He pulls the Audi up to the hotel entrance, glancing at his
watch. I give him a quick peck on the cheek and he smiles at
me, almost shy, shooting a quick glance up from underneath
his long grey bangs. "See you tomorrow," he says, "about two
o'clock."

I smile back into his pale, thin face. Edward's not a bad guy. He's got a lot of money, owns a company of some kind. Computers. Something like that. I wave and smile again as I climb out of the car, actually, I keep the smile plastered on for the benefit of the uniformed doorman and next the desk clerk, all the way to the elevator. I can let it go as the doors sigh shut, but a trace of it lingers on the corners of my mouth. Not such a bad day today, being touristy in Annapolis, eating seafood – chowder, crab cakes – and there's enough daylight left to take some pictures.

I discovered North Charles Street earlier, on my way to the Walter Art Museum and an afternoon of art through the ages. Without knowing anything much about architecture, I've become obsessed with beautiful buildings. There were so many along the way! Baltimore is an eclectic jumble of styles and periods, full of nooks and crannies that wait to be discovered. I hurry to my room, just grab the camera and run back to catch the elevator back down before someone else commandeers it.

The sun's just above the skyscrapers as I hurry along, still in my silk dress, the same blue as the early evening air, and mid-heel sandals not designed for hurry. Scuttling down the street as the light begins to fade, taking the pictures furiously. I frame the ornate storefronts, a church, businesses, they begin with skyscrapers and then drop to older levels. I like to discover their hidden angles, and look at them in opposition to the sky that they push against. It's never just glass and steel here (is this one neo-Baroque? neo-Classical?), even the concrete is ornate, doorways open to vast marble foyers. I snap and snap. The Baltimore & Ohio Railway Company, from Monopoly boards, B&O, from various angles, from just underneath the shadow of its doorway, then up against the doors and down the hallway to the now empty reception desk at the end, dwarfed by marble columns and a gallery above. My flash reflects against the glass doors and I push buttons on the camera to take it again without, although I doubt there's enough light to pick up much. Restaurants and bars and stores, all the way down to the museum again, then back to record the metal sculpture behind a government building.

Two films down and packed away, I'm just now noticing the way my feet are beginning to throb. I turn down another street, now just a block away from the hotel as the sun gasps its last violet breaths before disappearing from view. He's there on the sidewalk, along the side of an office building. He's wearing a loose red shirt, short-sleeved to show sculptured arms, and baggy jeans but I can see his strong neck. Full lips. Dreadlocks fall on his shoulders, just barely streaked with grey. I'm never scared in strange cities, even alone here as dusk is setting in – and maybe I should be – but here, with this purple falling over the buildings, I'm so taken with it, with the beauty and charm that seems to saturate the very air around me, I can't feel threatened by strangers.

"You look after yourself, young lady," he says. His skin is dark, chocolate brown, warm, his big eyes and generous features take in my silk dress, blonde hair and oh-so-much eye make-up.

"Oh, I will," and I smile into his earnest face, the lines around his eyes drawn into what looks like real concern. "I'm only going one more block," and I point to my hotel.

He nods approvingly. "Well, God bless," he says with a Maryland lilt. "You be careful."

I love their *God bless* around here, but I don't think I can pull it off, so I smile wider, he back in return, and he looks so warm, warm enough to touch, I'm almost drawn to lift my hand to his cheek before I stop the impulse. It's the mood of this place. But I hesitate only a moment, turning to continue to the hotel, still smiling.

My cell phone rings as I'm entering my room. "Hello?"

"It's Edward," he says, his voice is low and gravelly, like a good radio sports announcer.

"So it is," with a question in my voice. "What's up?"

"Listen, there's a meeting I forgot about, after lunch tomorrow, I won't make it over till 3:00 or 3:30," he says.

"Okay, Edward, I'll see you around 3:30, then."

His voice registers slight relief, "Good, good," then, "Damn!" he explodes. "I'm supposed to be meeting my partner and some . . . others." He stumbles a bit, and I think *why bother? Have I ever showed any interest in what you do for a*

living? You won't even tell me exactly what kind of business it is!
"For drinks in about ten minutes."

"Bye, then, or you'll be late." But I'm speaking into a dead receiver, he's already hung up.

I set down the phone and readjust to my hotel room, much the same in a generic chain in hundreds of locations around the world. I can finally kick off my sandals, sit in the generic armchair and watch TV. There's a bottle of wine I got earlier. I shrug out of my dress and take the bottle from the tiny beer fridge, flick on the television set and collapse in the chair. I could always go down to the hotel bar, like I did last night, flirt with the bartender and joke with travelling salesmen and conventioneers. Maybe it's all the walking today, but right now I just don't want to move. I stare at the flitting images of news reports, sitcoms and reality shows and drink a nice pinot noir. But at the back of my mind, he's hovering, the man on the sidewalk. Edward's never concerned about me, never even asks how I am. But then again, it's not really part of our deal, is it? I'm supposed to look out for myself.

He's never bothered to find out, never so much as wondered how I've been amusing myself until he gets here. Whether I feel safe. Even if I do, but should that matter? Edward leaves me alone till late tomorrow afternoon, so much time between my early morning swim and 3:30 in the afternoon. I wonder if he works around here, lives around here. My friend, I mean. My warm hearted friend. If I could find him, somehow run into him again. What would happen if I got all dolled up again for breakfast tomorrow morning, and as I'm coming down the sidewalk right around that same block, he was there? I can see him so clearly, rounded face, so dark, such gorgeous smooth skin, and the body of a man who might've once been an athlete, or maybe a construction worker, solid with big shoulders. I search my memory for his image, peering into the neckline of his shirt, trying to follow the line of his shoulders to the skin of his chest.

He'll be right there, and it'll be later in the morning, when all the office workers are already in their cubicles, leaving sparse traffic on the sidewalk around us. I'll smile, he'll nod and smile back. And I'll see it again, in his eyes, the connection, the understanding I felt. I know what people think, this well-dressed woman, travelling alone, walking alone at night, frequenting downtown hotels and bars. Two plus two is always four. But he understood the part about being so solitary all the time, and maybe in the slight shabbiness of his clothes I can guess at why, but it doesn't matter, only that I saw his warmth and heard a sweetness in his voice. He'll ask me how I got back to my room, politely, and I'll answer, *Just fine, thank you, that was sweet of you*, and hesitate as I walk by, I'll wait for another sign of interest, but I won't be able to wait for too long, so I'll probably turn back to him and ask *Would you like to go out for a coffee? Or something . . .?* with a small laugh.

He'll be surprised, but in a happy kind of way, pleased, he'll say *Well, all right, young lady*, with his musical intonation, and we'll go about a block or two, just enough time for him to take in my smile, my short skirt and Italian leather pumps. Maybe he'll laugh, shake his head. *Where should we go?* I'll ask, leaning close to him, looking in his dark eyes, smiling *You tell me. This is the first time I've ever been to Baltimore*, and he'll answer slowly, *I've got coffee at my place, if you want coffee. Or something . . .?* He'll look at my face carefully as he smiles, to see if he's got it right, using my words, and I'll simply tuck my arm into his, slide my hand into his hand with a squeeze. *I'd love to.*

We chuckle together as he leads me back to North Charles Street.

"I'm up there." He points to big windows above a bistro, stairs that walk up in art deco, it looks like a loft with big rooms, the art museum, the square with a tall monument, are just down the street.

"Looks beautiful," I tell him. "I bet it's full of light."

He nods; his face creases with pleasure. "You could say that, for sure. It's filled with light." He goes ahead to lead me between the buildings to an entrance off the back. "You be careful, watch your step." And he stops to give me his hand. We must be behind the restaurant here, a hallway that goes around the back of the building. There's a staircase at the other side, big and wide, worn wooden floors that look more comfortable than shabby, the banister heavy and ornate. I take two steps and his hand snakes around my waist from the step below, then drops to slip under my skirt and touch my cheeks lightly with his big palm. I hurry up the steps, that featherlight touch of his fingertips on my arse, I giggle and press up a little faster.

"You're tickling me," I tell him, and he laughs low and deep and tickles me on purpose, till somewhere between the second and third floor, here, the sunlight filters through dusty windows that look out on the street from the landing above, it splashes here in a pool of light and I turn, stop, take both his hands and pull them around me, I pull him down to lean over me, to kiss him, my fingers sliding under his waistband to hold the muscle that curves underneath.

"Baby." He just breathes it, our tongues find each other and we're lost to time, soft wet lips and tongues, pressing myself up to the hard muscle of his chest, exploring the contours of his arm with my fingertips inside his sleeve while his lips taste me softly, delicately, like he wants to carefully savour every single second.

"I want you so very much," I tell him, I whisper it into his ear and stroke the thin skin on the inside of his wrist. "Do you want me?"

"Baby, I haven't wanted anything this much in ten years!" It's spontaneous, and unmistakably genuine. We both laugh at the urgency of his voice, till he whispers, "Shh . . ." into my ear back, and I nod against his shoulder, still shaking with silent laughter. We listen to cleaners bump and bang around in the restaurant below, their distant voices joke and gossip through the stairwell. He talks to me, the words run together and his voice is deep, and full now of a seductive music.

"Baby, let's take that off," and my dress slips over my head, my fingers pull at the buttons on his shirt. His chest is big, rounded.

"You play football?" I ask him, and he's shy, sheepish in reply.

"Not for so many years." He lowers his eyes under thick lashes, I have to laugh at him. "I'm way out of shape. Getting fat."

"Oh, no," and my hands reach for him, we switch places in a

slow ballet. I ease into his lap, brushing his nipples with mine, pulling his arms around me again. "Not out of shape at all. You're so beautiful."

"No, that's *you* baby," he says, "*you're* beautiful," and I watch his thick fingers touch my pale hair, stroke my pale skin, feel my breasts and warm them, watch him flick his tongue over my nipples until they're small and hard.

Omigod . . . my chest against his, *omigod*, I feel it as it seizes me from inside, twists in my gut in a delicious thrill of wet desire, a stab of excitement and I gasp, I feel myself melting against the hard bulge of his cock inside his pants, and, "We should go inside."

He laughs at me, lifts me up out of his lap, steadies me when I can't find my way to stand for a moment or two. I laugh and point at the strained zipper of his fly. Some shred of common sense remains, I grab my dress from the step with one hand as he takes the other and we go upstairs, first he leads, then I start to run, giggling again, and he follows me up to the third floor, just down the hallway, and a big wooden door marked 3B.

"Is this the one?" I ask, and he nods, he opens it while I wait impatiently. Then inside it's as sunlit as I imagined, dark red carpet on wooden floors, old ornate furniture and kitchen cupboards. I'm rarely more than a few inches from him, for hours that melt into our very own space and time. The afternoon is spent in his brown eyes, inside his strong arms, I feel the different surfaces against my skin – wooden floor, carpet, kitchen counter, the sheets on his bed – because I won't go until I've tasted him over and over.

"What do you like?" he asks me once, and I just tell the truth, "Everything," and I laugh but I press against him so he knows it's true. "I want everything, that's all, I want to do everything with you."

I want all of you. I'm greedy for his warmth, his skin against mine, his lips, his warm skin inside of me, the way he holds me while he penetrates, slides in and out while the only sound is gasping breaths, his hands around me, the way he fills me up, greedy on this golden afternoon for his tongue in my mouth, between my legs, his fingers that stroke and push inside of me.

The hotel phone rings. It surprises me out of my imaginings,

the fingers of one hand are still wet, still touching my pussy,
and I reach for the phone without thinking with the other.
"Hello?"

"Hi, it's Edward. Meeting's over, and I'm about five minutes away, as it turns out. I thought, since I won't see you so
much tomorrow, I thought I'd drop by."

"Sure," and my voice is honeyed, I'm still bewitched and,
now aware, I need to hang on to the mood, because to fall out of
it, and straight into sex with Edward, that would be too much
of a crash.

So I take the second bottle of wine from the bar fridge, glad
that it struck me earlier, maybe out of some glimmer of fore-
sight, to take advantage of the two for one special. There's
some pinot noir left, but I want the second now, a sparkling
white, to keep me over the edge, to sustain some of this divine
state of mind for Edward's visit as I get ready for him. He's at
the door before I know it. I let him in, and hand him a glass of
my bubbly without a word, just a smile and his favourite view –
from behind, with the black lace panties and high heels, (the
ones that tie around my ankles). His face flowers into absolute
delight. It's such a small gesture, really, dressing – or undressing – for him, and I'm feeling so expansive. Edward is flabby
and white, has little imagination, but at the back of my mind,
just behind my eyes, the purplish dusk settles on the buildings
of Baltimore, and my big warm lover waits down there on the
sidewalk.

Edward's not sure what's happening to him. I am *inspired*, I
make love to his flesh in a way that was never before possible.
He's smart enough not to question any of it, just go with the
flow, and I let it all drop over him, the overflow, sublimely
generous, leaving till tomorrow to think about how I can make
one man so happy while my head's so full with somebody else.

Later, when Edward's gone, I'm filled with lassitude but not
tired enough to sleep. I pour myself the last dregs of wine, go
sit on the windowsill to peer down at the street, and wonder,
can I get that magic I felt on the sidewalk, down there behind
the courthouse as the night fell on Baltimore, there beside the
sculpture, (and I can see the tip of it now,) can I get that magic
to work for me again?

My Seven Lovers

Kim (San Diego, USA)

I am sitting on the bus after a long day at work (I'm a nurse in a small and dull hospital) and there are six men and one other woman here with me. They vary in ages, and each of them I find attractive, one way or another. I begin wondering what they look like naked, what kind of lovers they are. I start to imagine that they are all my lovers. Not at the same time, of course, this isn't some kind of wild bus ride orgy. Each is a secret lover.

I. Who Are My Lovers?

Steve

He's thirty, works as a medical engineer. He comes up with new equipment designs for doctors to employ – and he has lots of money, a good catch for any woman with marriage on the mind (which I am not). He's the younger brother of:

Curtis

He's forty-three. He's my boss at work (but in bed, I'm the boss and the one who holds the whip and uses it). He's married and has two daughters younger than me; it seems one of them briefly dated:

Tim

He's eighteen, a senior in high school. He gets hard pretty fast right after orgasm . . . again and again. *Oh, the young boys!* say the older ladies. Hey, I might as well have sex with a younger guy if I'm going to be with older men, eh? Speaking of older dudes, I don't know if you'll believe this, but you're just going to have to believe it because there is:

Hank

He's seventy. Yes, that's right. *Oh, wicked me.* He's a professor emeritus type; he writes books on political history. Sometimes I do work for him, and sometimes I let him fuck me. He has a lot of stamina and staying power for a man his age (I can't help but be impressed by that); he's quite fit, muscular, and probably the best fuck I've ever had (really!), next to:

Larry

He's fifty-two. He's my stepfather – or should I say ex-stepfather? He's no longer married to my mother, and now he's one of my lovers. He's been my longest lover, off and on, which I'll explain a little later. Yes, it sounds sordid, and it *is* sordid, but *I'm* sordid, and so is:

Ron

He's twenty-two, my age. He's your normal southern California guy with the tan, the muscles, the tattoos, and even the baseball cap. He doesn't have much in his head and that's fine by me. I like hanging out with him and he's a nice hard fuck, and so is:

Bethany

With all these men, I need a female lover too – variety, of course. Pussy (never "cunt", I hate that word) can be just as good as dick. Bethany is pure lesbian and if she knew I put dick inside me, she would probably vomit. She's twenty-five, a lipstick lesbian, petite and bouncy. You see, I'd never gone to bed with a woman, I wanted to try it, Bethany came along, it happened. I enjoy what we do in bed, so we do it a lot now and then, when I can fit her in my schedule with all these others.

II. How I Met My Lovers

Curtis

I've been sleeping with him for two years now, ever since I left Alaska and moved to warm and sunny southern California: San Diego. I'm not sure who made the first move, but I was attracted to the man and had sex with him in the office, and later in motel rooms.

Steve

Curtis' wife and kids were out of town one weekend so I spent the night with him. His brother made an unannounced visit. Curtis came up with some story that I was helping with extra work but Steve knew what was going on. Steve had his brother's looks. I slipped Steve a note: *Call me* with my number. When he called, I said, "I really *was* helping your brother with extra work."

"Yeah?" Steve said. "With what? Mid-life crisis?"

"I didn't want you to get the wrong idea."

"Is *this* why you wanted me to call you?"

"No."

"I didn't think so."

"I was hoping you'd ask me out on a date."

"Oh," he said.

When he picked me up that night, I said, "Forget the dinner and the movie, let's just fuck."

"You're very fast," he said.

"I don't like to waste time," I said.

A week later, Steve told me that he didn't want to fuck me if I was fucking his brother. "That's *too* weird," he said. I lied and said his brother was a one-time thing, that I didn't like seeing married men . . .

Tim

I met him on the beach. You got it: he surfs. His long blond hair is very cute. He thinks it's cool to be fucking an older woman – five years and I'm "older".

Ron

Met him at a party; he and two of his friends got me into a bedroom. I knew what was going on. The three of them fucked me on the bed. Ron stayed, looking guilty. He kept saying that he was very sorry that he and his friends raped me. I told him it wasn't rape, I knew what they were up to, I played along, I wanted to get laid just like he and his buddies did. He didn't believe me, maybe he thought he'd get in trouble. To prove my sincerity, I gave him a blowjob and later went home with him where we stayed up all night and screwed our happy heads off.

Bethany

She's a graduate student at the college where Hank is an emeritus. She had done some work for Hank; it was at Hank's house that we first met. I knew she was gay, I saw her give me The Look. I gave her The Look back. One time, we went out and had some beers. "Do you like to munch carpets?" she asked me. I told her no but said, "I'd like to try."

Hank

Okay, I saved the two sordid tales for last. Yes, the man is seventy and no, I never pictured myself ever in bed with a man his age. But it happened, and this is how: like I said, he writes books on the politics of the past. History and the behind-the-scenes matter of governments. "Some call me a militarist," he once said, "but I am, in fact, a realist. And," he added with a wink, "quite robust." An out-of-town friend, a man in his early fifties, came in for a visit and I wound up in bed with him. One time only. But Hank found out. "Why him," Hank asked, "and not me?" So I said to Hank, "I'll go to bed with you, one time and one time only." But he was such a fantastic fuck I came back for more, and more and more.

Larry

Well, like I said, he used to be married to my mother – not for a long time, something like two years. They were dating for a bit, went to Vegas, got drunk, got married, and the next time I had sex with Larry he said, "Guess what? I'm your Daddy now!" I hit him and told him not to joke. When my mother told me about the Vegas marriage, I was very angry at Larry. I told Larry that I would never sleep with him again as long as he was my "stepfather". Oh, he tried, though, and despite the fact that I really liked sex and liked sex with him, I did not give in. So the day the divorce was final, I went to Larry and gave him a big sloppy blowjob. "Oh, what I've been missing!" he said. "We have a lot of catching up to do," I said.

III. Six Cocks & One Pussy –
A Brief Description of the Genitals of My Lovers

Curtis

It is short, maybe five and a half inches, but it's very thick. *Thick is good.* I like the feeling of being stretched out. His balls are big and dangle to and fro when he walks around without underwear.

Steve

He's thick like his brother but about an inch longer . . . and his balls are small.

Bethany

Let me insert her pussy here, among all these dicks. Her pussy is shaved, unlike mine (but I've been thinking about it). It has tiny lips, unlike mine. It squirts when reaching orgasm, unlike mine. It tastes so sweet, unlike mine, which I know is a little bitter (or tastes so when I suck a cock straight out of my cunt).

Hank

Big, thick, meaty, veiny – with a huge bulb of a head. And it stays hard for two to three hours. This is why getting fucked by the old guy is so great.

Ron

It's uncut. I like staring at it, hiding under all that foreskin – and then peekaboo, it pops out!

Tim

It is curved like a banana. The curve does wonders on my clit and makes me have multiple orgasms.

Larry

It's an average-looking, average-sized dick except a small piece of the head is missing, and he has only one testicle. The single testicle thing is a birth defect, the missing piece, he told me, "is a war wound left by my first wife. The night she knew it was over she acted like everything was okay, so we fooled around, she was giving me head and then she bit me. She spit the piece of me out and said: 'Now you'll never forget me.' And I never have." And I said the woman must have been fucking crazy.

IV. Crazy

And so am I – I'm sure that's what you're thinking. In this day, this age, I have this many lovers . . . and none of them know about each other . . . I could have more, the opportunities present themselves but I manage to curb my enthusiasm. I work them into my schedule and try my best to avoid not having sex with more than one each on any single day. But there is one day I have to confess about –

V. Oh, That One Wild Day of Pure & Constant Fucking

This was a Saturday. It started early, real early – at 5:30 a.m. I was sleeping in Tim's bed and he woke me up for a morning quickie. That's always a nice way to wake up. Then he got into his wetsuit, grabbed his board, and said, "Gotta catch those early waves, babe."

"Have fun."

"See ya, babe."

"Bye," I said, watching his ass as he walked out the door.

I couldn't sleep. I dressed and started to drive home. I was hungry. I called Steve on my cell, knowing he would be awake and working on some kind of engineering problem.

"Meet me at I-Hop," I said.

"This is a surprise," he said.

"I need pancakes," I said.

"Pancakes sound good," he said.

We had pancakes and eggs and then went back to his place for a quickie. He said he was on a breakthrough and wished he could spend the whole day with me. I told him that was okay, gave him a kiss, and was back at my place by ten. I was just about to kick back and watch some morning cartoons when Ron called. He was in the area. I told him to come on over. I was suspicious about his "being in the area".

"Actually I'm on my way to the airport," he said. "I wanted to see you . . ."

"Flying? Where to?"

"Las Vegas."

"Gambling?"

"There's a girl there."

"Oh, I see."

"I wanted to tell you . . ."

"What's her name?"

"Rachel."

"Nice name."

"Are you mad at me?"

"No," I said, and smiled.

"You're always evasive about getting serious," Ron said, "and Rachel . . . she wants to be serious."

"What does she do in Vegas? Black jack dealer? Dancer?"

"She's just a teller at a bank."

"Well, go see her," I said.

"You're mad, I can tell."

"I'm not," I said, and I wasn't. How could I be? I had no right to be.

"We can still be friends," he said.

"We can be *good* friends," I said.

"Really?"

"Really," I said. "Let me show you what good friends can do for each other," and I got down on my knees and sucked him off.

I watched him drive away, from my window, his semen still swishing in my mouth . . . and I felt sad. I felt like I'd lost something.

I laid down to take a nap.

At noon, my cell rang. It was Curtis.

"My wife will be gone all day, she took the kids to see her mom," he said. "I'm alone here. Why don't you come over . . .?" His voice was low and sexy.

"Isn't that risky?" I asked.

"It's always been that," he said. "Hmm?"

"Well," I said. "I don't know . . ."

"I'm your boss," he said.

"This is my day off."

"You must do what I say."

I could not resist, of course. I told him I'd be there in an hour. I showered, brushed my teeth, washed out my mouth with Listerine, and drove to Steve's house. He asked if I was hungry for lunch and I said I was. He made sandwiches and we drank some wine and kissed for a while. Then he took me to the bed he shared with his wife.

"I want your arse," he said, "will you let me stick it in your arse?"

"Always, honey," I said. I let him fuck me this way even though I didn't care all that much for it; I let him do it whenever he asked because he said his wife would never let him but when he got to do it with me, he always got giddy and happy – and that made me happy.

I was driving home at 3:30 p.m. when Hank called my cell. He said he couldn't find a file folder he needed for his research. He sounded frantic. I told him to calm down and drove to his house. Turns out this was a ruse, he just wanted to see me, to fuck me. I said I'd give him a blowjob but he said he really needed to be in my pussy. After that backdoor action with Steve, leaving my arse stinging, some pussy action sounded nice.

While Hank fucked me for a couple of hours, my cell rang three times.

Leaving Hank's, I checked my messages. It was Larry. His messages: "Please call ASAP." I hoped nothing was wrong. I called and he said: "I just needed to hear your voice."

"What is it?"

"I miss you," he said.

"I miss you too."

"What are you wearing?"

"Nothing, I'm naked."

"You're driving."

"I'm driving naked."

"Touch your pussy for me," he said, "touch it . . ."

So I had phone sex with him as I drove. I listened to him come and smiled, feeling powerful.

I called him back when I got home and we had more phone sex, I played with my clit and he listened to me come.

An hour later, the cell rang and I figured it was Larry, ready for more phone, but it was Bethany.

"Let's have dinner," she said.

"Okay," I said.

"What do you want?"

"Your sweet pussy," I said.

"That's dessert."

"Whatever you want."

"I want to make dinner for you," Bethany said. "I want to cook for you, okay?"

"Okay."

I got into a really short yellow dress, thin fabric, no underwear or bra; I arrived at Bethany's apartment at 8:00 p.m. She was naked, but wore an apron and high-heels. I could smell pasta being cooked, and all the lights were out, except for two candles on the dinner table. And a bottle of red wine.

"Wow," I said.

"I want tonight to be special and romantic," she said, kissing me deeply and grabbing my left tit with one hand and my right arse cheek with the other.

I grabbed her too.

Our tongues tangoed for three minutes.

"Tonight *will* be, sweet thing," said I.

And *oh*, it was.

Nassau Hangover

Rene (Edinburgh, Scotland)

I, Rene Mountbatten, sat in a little corner of the, oh, so elegant hotel lobby. I made a wish for action – any kind of action. My mouth grated, dry as the Sahara – all the booze last night; my guts churned – too much food; my head thumped – a terrible flight.

My husband, Ben, had told me that he wanted to play cards with some idiots who were on the plane. Hated cards. I had wanted a good shag and it was plain he hadn't.

A man sat near me and flicked through a *New York Times*. This was my chance. I did not want to talk to women today; I spent my life with women. Three daughters and a surgery full of nurses and receptionists are enough for anyone. I am a sexist, bad, socially inappropriate bitch and need deep voices today.

He introduced himself as Solly Wittenberg. "My wife's originally from Montreal. Jean. French. I'm from Buffalo. We live in Detroit." A nice little potted bio. Couldn't have been much shorter.

The specimen of American manhood was incredibly sexy. Why and how? An orderly bulge vibrated between his pants. His face was the kind with hollows under his cheeks. I'm a sucker for hollow faces. His lips curled as if about to smile. My headache was suddenly gone. Instead, I had an ache somewhere in my lower belly, an ache crying out for some medicine.

I tightened against the fine cotton of my shorts. He breathed as if a mass of electrons zapped in random – fizz, buzz all over him, vibrant. He floated across from me, his body hardly putting any weight on the seat. I imagined the tight soft depressions in his behind; I dreamed his clean-man air. I wove fantasies of touching him, sucking him, tasting him, swallowing him. I pulled his skin inside me, my skin inside his.

I cried in pain deep inside myself while they talked about the European Union, Scotland . . . I heard my own voice prattling on about the medical services in the UK compared with those in North America . . . and he was getting pissed off. All I could think about was the movement of his back as he thrust deep into me.

My family had often told me that I don't have conversations but give lectures. No foreplay is as good as listening to a man's voice and having that same man listen to my voice. I had to keep him with me. He had an aura of expensive body lotion. His hair curled and trembled off the tight skin of his face. I sensed myself feeling it between my fingers, comparing it to the fine curly hair he must have around his balls and cock; I imagined myself familiar with all his sweat and pores.

I said, "There's a part in Fay Weldon's book *Darcy's Utopia* when a character says . . ." Shit, this sounded boring. He was going to leave.

He replied, "Fascinating. Interesting. Something to be considered." By the blank daze on his face, he was praying to some god to take this dull, tedious woman out of his life. Beam me up, Scottie.

Oh, this man will have a long, thick, firm pink dink; I tasted it, the flavour made the skin of my mouth soft, warm; flesh, flesh, flesh. Lust always turned me into a guppy: mouth, no brain.

He asked politely, "You vacationing with your husband?"

"He's around. Ben. Playing cards. Something like that." I itched to get down and unzip him. Nothing filled my head but sex, sex, sex. All the time sex. Other people have proper thoughts about politics, business, art, work, brain surgery, economics, buying bread. He has deep brown cow's eyes. If he closed them, I could lick the lids gently. Run tiny kisses up the uneven bridge of his nose." . . . our problems in Scotland . . .

"I sounded so authoritarian, so full of bullshit. Buddy, you are talking to the original nut here. He stood and held a hand out for me to shake. Such manners! I took it, shook it. I did not bend down, kiss it, infuse the jasmine of his flesh into my head, slide it right up between my legs. He pulled me up. We held hands for a moment too long. Too long in the best Harlequin fashion we were locked in gentle combat.

"See you around, no, doubt," he said.

"Hopefully," I said and regretted my shorts and shirt, my socks and my shoes; regretted the hotel, wild for a jungle, wild for a deserted beach, a wild underbrush. Blink. Life is real. Life is wooden. "See you around." Stood waiting until he was gone as if I were a statue, frozen to the spot. The Greek statues were blind. If I had no eyes I couldn't see him, couldn't imagine sex with him.

Perhaps it was time to find husband? Must be time for lunch. In the daytime cave of the bar my "better half" sat with three other people – two women and a man. They were vaguely familiar. They had been on the same plane. I hadn't talked to them. He talked to everyone, bouncing up and down the aisle like a bad child. Mr Sociability when it suited him.

He half stood. "Hello, love, this is Jack and Linda and Linda's sister, Fiona. They're from Hamilton. My wife, Irene. We're all playing."

Play? What? Where? With whom? Why?

"Poker. Playing poker. Want to play?" he said without much enthusiasm, his words slurred.

They all appeared to have had a bellyful to drink and seemed *happy*. I did not want drunken, *happy* talk.

"It's almost time for lunch," I said, detecting a very definite whine in my voice.

He laughed. "That's Rene! Always looking after my precious tummy." He focussed on cards as he talked.

"Well, it's time for lunch and I'm hungry. Are you coming soon?"

"No, I'm playing cards right now, can't you see? When the game is finished, then I'll have lunch. Not before." His voice cut through me, cold as ice. This was going to be a fantastic, exciting, thrilling holiday. When he spoke in iambic pentameter, I knew it was going to be bad.

"Fine. Can I have the room card, please? If it's not too much trouble and doesn't interfere with your game too much. I have a need to freshen up before lunch." I was excessively polite. He handed me the security card.

Had to pee. Wondered if I could find the room again in this labyrinthine place. Strayed along identical corridors. A sign said rooms 302–350. The door to my room was open. Their suitcases stop between the beds. I went in. The man from Buffalo sat on the toilet. The extractor fan buzzed.

"What the hell are you doing in my room?"

He didn't seem at all perturbed. "I would imagine it's clear enough what I'm doing. I had to go and the door was open. Guess the maids left it open. They were occupied, must have thought it was my room. My wife has the keycard to our room. They only give you one. Something faulty with the machine. Nothing works in this hotel. When a man has to go a man has to go." I didn't mind a stranger using the room for a fast pee but this wasn't right, not right at all.

"You should go."

"What harm am I doing?"

"It's my room and I want it to myself."

"Are you giving me time to wipe my arse? Finished, anyway." He did the necessary, washed his hands and left the room without saying anything.

Now I would have the room to myself. My own hotel room, this home for the next two weeks. The holiday was all paid up, the plane did land, his mother had been bribed to keep the children so we can have this "second honeymoon". Second honeymoon? Knew it was a stupid idea. Wasn't the first honeymoon in "Romantic Bermuda" bad enough? One long fight. Ben and I did just fine when we saw little of each other. I would not play cards on holiday. Not cards. I sprayed the room with Xanadu. Peed. That was better. God! I'm beautiful – so the dressing-table mirror announced. Took off my blouse and bra. God, I'm beautiful. Ben didn't know what he was missing. Silence. Peace. Cupped my hands and sniffed them. The man was on my skin. My own sweat wafted up to me. Peace after the roar of the engines. Rubbed oil on my nipples and they stood out red and hard. I had to have the most beautiful nipples in the world. Turned round to look at my butt. Not bad for a lady of thirty-something with three children. Not bad at all. Not a rear-end to be ashamed of. Took my new bikini out of the case and dragged off my shorts. This totally beautiful naked woman. God, I'm beautiful. I lay on the bed and concentrated on how the holiday should go.

For a start there would be a knock on the door. I would be naked.

"Who is it?"

"It's me, the man from Buffalo. Forgot my book. Can I retrieve it, please?" His voice soft and polite.

God, this man is too polite. Politeness deserves politeness in return. He used my toilet uninvited and I will answer the door naked.

He drifted past me as if he was used to people who answered the door naked.

I reclined on the bed, leaned on one elbow. I was in the mood for . . . whatever.

"I left it on the chair beside the bed." He found it and stood holding it. "Going swimming?"

Stupid question. His short tight blond curls glistened in the shuttered afternoon sun. He had to have the blondest hair ever seen on man. Not fair for a man to have such beautiful hair. I ran my hands up and down my legs, stroked a nipple. "Getting changed. Felt tired. Needed a rest. You flew in today? Is the book any good?" I combed the rich, black hair between my legs with my fingers. The curtains drifted in and out in the gentle breeze of the air-conditioner.

"Detroit. The book is good. Took your suggestion and picked up *Darcy's Utopia* in the shop across the square. They have a good selection. Started it when . . ." He indicated the toilet.

I nodded. "How nice. Yes. Nice. What do you do?"

"Flower business. What do you do?"

"Nice to have a flower shop. What do I do? Doctor. Skins."

Long, long legs finished somewhere under his arms. I would have given my right arm to have legs like that. He wore short, short, blue shorts and every fold of his body knobbed plain under them. He sat on the edge of the bed and fondled the cover. A long slow shrug. Every cell of my skin tingled, exploded, effervesced.

He said, "It's cool here. We're in the other block, the annexe
. . . cold there but cool here."

I shifted over slightly so he could have some room. "How
was your flight?"

Oh, this conversation was moronic. I knew it and I knew he
knew it. I would have to create something better than this.

"Same as yours, I guess. Boring."

I stroked my belly, imagined it was his belly. "Husband is
playing cards. Hate cards. Not much point in coming on
holiday and being bored, is there? Especially when it's a second
honeymoon."

"Yours, too?" he said. "It's our second honeymoon too."

"Funny that, isn't it? Both on second honeymoons and my
husband playing cards. Well . . . now he's shit-faced."

"My wife departed on a bus tour. Detest them. Usually I
ends up in some bar picking up someone to talk to. She's
amused by talking to strangers. Never talks to me. Well . . .
sometimes talks but never listens. Same, every holiday. Talk,
talk, all the time."

"That's nice. Better than playing cards. What's her name?"

"Lisanne. And yours – I mean your husband's?"

"Ben."

"That's nice. And yours?"

"Rene." He toed off his sandals and rested back against the
pillows. "You smell nice," he said.

"Thanks." I bent over and sniffed behind his ears. "So do
you." He had large strong ears. I liked ears. Ears are the nicest
part of a man I sometimes thought. I licked the lobes one by
one. "Ummm. Now you."

He lightly feathered each nipple with his lips and then licked
them; he rolled them round in his mouth, turn about turn. So
delicately, it was hardly a touch. He folded my breasts together, the dark line between them concentrating the oil I had
used earlier. He ran his tongue down the valley, down my belly
down to my belly button. I took in a deep breath. Lovely. I
nibbled up and down his strong thick biceps. He tasted of clean
flesh, chocolate, mineral water, gin, honeysuckle . . .

He slipped off his shirt and lay back on the bed. His giant
hard-on pushing against the denim of his shorts. I got up and

locked the door. Let Ben Dearest come and bang on it. He should have taken up the invitation when it was offered. I worked too hard to miss one day of holiday. The only sound was the hum of the air conditioner and the occasional crackle of starched sheets.

Solly was smiling and drinking in my body. Oh, I could tell he liked it. I sat on the bed and looked down at him. Unzipped his shorts and tugged them down. He was beautiful. He was plainly a man who kept himself fit. Not a spare bit of flab on that body. Tight. The muscles of his abdomen rippled as I ran my fingers up and down them. His balls were neat and tucked in. His circumcised cock rested like a tree trunk, thick, solid, against the hollow of his belly. I bent down to nuzzle him. Big on nuzzling, I was, like a cat. A man had to smell right for me. Yes, male musk, clean sweat. I licked his cock up the shaft and finished with a kiss on the tip of his nub.

"No way. My turn, first," he said and sat up. He stretched me out so I was exposed on the bed absolutely straight. He kissed me, running his tongue round and round just inside my lips. He lifted my arms right above my head and kissed under each arm in turn. He sniffed me like a dog sniffs a tree.

"I always sniff. Scents really turn me on."

"Funny. Me too."

"You smell like jasmine."

"You smell like vanilla."

He moaned and sucked my nipples, rolling them round and round. "Your tits taste of brandy."

I sighed. I was going to rise off the bed and fly like an angel. It had been so long since I had a good fuck I could come any minute. All of my body cried out for it. Cried. Wept. Moaned. Shouted.

He crouched down between my legs and opened me like a flower. He divided the thick black hair so he could see what he was doing. In the mirror of the sliding door of the wardrobe, I saw this gorgeous man bending over the body of this beautiful woman and I was amazed that it was Rene. He spread my lips gently to expose my clitoris and ran his fingers down it as nimbly as warm water tumbles over pebbles in a tropic stream. I raised my body to his face. He wet a finger and just touched the tip of my clitoris. Then the tip of his tongue contacted it. He rolled his tongue into me as if it would reach right into me as far as my cervix. Now he was pulsing his own rhythm, he was moving with me, his tongue circling, circling and rolling against me. He relaxed away from me and I tried to tip his head back to its place but he sat up and kissed me. I tasted myself and him mixed: his lips and the slightly sweet love juice of my own. My orgasm was building up from my vagina into my chest, right into my head. He reached over and fumbled in the pocket of his shorts and took out a small packet.

"Well done," I said.

"Always prepared," he said.

"Me too, but they're in the suitcase." I sat up on his thighs. He opened the packet and took the condom out. I laughed. "Good god! What on earth?" He had a blue condom, with gold spots.

He smiled. "Way out. Blue spotted. I mean . . . Couldn't resist it."

I slid it onto his cock and it became a leopard spotted thing. His balls were tight and so close to his body there was nothing spare, nothing hanging loose. I kissed the tip. The rich, aromatic taste of jelly babies. Good.

"Time to get down to things." Down to it he did. He bent me over the edge of the bed and pushed his cock into me, right into me until it was part of my own body. I knew I was coming, coming with the largest orgasm ever. He supported himself with one hand and the important finger of the other hand did its thing on my clit. Nothing, but nothing would stop me now. He readjusted his angle and I grabbed his hand and replaced the finger at my clitoris and now he was in the rhythm and I was sure that he was coming and nothing mattered but that great dick inside me and he was coming into me and I was coming and I pulled his hand away so he could concentrate on his own orgasm and fingered myself so I came with him and I did and did and did and went on coming and coming, using his spent dick like a dildo. He was wonderful. Wonderful.

He finally let his cock slip out and went into the bathroom to do the necessary. I stretched, collapsed on the bed, tried to find my body again. It was all in bits in the galaxy somewhere.

He returned to sit beside me, a towel wrapped round his waist. He ran a hand up and down my body. "Do you think we should bother with our spouses or just disappear and leave them to themselves? Your husband and my wife."

"Well . . . see them later, perhaps. Depends how we feel."

"Sure."

"We could both go for a swim." I liked the idea of a swim.

"Then perhaps . . . see what happens." He absently stroked my breasts.

"Sounds good to me. Isn't it funny about the second honeymoon bit?" His cock was again hard and sticking out making an umbrella of the towel." We are to be on our own, more or less. So it seems. We should amuse ourselves. It could well be a second honeymoon but not you and your wife and me and my husband."

Yes, this is what would happen. I willed it to happen. Perhaps later I would hang around the pool and see if I could bump into him. And if I didn't, so what? I would have him in my mind and it most likely would be better than anything that would be real.

It's All in the Mind

Corinne (Atlanta, USA)

Although in reality my bachelorette party was quite a bit tamer that this fantasy, sometimes I get carried away and have fond memories for the party I didn't actually have. On nights when Ben's away, I'll put on the slinky slip dress I really did wear to my own party, turn off the lights, and lie in bed, dreaming of what might have been. I had a perfectly fun party, mind you, filled with plenty of good friends, the best friends a girl could ask for. But still, every once in a while, I like to pretend that I'm still single and carefree, ready for sexual adventure at any moment. And since Ben doesn't really know much about my real party (both of ours are just kept on a private premarital moment basis), I'm free to fantasize about those wild days in any way I want. So the first bit really happened, but the wildness, well . . . draw your own conclusions.

I was getting married for the very first time, at age 32, a bit behind all my other friends, who had been settled in with their husbands and SUVs for a few years, and was grateful to finally be settling down with Ben. He was worth the wait, let me tell you, tall and handsome and strong, and sweet as can be, the answer to my dreams. I was thrilled, but hearing his friends talk incessantly about his bachelor party when they thought I was out of earshot had gotten me a little worked up, if you know what I mean. Oh, they tried to hide it from me, ceasing their conversations when I entered the room and sending secret messages to Ben. But still, I knew something was up and just a small bit of spying led me to the conclusion that the weekend of Ben's "boys,' night poker" was going to be a lot more tits and arse than full houses. And part of me wanted the same thing, a last corral, a night out with my favourite girls to see if we still had our magic, to get in trouble just one more time. So I called Stacy, my best friend, and she quickly got on the phone, something she'd been forbidden to do, and in no time, my bachelorette party was arranged. Aside from knowing the time, I didn't know where we'd be going or what would happen, but I was thrilled anyway – Stacy's never thrown a bad party in her life.

These were my oldest friends, and some of my best ones, but over the years we'd grown slightly apart. They were almost all married, and secretly saw me as the loser girl who'd had to wait such a long time just to find a guy to ask me, whereas I'd more than savoured my freedom. Some of them had been virgins when they married, or their husbands had been their firsts, whereas I could barely remember what being a virgin was like. Not that I'd been with tons of guys or anything, but enough to know my way in and out of bed with a guy, to know what I liked and what I didn't, to feel that I wasn't giving up my youth or my body to have Ben next to me for the rest of my life. I was thrilled to be marrying Ben, but every few nights I'd wake up in the middle of the night, chilled to the bone with sweat and fear, my dreams taking a shadowy turn, making me wonder if I was making the right decision. I had deliberately dropped my control freak ways and let my friends plan everything, leaving myself free to ponder the intricacies of my new life and status. I still wanted the thrills, the fantasies, the crazy ups and downs that dating and flirting brought. I consoled myself with the thought that our bachelorette party would be just as wild as any man's bachelor party, but I was really only humouring myself. Little did I know that I was actually right.

The night of the party, Ben's friends picked him up in the early evening, giving me time to fret over what to wear. What does a girl wear to her own bachelorette party? I was clueless, and obviously should have thought about this earlier, but my mind had been otherwise occupied. I combed my closets, dismissing all my usual fun and cute shirt and skirt combinations as too young-looking; tonight, I simply wanted to look sexy. Eventually I settled on my favourite lacy slip dress, in black and leopard print, with a real slip underneath, sexy and fun and smooth against my skin. Thankfully it was summer so I could get away with such attire; if anyone questioned me, I'd say it was too hot to wear anything heavier.

When Stacy arrived, she was squealing with excitement; I've known her my whole life so this was nothing new, but she was almost more excited about the party than I was. What had she planned that would have her hopping up and down like that? She ushered me into the kitchen to make a round of our signature drink, a mix of various juices and plenty of alcohol, and it was just like high school again as we drank and talked and giggled, but we had much more to laugh about tonight.

We headed out with Eileen driving, and I was shocked to find us at Pizaazz, our favourite club – I'd thought we'd be going somewhere new and unusual. But my closest friends greeted me there, dressed up and ready to have the time of their lives, or something close to it. Most were married or had steady boyfriends and while we still went out and had fun, it wasn't like our single days, where we'd often drink ourselves silly and then stay up till dawn watching old movies and painting our nails, girl bonding of the highest order. Me, I didn't quite know what to expect, having tried to not micromanage this night as I do everything else in my life.

We ordered fruity, girly drinks in bright bold colours and went around the room sharing our fondest of my hellish dating moments – from the blind date with the guy who was over a foot shorter than me, to the one who immediately started talking about the upcoming baseball season after he came, with no apology or segue. Then came the gifts – mostly "naughty" items found in the tackiest of sex shops, like penis-shaped chocolates and a veil with little penises pinned all over it. Anything goes when you're getting married, I guess.

We were having so much fun, just like the old days, when all of a sudden Stacy leaped up and said, "It's time." She pulled a black satin blindfold from her pocket and proceeded to wrap it around my head. I couldn't see a thing but could sense the commotion in the room. "Get ready, Corinne, because we have a very special treat for you."

They spun me around – just once, thankfully – and then undid the blindfold, presenting me with one of the most gorgeous men I'd ever seen. I figured there would be a stripper – these were my friends, after all – but one who looked like this? He was young, probably early twenties, and muscular, but not overly muscular like a bodybuilder – they sometimes look to me like their muscles are on the outside when they should be on the inside. No, his muscles gleamed and strutted, pushing gently up through his skin. He had dark brown hair, and a natural-looking tan, and he was tall. And most of all, he was smiling right at me; not a cheesy "I'm here to please you" smile, but what seemed like a real one. I melted into the chair and smiled back, drunk on the gloriousness of having my very own stripper. He had on black jeans and a white ribbed tank top, leather jacket slung over his shoulder.

The music started up right away and we all sat and watched as he expertly moved across the floor, occasionally approaching us and shimmying right up in one of our faces, maybe touching a strand of hair or stroking a cheek, the consumate seducer, knowing full well the effect he was having on us. When I glanced around at my friends, many of them were fanning their necks with the programmes Stacy had made, clearly affected as well. And I just sat there, stunned, my panties suddenly very, very wet. I wanted him, not for a lifetime, but I definitely wanted something more than a mere striptease from this gorgeous hunk, who seemed to be making special eyes at me while he worked the room.

He beckoned me forward with a crooked finger, and on shaky legs I stood up and walked close to him, and let him whisk me around the room, occasionally catching a whiff of him – sweat and salt and man, all rolled into the perfect aphrodisiac. He put my hand flat on his chest and held it there a moment, then lifted me up and carried me back to my seat. Everyone oohed and aahed and tried to get a closer peek as he lavished me with attention. I wondered if my wedding day would be like this – all eyes on me (probably) and feeling like the sexiest, most desired woman ever (maybe). But there was also something else; I wanted this man, this stripper, this hunk who now seemed to only have eyes for me.

It didn't make sense, logically, but so what? I felt young and wild and naughty, like I was sneaking out of my parents' house to make out in my boyfriend's car, yet this was almost worse because I was old enough to know better. But I knew none of the girls would blame me; he was too hot to resist, especially when he picked me up, *in the chair*, and carried me into a back room. "Excuse me, ladies, but I just need your friend Corinne here for a few minutes and then I'll bring her back to you, good as new."

After that stunning exit, he moved us to our own small room, one I hadn't noticed before, and began telling me again how hot he thought I was. He also started showing me, running his hands up and down my filmy dress, then up, up, up my skirt until he reached my now wet panties. With one hand he pressed my panties up against me, almost entering me, and with the other he stroked his cock, clearly visible through the white fabric. He pressed up against me, so close I could feel his hand moving along his cock, and I leaned back in the chair, knowing he'd catch me if I started to tilt. His fingers slid underneath the edge of my panties, and I didn't stop him. They stroked along my lips, teasing the wetness there, and I spread my legs almost involuntarily. This was the most hedonistic thing I'd ever done, pure sexual arousal, raw and concentrated, without the baggage of dating and waiting and trying to make a good impression. The only thing I needed to do for this anonymous man was be wet, want him, let him in, and I did. He pushed his fingers deeply inside me and though basically pinned to the chair, I arched up to meet him, his cock pressing against my stomach, its starchy, sweaty smell reaching my nose and making me lick my lips. Part of me wished we were somewhere else, somewhere more private, with a bed, a more traditional place so I could lie down and truly let him have his way with me, but I also knew if we were in a bedroom this wouldn't be happening. It was only the club, the party, the sense of this being the last day before the first day of the rest of my married life, or close enough to it, that allowed me to go this far.

But what about him? What did he do every other night – seduce a new girl for money? Great life for a guy. So used to dealing with practicalities before I could get off, my mind kept wandering afield but I reined it back in, tuned it out as he pressed deeper into me. As much as I might have wanted to think cynically about him, I couldn't. He wasn't some random hooker, a common whore, but the first guy since Ben to make me feel this way, alive and electric with desire, my skin tingling. I pushed any possible doubts out of my mind and simply revelled in the way he touched me. I could see my friends peeking into the room but I didn't care. I closed my eyes as he whispered into my ear, a steady flow of dirty words that I knew weren't really true but sent me orbiting nonetheless.

"You're the hottest girl here, the hottest bride I've ever seen. I've been hard since the minute I saw you. I want to make you come so hard you'll feel it tomorrow morning."

I took in his words, felt the visceral impact when he told me he was going to squeeze my nipples and slide his hard cock into me; they are simple but incredible words, powerful enough to make me wet the moment I heard them, the moment his breath hit my neck right below my ear. I wasn't about to go all the way, because I didn't need to; just the suggestion of it, the knowledge that in a fast move he could be up inside me, his hard, huge dick stretching and plundering me, taking me in a way Ben is far too considerate to do, was enough.

I leaned back, my hair falling in a long row behind me, willing him to suckle my neck. Like some magical sexual fairy, he moved from my breasts to my neck, which by then was ticklish and itching to be bitten, clawed, scratched. He sank his teeth into this most tender of flesh, with no warning that his bite will be so harsh and sharp. He seemed to anticipate what I needed before I could verbalize or even think it, teasing my neck with tiny testing bites that built one on top of the other in the very same spot. His bites fulfilled some special sexual need I have, complete in itself, and when he licked softly over the reddened skin, I felt like I could die right there.

"Was that enough for you?" he whispered with a growl, clearly certain that it wasn't.

Suddenly, what was enough just moments ago is far from it, and I wanted more, any possible guilt at going this far assuaged by the knowledge that Ben was probably off doing much the same, or at least he would if he could, and besides, once we were married I'd be loyal to him for the rest of my life, just as

I'd been loyal to him for the three years we'd been together. And what's more, even if my conscience had wanted me to, I couldn't have stopped there, especially not when his fingers pressed against my wet panties, pushing the fabric right up against my eager cunt, then taking his other hand and drawing it to his hard cock. We stroked each other through our underwear and when his fingers slipped inside my panties, I spread my legs eagerly, not caring where or who we were, simply that I needed him inside me. While his fingers entered me, pressing deeply where I needed him the most, he straddled me, and I could feel his cock, his strong legs as he gave me the most intimate kind of lap dance imaginable, his body locked on mine.

I nuzzled his chest, rubbing my lips and cheeks back and forth against the strength of him, then licking my way towards a small, pert nipple that seemed to call out to me. I licked it at first, felt it get slightly harder and tighter, then brought my teeth around it. He hissed and grabbed my head but didn't stop me, so I kept it up, teasing and working his nipple as guys had done to me before. I wondered if it felt the same for him, if with every twist and bite of my teeth he felt a deep urgent pull in his groin, a need that drove him mad with desire. My guess was yes because after a moment he did stop me, pulling my head up and staring directly and intently into my eyes. "I want you. I know this is my job, but please believe me when I tell you it's not like this with all the girls. I give them a little tease, a little show, and then I'm home, but you, you're incredible, irresistible. Your husband is going to be a lucky man, but for tonight, I want you, I want to slide my cock into you and fuck you like you've never been fucked before. I want to make you come right here in this chair."

Nobody had ever talked to me like that before and I was so tempted that I almost gave in. "I want you, too, but I just can't let you fuck me; that would be going to far. But pretty much anything else is fair game . . ." I trailed off as I wrapped my hand around his dick, moving my gaze from his warm cock to his blazing eyes which seemed to want to penetrate me in their own way. He brought his fingers from my cunt to my mouth, and I suckled my own juices from them, then pulled his fat fingers into me while he pushed them towards the back of my throat. I automatically reached for his cock, wanting it in my mouth, to taste it if I wasn't going to have it inside me, but he pushed me aside and kneeled before me. He edged my panties down my legs and off, then pushed my legs aside and began licking me, long, warm strokes along the length of my slit that ended in a slow finish at my clit and had me gripping the chair and biting my lip so as not to scream out. His tongue and lips expertly worked me, licking and plunging and nibbling, pressing harder just when I needed it. My legs trembled as he tugged on my clit and when he pushed a finger inside me, I came, shaking against the chair as he stayed with me for the ride. He licked up every last drop of my juices before moving to kiss me, giving me a taste of myself.

When we finally emerged, sweaty and a bit red-faced, my friends all had drinks in their hands. He left soon thereafter, and I rejoined my friends like none of it had ever happened.

When Ben gets home and finds me in the slip dress, he always gives me a funny little look, his eyes asking "Why are you wearing that sexy thing just to lie around the house?" That's for me to know, and him to hopefully never find out!

Corporate Blonde

Violet (Vancouver, Canada)

Thanks to an ultra-strict upbringing, and the fact that I still live at home, what little sex life I have takes place mostly inside my head. I've got a vivid imagination, and it serves me well on long, cold, lonely winter nights – any nights, and most every day, for that matter.

Since I don't go out a lot, I don't meet a lot of people outside of work, so it's the people at work that I usually fantasize about, along with movie, TV, and pop stars, of course. And the only woman I've ever kissed in my life was my grandmother, and the only woman's legs I've ever caressed have been my own, but that doesn't stop my dirty little mind from percolating with naughty thoughts about wild lesbian sex – lesbian leg sex, no less – with my gorgeous boss.

Laura Danton is the head of the project team I'm currently assigned to. She's a cool, uber-professional blonde babe with a slim, sleek figure which she always keeps tightly wrapped in the latest and most expensive fashions. She's a great boss to work for, if a little distant with new employees like myself, but it's her long, slender, stocking-clad legs that flow out of her dangerously short skirts like shimmering black or white twin waterfalls that really make me admire, and mentally seduce, her.

I lie back in my warm bed, or hot bath, and touch myself all over, thinking about Laura and me working late one night, when I just happen to notice a run in her silky, shiny, shadow-black stockings . . .

She'd just propped her ballerina legs up on her gleaming desktop and crossed them, and right away my leg-sensitive eye picked out the one inch breach in the sheer, black stocking on her right leg. The tiny tear exposed a small section of her brown, lightly muscled calf. I gulped and stared fixedly at those tawny legs, at that wicked violation in the structural integrity of her sexy leg coverings. Thoughts of work sailed out of my dizzy head and thoughts of making love to those luscious limbs cascaded in.

She looked at me as I gazed blankly at her entwined, silk-sheathed legs. "Is there a problem, Violet?" she asked.

I blinked several times in an effort to clear my foggy brain, and my lustful leg musings partially dissipated. I crossed my own legs and gladly felt a well-known wetness. "Huh? Oh, no, Ms Danton. I was just thinking about something, that's all. Sorry." I stared down at the files that were strewn all over the table I was working at, my face flaming red.

"Laura," Ms Danton said.

I looked up. "Huh?"

"Laura. Call me Laura. 'Ms Danton' makes me feel like I'm a thousand years old, when I'm only twenty or so years older than you are," she remarked with a smile.

"Uh, okay, sure, Ms – Laura." My eyes froze again on that winking rent in her night-shaded stocking. I could almost feel and taste the warm, firm, sun-kissed flesh that lay exposed by that heavenly tear.

"You sure there isn't anything wrong, Violet?" Laura asked again, her azure eyes boring into mine.

I glanced back and forth between her graceful, folded legs – that erotic run in her shimmering stocking – and her beautiful, quizzical face. She was wearing a flawless, pearl-white, silk top and a short, black-leather skirt, and, of course, those shiny, noir leg-wraps. Her black stilettos lay discarded somewhere beneath her desk.

"Well?"

I sucked some humid air into my overwrought lungs, fought to steady my spinning head, and decided to make my move. Coming on to your boss is a perilous, potentially career-ending manoeuvre at the best of times, even more so when you're not even sure that she shares your affinity for girls, as well as boys; but Laura's gorgeous legs were driving me crazy, and I just had to find out if I could possess their lithesome beauty or not. So, I stood up and walked slowly and shakily over to her desk.

"Um, yeah . . . Laura," I mumbled, "there is something wrong. Y – you've got a run in your stocking." And I reached out a trembling digit and touched her bare skin. Her leg jerked, then quivered slightly as I ran my slender finger back and forth along the sliver of bronzed flesh that had been exposed by the break in her inky stocking.

She bit her lip. "D – do I?" she stammered, making it the first time that I'd ever seen the in-control career woman flustered.

That made two of us. But I knew what I wanted, and although I'm only nineteen years old, I'm not shy about going after something I want – till I get it. I gently caressed Laura's smooth skin, brought a second finger into play so that I was blatantly fondling a small portion of her slim leg.

"You sure do," I breathed in answer to her rhetorical question. "And I think it's getting bigger." I pushed against the clingy edges of the small tear with my twitching fingers, expanding it, exposing and stroking more and more of her naked, sun-burnished leg flesh.

She gasped, and her eyelids dropped down to shade her sky-blue eyes as I reverentially rubbed her calf with my long fingers. Her legs shook and grew goosebumps, and as I stared meaningfully at her, my bold digits working their erotic magic on her to-die-for legs, I saw her nipples flower to arousal and indent the thin material of her top.

Yes! The oh-so-hot, yet outwardly oh-so-cool, mature babe was getting as turned on as I was. She licked her glossy lips with a pink, kittenish tongue, and let her appraising eyes wander up and down my girlish figure, before refocusing on what was truly important – my fingers and her leg. I swallowed hard and pushed my whole hand through the opening in her ravaged stocking, rested it on her sublime leg and squeezed.

"Yes, Violet," she murmured, dropping the file she'd been holding and cupping and kneading her firm tits, discarding all pretence that we could ever keep things on a strictly professional basis from here on out. There were some things even more important than business, after all.

"Yes, Laura," I agreed, and savagely grabbed up and tore the shiny fabric of her stocking with both my hands, ripping it until it lay shredded from ankle to skirt. I wasn't holding anything back; I wanted those seductive, golden legs in my hands and mouth – now!

"I want to suck your toes!" I yelled, my soft hands sliding all over her brown skin, caressing and fondling her glistening limb.

She was taken aback by my towering need. "Uh, well, Violet, I'm, uh, expecting my boyfriend anytime soon. He was –"

"Fuck your boyfriend!" I shouted.

She stared wide-eyed at me, then hastily nodded her head. She pulled her legs away from me, swung them off the desk and onto the carpet, then stood up and quickly unbuttoned and shrugged off her blouse, unzipped her skirt and let it puddle at her stockinged feet. Then she unhooked and tossed aside her satiny, white bra and stood there a moment, letting me admire her nude, sun-buffed upper body, her firm, ripe boobs and jutting, mocha nipples. There was just one problem: her luscious legs were now hidden behind her desk.

"I want your feet and legs!" I demanded, like a petulant school girl, my pussy going from damp to drenched.

She cleared papers and business bric-a-brac off her huge desk with a couple of wild swipes of her arm, climbed on top, and then slid down into a sitting position on the very edge of the massive slab of varnished wood, facing me, her dangling, dancer's legs only inches away. I quickly gripped her fleshy thighs and pushed her legs open, inserted my overheated body in between the gorgeous pair of them. Then I brushed her lips with my lips, and she responded, and we kissed urgently, hungrily.

I mashed my mouth against hers, as I ran my joyous hands up and down her slick, stocking-clad thighs, reveling in the silky, sexy feel of her sensual leg wear. She grabbed my head and riffled her fingers through my short, orange-streaked, black hair, and we Frenched each other, our tongues swirling together angrily, frenziedly slapping against one another.

I pulled my head back and dropped to my knees in front of her – in front of her legs. I knelt at her feet like pagans kneel before golden idols, encircled her shapely ankles with my fingers, brought her delicately arched peds together, and began kissing and licking them.

"God, yes!" she moaned, clutching her pert titties and squeezing them, rolling her plump nipples as I licked at the bottom of her stockinged feet.

I dragged my tongue along an erotic course from her heel, up her arch, and into her toes, again and again, first one foot and then the other. I held on tight to her trembling legs, her jumping feet, and stroked her ultra-sensitive soles with my incessant pink tongue. Then, when the bottom of her succulent feet were painted all nice and wet with my hot saliva, stocking and skin, I tilted her feet towards me and went to work on her silk-sheathed toes.

"God, that feels good," she whimpered, sliding a hand down into her tiny, white panties. She started fingering herself, frantically polishing her flowered clit.

I made it tough for her, kept her legs together by pressing her feet together, but she still managed to buff her swollen nub with one hand while she groped her boobs with the other. I licked all over and around her slender, wriggling toes, before sucking them into my mouth. I gobbled up all of the toes of her right foot and tugged on them, slashing my tongue across the vulnerable underside of her foot-digits as I sucked and sucked on them, anxiously crammed as much of her exquisite foot as I could into my mouth.

"Suck on my toes, Violet!" she screamed, her long, blonde tresses falling across her lust-contorted face like a shimmering curtain, as she desperately rubbed her engorged clit and plucked at her hardened nipples.

I disgorged her right foot and swallowed up the toes of her left, redoubled my erotic foot-in-mouth massage. I pulled on her toes, tongue-lashed and slathered them with spit, greedily sucked on them through the saliva-clotted material of her shining, black stockings. Then I unmouthed her left foot and pushed both of her feet together, sole to sole, and ran my thick tongue up and down the twin rows of wriggling toes, gleefully lapping at all of her outstretched toes at once, up and down, up and down, over and over.

"I'm coming!" she cried, her hand shifting to hyper-speed in her panties. Her head lolled back on her shoulders and she screamed with all-out release.

I quickly twisted her feet around and jammed both of her big toes into my gaping maw. Her streamlined, built-for-sex body was jolted with orgasm, and her supple, delicate legs and feet jerked around in my loving hands as I desperately sucked on the two largest of her beautiful toes.

Then, seemingly out of nowhere, a man suddenly burst into the woman-scented office and raced over to Laura and me. His long, hard cock jutted out of his unzipped pants, and before I could even react, he started fisting thick ropes of white-hot semen out of his raging dick and down onto Laura's drenched feet – and my face.

"Yes! Come all over my feet, baby!" Laura yelled at him, her body still undulating with the aftershocks of orgasm.

The spurting guy was obviously Laura's boyfriend – the one she'd mentioned earlier, just before I attacked her legs – so I didn't pull away from her sodden feet as he coated them with jism. Instead, I continued to suck on her toes, her anguished boyfriend spraying his molten man-juice all over them and me.

"Lick the come off my feet, Violet!" Laura commanded, grabbing her boyfriend's straining cock and stroking it madly, jacking the last few bursts of heated jizz onto her delightful feet.

I swirled my tongue all over the tops of her stockinged feet, eagerly lapping up her boyfriend's simmering goo. I tasted the salty spooge and swallowed it down, not satisfied until Laura's pretty feet were one hundred percent sperm-free. Then I smacked my saucy lips and smiled up at them, my hands squeezing and kneading Laura's lovely feet.

"Hi, I'm Eric," Laura's boyfriend said by way of formal introduction, then tacked on the understatement of the year: "You like feet?"

I nodded. I fucking loved feet, and would've loved legs – Laura's lush legs – if Eric hadn't interrupted our girlish fun. Still, I wasn't about to complain. Eric was a tall, muscular, good-looking guy of around forty, with curly, salt and pepper hair and a handsome, seven-inch prick that was still hanging hard out of his open fly. I smiled impishly at him and pondered the sexual possibilities.

"How 'bout cock?" he asked.

I stared into his warm, brown eyes and replied, "Sure I like cock – in my cunt."

And before you could spell "menage a trois", Eric was out of his duds and Laura out of her torn, dripping stockings and drenched panties. They stood nude and lewd right in front of me, and then passionately kissed each other, Laura working Eric's rod with her hand while Eric squeezed my boss's tits.

I scrambled to my feet, anxious to join in the sexual fray, and they helped me out of my dress, out of my matching lacy, black bra and panties. I'm built along Laura's lines: trim and tight, but paler by comparison, with slightly smaller titties that are capped by stiff, ultra-pink nipples. My cunny is shaved bare and smooth as a baby's bottom, except for a tuft of soft, black fur right at the top. My taut, heart-shaped arse never fails to get compliments, and such was the case here, as Eric and Laura grabbed a butt cheek apiece and squeezed and fondled my bum, as we all leaned in and three-way Frenched. We recklessly twirled our tongues together, the lusty couple feeling up my hot, tight butt. Then I squealed into both of their mouths when I felt someone's finger slide down my crack and into my cunny.

"Violet got us off," Eric remarked to Laura, "so I think it's only fair that we get her off."

"I agree," Laura responded, smiling slyly at me. "I've got a confession to make, Violet. Eric's actually been hanging around the office for the past two hours, patiently waiting to witness your wicked little foot seduction. He watched the whole thing from the door." She ran her silver-tinted fingernails up and down my bottom. "You see, I've been watching you watching my legs with your tongue hanging out for the last couple of weeks. So, I thought I'd keep you late tonight, cut a small slit in my stocking – give you an opening, so to speak – and then Eric and I would see what developed."

"What?" I gasped, momentarily stunned to learn that I was prey rather than predator. Then I shrugged my shoulders and kissed Laura, thanked her for ensnaring me like she had. You don't get to be a first-class manager without being a shrewd judge of character, I now knew.

"Okay, ladies," Eric interjected. "Enough tell and kiss. How 'bout we get down to business?"

"Good idea," the sultry blonde capitalist agreed, and she provided Eric and me with directions such that I ended up flat on my back on her desk, Eric's hard cock shoved balls-deep into my sopping cunt. Laura climbed onto the desk with me, positioned her pussy over my face, and gripped my bare feet around the ankles and pulled them back so that she could play with them while I ate her out and Eric banged my twat.

My head spun and my body tingled with the awesome eroticism of it all; with the sweet smell and tangy taste of Laura's soaking wet cunny; with the clit-gratifying sensation of Eric sliding his steely fuck-pole back and forth in my stretched-out, steaming pussy; and with the pure-heaven feeling of Laura's slippery, darting tongue painting my small feet with her superheated saliva.

"Fuck, she's tight," Eric groaned, as he slammed his engorged schlong in and out of my gripping snatch. He pummelled my pussy and pushed my legs forward as far as they'd go, allowing Laura to shove her pink tongue in between my wriggling toes.

Laura made unholy love to my electrified feet with her mouth and tongue, as her stud of a boyfriend fucked me silly. She bounced her blonde head back and forth between my peds, vacuuming all of the outstretched toes on one of my feet into her mouth and tugging on them, and then doing the same to my other tender tootsie. I moaned into her dripping cooze, vainly struggled to lap at her pussy, overwhelmed by the sheer sensuality of our leg-inspired threesome.

Eric jolted me faster and faster with his frenzied cock-thrusts, then hollered in warning, "I'm coming, girls!"

"Jerk him off with your feet, Violet!" Laura screamed.

Eric tore his dong out of my gash and Laura shoved my legs forward and slapped my feet together over her boyfriend's greasy pole. I grasped his rod between my spit-slick feet and pistoned his cock with them, as Laura excitedly rubbed my engorged clitty with her fingers. Eric let out a roar that could've been heard two buildings away, and I felt his sizzling seed splash down onto my tummy as I continued to vigorously foot-pump his dick. Laura's expert clit-buffing then brought me screaming into the gaping abyss of my own depthless orgasm.

"Ohmigod!" I shrieked into her pussy. My cunny burst into flames, and my entire thrashing body was consumed by fiery ecstasy.

I writhed around on the brilliant desktop like a girl possessed, my arched feet still clinging to Eric's blazing cock as he spray-painted my stomach with heated spunk. Laura jammed her fingers into my gushing cunt, frantically polished my button with her thumb, and I came and came and came, the whole world crashing down upon me, leaving me devastated, wasted.

"I think she really enjoyed that," Laura gasped, her thighs still pressing against either side of my head, her puffy, pink pussy lips only an inch away from my gaping mouth. She pulled her fingers out of my smouldering snatch, my feet off Eric's ruptured cock, and licked warm, sticky sperm off my rippling belly in long, hard, wet tongue-strokes.

When she'd finished cleaning me up, she and Eric kissed, Frenched, swirled come between the two of them. I tentatively licked at Laura's glistening twat, weak as a kitten, having been left with barely a leg to stand on.

. . . Now, I'm not sure how Laura's boyfriend got into my orgasm-inducing female foot-fantasy – since she doesn't even have a boyfriend, as far as I know – but in a fantasy, unlike the real world, thank goodness, anything is possible: right?

Toyboy

Blossom (Dublin, Ireland)

I took out my key, unlocked the door, and walked in. The house was cool, still, and silent as usual but, unlike most days, it was filled with the homey scent of cinnamon and cloves from the apple cake I baked the night before.

"I swear I must be psychic." I shut the door and locked it behind me. "Somehow, I just knew that he'd arrive here this morning. And finally, now I'm back home, too. I thought the day would never end."

I was so horny I didn't know how I'd managed to make it through the tedious workday without touching myself, but I was glad I waited. My first orgasm of the day would be with him! The first ones were always the best and this would be a real first in more ways than one. I took a very deep breath, wished myself luck in the mirror, and walked down the narrow hall to my bedroom.

I stepped tentatively into the room and looked straight ahead. There he was! He was lying on my bed, his head and neck supported by pillows. And that smile! He'd had a big smile on his face when I'd settled him and left him there in the morning, but I could almost swear that it was even bigger now. He looked so happy – perhaps even as happy as he was about to make me.

I couldn't wait much longer. Dinner would have to be postponed till, hopefully, very late that night. First things first! The hunger that most needed satisfying was definitely not for food. I smiled and told him that I'd take a quick shower and be right back.

I hated to leave him, even for mere moments, but my

deflowering had to be special and perfect, a memory I'd treasure. A shower would wash the nervous sweat from my body and refresh me, perhaps even soothe my frayed nerves a bit. I was sure that it was what I needed to do. It wouldn't take long, and afterward we'd have all night, and if all went well, countless days and nights to come.

I blew him a shy kiss, rushed into the bathroom, and turned on the water, letting it warm up as I used the toilet. The thought of him, lying there so close, waiting for me in my bed, had me more aroused than I even realized at first. My senses were so heightened that I gasped and shivered when I accidentally brushed my clitoris with the toilet paper.

I climbed into the tub and stood under the hard, pulsing spray, letting myself get wet all over, except for my long hair that was coiled into a bun at the nape of my neck. After washing my face, I caressed my curvaceous body all over with creamy perfumed soap, bought the week before, in anticipation of his arrival. I paid careful, gentle attention to my private parts that I would soon be sharing with him for the first time.

Instead of taking the shower massage off the wall and aiming it at my nether lips, as I did most evenings, while leaning against the tiles or reclining in the deep tub, I left it in its bracket on the wall. I just stood there for a few moments, enjoying the rhythmic bursts of warm water as they hit my upper body and cascaded soothingly down to my toes.

One strong jet of water struck the very tip of my taut nipple and brought tears to my eyes, but I soon forgot the sudden sting. My body was aching for sex, and ready, so ready. It wasn't just my stiff, sensitive nipples that told me that, but also my quickening pulse and my labia and clitoris that were swelling, throbbing, and becoming coated with a slick, viscous fluid that could never be mistaken for water.

I turned off the shower and got out of the tub. I quickly dried my tingling skin with a big, fluffy towel while looking at my glowing, bright-eyed face in the mirrored door of the medicine cabinet. My hot, quick breath fogged the glass as I watched myself unfasten and shake free my mass of long, dark curls.

"Well, here I am." I smiled encouragingly to myself, trying

to erase years of insecurity and self-doubt. "I'm a luscious, desirable woman, a Rubens nude come to life. He won't be disappointed."

I sensuously creamed my skin with moisturizer scented with the same fragrance as the soap, then completed my toilette by spraying a cloud of the matching cologne into the air and walking through it. After taking several deep, anxious breaths, I opened the door and stepped out into the bedroom, naked, shy, and nervous, but ready. Most definitely ready!

My lover was still lying there, just as I knew he would be, tucked snugly under the blue flowered comforter. I walked to the window and drew the curtains. It would be quite a while before sunset and I felt too shy to be so exposed and on display in such harsh, unforgiving, bright light.

I turned away from the window and faced the bed, my hands kneading my heavy breasts. I walked back to him, slowly, luxuriously caressing and fondling the abundant flesh of my soft hills and valleys. I looked down to watch my hands tenderly touching my body, but I'd made the room too dark. I wanted to be able to see myself and I wanted to be able to see him. I needed to see the two of us together. I lit two candles on the dresser and a large pillar candle on the bedside table.

"That's much better. Not too bright, but just enough. All the better to see you with, my dear," I murmured to him.

I shyly pulled up the comforter as I slipped in, next to him. The candlelight was soft and flattering, but I was still feeling somewhat bashful. After all, I'd never been naked in front of any man before.

He didn't seem displeased when I asked him if he minded if I readied myself a bit with my vibrator, so I reached under the pillows and drew it out. I slipped it beneath the covers, spread my legs, pointed it at my centre, and turned it on. Just the sound of the strong motor humming, excited and dampened me before I even parted my lips and lightly touched my clit with it.

"You do know that I'm a virgin?" I confided with some embarrassment, moving the small yet powerful machine away from my hardening bud as I spoke. "I'd feel less anxious if I could widen myself with this." I showed him the dildo I kept secreted with my vibrator.

When he kept on silently smiling that inscrutable smile of his, I took that as acquiescence. Lying with his warm arm behind my back, I repositioned my whirring machine. With my right hand on the vibrator and my left holding the dildo, I began to prepare my sex for penetration by his phallus.

And did I ever need preparation! I took my hand off my trusty vibrator, left the dildo clutched tightly inside me, and lifted the covers to take a peek at him. I stared at his swollen, standing organ. It was massive! It was positively frightening!

It appeared to be at least nine inches long with a big, bulbous head and a hefty shaft traced with bulging veins. It was nearly puce in colour and incredibly firm, I discovered, as well as huge. The fingers of one hand could not span its circumference. I had to use both hands, and when I squeezed, the monster barely yielded to the pressure. I was sure I needed plenty of time to prepare myself to take that tremendous member into me, that is, if it were even possible.

Nervously I picked up my massager and resumed teasing myself with it. My swollen folds parted as I gently pushed the dildo further into my sheath. I began moving the cylinder in and out of my increasingly-slicker and more-welcoming canal. I closed my eyes and focused all my attention on that one small area of my body that seemed to be all that existed in the entire universe.

As the plastic phallus pushed in, parting my hidden walls, I revelled in the sensation of being completely filled. As it was drawn out with twisting motions, I suffered the aching, teasing sadness of my folds collapsing in upon each other, contracting in their loss. The vibrator danced around my clit as alternating waves of joy and sorrow, fullness and emptiness, the emotions of my very flesh, rippled in and out of my clenching sex.

The erotic sensations were so intense that I was in danger of becoming lost in my private reverie of voluptuous abandon. Unlike other occasions when I was alone and hungry, this time my sole purpose was not to pleasure myself to orgasm. I had to remind myself that now, with each rhythmic probe and twist, I was making my sheath wider, more lubricious and welcoming. I had to be mindful of the task that went beyond my own immediate gratification. My goal was to prime myself to take his big, hard penis into me.

Thinking of his size, especially his considerable girth, reminded me of the need to widen my nether mouth as much as I possibly could. With that in mind, I began circling the dildo as firmly and widely as possible, round and round inside my pussy. With each determined circle, with each hard revolution, I was loosening my tight entrance and widening the swollen tunnel of my uninitiated sex. It was truly a labour of love.

When I felt ready, I turned off the vibrator and put it aside. I drew out the dildo, moaning in pleasure as I felt the firm tug on my folds of inner flesh. The plastic cylinder was as warm as my swollen cunt and covered with my slippery secretions. Rolling over to face him, I smiled, licked my lips and got onto my hands and knees. With pendant breasts swaying heavily beneath me, I moved down on the bed till his erection loomed directly in front of me.

After one last shy look up at his face, I lowered my head and opened my mouth wider than I ever had before to encompass his glans. I began to lick and suck. I sucked and sucked, coating his sex with my saliva. My fists travelled up and down his shaft, my motions at first light and slow, getting firmer and faster as the suction of my mouth increased.

After a-while, I tired. My mouth and neck were not accustomed to such strenuous exercise. My jaw complained audibly as I forced it open even wider so that I could release his penis. It bobbed up proudly, glistening in the candlelight.

I had not expected to feel such vast and varied emotions. I was excited, aroused, and filled with such aching desire, but that bulging tool of his was so immense. The virile masculinity of it made me feel small, soft, and feminine. It looked so dangerous and powerful in contrast with my own fragile vulnerability. It frightened me almost as much as it enticed me.

I picked up the vibrator and paused to allow myself one more look at the instrument of my imminent impalement before rising up and straddling him. I knelt above him on legs that were shaking with equal measures of anxiety and anticipation.

"I'd better do this myself," I breathed as, with determined

fingers, I stretched my labia wider and wider until my slit was splayed open as far as it would go.

I wanted his entry into me to be accomplished with as little pain as possible. Happily, the escalating pulsations and spasms of my cunt focused my mind more on my hunger and less on my trepidations. But still, I wanted to be careful.

I thrust three fingers of my left hand into the hot flesh of my soaking sex. I pulled them out, dripping with my thick juices, and lubricated his entire penis. Again, I delved deeply into myself, this time spreading the copious secretions over my swollen lips that would soon envelop him. One more time, I plunged into my cunt and used the viscous fluid to wet my own little erect phallus. After that, I was sure I was ready.

I inched further up on the bed, pulled my lips wide and positioned myself in a tense squat over his erection. I teased myself with the vibrator causing more love juice to dribble out of me and drip down the length of his prick. Determinedly, I lowered myself till I felt his hard cock pressing firmly against my spread lips. I looked up at him for encouragement and found that I didn't want to look away from his face. I felt the connection between our eyes echoing the connection between our sexes.

Panting, I lowered myself determinedly onto his prick, then withdrew, only to push down and swallow him again. Up and down I went, a bit further each time, all the while with my eyes locked on his. I could feel my cunt stretching – it stung, but I stubbornly persisted until I sensed an obstruction inside me, a barrier that wouldn't allow him any further into me.

"Damn! I'd better take care of that," I muttered. "With all the wanking I've been doing, I'm surprised it didn't tear before now."

With my vibrator on high speed and pressed directly against my clit, I rose up and then thrust myself down hard and fast. Crying out in pain, but even more in joy, I impaled myself completely on his cock. I finally had him inside me to the balls.

I felt torn and sore, but still I rode him, gently and slowly at first until my growing pleasure gradually overcame my pain. Soon my tension and lust were so strong and uncontrollable, I was bouncing furiously up and down on his tool. The bedsprings were squeaking madly. My panting became louder and more ragged. I threw my head back and sweat flew into my eyes, stinging them, but I couldn't have cared less. I couldn't bear to even think of ending that incredible fuck for anything in the world. I just kept fucking and fucking and fucking with all the energy and enthusiasm and lascivious horniness I possessed.

But all things, including wonderful fucks, must end, and for me, the ending was spectacular. I exploded in a magnificent orgasm, totally consuming my entire body. It was, by far, the biggest and best I'd ever experienced.

I felt as if my insides had shattered and burst and gone shooting up and down, from one side to the other, all throughout my convulsing body and inside my exploding head. My spasming cunt gripped him voraciously, repeatedly. My clenching muscles clamped, vise-like around him, keeping him captive. It felt like we would never come apart, just remain that way forever, lustfully locked together.

The overwhelming sensations kept going on and on. Just as the dizzying contractions began to weaken slightly, another climax built up almost immediately and broke, crashing and tumbling through my body. Suddenly, I realized that my vibrator was still pressed against my clit. I couldn't take any more stimulation. The extreme, intense pleasure had crossed the threshold of my endurance and become pain. I threw the vibrator aside but kept his prick tightly imprisoned inside me while the spasms slowly subsided, leaving a glow of pleasure behind.

Sighing and breathing heavily, I leaned down and laid my head on his chest, feeling content and at peace. After a few moments of well-deserved rest, I wearily pulled myself up off his still-rigid cock, then bent down and licked it clean, relishing my own sweet taste. I moved up on the bed and lay down next to him, sore and shaking, but happy and satisfied beyond anything I had ever known. The wonderful feeling extended to all aspects of my being – body, mind, and soul.

I was no longer a virgin, could never again be called an old maid, or that hideous word, spinster. If my aching insides weren't enough to confirm my deflowering, the spots of blood on the sheet and the pink tinge to the juice I'd lapped off his phallus proved it.

My bedroom was totally quiet and still again. It seemed strange to me that this place of ecstatic pleasure and voluptuous sensuality hadn't changed in some palpable way. It was still the same familiar, calm and peaceful room of my maiden years even though I had changed so much myself.

I smiled and looked over to my right to see my lover lying there, smiling as broadly and contentedly as I was. I reached out and touched his face, his hand, his arm, his leg, and then very gently and lovingly, caressed his sturdy phallus.

It was then that I found myself wondering, "If a life-sized doll with an attached phallus is this fantastic, how much more incredible would a flesh-and-blood, living, breathing, loving man be?"

For the time being, at least, I could only imagine, although I hoped, with all my heart, not to mention my body, that one day soon I'd be lucky enough to find out. But until that day came, I knew I'd be OK. I'd do just fine whether I found a man or not. After all, I had my very own toyboy!

Butterfield 8 For 4

Lena (Oakland, USA)

As Addison spoke with the restaurant hostess, I watched a group of people near the bar – three men and a woman. They were all attractive people but that's not what held my attention. I saw, even from several yards away, the glimmer in her eye and heard the lilt in her voice. I became her, just for a few seconds, because the situation she found herself in was the one to which I often masturbated: one woman surrounded by men. I envied her and wondered if her evening would turn out anything like my fantasies. For her sake, I hope they did, for I held little hope that mine would ever live up to my own imagination.

Please understand that I am not disappointed – not really – that I am not likely to live out my three-to-one ratio fantasy where every man wants to fuck me and, because all of them are irresistible, I give every man that opportunity. In fact, in my fantasies, everybody is dying to experience what's under my unprepossessing clothing and, for some reason, I am eager to reveal it.

In real life, though, I am pretty but shy. I am the quintessential good wife with the requisite number of children (two), the charming house (mortgaged), and the attentive husband (when he's not preoccupied with his job). As I watched the men in the restaurant usher the lucky woman to their table, my mind wandered to a place it shouldn't – a place very much at odds with the anniversary dinner I was about to share with Addison.

But Addison had encountered someone he knew and was shaking hands and exchanging greetings, so my mind had all the permission it needed to reconstruct the evening according to my wanton and forbidden fantasies. It would have to begin, I decided, before we left the house that night . . .

"Are you sure this is what you want me to wear? I feel kind of slutty."

I stand before my husband in a mini-skirt and thigh-high boots. My long blonde hair hangs in graceful waves around my shoulders. I know I look great but my usual look is not quite so blatantly sexual. I need his assurance.

His eyes sparkle. "Perfect," he replies. "Everybody who sees you will wish they were me."

He kisses me and runs his hand along my thigh. I kiss him back, enjoying the precious time we've arranged for ourselves this weekend. The weekend babysitter has just arrived and, after dinner at Butterfield 8, we are off to cloister ourselves in the Peninsula Hotel downtown. I can't wait to have him all to myself, with no screaming children and no obligations.

Butterfield 8 on a Friday night teems with hipsters, curiosity seekers, and those who want to be seen. The food is only one of the reasons we like to patronize the place – the spectacle of humanity never fails to disappoint. Even the wait staff provides unwitting entertainment.

As we make our way through the crowd to check in with the hostess, I avert my eyes from all the stares that come my way. My outfit turns as many heads as Addison predicted, and though I am accustomed to admiring glances, drooling stares are relatively new to me. I'm not sure I'd want it every day of my life, but for tonight, it is strangely invigorating.

Addison speaks with the hostess as I look around. My eyes widen when I caught sight of Jeff and John at the bar.

"Addison!" I nearly shout to be heard over the din of the crowd. "Look over there! Jeff and John are here!"

"Well, let's join them! Our table won't be ready for a few more minutes."

Neither of the men have ever looked at me the way they do tonight. I am reminded of those cartoon wolves, the ones with the gleaming eyes and teeth. I giggle at their stares as I approach.

"What the heck are you guys doing here?" I say, giving them each a hug.

"We've gotta eat, too, you know," Jeff says, laughing. "With Amy gone, I have to fend for myself."

"Most men would just open a can of tuna," I tease. "I didn't realize Donna was gone, too. . ." I say to John.

"Yeah – visiting Bruce and Jane down in Tampa."

"So, we've got you all to ourselves," Addison says, grinning.

"You look stunning tonight, Lena," Jeff observes. John agrees. I bask in the attention.

The air in the bar changes for me at that moment. A hush seems to fall, as if somebody had thrown a thick blanket over the crowd to muffle the dull roar. I look from my husband to Jeff to John and back again. My imagination is surely working overtime. It is just a coincidence that they are here. Without their wives. Assessing me like I was prey. I had to know for sure; my fantasies are too good to be true.

"Did you guys know we would be here?" I ask Jeff and John.

Addison answers. "Yes, honey. I thought we'd surprise you."

"So we're all having dinner together?"

"And whatever else comes up," Jeff winks.

My heart races. My pulse pounds in my ears. Addison stands there, beaming, proud of me and eager, apparently, to share me with his best friends. Amy and Donna virtually never travel without their husbands, so the situation is a once-in-a-lifetime set of circumstances. I am suddenly very aware of my pussy.

"Taylor," comes the growl of the hostess. "Table for four."

As we walk to our table, men and women turn to watch me pass. The attention fuels my confidence – I walk taller and even sway my hips as a result of the multitude of gazes. I am a high fashion model on an exclusive Paris runway, secure in the knowledge that I strike awe in my audience.

The women are especially disconcerting. I read envy in their eyes and slowly realize that a woman with three men is indeed an enviable situation. I savour their stares and let my eyes linger on their men, just for fun.

I've never been so wet in my life.

We are seated at one of the restaurant's best tables, a

banquette that faces the centre of the room. The men let me slide in first and all I can think about is being careful not to leave traces of my moistness on the leather cushions.

I can barely focus on my menu. The talk among the men seems harmless enough but I can't concentrate on that, either. John decides I need a drink. I don't hear what he orders for me. When the waitress returns with a tray of drinks, she puts a pink concoction before me and leans in toward the table.

"A pretty drink for a pretty lady," she purrs, winking at me. She is tall and voluptuous, a short-haired blonde pixie with innocence long ago lost. I smile back, uncertain how to flirt with a woman.

"Whoa, you got it goin' on tonight, Lena," John declares after the waitress leaves. "Even the women want a piece of you."

"I'm sure she flirts with everybody," I say, trying to sound dismissive but smiling at my own excitement.

The men laugh uproariously and Jeff touches my hair. "I think she's hot for you."

"Well, I've got enough to handle right here at this table," I joke.

Addison orders dinner for me and when the waitress delivers it, she addresses me directly. "How are you doing tonight, sweetheart? Was that drink okay?"

"Oh, yes. It was fine. Thank you."

"Good. Beautiful women should always be kept happy," she says, running her tongue slowly over her lips before sauntering away.

"If she could, she'd take you right on this table," Jeff teases. I am too embarrassed to respond.

"I have an idea," John whispers to me. "Why don't you go to the ladies room and take off your panties? I'm sure they must be soaked by now, anyway."

Out of habit, I look at Addison, whether for support or defence, I am not sure. Not having heard John's suggestion, though, Addison only looks at me sweetly and smiles, raising his eyebrows in eerie encouragement.

"Go ahead. You know you want to," John urges.

"Would you excuse me, John? I need to go to the ladies room," I announce so the table will hear me.

"Of course," he replies, sliding out of the booth to let me out.

My walk to the restroom leaves me tingling and shaky. Heads still turn, eyes still stare with longing. Am I dreaming? What kind of night is this? I am so wet, I truly believe my juices are running down the insides of my thighs.

Inside the stall in the restroom, I lean against the door, close my eyes and try to slow my breathing. The broken lock prevents it from staying closed, so my weight against it is the only way to ensure privacy.

Should I really take my panties off? My skirt is so short. Should I risk it? Is John telling the table right now that I am in here taking off my panties at his request? I like it, damn it. I like knowing they are talking about me, getting hard for me, fantasizing about what they'll do to me. Maybe they'll even share their plans with the waitress!

I slip out of my damp panties, forgetting to hold the door shut. As it creeps open, I look up to see the waitress standing there with a cigarette, smirking as she watches me. My pussy throbs. Nobody else is in the restroom and a heavy silence hangs between us. I stare back at the waitress at first with shock but then with intrigue. I open my mouth to speak, but to say what? Spew curses at her? Politely excuse myself? Invite her into the stall? My mind is a jumble of erotic possibilities.

I freeze, panties in hand, the hem of my skirt around my waist. Oh, God, I wince. Why don't I invite her in? Why do I behave like a frightened suburbanite? Just as I start to speak, the waitress turns around and casually walks out.

My panties hang in limp defeat from my motionless hand, as if I've tried to signal surrender with them but the other side hasn't been watching.

My drink sloshes around in my stomach and disrupts my thoughts until I can think of nothing else to do but return to the table. Wadding the panties up into a ball, I stuff them into my tiny purse with a sigh.

I stifle a big giggle as I walk past the curious diners. My pussy tingles with arousal, especially now that it is free. I like having this new secret – no, these two secrets! – safely tucked into my mind. *Hello*, I imagine myself nodding at the gaping clientele. *Yes, it's true that there's even less between you and my pussy than ever before. And, by the way, I almost had sex with a woman!* Cool air circulates under my skirt. It really does feel better to have those panties off!

I make eye contact, almost accidentally, with a beautiful Italian man dining with a woman (his wife?). His dark eyes assess me so completely, I almost lose my balance. I can't remember the last time a man so thoroughly undressed me without laying a hand on me. His companion shoots me a venomous stare.

As I slide into the booth to join the three men, my skirt threatens to rise above the line of propriety. I don't trouble myself about it. My damp thighs are drawn to the leather seats. I have a sudden urge to smear my juicy centre on the seats as I slide . . .

"Well, you were gone much too long," Jeff says when I am back in my place.

"Did you talk about me?" I venture, giving in to the giddiness that hovers on the edge of euphoria.

The men laugh. "Oh, yes," John assures me. "But it was all positive." They laugh again. He puts his mouth close to my ear. "Did you do what I asked you?" I nod discreetly.

"Is everything all right?" Addison asks. He senses I am not completely myself.

I feel myself blush. "Well, a weird thing happened."

Eyebrows go up and heads lean toward me.

"Our waitress was in there."

I pause. The men wait. Finally, Addison says, "And?"

"I think she was looking at me."

"What do you mean 'looking'?"

"You know, through the door."

I can't tell them what really happened – I don't want to sound as culpable as I know I am.

"Did you like it?" Jeff asks, smiling.

"It was just weird."

But I can't get the scene out of my mind. And when the waitress brings our dinners, this time staring boldly at me without saying a word, the men take notice. The silence amplifies the woman's obvious interest in me.

My internal temperature rises and I increasingly feel as if I am sitting in a puddle. Wet and fidgety, I poke at my food mostly to distract me from everything else I am feeling.

To make matters worse, the handsome Italian makes no attempt to disguise his fascination with me. Every time I look in his direction, his dark, velvety eyes are staring at me. I can only imagine how outraged his companion must be, both at him and at me, but what can I do about it? Apparently, John has a solution.

John's hands are suddenly groping my knees, though his gaze is fixed forward; on the Italian, in fact. He says nothing, but firmly takes hold of my nearest knee and pulls it toward him, forcing me to open my legs. The man's gaze immediately shifts from my face to my crotch.

I am so stunned by John's actions, I don't have time to react. He's not only helped himself to my body but put it on display for another man to view. I've never in all my life exposed myself in public, let alone to a stranger. How much of my pussy can the Italian see? What must he think of me?

For the second time that night, I am amazed to discover that shame quickly dissolves into excitement. I like being the object of so much lust. Yes, there was a certain amount of power in it but also a liberation unlike any I've ever known. *Look at my pussy!* I want to purr at the Italian. *Isn't it pretty? What would you do with it if I let you have it?* And how I wonder what he *would* do with it.

Despite my clothes, I might as well be naked. I've been laid spread-eagled on the table and am relishing every moment. In my mind, all sex flows from me. My body vibrates like a guitar string strung too tight and strummed incessantly.

Thankfully, the Italian is worldly enough not to flinch at the sight John forces upon him. Though he lingers on what is between my spread thighs, he shifts his gaze before his companion follows it. The corners of his mouth turn upward just long enough for me – and John – to know that he's seen my glistening pussy and enjoyed the opportunity.

Neither Addison nor Jeff seem to be aware of what John has done. They eat their meals, blithely unaware of anything for the remainder of the evening. Their provocative banter continues while I virtually drip for the Italian.

After the men finish their dinners and I explain that I just didn't have much of an appetite, they decide to skip dessert.

"I prefer to take my dessert at the hotel," John says. "Behind closed doors and over a period of several hours."

"So, how are you feeling?" Addison finally asks, breaking the silence on the way to the hotel.

"Fine," I reply. My grin is unstoppable.

I know he wants to know what I am thinking. He probably wants to hear that I am excited or looking forward to what is ahead of me tonight. But no words can adequately describe the incredibly delicious anticipation I feel. Where can I begin to tell him about the whirl of thoughts and emotions inside me at this moment?

"Fine? Is that all? This from a woman who's going to be fucked silly by three men who think she's the most beautiful female on the planet?"

I smile at his enthusiasm and eagerness to please. His erection is very obvious. Even his voice is somewhat breathless. "Yes," I say. "Just fine." The car seat practically steams from the heat of my pussy.

John and Jeff lounge comfortably in the Peninsula Hotel lobby. Addison has driven quickly and not encountered much traffic – how do John and Jeff arrive so much sooner? Based on the twinkle in their eyes, I can only assume that the power of the libido has overcome the limitations of their respective cars. They get to their feet when I and Addison enter the lobby.

The woman at the reception desk smiles in that warm but detached way that customer service people are trained to do. Once the four guests have all collected before her, however, her somewhat vacant smile morphes into something else. As if reading the group's intentions, that familiar spark seems to light her eyes. Everybody's colour is a bit deeper, their voices slightly higher.

"May I help you?" the strikingly attractive woman asks.

How have the gods conspired to put so many beautiful women in my path tonight? Not only are they beautiful, but they eye me with the kind of wanton desire I've only fantasized about. Everybody seems to sense that I will be fucked by three different cocks. Rather than judging me a wanton trollop, people are drawn to my unleashed sexuality. The circumstance somehow affirms my sexual nature – if I am courting three cocks, I must surely be worth fucking.

The receptionist gives me the once over but it is unlike the kind of cold assessment I am used to getting from women. This one feels more like the one I got from the voluptuous waitress. My skin tingled.

"Yes, you can help us," Addison says as he turns to me. "Why don't you tell the nice lady what we want, sweetheart?"

My body temperature climbs several degrees. I hesitate, looking from one man to the next, hoping to be rescued, but all three of them smirk in response. My shyness peels away from me in layers, falling to the floor like unnecessary clothing.

"We'd like to check in, please. The name is Taylor." My throat is too dry to swallow.

"All four of you?" The pretty brunette asks with a tilt of her head.

"Yes," I say slowly and more quietly. I don't know whether to be annoyed or turned on by this woman's implied assumption. I can't even look at the men's faces – their amusement is palpable.

The receptionist types something into her computer and accesses the information she seeks. "Oh, yes. The honeymoon suite." Her smile lingers long after she speaks. She writes something down, then retrieves the key to their room from the cubbyholes behind her.

Handing the key to Addison, she says, "Enjoy your stay," with so much implication, I blush from head to foot. As the men walk away, the woman discreetly slips a small note card across the counter to me. Wordlessly, I take it and turn away.

On the way to the elevator, I pause to look at it. It reads "Fuck'em each once for me."

The heat among the four of us approaches the incendiary level by the time we reach our suite. I will always remember that it is Addison who approaches me first, kissing me softly over my face and moving to my lips with sensual slowness. As his mouth meshes with mine, hands explore my body. Zippers unzip, and fabric slides along my skin. Hot breath caresses me.

Though the room isn't dark – someone flips a wall switch when they enter the room – I can't discern faces at first. As all of the men touch me, I become a goddess under their worshipping adoration. I feel loved, desired, profoundly sexual.

Several hours pass in a blur of unrestrained hunger. Cocks penetrate my pussy and my mouth. Tongues dance over my tits, coaxing my nipples to their fullest. The men take turns with me, each one lovingly fucking my brains out. I hear myself shouting with pleasure and know I am as much out of my body as I am in it. I can't stay inside myself – the euphoria surpasses my capacity to withstand it.

There is a pause in the action sometime around midnight. I lose track of all orgasms, my own as well as the men's. Addison slips out for a pack of cigarettes and suddenly my lust mixes with panic. It is one thing to give myself to these men when Addison is present but quite another to enjoy them in his absence. I am a schoolgirl, considering the ramifications of giving one a blowjob or letting another eat my pussy. Having my husband gone, even for a little while, makes me feel naughtier, which in turn makes me wetter.

I let myself focus for the first time tonight. To my delight, I discover that Jeff is hung like a horse. His big, thick cock mesmerizes me as he approaches and still glistens from my juices. I am vaguely aware of being penetrated by something large but don't realize exactly who has wielded the object of my pleasure. Now I know it is Jeff and don't protest at all when it is apparent that he is taking me again.

"I've been hard ever since Addison proposed this whole idea," he confesses as he holds open my thighs and pushes himself into me. As I gasp, he continues. "I just can't believe I get to fuck such a beauty." He rams me hard, as if punctuating his comment. I admire his muscular physique that now shines with a thin film of sweat. I am consumed by the urge to run my palms over every developed contour of his finely shaped body.

Seconds after he sprays yet another round of come onto my tummy, John moves in to take his place. If Jeff can be defined by his size, John's claim to fame is his exceptional hardness. He has yet to orgasm and we've all been fucking for more than two hours! His endurance captivates me as I see that his rock-hard member has a mind of its own.

"All I could think about was having you to myself," he says as he kisses the insides of my things. "I want to please you until you can't stand it any longer." His mouth tickles my clit. Even the way he licks me makes me feel that I have powers even I don't understand. He brings me to orgasm quickly and the moment the tremors subside, he slips his throbbing erection inside me and pumps away. Addison walks in on the scene.

Having him see me get fucked by someone else, someone he knows and has even encouraged, makes me spread my legs wider. I catch his eye and hold it, revelling in the excitement on his face. John fucks me incessantly – so long, in fact, that the other two men can no longer contain themselves. Addison feeds me his cock, which I accept gratefully. Jeff stares at the scene and beats off, spraying his stuff on the bedsheets.

I don't know when we all fall asleep. Time has become meaningless many orgasms ago. Light dapples the sheer curtains and I turn languidly to greet the morning. Our bodies lay like rag dolls across the two beds and I smile with the memory of the previous night, knowing it will never be like this again, that the moment I return to predictable but loving monogamy, all I will have is this masturbatory fodder and an indelible smile.

"Honey? You okay?" Addison said to me, shaking my shoulder gently. He thought he was jarring me from some kind of reverie or daydream, and I didn't have the heart to tell him that I'd just thoroughly screwed him and his two best friends. My panties were wet and I was sure my eyes were glazed over, but I managed a smile and came back to the reality of Butterfield 8. For two, not four.

"I'm sorry to have kept you waiting. I would have introduced you but then we never would have gotten rid of the guy. He probably would have joined us for dinner!" Addison said as we headed for our table.

I fought the urge to tell my husband that I could take as many men for dinner as he was willing and able to provide. Maybe I'll work up the neve to tell him on our *next* anniversary.

Blue Eyes

Heather (Glasgow, Scotland)

Bottle of red wine in one hand and a glass in the other I strolled to the window for perhaps the hundredth time in half an hour. Was I restless, was I confused? Yes. Only the day before I had moved my stuff consisting of four carton boxes, one suitcase and a microwave into this small damp Glasgow flat.

I called it coming back to my Scottish roots but in truth I was running away at twenty-seven; having qualified as an interior architect two years ago, I hoped that my job chances would be better in Glasgow – I'd found nothing in the over-crowded London market apart from Mark, my dead-end ex of approximately two weeks.

Mark had been a rocker – well, he was in a rock band of sorts. What can I say about Mark except his cock was huge, and yeah, the sex was great – he had a personality about as interesting as a snail and an IQ of zero.

Did I love him?

No. I've never been in love, sometimes wonder what the word actually means. Is it created by fairies? This magic little gift that only the good girls get. Then, in that case, I'm bad.

Hey, I'm worse than bad – I must be as bad as they make 'em.

Do I miss him?

No!

Do I miss the sex?

Yes.

I took another gulp of wine. It helped dull the pain. I pulled the curtains back and stared out at the road workers who were, to my untrained eye, fixing some sort of power line. Even although it was six o'clock in the evening, it was still bright on this overcast day in March and the workers below had become like a little TV show to me. Dressed in yellow jackets, jeans and high sturdy boots, they were something to occupy my thoughts other than my ex, my non-existent finances, and the dire economy. They weren't nice-looking men, not one male strip-a-gram among them.

Wait! That had been the case until a second ago. The man who now walked into their midst was gorgeous, a male Greek Adonis – better, Michelangelo's David walking and breathing in the flesh.

My thighs clamped and throbbed alarmingly, my glass shook and a trickle of red wine spilled on the carpet. Hell! I would have to get someone in to clean it, but I would worry about that later.

My eyes wanted to return to the perfect male specimen below and I let them.

He was tall with jet black cropped hair. A few X-rated thoughts ran through my head, just looking at him. Hungrily I watched him, momentarily absorbed in the way his T-shirt so nicely outlined his wide shoulders and strong back, and then there were those jeans, lovingly cupping his long, well-defined legs, not to mention the best-looking butt I'd ever seen.

Suddenly I wanted to kiss that butt, to run my tongue along its smooth moonshine crack.

I sighed lustily, then shrugged it off. I had given up on men. A shame, really, because he definitely had a body designed to tempt women – sort of sinner and saint all packed into one very well-put-together unit.

My pussy was hot and wet. Sometimes – well, most of the time – the little horny organ between my legs had to be obeyed.

And so it was that I obeyed her now.

Placing my glass on the windowsill, I gave way to the fantasy building in my head. A fantasy that I had always had; although the time and often the location changed, the dark-haired, blue-eyed man never did.

In the fantasy I was running – from what and from whom I don't know. My hair spiralling out behind my body, the wind on my naked flesh cool. Suddenly I fell but there was danger:

what and who this danger was I had no idea. But then it didn't matter, a strong, long-fingered, firm hand grasped my own, pulling me to my feet. Then we were running and running: me breathless and him, this tall dark stranger, not breathless at all. Pulling me along to keep up with his pace, his powerful strides cutting and flattening the soggy plant life beneath his furry boots.

Then I stumbled.

And suddenly strong arms encircled me and I was warm and secure against a hard chest. His heartbeat beating rhythmically beneath my cheek while his strides on the hard earth jolted through my entire body beneath the moonlit darkness.

There was danger still but nevertheless I felt safe in this stranger's arms. Turning my head, further into his chest, so that I could breathe in the animal scents of his furs, I was aroused: then it came to me suddenly. In my fantasy, I had gone back in time; I was a modern woman saved from some kind of prehistoric beast by a cave-age man.

I shivered in anticipation, wondering what this man – when the time was safe – would do to me. Would he kiss me? Would he make me his wife or would he ravish my body?

Eventually we came to a cave. It was still dark and terribly cold. He lay me down on a bed of furs and left me alone. My breath came in short bursts, grey and icy under the moonlight; I was afraid and excited all at the same time.

Would he come back or was I alone in this strange new land?

A shuffle, followed by the sound of sliding stones, and then his large frame in the entrance of the cave blocked out the moonlight.

I was saved.

My skin tingled, for what would my primitive rescuer take as his payment?

Me, my body, my soul or – worse – my heart?

A spark, the sound of flint hitting stone, and then a small fire jumped into life. My rescuer's back was to me, his shoulders were wide, and the frame beneath the deer skins muscular.

The fire crackled and he turned to me. Suddenly I found myself snared by a pair of blue eyes, as icy cool as the frozen landscape that was his home. I swallowed while the firelight continued to play off his sculpted face, pushing tiny shadows here and there beneath his strong nose and square chin.

He pulled back the furs covering my trembling body. I trembled all the harder from a combination of cold and nerves.

What did he have in mind?

Pulling off his boots and stripping away his trousers, he turned to me, completely naked in the firelight.

My eyes widened, and I had to resist the urge to pull the furs back up to my chin. His blue eyes were hungry for me, his wide shoulders giving way to a flat abdomen sporting a six-pack, then there were his slender hips and long powerful legs. His groin – oh, his delicious black hairy groin – caused my temperature to accelerate. He was hard, his cock standing up proud and erect from a mound of curly hair. I blinked for, truly, in my entire life I had never seen a cock so large: ten inches long and so thick that it would be impossible to close my fingers around its tip.

He undressed me, his fingers warm against my cool flesh. I shivered more from anticipation than actual fear, for my pussy was wet, the moisture clinging uncomfortably between my legs. I wanted his hard cock in me, I wanted this prehistoric man to fuck me.

No ceremony here, no cute foreplay to get me aroused; when I was naked he grunted with satisfaction and pushed me back against the furs. Pushing my thighs apart with one large hand, grabbing my breast with the other, he moved over me. For a moment I felt the furriness of him against my thigh; then he was entering me and there was nothing gentle about it.

I gasped and cried out, my fingernails digging into his back, while he gripped my butt and moved back and forth over me, plunging into me time and time again, with a force that rocked my world. In no time my body was soaked with perspiration. He was rough and hard.

And I loved it!

With a cry I arched up against him, pushing his cock hard against the tender back wall of my pussy; then I climaxed, my thighs throbbing as wave after wave of sweet fiery emotion touched every cell in my body. He continued to move over and in me, his breath fanning across my face, now and again a glimpse of blue eyes in the darkness; then, withdrawing his cock, he turned me around so that I was facing the floor, the fluffy furs tickling my nose. He parted my thighs, lay over me so that his weight was pushing me down hard against the ground, and then . . .

Hell! My cell phone rang, interrupting my train of thought just as my fantasy was getting interesting. I pulled my hand from my panties and reached for the slim flip phone in my handbag.

"Oh, hi, Mum."

"Have you settled in yet?"

"I just got here."

"Have you unpacked?"

I looked around at my stuff still in the cartons. "Yeah." There was a rat-a-tat-tat on the outside door. "Wait, Mum, I'll call you back, okay? Someone's at the door."

I snapped the phone, and the most devastating sight I'd seen in a long time greeted me. Devastating for what? My libido, that's what! Six feet two inches of prime male flesh filled my doorway. Maths had never been my strong point but I clocked him at around thirty-two, give or take a couple of years. Certainly not much older than me.

"Hi." The dark haired man extended his hand. "I'm Blake and you must be Heather?" At my nod, he smiled warmly. Perfect white teeth flashed, and the soft skin around his eyes crinkled. Damn and blast that he was wearing sunglasses, for I couldn't see their colour. "I just wanted to let you know that sometime this evening, and possibly tomorrow as well, the power will be out in your building."

My skin tingled; his sexy deep Scottish accent washed over my body like a caress. I cursed that I didn't have one; then, having been born in London to a Scottish mother and English father, there was fat chance of that.

When I looked up, he was grinning. I blinked but, nope, he was still grinning.

"What?"

He smiled warmly "I just said, it's probably a good idea to get a flashlight."

I nodded. If the power was going to be out, it certainly made sense.

"Hello, Earth calling pretty lady in the doorway."

"Sorry." I blinked again. "I was away in my own little world. What did you say?"

"I said, don't leave it too late. The lights will be going off around eight – and, the next time you decide to touch yourself, make sure you've closed the curtains properly."

I flushed scarlet to the ears. "You saw that? I mean, you saw me . . ."

"Lady, I saw everything."

Shit. I closed my eyes and raised my head to the ceiling, praying for inspiration. What must this guy think of me?

"Don't be embarrassed. We all do it."

I looked at him, and saw my mortified reflection reflected back in his dark shades. "Yeah but not in public."

"I enjoyed it."

His voice was low and sultry and sent shivers down my spine. He turned on his heel, but not before I'd seen that he was aroused; his tight-fitting jeans hid nothing.

Out of breath and panting, I was struggling up the stairs of my building shortly before eight, with a bag of shopping in one hand and a new torch in the other. The blasted elevator wasn't working again, but when did it ever? There was a crack, a low hum and then the lights went out. I was left alone in complete darkness, my heart accelerating out of control, a half-eaten packet of potato crisps my only companion.

In a moment of inspiration, it came to me that I had my brand new flashy torch, thanks to sexy worker guy, complete with batteries. All I had to do was get the little things in the torch and Bob's your uncle. Rummaging in the bag until I found the necessary, I placed the torch on the step. A cat screeched; swirling around, my foot collided with it. I could only stand there breathing hard, cursing the cat as the torch clunked and clicked away down the stairs.

There was no point retrieving the torch; I reasoned it would probably be lying in a thousand pieces somewhere. The bottom of my shopping bag split open just as I stepped onto the next step. My foot squashed in what could only have been yogurt and, with a crash, I fell. Sitting alone in complete darkness, in sticky cold yogurt, I felt like crying. Out of nowhere a strong, long-fingered, firm hand grasped my own, pulling me to my feet.

I gasped and fell against a brick-hard chest. Something about the whole thing was so familiar yet different. It came to me that the man reminded me of my prehistoric fantasy.

Suddenly I was aroused and hotter than an inferno.

Gently he steered me along the corridor in the direction of my doorway. How could he know where I lived? I wondered, but I was far too horny to give it adequate thought. If I didn't take my chance now I would lose it. I stepped away from him. His breathing in the darkness slowed. It was a moment before he reached for me and, when he did, his hand collided with my breast; quickly he jerked it back.

I bit back the sigh in my throat and waited. This time, when his hand reached out it encountered my face. Turning my head into his palm, I kissed the sensitive skin there and ran my tongue along his middle finger before taking it fully into my mouth.

He gasped but didn't say anything.

Good! My prehistoric man never spoke, nor should he if the moment was going to be perfect.

With a grunt he pushed me up against the wall, his hands eagerly exploring every part of my body. I shut my eyes; in my head I was in a different place, a cave in an icy, untamed land.

His hands tugged at the front of my zipper. Pulling my hair back, he kissed me hard on the mouth; then, grabbing my butt, he pulled me against his erection.

I tried not to whimper, not to speak – it was so much sexier – but I was wet and horny for him, there was no denying that.

With a grunt, he pulled down my jeans, jerked his fingers in my panties and ripped them in half. As easily as if they were made of paper rather than lace. Breathing hard, he rubbed his hand through my pubic hair. I never shaved and, judging by the grunts coming from him, he seemed to appreciate that fact. One hand stroked up beneath my jumper and cupped my breast through my bra, while the other parted the lips of my pussy and slid a finger inside my warm creamy centre.

I shut my eyes tightly and fought the urge to buck up against him. His finger was moving quickly in and out of me now, hitting all the right spots, his other hand wreaking havoc on my erect, stiff left nipple.

Giving into desire, I gasped and pulled him firmly towards me; tangling my tongue with his, I melted in his kiss. I never kissed my prehistoric lover in my fantasy but then, this was a real living, breathing man before me, and I had to have . . . all of him.

As if sensing this, he slivered his tongue down my neck and buried it in the sweet flesh of my pussy. I felt my pussy contract when he pushed his tongue inside me. His tongue was hot and hard as it drove in and out. I gasped and bucked against his mouth.

Even in the darkness I could feel his cocky grin as he took me deeper into his mouth and tenderly sucked and nipped my horny little mound. I was dying, swimming in a sea of pure erotic sensations, then suddenly his mouth was back on mine, his cock freed from his jeans, warm and hard, resting against the soft skin of my stomach.

Before I could think, he grabbed my buttocks and, using the wall for support, plunged his hard shaft into me.

Ah, pure bliss, having him there in me so hard and strong. I felt as if I would burst from the sheer size of him.

And yet I didn't!

Instead, something magical happened in the darkness on that deserted stairway, as his cock continued to plunge deeply into me and his balls gyrated against my thighs. The pain was extreme and immense, like nothing I had encountered from smaller cocks before, but then suddenly it gave way to such mind-blowing pleasure.

For I had two options in that moment while I was rammed up hard against the cool wall and he thrust into me. They were give up the pain and enjoy it or suffer.

I gave up the pain.

A moment later, I was coming, my hairy little mound tightening around his hard shaft. With a cry from his parted lips, I felt his seed warm and infinitely sticky enter and fill my pussy, my womanhood. But then something totally unprecedented happened. I was coming again; wave after wave of pleasure coursed through my body until I believed I would die from it. I came again!

Burying my head and my grin in his neck, I laughed. Multiple orgasms really did exist – they weren't just conjured up by fairies for good little girls or a figment of a man's imagination.

Was I happy?

Yes – and, a lot more, for the first time in my life I was fulfilled.

When I had come back to myself, he gently helped me dress and then escorted me back to my doorway.

Strangers in the night, we tenderly kissed; then he was gone, his footfalls quieter, his feet taking him further away from me.

I showered, but not between my legs, however; unconsciously, I wanted to leave his salty aftermath there. Just as I stepped out of the shower, there was for the second time a rat-a-tat-tat on the outside door. Tucking a towel around my breasts, I went to answer it.

When I looked into the bright corridor – for the lights had come back on – no one was there. I still do not know what prompted me to look down, but when I did I saw my shopping neatly collected in a pile on my doormat along with my torch, a little worse the wear but still functional.

Next day, as I chomped on a piece of burned toast, another overcast day greeted me, the tall Glasgow tenements seeming as grey and oppressive as the weather. The little yellow-coated workers were still there, but to my disappointment sexy guy was nowhere to be seen.

Fifteen minutes later, I was walking through the persistent drizzle, a cup of Starbucks coffee from Union Street in one hand and a newspaper in the other. When I pulled up short, the man before me did the same. When I looked up, my eyes encountered a pair of dark sunshades. Man, was the guy egoistic, was my first thought; my second was he had a right to be, for he was as gorgeous as the first time that I had met him – better, even, in the light of the day, if that was possible.

I tipped my cup. "Hi."

Blake tipped his cup – also from Starbucks – and, pulling the collar of his yellow worker's jacket up, walked on by.

In that second I wanted a thunderbolt from God to incinerate him; then in the next I remembered how gorgeous his fingers had looked clasped around the plastic cup. In the third I wanted those very same fingers to probe me. In the fourth I feared that I was losing my head. In the fifth I wanted him to fuck me and I *knew* I was.

He hadn't shown any interest in me; in fact his cool rebuff told me all that I needed to know. Pulling up my hood – due to the drizzle which had became a downpour – I sipped at my coffee and considered the facts. He was a hunk, and what did that mean? He probably had a long-legged, busty, blue-eyed blonde girlfriend and therefore no interest in me.

I was blonde but, at five foot two, certainly not long-legged; nor was I busty.

That night, around eight, the lights went off. My palms were sticky and my pulse rate sporadic. Should I?

There was only one way to find out. The corridor was as dark and as empty as the night before. Would he come? I hoped and prayed with my whole heart that he would.

And still I waited.

Then I thought I heard footfalls on the stairway. I couldn't see through the darkness. My pulse rate accelerated. Had I imagined it?

Suddenly, strong hands encircled my waist and pushed me up against the door. My scream was cut off by a warm probing tongue.

I smiled and wrapped my arms around the large man's neck, for I recognized that tongue. It was my lover of the night before. While his lips devoured mine, I reached behind and pushed open the door. This time, I wanted to have him naked, gliding over me, just like my prehistoric man in the cave; I wanted to feel every piece of his flesh.

The apartment was dark, but the light coming from the street lamps below allowed me to make out the shapes of the furniture easily enough.

I took his hand to lead him through to the bedroom. He had other ideas; sweeping me up in his arms, he dumped me on the sofa in front of the window. Sitting there, I had to watch him undress, the orange glow from the lamps reflecting off of his muscular skin. It was extremely erotic; sliding my fingers under my skirt, I began to fondle myself; slipping my fingers in and out of my wet pussy, becoming hotter and hotter with each piece of his clothing that fell to the floor. When he turned, I caught a glimpse of his cock and almost climaxed right there. For it was huge and thick: another thing this man had in common with my prehistoric lover. I hungered to touch it, to feel it. I got my wish; stepping up to me, he tangled his fingers in my hair, tipped my head back and pressed his huge cock into my mouth.

My lips parted, but this was no mere blow-job; the man was actually fucking my mouth. Using it as if it were a pussy, he pushed his cock in and out, quickening the pace.

I was wetter than ever before in my life. He had taken all control away from me and I loved it. I shoved several fingers into my pussy and my left hand cupped his buttocks. I sighed, feeling the strong muscles bunch and contract with each of his thrusts under my palm.

It was heavenly.

He withdrew his cock from my mouth, and my tongue followed it. Hungry for more, I placed my lips against his groin and kissed the furriness there. He bent before me and kissed my lips, oh, so tenderly. His tongue gently probed my mouth; I thought that my heart would break. Then he pulled my jumper off and pulled down my skirt and pants until I was sitting there naked before him. He parted my thighs and slithered his tongue from my hip down my right leg to my pussy, while his other hand squeezed and kneaded my breasts.

A moment later, I gasped when he buried his face between my thighs. Expertly he slithered his tongue in long languid strokes down the length of my pussy and back again. He nibbled on first one lip then the other, before pulling them wide open, plunging his tongue deeply into my warm creamy centre. I gasped as I felt his tongue wiggling and moving deep within me. The little guttural sounds he was making deep from the back of his throat got me as horny as hell. Sliding his tongue a few times over my clitoris, he parted my lips and plunged his cock into me.

He was hard, his stroke powerful; I gasped.

In fact, I was making so much noise the neighbours could probably hear but I wasn't in any state to think about that just then.

He continued to thrust into me. With each thrust I was pushed further against the back of the sofa until, in the end, he was standing, gyrating into me, supporting my parted legs high up around his waist.

My breasts were bouncing wildly out of control. Slipping a hand down, I cupped his jingling balls and gently squeezed, then I fiddled madly with my breasts. My clit was swollen and poking between my lips; I could feel it rub against him.

Watching his magnificent muscular body, I climaxed, my milky come exploding over his balls, down my thighs and onto the floor.

He shuddered and, with an animalistic groan of male satisfaction, delivered his seed into me.

I still hadn't come properly back down to earth when the door closed softly a moment later with a gentle click.

Next evening, I knew from the clock on the wall that it was eight. The lights hadn't gone off and they probably wouldn't either. The little yellow-coated workers were gone and that could only mean they had fixed the problem. Pushing the crossword I hadn't been able to get into to the side. I paced the room. I flicked off the lights, and unbolted the front door; naked, with a bottle of red wine in one hand, I sat down to wait.

The tick, tick of the clock was maddening. Pouring myself another glass, I strained to see through the darkness. There was a flash of light from the corridor behind, a glimpse of a tall man, and then darkness again.

I could hear his breath. I stood up, hands out before me; I came to his chest. He stood there silently as I slowly undressed him. When he was naked, I swirled my tongue around the tip of his cock, smelling his desire that was salty and something altogether man.

Pulling me to my feet, he kissed me then with a thoroughness that left me shaking; then, flipping my legs out from beneath me – for he was so strong and I like a doll in his arms – he lay me down on the floor. Taking my glass he poured droplets of wine into my mouth.

I gulped, while his hands rubbed the wine running down my chin, over my shoulders and breasts. Then he plunged a finger into my pussy, the lips opening easy for him while he dribbled wine over my breasts.

I shivered; the wine was cool and my skin hot. He rubbed the wine in over my nipples, making them even harder, more sensitive to his touch.

With his tongue he licked it off. My thighs clamped around his finger and my nipples tingled unbearably. He bent and took my left nipple between his teeth and bit down. I bucked against him, wanting the muted pain along with the pleasure.

I moaned when he poured the whole glass of wine over my stomach, then whimpered with desire as he lay his body over my sticky flesh. I parted my legs, inviting him, and when he entered me, stretching me with his fullness, I buried my head against his shoulder. I could feel warm sensations begin to work their way outward from the centre of my groin. Each stroke took me to a new and higher plateau of pleasure.

Just as I was about to climax, he withdrew from me and turned me to face the floor; just like in my fantasy he spread my thighs wide and then hard, almost brutally, he moved into me, his thrusts hitting the back wall of my pussy. His hands spanked my buttocks; male grunts filled the dark room. It was good – it was better than good, it was fantastic.

But something was missing!

Blake's face appeared before my eyes as the man above me continued to thrust into me. It came to me then, I couldn't do this. I had hardly met Blake but it was him that I wanted, not this fantastic faceless lover of a man.

Hell, my prehistoric cave-man had a face; this guy was just a body. I wanted Blake.

I shivered. Every sweet impulse shut down as if it had never been there. Sensing this, he withdrew.

I stood and pulled on my jumper. "You should go."

Silence.

I flicked on the light and turned, expecting to face a put-out man. I gaped. sitting before me buck-naked, looking unbelievably sexy, was Blake. He had been my secret lover all along. When he looked up, I was snared by a pair of icy blue eyes.

I could have laughed with joy. Blake was my prehistoric lover, living and breathing in the flesh. In fact, the man of my dreams and the man of my flesh were so similar, they could have been twins.

He stood. "I'm going. Look, listen . . ."

"No!"

He ran a hand through his black hair. "But you just said."

"I know. That was before I knew it was you. See, I was thinking about you. I wanted, well, to ask you on a date maybe. Hell, I'm making this worse, but do you like me? Oh, tell me to shut up."

He grinned sexily. "I'm crazy about you."

"You are." I licked my lips. "In that case, how do you take your eggs?"

"Scrambled." He tugged my jumper off and entered me before we had even tumbled to the carpet.

Dirty Girl

Jade (Derby, UK)

Personally I blame it on the nuns.

I didn't have a Catholic upbringing, my parents weren't even lapsed, but when I was fourteen everything changed. When they caught me in their bed with the next door neighbours' oldest son, a bottle of vodka, a joint and a Polaroid camera (what can I say, I'm easily led) they decided some repression was exactly what I needed.

And after that shock, my mother's subsequent turn to Valium and my father's consequent turn to an even younger mistress, they decided religion could be the answer for us all.

To say it didn't work is rather an understatement. At eighteen, when I finally escaped the ridiculously strict convent school, the years of repressed bad girl behaviour came out with a vengeance.

So now, more than a few years later, not only have I done pretty much everything with everyone (except a nun, which, admittedly, remains a huge fantasy, but is another story . . .) I have all the conditioned guilt to go with it.

So my fantasies aren't exactly conventional.

But fortunately I seem to have found someone even less conventional than I am.

Or should I say that he found me?

It always starts in the shower. I'm using some lavender shower gel that's supposed to be relaxing me, rubbing it slowly over my body, but it does nothing for my knotted shoulders. I just can't relax, and I know that I need someone's sensual touch to release the tension inside.

I try not to think of my ex-boyfriend. I know that I am right to be alone, no matter how much I miss the sex. Splitting with Greg hardly left me devastated – you could hardly describe him as my soul mate – but what he was lacking in romance and intellect he more than made up for physically.

Well, at least he had at the start.

We had spent days in bed, lost weekends and almost friends as we'd explored each other's bodies, his hands running across my skin, fingers deftly making me squirm; he'd been the best lover I'd had.

But that was before *he'd* come into my life. Just answering the phone that day had changed everything, and Greg had suddenly seemed boring in comparison, our relationship dull and uninspired. Nothing had changed the feeling, no matter how hard I'd tried (and, believe me, I bought half the sex shop trying).

There were so many regrets, all too late now.

I know that if I'd wanted I could have stopped him leaving, told him some bullshit to make everything better. He'd caught me on the phone, had heard just enough to be suspicious, and that had been it. I could have tried to explain – God knows, with my imagination I could have thought up some story to make him understand. I could have tried to convince him to stay.

But if Greg had stayed then he'd have wanted the phone calls to stop.

And I couldn't let that happen. They were my secret; my forbidden exploration of something more than anyone else had ever given me.

When it came down to choosing between them, Greg didn't have a hope. The phone calls couldn't end.

But ever since Greg had left it seemed like every muscle in my body was tense, waiting in nervous anticipation for something to happen, for *him* to take it further.

I climb out of the shower; the lavender gel is doing nothing for me except making me smell like a pensioner. I groan as I see myself in the mirror. Without Greg and without sex I'd turned to food to satisfy my appetites. All I'd wanted was a good fuck, but all I'd had was chocolate, and it was definitely starting to show.

I had to be positive. I wasn't chubby, I was voluptuous, a body made for pleasure – each part perfect for caressing, kissing and nibbling. All I needed was a man.

And there was only one I wanted.

I rapidly dry myself, rubbing the harsh towel between my legs roughly, trying to resist the temptation to pleasure myself now, knowing that I'm testing my willpower as I reach for my body lotion and revel in the coolness against my hot skin. I tell myself if I wait until later I'll have more time, something better than a hurried wank, and put the body lotion back, before it drives my body wild. Later I'll be so ready, waiting for the satisfaction I've been craving so long.

It's the only thing I miss about Greg, the regular sex. Although he might have acted like an emotional cripple, he still had a hard cock that was always ready for action. Since he'd gone my libido had seemed to go through the roof, and I was pleasuring myself to the point where I was in danger of getting Repetitive Strain Injury if I didn't get a *real* man *real soon*.

I dress quickly, before the temptation becomes too much, drying my hair quickly as I brush out the curl, getting myself ready for my respectable job in the city. If only they knew what I was really like, I think, smiling at what they would think. Everybody at work thought I was so serious, so in control, probably thought I was some frigid spinster. I had perfected this facade long ago. But they were wrong.

My breath catches as the phone rings. Another reason why my lust levels have so suddenly increased.

The funny phone calls that were more exciting than upsetting, that I probably looked forward to more than the caller did. I could feel myself getting wet at the thought, and chide myself, trying to dispel the sensations suddenly overwhelming my body. I don't have time for this now.

I try to ignore the continuous ringing, wishing that the hairdryer could drown out the tempting siren. I can't do this now. I can't be late for work – I've never been late for work. It's not the me that everybody knows and expects. But I know my willpower will break before his ever will. It was as if he knew when I was home alone, as if he knew when I would be too weak to refuse his advances. I tell myself that I wish he wouldn't phone, that I want to break this perverse addiction. I know that the only way I can break it is if he stops; I don't have the strength to resist by willpower alone.

But I don't mean it, and if he stopped I know I would be devastated.

And I think he knows it.

I put the hairdryer down. It's useless to think I can fight the feeling growing so urgently inside me; this thirst needs quenching immediately.

I pin my hair up, then walk down the stairs slowly, letting the anticipation build, feeling the adrenaline coursing through my body. I sit by the phone, legs unable to hold me up much longer, shaking with excitement. I answer with a trembling hand.

"Are you alone?" the man whispers, and I fight the urge to reply. His voice is low and husky, and reminds me of melted chocolate with its melting liquid quality. He pauses, giving me a moment to let my thoughts run wild as I try to guess what he would say next, which erotic scenario he would help me explore this time.

"I know you're alone, otherwise you would have hung up by now. You wouldn't want anybody else to know what's going on, would you? You wouldn't want your friends to know what a dirty girl you are."

I smile. He knows me so well without even having to say a word. Every dirty thought I had ever had he knew, every fantasy I'd ever written off as perverse, he was ready to illustrate and magnify. He was the voice of my libido; he was my imagination exaggerated; he was every obscenity that tempted me personified.

He was like my sexual conscience gone mad.

Sometimes I wanted to ask who he was, but didn't dare ruin my fantasies of him, so let him carry on uninterrupted.

"So have you showered and moisturized today, prepared yourself for me? Did you shave yourself for me, made yourself neat and tidy as if I could see you? Did you touch yourself and think of me as you rubbed in your body lotion? Are you dressed today, or are you sat there naked, waiting for me? Are you waiting for me, are you touching yourself already?" He stops; his breathing ragged, and I can hear his zipper opening.

"I think that today you're dressed, that today you thought you would ignore me. You thought that today you wouldn't let your clit control you, that you would act as repressed as everyone else, that you would pretend that phone wasn't even ringing. Like a good Catholic girl. But you couldn't, could you? Because you're not good. Because your clit began throbbing as soon as the phone rang, each ring, each throb calling you to me. Because my power is stronger than your will, and you know that I give you more than any other man could, without touching you. Because deep down you know you are my whore, and you love being treated this way."

He pauses, and moans softly. I know his power over me turns us both on so much. Every word is like a touch to my body, and I feel my face grow warmer as he voices my darkest secrets.

"So, where will we start? I think you should start by undoing your blouse, but don't take your bra off yet." He says it so casually, as if it is nothing to ask someone he's never even met to take her clothes off, as if this situation were completely normal.

I obey without question or hesitation, slowly opening each button of my shirt as if he is watching to see I'm doing it properly, and then stroke my breasts at the top of my black bra. Already my nipples are hard, and I long to touch them, but I know I must wait until I am told to.

I know the rules already, and dread the result of breaking them.

"I bet your little nipples are standing out like press-studs, aren't they? Touch them, softly, drag your fingertips across them quickly. You want to rub them, but you can't, not until I tell you."

I silently comply, making my nipples ache with the need to be touched more, sending sparks of desire snaking down from my breasts to my clit. But I can't touch myself more yet; I have to wait until he says I can, he is in charge, and I readily submit to his control. The delay seems endless, and I'm ashamed how erratic my breathing already is. But the embarrassment only turns me on further; the thought that he can humiliate me how he liked merely made me wetter.

Sometimes when I touched myself, in the moment before I came, I couldn't help the unbidden thought entering my head that I wanted to be humiliated. In my darker moments of fantasy I dreamt of someone catching me touching myself as he filled my head with words of fantasy, of someone to take it further.

But, for now, his voice was enough.

"Now pinch them through your bra, pinch your nipples so hard I can hear you whimper." His voice is hoarse, and I know he is as excited as I am, if not more so.

I quickly pinch myself, and whimper loudly down the phone, wanting to hear the effect it has on him. I heard him gasp just as loudly, and instinctively know what's coming next.

"I'm touching myself, I'm rubbing my cock, talking to my dirty girl. You make me so desperate." He moans again. "Now take your bra off, but don't touch yourself yet."

I instantly slip my bra off, and lean against the wall to feel the coldness against my bare back. My skin feels like it's on fire, and the wall only provides momentary relief of the heat that is consuming me.

Looking down, I see my breasts are heaving with desire, my nipples hard and so erect. I wait, hand poised above my breast, but not yet touching. I can't help rubbing my thighs together, wishing he would let me touch myself now, but at the same time dreading the moment it's over.

"Now slowly stroke around the outside of your breasts. How much do you want to touch yourself now? How much do you wish I were there to sink my cock deep inside you? Think about my hands on your body, imagine that it's my hands getting closer to your nipples, circle slowly the soft skin around them, and then touch them. Imagine that my mouth is on your nipples, teasing them with my tongue, nipping them softly, until you grab my head to make me bite you harder."

My head is flooded with images of the faceless stranger doing what he wants to me, and I sigh loudly as I pinch my nipples harder.

"Now imagine that I'm watching you, as your hands slide

down your belly, as you start to open your skirt so damn desperately."

I can't help doing exactly what he tells me to do, and undo my skirt, urgently tugging my panties down around my thighs, feeling the sticky wetness on them as they rub against my inner thighs.

"Slip your panties off and lie on your back. Now open your legs, but don't touch. Just think about the air touching your most sensitive parts, and think of me knelt between your legs, looking at your body."

I have always been shy about letting men look at me, but now I open my legs as wide as possible, so wide there is no need to part my lips with my fingers. Suddenly I relish this feeling of exposure and squirm with lust-filled embarrassment as I think of a faceless man watching me. The cold air seems like a lover's caress in the most intimate places, and I slowly trail my fingers up along the inside of her thighs, trying to prolong the moment until I have to touch myself, until I can control myself no longer.

"Now stroke the inside of your thighs, and slowly work your way up to your clit. Think about your clit throbbing, aching for my touch. And now touch, but not hard yet; just catch it gently with the tip of your nail. Now open your legs further and drag your finger down to your hole, and then back to your clit, and back down again, until you are slick with your juices."

I do, barely able to open my legs further than I already had, groaning as I feel how drenched I am. I move my finger from my hole and back to my clit once more than he had said, then pull my hand away urgently as I feel how close I already am. This was why I had to let him control me; he could make me last longer than I ever could.

"If I were there I would lick you clean, stick my tongue deep inside you then suck on your clit until you exploded in my mouth."

But you're not, I want to protest, wanting to dare him to take it further, but can say nothing as the thought of this faceless stranger lapping me to orgasm invades my head, making me pant with desire.

"But I'm not," he says, as if he can read my mind. "So instead you can kneel up for me."

I kneel. This is different; usually he just makes me touch myself, listening to me come. But I trust him, knowing he can only increase my pleasure.

"Now wet your finger with your juices, then reach under yourself, and push your finger inside your arse. Can you make yourself squirm like I could?"

He stops talking, and I can hear his hand rubbing his cock faster and faster. I've never done that before; the idea of anal sex had always seemed somewhat seedy and, although boy-friends had discussed it, the look of disgust on my face had stopped them suggesting it again. But now, now it's different. I can't stop myself doing exactly what he wants; for *him* I could do anything.

"Imagine that your finger is my cock, invading you every-where, taking you like never before."

I obey, struck by the thought of the faceless man taking away my remaining inhibitions, fucking me from behind as I touch myself. Suddenly I want him to take me up the arse, to give him that prize as if it were my final treasured virginity.

For him, I want to do everything.

"If I fucked you, you would know you had been fucked. I would take you in ways you haven't dared dream of. I would make your cunt ache so you were begging me to fill it. I would make your clit throb so you would lie on your back with your legs spread wide, touching yourself while I watched, like the wanton whore you are."

"Now," I moan. "Now."

"Now touch yourself, think that I'm fucking you now, now I'm fucking you hard and every way and rub yourself faster, so that I can hear you scream as you come."

I can't take any more, and I roll over on to my back, opening my legs wide and using the heel of my hand to rub myself harder that I'd ever thought I could stand. I can feel it building, and I pinch my nipples with my free hand, letting the pressure build. I hear him come loudly, and stop fighting it, almost screaming down the phone as the heat consumes me, my clitoris throbbing over and over again.

I collapse against the wall, holding the phone close as I hear his breathing return to normal. I'm still gasping heavily as I try to find my voice, try to find the will to stop this and get back to real life.

"Stop calling me, or I'll call the police," I order, barely able to speak, knowing my threat is empty, but knowing that this has to stop somehow.

"You don't mean that," he tells me, laughing. He hangs up before I have the chance to slam the phone down on him.

He's right. I'm his dirty girl, and I like it.

At the Window as He Watches

Dara (Hoboken, USA)

I'm so hot. I'm standing at the kitchen window, expanding my chest, trying to get some air, this torrid, sultry night. Immediately, I notice the man, lounging spread-eagled on the bench across the street. I admire his strong muscular thighs, barely covered by his tight shorts. His broad chest glistens seductively under the streetlamp; his arms look big, hard, dangerous.

Our eyes meet and lock. He smiles slowly – or perhaps it's a leer. His gaze wanders lecherously over my body. I grow hotter as he examines me, his eyes travelling over my contours, lingering on my tender, private places. My very flesh feels his sharply focused eyes on me. My discomfort grows into embarrassment and a sense of violation.

I squirm uncomfortably, but I have to keep looking at him. I have no choice but to stand there and pose for him. He commands it. He exerts some intoxicating, mesmerizing power over me. I sway precariously. It's not just from the heat, but my growing weakness, my burgeoning helplessness are making me feel faint.

Hypnotically, I lower the straps of my nightgown. I feel he ordered me to and, even more strangely, I have no doubt that I have to obey. The gown slides down over my damp, limp body. I have no power to stop it. He doesn't even let me shield my breasts and pubis from him. I see him very slowly, severely shaking his head, lifting his eyebrows, challenging me to dare disobey him, to even think of fighting him.

I can't. It's impossible. I have no will of my own. My arms drop defenselessly to my bare sides, leaving me in bold and brazen display, just as he desires. He smiles triumphantly and solemnly nods his head.

I burn in the painful heat of his stare, searing my soft flesh in ever-decreasing circles as he scrutinizes my breasts. He carefully goes over each and every tiny pucker of my areolae, then sharply flicks my tense nipples, making me gasp.

I feel him handling me, maliciously moulding my mounds with demanding, hard hands. His cruel palms and his coarse, probing fingers examine me much more thoroughly than any doctor ever had. I groan in discomfort and he returns his attention to my nipples. His strong fingers pull, stretching them to the point of pain. No lover has ever done that to me. Logically, I know I'm torturing myself with my own fingers, yet he controls them. He owns them. He owns all of me.

The pain in my nipples is becoming unbearable. I can tell he knows he's hurting me by that cruel, self-satisfied smirk on his face. I attempt to call out to him, to beg him to stop, but I can't, and he doesn't stop. He just won't stop. For his sadistic pleasure, I'm forced to keep on pulling and twisting my poor nipples that won't even allow me the relief of going numb. I don't think I can take any more. I hear him laughing heartily at my abject helplessness, my complete defencelessness. I know there's no way to fight him, no way to stop him.

It's so horrible, so demeaning, but then again, it's wonderfully arousing. I've never felt so confused, so completely controlled and yet so wildly alive and free. Despite the pain, or perhaps because of it, deep down, I don't want him to stop. He's opening and exposing my submissive nature as no one ever has. He's discovered my deepest, most shameful secret, my hidden dark need for domination, my desire for humiliation and subjugation. No lover has ever tapped this profound well of enforced erotic freedom. No man has ever treated me like this, and here he is, a total stranger, doing this to me. That's the best part – the most amazing, erotic thing!

This is my fantasy come true. And who said women don't want their fantasies to actually come true? The dripping and pulsing between my trembling legs proves that theory wrong – certainly for me.

He whistles and snaps his fingers to reclaim my absolute attention. He knows my mind was wandering. He won't allow me even that privacy. I know he's going to punish me for my lapse. I feel ashamed and elated. I hang my head and feel my blush rising quickly and profusely from my chest to my face. The intense rush of heat feels like I just opened an oven door and looked right in.

The powerful man sharply nods his head. I know immediately what my punishment is to be. I lean out over the windowsill. My unsupported breasts drop heavily from my body. He knows just how to humiliate me. I feel much more than exposed. With my tits hanging down like this, I feel pathetic, sloppy, bovine.

He isn't finished. It gets worse. I'm forced to lift them by the nipples. It hurts like hell! They're so heavy and swollen, my nipples so hard, stretched, and sore. This is torment. I can't possibly do any more, but he forces me to shake them for him.

I can't do this! I'd say it hurts my pride, but I don't think I have any left. I'm just his toy, his slave. He grins and scrutinizes every yank on my nipples, every hard drop of my boobs, every bounce, every jiggle, as I perform the demeaning display for him. My nipples are burning and all this shaking is killing my tits!

As I tightly clutch my nipples and heft my aching mammaries up and down, I try to pretend I'm someplace else, doing anything else, but he won't allow my mind to wander again. It was my wandering mind that got me into this predicament in the first place. He's making sure I know that. My awareness is essential to him. It makes me all the more submissive, all the more ashamed.

I can't stand any more of this pain and embarrassment. I implore him with teary eyes to allow me to stop, but he doesn't. He lets me know that he's thoroughly enjoying the show especially because I don't want to do it.

Suddenly he commands me to stop. Immediately I release my poor nipples, but I can't enjoy any relief, for my big tits drop so hard that the pain and shock make me gasp. Even worse, I'm mortified that he sees the cruel work of gravity on me. His wicked laugh mocks me and my sense of being used intensifies as he points out that he's firmly rubbing his crotch – getting off, at my expense.

He can't possibly expect any more of me. I don't even know who he is. He's an anonymous stranger. He has absolutely no right to order me around like I belong to him, body and soul. It isn't logical for him to be able to control me, to make me perform such lewd, exhibitionistic acts for him.

But then, why am I obeying? He knows he can demand anything of me and I'll do it. Whatever he says, whatever he wants, I know I can't resist. I'm incapable of fighting him. Whatever his power is, it's vastly superior to my own will, my own pride. This power he has over me is the ultimate turn-on. I've often heard that power is an aphrodisiac but that referred to a different sort of power, the kind involving business, politics, money. Those things never made me hot. But this is much different. This is the only kind of power that's ever aroused me. His power is in his silent strength and cool control, his strength and control, his absolute power over me.

I don't really want to listen to him or even to my own thoughts. I don't want to have to think. I don't want to involve my brain at all. All I want to be is a body, a horny animal. I want to leap on top of him and fuck him to death!

But no, what I really crave is for him to take me by force, mount me like a wild animal. I want him to do bestial, painful things to me, brutal things that no one else has ever dared to do. I need him to humiliate me, torment me, punish me, force me into total submission to his inhuman lust. Lust to match my own.

His slow hand creeps under the elastic of his ever-tighter, tighter shorts. I lift my breasts with cupped hands, in offering to him. My gesture tells him everything he wants to know. I am his, completely, utterly. He acknowledges my total surrender with a superior smile, letting me know it isn't over yet. There's much more to come.

He teasingly lowers his shorts' elastic and his massive erection springs out. He chuckles to see me wide-eyed and open-mouthed. I run my tongue longingly around my lips. He proudly wags his magnificent prick at me. My randy tongue goes to the side of my mouth where I involuntarily clench it between my teeth, pressing it hard against my cheek.

The saliva gathers in my mouth. He sees me gulp it down. He knows exactly what I want in my mouth, what I want to feel, hot and thick, down my throat. His teasing, taunting, and posturing is driving me crazy with horniness! His show is forcing me to helplessly press my damp thighs together, making me move them back and forth over each other, against each other, giving my cunt lips a clandestine, desperately needed massage.

I can see that he's highly annoyed by my weakness and lack of self-control. To appease him, I widely spread my legs, too far apart to touch each other, but there's simply no way to stop the squeezing, gripping, clenching in my cunt. No way, at least, until I realize and become afraid that if I don't stop my secret masturbating, he'll know and surely become increasingly vicious.

My face colours deeply, showing the embarrassment I feel at my transparent weakness. I know he knows. I knew it even before he started shaking that thick, hard cock at me. It's as if he's brandishing a disciplining rod and threatening me with severe, cold-blooded punishment. The feeling is so intense, I want to turn, bend, and present myself for chastisement or whatever else he wants to do to me.

My inner muscles stop contracting immediately. I freeze in terror. That satisfies him for the moment. He sits there, stroking up and down the impressive, frightening, length of his tool. With his other hand, he hoists his heavy balls, hanging them over the elastic of his shorts. He fondles them with his large hand, showing that he can be gentle, even if only to himself. He smiles up at me, then spitefully stuffs himself back into his shorts, grinning smugly at my transparent disappointment.

He has my cunt watering and he knows it. It's pulsing and throbbing at his domineering selfishness and undisguised superiority. I want him with a need that comes from somewhere so deep inside that it terrifies me. My craving is huge and primal, beyond my comprehension. My desire is so overwhelmingly raw and primitive I can neither control nor explain it. It makes no sense, for it's beyond and below thought. My body pays no attention to my own orders, but is a willing slave to him and his every whim.

My eyes are glued to his crotch until a sudden jolt (it has to be from him) makes me look back up at his face. His face is very handsome, but marked with a vicious and demanding expression. He nods at me, sharply and meaningfully.

I turn slowly till my back is toward him. Mechanically, I

bend at the waist and stand still, awaiting his next order. I try frantically not to obey his obscene command, but I have no choice. With the shaking fingers of both hands, I spread my cheeks for him.

My face is burning with shame. He wants to see my anus and I'm giving him exactly what he demands. I'm not just exposing my most private self to him, but I'm displaying a part of my body that I wouldn't even want to look at, myself. He doesn't really want to see my arsehole, he only wants to prove to me that I would do absolutely anything for him.

He's right. I would do anything for him, no matter how degrading, how shameful. Here I am, sticking my naked, spread arse out of my window, exposing my bumhole to all of Manhattan. I'm displaying a part of myself that I'd be too embarrassed to view in a mirror, much less show anyone else. I'm doing it just because he's telling me to. This is all beyond strange, beyond arousing!

I can't believe what he's making me do. How long will he keep me here like this? This obscene pose is physically awkward, as well as humiliating. Surely he's seen all there is to see. Why is he forcing me to continue offering him such a mortifying view?

Of course, I know the answer before I even finish the question. He's on the biggest power trip I've ever seen. He just wants to continue showing me that he can keep right on forcing me to do absolutely anything he wants, anything at all, bar nothing! He wants absolute control and he has it. I'm so embarrassed, I just want to disappear.

Finally, he allows me to drop my straining hands. He keeps me bent over for awhile longer, but at least I can rest my hands on my knees. My back is aching!

Thank goodness, at last, he's letting me straighten up. I want to arch my back to soothe my sore muscles, but that isn't in his plans. He's making me turn around to face him without a moment's rest. I see the smug, self-satisfied look on his face and it's really pissing me off, but what can I do? I have no control over him. I'm trying very hard to keep my face expressionless, but I know he can see the anger seething in my eyes.

He keeps right on smiling! He's driving me fucking mad, damn him!

After what seems like ages, he bends to look down at his hand that is repeatedly, lovingly stroking that hefty bulge in his lap. He looks up at me again, slowly nods his head, and stares menacingly at me. I know that any attempted refusals on my part would be in vain.

So, I fetch the high wooden stool with the reclining back and put it directly in front of the window. I climb up onto it and try to settle as comfortably as I can. Although I can already guess what his next order will be, and I dread following it, I look out at him and await his instruction. He stares at me and allows my anxiety and discomfort time to build.

Now I know he wants just what I was afraid he wanted. I raise both feet to the dusty old windowsill. I have to fight a strange urge to scrawl something in the dust with my toes or to streak the dirt around in an abstract design. I guess I'm just trying to forget what I know I have to do, to forget where I am and whom I'm with – anything to take me away from the further humiliation I know I'm about to endure. I have to have some control back. I need to have some, even just a little bit.

Well, I'm getting nothing. He's forcing me to look back up at his face and I'm feeling stupid that I even tried to fight him. Now, I'm spreading my legs for him. My feet are at opposite ends of the sill. I feel the stretch and strain in the tendons of my groin and upper thighs.

Although my eyes are focused on his face, as he demanded, I can still see his beckoning cock. Both his grin and his erection are growing. He pulls his shorts away from his body to allow his monster room to expand. The angry red head of his prick on its thick, veined shaft is swelling over the elastic and seems to be staring right up at me.

My mouth opens involuntarily, my pussy twitches. I lick my parched lips. I want to suck that big, fat cock, run my teeth along its hardness, lick it, nibble it, roll my tongue around it. I want to milk him dry and feel explosions of warm, thick jism spurting down my throat, dripping over my face, my tits, my belly.

I try to inch my thighs imperceptibly closer to each other to give myself some relief. He's been teasing and manipulating me, making me very angry and frustrated, but above all, getting me insanely, desperately horny! Shit, am I horny!

Of course, the fucking bastard knows exactly what I'm doing and stops the progress of my legs with a warning finger. I'll give him the damned finger! Oh, God, if I can't have his prick, I want his fingers, his tongue, something – anything stuffed inside me!

I slide back on the stool, just as he commands, and obediently lean back so he sees I'm ready to proceed with the command performance. I run my index finger slowly down the midline of my body till I reach my hairy acre. I run my fingers through the thick, dark curls. A finger gets caught in a tangle and I wince at the sharp pain of the hairs being pulled.

He, of course, shows amusement and just to tease me, lowers his shorts further. I draw my breath back sharply. His fully erect prick is a beauty. He's beginning to hypnotize me with his wanking hand that's moving relentlessly up and down his rearing organ. He seems a bit detached, off in his own world, so I do nothing more for the moment. I sit still, anxiously awaiting his next instruction.

Suddenly, he blinks and it seems to rouse him from his private reverie. He nods and I jump. What is it in his nods that they hold such power over me? I don't know and I can't help what I do next. I'm cupping my crotch and squeezing. It's awkward and uncomfortable, but somehow I'm managing to do it. I have to do it.

My cunt is pounding. I want so badly to snake my finger up into my slit. I just start to slowly insinuate it between my puffy lips when he stops me. It's not time for that yet. Now, he wants me to hold myself open for him, so I obey. With two fingers on either side, I stretch open my pussy for him. I'm sitting here, displaying the inside of my wet, gaping cunt just because he told me to.

Oh, God, he's showing me his balls again. He's lifted his big, heavy bollocks up over his shorts to show off his entire package. One hand is squeezing while the other's stroking, pulling, twisting, steadily, maddeningly.

I am open. My cunt is so open, so open and wet and hungry for him. I'm craving him so intensely that my pussy is a spasming cave of convulsions. These mini-orgasms are taunting and teasing, not satisfying me. They're making me more and more desperate for a really good fuck!

Damn that bastard! He's much worse than a cunt-tease. He's sneakier than a voyeur, more full of himself than an exhibitionist. He is driving me fucking mad, contentedly playing with himself like that. He's a controlling son of a bitch. He's tormenting me and I'm loving it, absolutely revelling in it – and detesting it, and him, at the same time.

With my lips still spread wide, I pull up the hood to expose my stiff female phallus. It's sharply sensitive and when he has me run my fingernail over it, he seems fascinated by the pain he sees registering on my face and by the jagged twitching movements of my body.

Finally, he's making me slide my middle finger into my pussy. I can feel my muscles contracting gratefully around it. Just as I begin to push it in and draw it out to relieve the unbearable tension inside me, he stops me, then gestures with a quick jerk of his head.

Following his direction, I withdraw my reluctant finger and hold it up for his inspection. He makes me suck it dry. That's a thing I normally like to do, for I love the sweet flavour of my juice, but he's watching me do it. He's staring at me while I lewdly savour myself. He's watching me so closely, so intimately, making me feel absolutely naked. Hell, I am naked, far beyond exposed. I'm sucking for him and it's just not the same as doing it to satisfy my own desire. It's much baser, it's worse and, because of that, it's so much hotter, so much better.

He moves his eloquent head down and to the side. Obeying, I lower my legs to the lowest rung of the stool, climb down, and walk to the fridge. I'm opening the door, bending down to the lower bin, once again being reminded of the heavy, naked weight of my breasts.

I pull out the bin, reach in, and grab the largest cucumber I have. It's his decision, not mine, to pick that precise one. I swear he made me pick the biggest one. It's really long and thick – I wish it were his prick and not just a damned cucumber. I quickly walk back to the window, climb the stool, and settle back into the required position.

He's wagging his big cock back and forth at me as a reward for my alacrity and obedience, or perhaps it's just a cruel tease – "this is mine and you can't have it". I'm not sure which he means to convey, but I feel both. Maybe that's what he wants me to feel. Probably. He sure does know exactly what he's doing, what he's doing to me.

He's made me his puppet. If he were in my apartment right now, rather than across the street, he'd make me his abject slave. Actually, he already has. I guess I'm safer with him not so close. Look what he's doing to me from a distance. I wonder what he would do to me if . . .

He's demanding my attention. Instantly, my mind stops wandering. I'm watching him stroke and squeeze in a consistent way, a regular rhythm, not slow, not fast. He has a lot of control over himself, as well as over me. My God, he'd be a great fuck! I can tell that he's an animal who'd last for hours. A man who could fuck my brains out and make me come and come and come till I had to beg him to stop. No one's ever been able to drive me to that. Not so far, anyway. I think he can. I know he can. I'm sure he's the one, the one who can give me more than I can take!

He's beaming as if he heard me say those words aloud. Feet back on the windowsill, legs far apart, I'm spreading myself wide open with my left hand. I'm rolling the smooth end of the cuke around and around my slick labia before attempting to push it into me.

It's really huge! So big, I have to insert it in little increments. A tiny bit further each time. A little bit deeper, stretching the yawn of my tight, hungry cunt. My tender pussy is stinging sharply, but I persist in fighting my tightness and my fear. It's so thick. But I know I have no choice – I have to take it for him, and besides, the reward will be much, much greater than this temporary pain.

With each push, I drive it farther into my sheath and with each stroke out, more slippery juice covers it, making it easier to coax it farther in. As he moves his hand, so I move mine. Our hands are dancing together to the same primitive music, our bodies in heat and in sync.

As his other hand fondles his balls, so mine manipulates my clit. Our eyes are locked together and our breathing is in tandem. Just like a bicycle. Just like riding a bicycle. Just like fucking. It feels like we're actually fucking each other. In/up, out/down, in/up, out/down.

So good! So fucking good! So bloody fucking hot! Looking into his eyes, watching his quick, blurry hand, shoving it in, feeling so totally stuffed, then feeling the phallus pulling my walls so deliciously, leaving me so achingly empty, waiting for the next welcome, hard thrust, all the while, pulling my clit to bits!

"Fuck me! Fuck me!" I'm mouthing wonderful obscenities to him as he calls me his horny bitch, his slut, his fucktoy. He's growling at me, telling me how fucking great it is to be banging my hot, wet cunt.

It's a brutal, vicious, bestial fuck and I feel so uncivilized, so animal. We're so dirty, so filthy, so bad! Our hands are flying. He closes his eyes, scrunching them tightly, throwing his head back, the sweat's pouring from his face. Maybe he's telling me that I can close my eyes, that I should close my eyes, but now I want to watch. I want to watch my voyeur, my sweet, cruel, demanding voyeur. My master.

So I'm watching him as I'm fucking myself. It's making me even hotter, watching him, seeing his hand, a blur in contrast with his slow ball-handler. My hands are on automatic. My mind is fixed on only one thing, watching him right now while he's too lost in himself to be watching me. My eyes are wide open because I have no need for fantasy. He is my fantasy. He's pushed me to a strange, dangerous place I've only dreamed about.

I'm lost in watching him as his hand speeds up and then slows way down to clench his spurting prick, watching his spunk flying up out of him and arcing down to splatter on the sidewalk in front of him, then up again and down, then up again and down.

That torrent pushes me up over my own climax and now I have to close my eyes. I have to close my eyes and just feel. Just feel that natural dildo, forcing my sheath apart when the walls just ache to collapse, close down upon each other, clench and grip and squeeze. Just feel the piercing, shocking moment when my clit can't take any more and its jagged sharpness slices through the rounded rollings of my cunt.

Coming! Coming! Coming! Over and over again!

Finally, totally depleted from my shattering climax, I groan and pull the dripping artificial penis from my worn-out pussy. I relax as the contractions inside me become softer and farther apart. I wait for my pulse and breathing to get closer to normal. I can hear myself sighing in relief and contentment as the sweat drips down my body.

My dreamy haze begins to clear and I straighten up and look out the window at him. He's sitting there, with his big arms folded across his chest and a broad smile of satisfaction on his face. All I see is a look of tired, contented pleasure, no more threatening stares and leers, no more demanding, severe expressions of dominance and mastery. I can look at him as I would look at any lover lying next to me in bed. Now he is truly gazing at me in the same way, now that our game is over, now that we're both sated.

He rises from the bench. His flaccid penis and emptied balls fall heavily over his damp shorts. He pulls out the elastic from under them, adjusts himself carefully, and tugs the tiny shorts back up to his waist. He winks and waves, grandly blows a kiss at me, then turns and begins walking away.

I lean out the window, this time, because I choose to, and watch his lovely, tight arse receding into the distance. I watch as his fine body gets smaller and smaller, till he's too far away for me to see. I remain here a while longer, feeling the sweat evaporating and cooling my hot body. With him no longer in my sight, the lascivious and decadent experience seems almost like a dream.

But it hasn't been a dream. In my hand, the glistening cucumber, as hot as my cunt, tells me it all had to be real. I begin walking out of the room and the dripping onto my thighs confirms it. I feel so deliciously content. I'm even moving differently than I usually do when I'm alone. I feel like a sleek jungle cat, slinking, gracefully prowling. I feel beautiful, desirable, sexual, alive!

I love this sultry, sexy feeling, I don't want it to end. I need this every night. I need him to come back and play with me again. I pray he comes back. Please, he has to come back to me. I'll be watching for him at the window. I'll be waiting.

Captivated

Wendy (Nottingham, UK)

My name is Wendy, I'm twenty-four years old and I'm from Nottingham, England. I'm studying for a Masters degree in business psychology and I've had two previous sexual partners. Both men. I say that with some regret because I've always wondered what sex would be like with another woman. I suppose most women have thought about that at some point in time. However, I like to think that my fantasy is a little different because I would like to be held captive by another woman, to be completely powerless against her and to be ruthlessly dominated. It's the contrast between a soft womanly body and a merciless female mind which excites me. The two opposing halves of the female psyche rubbing up against each other and making sparks fly. I guess you could say that fantasies are all about vixens and very willing victims!

One of my favourite things to imagine is that I'm lying in the back of this rusty old Transit van. Actually I'm tied up. There's an old musty mattress in there and a threadbare carpet that smells of engine oil and grease. My movement is restricted by the baling twine tied roughly around my wrists and ankles and secured to some kind of make-shift hooks welded to the tops of the wheel-arches. I am completely naked apart from a black lacy bra and panties and silky black hold-up stockings, a birthday gift that morning from my flatmate Simone. Will Simone be wondering why I haven't made it home tonight? Would she have called the police? I can't see anything through the torn piece of rag that has been used as a make-shift blindfold. I can hear a diesel engine running rhythmically and the dry stuffy heat from the vents in the passenger compartment is starting to make me feel increasingly uncomfortable. I wonder how long I've been here and if I'm ever going to get out. What if no one knows I'm missing? How would anybody find me? Still, in spite of my anxiety, I find myself thrilling with the sheer anticipation of what could happen next.

Suddenly I hear the slow but purposeful "tip tap" of footsteps approaching the van. Is it a curious dog-walker or a police officer? I wonder how the hell I would be able to explain my predicament to a strange man and fear grips my stomach. The footsteps approach the back of the van and I strain to hear more. Next there's the sound of a key being placed in the lock and the door opens. I feel a welcome rush of cold air from outside mingling with the stifling air inside the van and hundreds of little goose-pimples raise up along my arms and my thighs, but that's not just due to the colder air. Someone's in here. Someone sees me exposed like this. I hear a mocking laugh and a low voice speaks to me.

"Oh, please don't get up!"

"Let me go!" I beg.

"Don't talk!" A swift reply, hissed in my face. I recoil.

"Good girl," says the voice approvingly. "Now I'd better make sure you stay nice and quiet."

Through my blindfold I see the outline of a shadow move and I feel someone crouching over me. A gag is placed in my mouth and I catch a whiff of scent, quite musky and somehow familiar.

"Just do as I say and you won't be harmed," commands the voice, now an unmistakeably female voice. "Now let's play a little game, shall we?"

My mind is just registering the fact that I'm totally at the mercy of another woman when I feel her shift position and straddle me. She's wearing something skin-tight and slippery. The warmth of her legs enveloping mine contrasts starkly with the goose bumps still prickling along my naked body. I feel her weight pressing me down against the floor and I realize that I'm trapped here.

"We are going to play a little guessing game," she announces.

I strain my eyes to see if I can make out any of her facial features through the cloth but I can't. She could be anyone, my best friend, or a complete stranger. She is as hidden from my gaze as I am exposed to hers. Then I feel it, something cold and metallic with a smooth curved surface, brush against the sole of my left foot. I have always had rather sensitive and ticklish feet and this sends a shudder up my spine.

"Mmm, you like that, do you?" she asks. "Let's see if your other foot likes it too."

I shudder again, though not quite so much this time as I know what to expect. She returns to the left foot but this time I feel the tip being dragged slowly along my instep to the heel then around and up the inside of my leg. It feels like some kind of metal tool, like a spanner or such like. I feel the tickling sensations rising slowly up my body. Gradually I start to find myself enjoying the new sensation after the monotony of the waiting and the wondering. My fear starts to slip away as I surrender my body to the metallic caresses of this all-powerful stranger.

She moves the tip of the instrument in a meandering fashion up past my knee. I shudder again as the metal touches the bare skin at the top of my stocking. Then she stops and removes it when it reaches the top of my thigh.

"Looks like you enjoy having a tool stroked across your body, don't you!" she murmurs. "I bet you like a firm tool rubbed against your pussy too you little slut!"

As I am about to try to make some kind of response, I feel a colder and wider but similar metallic object pressed against the bottom of my panties and drawn slowly upwards against the taut satin fabric. I can't help but shift my position and open my legs a little bit wider in response to this. She draws it up and down my panties in long constant strokes and I feel the lips of my pussy gradually beginning to open and moisten. She circles around my clitoris and I feel my back arching and my hips raising to meet the strokes and guide the tip to where I want it.

"Oh, no, you don't," she says, "I can see what you're doing. I'm in charge here and I'll decide if and when to tease that firm little clit of yours."

I'm pushed back down flat and feel her shifting her weight

forwards to press me all the more firmly into the mattress on the floor. I feel her hot breath moving over my chest and then blowing onto my right breast. Her gloved left hand cups my left breast then takes a hold of my nipple and tweaks it gently. Mmmm! She seems to be wearing tight-fitting gloves made of the same slippery and shiny material as the overalls that she must also be wearing. She leans forward and her long slender gloved fingers slowly ease my bra straps outwards across my shoulders and down my arms, exposing my breasts to the cooling air. My nipples are hard and tingle with expectation.

She swirls the tip of her tongue around the tip of each nipple in turn and I feel them standing to attention. She takes each one fully into her mouth, nibbles around the areola and then lets it slip out of her mouth, covered in saliva. She then begins to blow gently around each breast, her hot breath causing the saliva to evaporate, leaving a delicious cooling and tingly sensation behind. By this time I have to admit that my pussy is soaking wet and each nipple is sending delicious signals rushing down my spine to my clit.

Then I feel a metallic object being placed around first one nipple and then the other. It's some kind of spanner that encircles and grips both nipples simultaneously. The constant cool sensation all around the base of each nipple is interspersed with the flicking of her tongue and the sucking of her moist lips. It's almost as if the electricity of the nerve impulses is being conducted from one breast to the other by the metal. She begins to bite the tip of each nipple, dragging her teeth along its length as she does so. I whimper as the sudden sharp pain combined with the other sensations heightens my arousal. By now I have forgotten the strange situation in which I have found myself and open myself up to the unexpected. I am enjoying these new erotic sensations and I am ready for even more. I know deep down that I will do whatever she tells me to. I want to be a good girl and I want to please her.

She moves away from me for a moment and I feel her gloved hands circle my ankles. My toes splay outward in pleasure at her touch as gently she drags the tips of her fingers up my legs, with her thumbs tracing the outline of my inner thighs. Her fingers then start to press deeper and more deeply into my skin.

I can feel her sharpened fingernails through the tight-fitting material covering her hands. I know there will be bruises on my skin tomorrow. My heart is racing now and my breathing is increasing, my chest rising and falling with ever increasing amplitude. What next, I wonder?

As the steady pressure of her hands reaches my hips she slides her thumbs under the edges of my (by now soaking wet) lace panties and begins to pull them down gradually over my thighs. I am completely captive. She moves her thumbs along the edge of the inner lips of my pussy and I push my hips forwards and upwards to try to increase the pressure on my clit. As I do so she pushes her index finger deep inside me and I let out an intense moan. My hips rise up to meet her touch. Next I feel her finger slide along the slippery walls of my inner tunnel as my muscles relax and my hips lower. I am completely hers. I feel her press down hard against my pubic mound and hear the sound of her husky voice in my ear.

"You want me to fuck you don't you?" she teases. "But you're not quite ready just yet."

I moan in frustration. I want to beg her to please, please *fuck me* but with the gag pushed in my mouth it is impossible to say anything vaguely intelligible. I know she senses my arousal and part of me is ashamed that I am so obviously her toy, her plaything. Then I feel something else being tied around me, this time around my waist, and something else cold and metallic being pulled tight against my clit. I hear a low rhythmic buzzing. This seems to alternate with the constant clanking of the van's diesel engine, which is still ticking over. Soon I can feel the buzzing being transmitted through my clit and up my back, where it mingles with the stiff impulses from my breasts. I can hear the pitch increasing as she turns up the frequency of the vibrator. I begin to squirm and wriggle from side to side, or at least as far as my restraints will allow. I am murmuring to myself and starting to lose control of my body. I am completely at her mercy now and she knows it. The vibrations are driving me wild. My excitement is increased by the thought that it is a woman who has me prisoner here in the back of this dirty old van. It is a woman who has tied me up, it is a woman who has gagged me and it is a woman whom I must now obey to the depths of my being.

"Would you like me to turn it up some more?" she asks.

I groan with pleasure and manage to nod at my mistress.

"First, you must do as you are told and change positions for me," she commands. "I want you to get on all fours but you *must not look at me.*"

Right at this moment I would do anything to please her. She releases each arm and each leg in turn allowing me to turn over and comply. Then she secures me in a kneeling position, legs slightly apart and arms tightly fastened above my head to some point in the roof of the van.

"Before I fuck you I must check that your engine is oiled and ready to move up a gear."

The vibrator strapped to my clit is still buzzing away and I feel that I cannot take much more but still she continues to take it up to another level. Her left hand grasps my left buttock. Her right hand pushes between my legs and her fingers press against and move along the contours of my dripping pussy. I want something inside me now and I want to be fucked hard. Two fingers dip into and probe my hidden depths. She rotates her fingers back and forth as she withdraws them oh, so slowly. Then I feel the oily tip of her index finger press against the entrance to my arsehole. I push back and my arse easily accommodates her finger. It's a strange, totally new and very arousing experience for me. I have always dreamed of being fucked up the arse. Now my wish might just come true . . .

Whilst fingering my arse with her greasy finger, she leans forward and I feel her hard nipples pressed against my lower back. I moan in pleasure and she punishes me by squeezing my left breast hard and twisting my nipple. I let out a yelp but this just seems to encourage her. I feel a stinging slap against my buttock and I wince in pain.

"You *bad girl!*" she shouts. "Face the front and don't let me catch you trying to look around at me again!!"

I feel an even more forceful spank on my other cheek followed by the sensation of the resultant heat spreading out across my arse.

"*Now* I am going to fuck you." she whispers. "Up the arse and you're going to like it."

I hear what sounds like a power tool being revved up. Her left hand returns to my left buttock and she removes what are now two oily fingers from my arse. I feel something smooth and much, much larger press against the crack of my arse. I experience a brief moment of fear.

Oh, no, she won't try and put that thing up inside me, will she? I think.

But then I hear the sound of the electric motor again and the tip of the huge dildo moves back and forth, very slowly, and gradually begins to inch its way into my arse. Its surface is very oily and slippery and there is very little friction at all. I gasp as I feel myself opened up and completely controlled by this machine. The buzz and whine of the motor increases and I am deeply penetrated, fucked to my very core. My arse is hers. My mind swirls off into an almost altered state as I am overwhelmed with the simultaneous pounding sensations from within my arse and the buzzing from outside of my clit. The bonds tighten around my wrists and my gag is dripping with saliva where I have bitten against it. My tongue is swollen as I gasp for breath and I wonder how much more of this infliction I can take. I know that soon things are about to reach a crescendo and I am going to climax like I never have before.

As the sound of the motor reaches fever pitch I feel the heat in my pussy start to rise up through my whole body. I'm throbbing and throbbing along with the buzz of the machinery. My legs tense and my body starts to shudder as I am driven to the point of no return. Overwhelmed by the rush of pure ecstasy. I cry out with abandon and I come and come and come.

I am utterly broken.

Just then I feel her cradle my head and feel her fingers moving, brushing softly against my hair. "Sweetheart," she murmurs gently.

I feel the tension on my restraints loosening. I feel the blindfold come undone and as it falls down over my flushed face. I remain quietly obedient and keep my eyes tightly closed.

"Now comes the end of the guessing game," says my

mistress firmly. I turn slowly, squinting against the unaccustomed light, and look up into the face of the woman who has so thoroughly fucked me. Fucked me and made me her slave.

"I hope you liked this surprise birthday present." She smiles wickedly. "Maybe next time you can do the same for me?"

I stare up in shock at my mistress's viciously heeled boots, up her rounded thighs and marvel at the sight of her curvaceous figure barely held in check by a tight black PVC catsuit. The zip is opened all the way down to her navel and I can see lusciously full breasts with a hint of darkened erect nipple peeking out through the opening in the shiny black fabric. I'm amazed to discover that I know this woman. I've known her for years! It's my flatmate Simone, the very one who'd bought me the black lacy bra and panties that I had been wearing that day for my birthday.

"I always said that your best birthday present would be living out one of your fantasies," she purrs. "Now tell me if I was right?"

She was right.

Cognac

Ciana (Fairfield, USA)

The hotel was the most extravagant yet for the annual party a group of Simon's associates held. I knew a few wives, and did my best to mingle while Simon played the "must" politics. It did not take long to complete the rounds and run out of familiar faces. I looked for Simon, but saw he was involved in conversation and so I decided to find a safer harbour to bide my time.

As I slowly made my way to the grand bar at the back of the ballroom, the tall blond bartender caught my eye. He looked a bit younger, and more attractive than anyone has a right to be. The real killer was that lop-sided grin; the one that makes a woman's knees go weak. It was impossible not to return a smile and acknowledge the impact of his silent flattery.

With a polite greeting, I named my drink, something stronger than my usual, something more appropriate for such a . . . tedious occasion. The bartender stared back for a moment, the edge of his cocky smile lifting, deepening the crease of his suntanned cheek before he turned his back to pour. I found myself sizing him up, the stylish cut of his hair, the broad shoulders in the short white jacket of his uniform, the hard buttocks that filled the seat of those black, perfectly creased slacks so well. When I looked up I realized he had been watching my bold perusal in the mirror. This time he gave me a more seductive grin. Embarrassed, I feigned a cough and looked away.

"What's your poison?"

Startled by the voice, I turned. The speaker was a saucy, voluptuous brunette with pouty lips and a pair of gorgeous, expressive brown eyes. I placed her age somewhere between the charming bartender's and mine. She wore little make-up, and her short layered hair was carelessly tousled. Her dress, her informal manner, all indicated a distinct earthiness. And when she did not fabricate a smile, I took it as further evidence of her easy casualness, her total lack of pretence. I had no doubt we could be friends.

"Cognac," I answered, meeting her gaze.

"Same," she informed the bartender, her glance falling below his waist briefly before she returned her attention to me. "Meg. My name is Meg."

"Hello, Meg. I'm Bella."

"Great party, isn't it?"

The question sounded tentative, a gauge. When I sent her my best get-serious look, she chuckled, sounding relieved at not having received the standard polite bullshit.

"Are you staying here, at the hotel tonight?"

"Only way Simon can get me to attend these socials."

She laughed, with one of those sexy throaty laughs that melt men.

Before either of us could say more, the bartender set her drink down on the counter then casually leaned on his elbow with all the confidence in the world. He looked from me to Meg, his lascivious thoughts no secret. His glance inched to her full breasts, swelled high in her strapless black gown. Who could blame him? Carnality exuded from the woman, and there was no lack of want there either.

When Meg, unruffled by his boldness, continued to sip her cognac, the bartender made a small sound of desire then returned his attention to me. Gone was the previously playful smile, replaced by a candid expression of pure lust.

When a guest broke the sexually charged atmosphere, I became aware of the hot moisture our silent but intense exchange had generated, and shifted for comfort in suddenly dampened panties.

"Yeah, me too," Meg announced in a soft voice.

Discomfited by the frank and unexpected admission, I cleared my throat and took another sip of cognac.

Meg studied me through slanted eyes, then really floored me with her next comment. "Bella? Let's fuck."

I stood frozen, mouth agape, mind racing to distinguish fact from imagination before I was able to force my eyes to blink and collect my wits. Slowly absorbing her advance, I allowed her candour to encourage mine. When I met her eyes, it was with equal forthrightness, and we established an understanding.

"Are you here by yourself?" I asked as an afterthought.

"I am now. My brother's date showed up after all."

I turned and searched the room. Simon was speaking to a squat, balding man but his gaze was fixed upon me. We made eye contact, then his glance moved to Meg.

"Is that your husband? Not bad," she remarked.

Now that the course had been set I was simply too aroused and too anxious to dally. "Let's go," I said decisively when she continued to regard Simon with a calculating expression.

Meg shot me a rapturous look, and then quickly downed her drink.

We had only taken a few steps when, as if prompted by an unspoken signal, we paused as one and turned for a last look. The sexy bartender was wiping a wineglass but we seemed to still hold his undivided attention. He squinted in return, a hedonistic squint combined with regret. Meg and I sighed simultaneously, like a couple of lovesick teens, then turned and left with shared reluctance.

As she led the way out of the ballroom, my focus remained on her voluptuous bottom, quivering underneath the jersey fabric of her formal with each step she took. More hot steam pooled between my legs and I hastened my stride.

We rode the elevator in silence, oblivious of the elderly couple who had followed us in. Meg stared at my shapely leg, visible up to the upper thigh through the long frontal slit of my evening gown. As for me, I shared the bartender's appetite for her heaving breasts. By seconds, the moistened gusset of my panties was growing more uncomfortable.

I let Meg enter the room first. Just as I shut the door, we reached for each other, hungrily, without the usual formalities between two strangers. Driven by lust, there was no feminine gentility when our mouths parted and our tongues began an urgent, passionate acquaintance.

As we kissed, we tugged at clothes anxiously. Meg snapped open my bra, and we separated, both pulling at the straps to rid me of the restraining undergarment. My eyes fell on her curvaceous body wrapped in black corset and lace-top stockings. Her large erect nipples, popped over the half cups, looked ripe enough to make my mouth water. Mesmerized, I licked my lips and swallowed before I started to drool.

Meg literally shoved me onto the bed with a growl then came down herself. "Your skin is so soft, so creamy," she murmured, anxiously caressing my arms, chest, tummy while her glance took a slow tour down the length of my long legs. Turning back abruptly, her eyes locked on mine and, without preamble, she shoved an elegant finger deep into my flaming centre.

"Aaahhh," I sighed and raised my hips high to greet her.

"That feel good?" she asked, and covered my mouth with hers. Her tongue blasted through my parted lips in a mission of invasion. She took as liberally as I gave, and offered the same in return. All the while, my body pushed and churned on her comforting hand.

I moaned my loss when Meg tore her mouth away to posture herself for a more significant seizure. Welcoming the pain of passion, I clenched her hair and encouraged her hungry assault on my breasts.

"Delicious," she cooed as she switched from one insistent nipple to the other.

I squeezed the breast she was suckling. It encouraged her to work harder. "So you like sucking tit, hmmm?" I teased.

With her lips pursed tightly around my taut peak, she could do little but moan.

"Me, too," I agreed and, unable to resist any longer, reached for one of her heavy succulent mounds, only to have my hand pushed away.

"You'll get your turn," she teased and slid lower. "I want to taste your pussy."

The sound of the door opening gave us only a momentary pause. "What took you so long?" I questioned when Simon entered.

"You know business, hon," he answered, removing his tuxedo jacket.

Meg turned her head, but kindly kept her finger buried. She regarded Simon, one thick eyebrow arched with interest.

After the introductions, Simon removed his shoes and stretched out by my side. "Did I miss much?"

"A lot more to . . . come," I replied.

He chuckled and gave me an affectionate kiss.

"So, Meg, what's a nice girl like you doing in my bed?"

Meg gave him a brazen once over, then leaned across me. "Getting a good lay, I hope."

"You got it, baby," Simon promised and took that edible pouty mouth of hers with his. While he kissed her, Meg did not neglect me, her slender finger burrowing even deeper into the heat and humidity it worked to promote.

Releasing Meg, Simon asked, "What did I interrupt?"

"I was just about to taste Bella's pussy."

"Then let me help."

He spread my delicate nether lips, gently, wide, using thumb and forefinger. Together, they stared long and hard at my vulnerable clit while it cried for attention. Then Simon's heavy tongue came down and took a single slow lick, leaving me quivering.

"Mmm, that there is pure honey, Meg."

Meg shot him a glance then dipped her head and snatched my swollen nub between velvet lips. My body responded instantly, welcoming the impatiently longed-for onslaught.

Simon's eyes remained on my writhing form as he first removed his bow tie then eased my legs wider apart. Meg accepted the invitation and carefully moved to lie in the "V" he had provided, her finger never slipping out of my honeyed nest in the process. I, in turn, bent my knees deeper around her and provided her with a more splayed access.

Settled, with her warm breath fanning my pubic hairs in a pleasant distraction, she extracted her buried finger. Before I could feel its absence, a soothing plump tongue slipped in to take its place, intoxicating me. I took Meg's head in both hands and pushed my crotch to her face. She held nothing back, huffing and slurping as she reached farther and farther into my depths. It was heaven.

I cried deliriously when she next removed the essence of my

pleasure, that nimble tongue of hers. Then cried again when she filled me with two fingers in its stead. And when she took my greedy clit once more, I became lost in the climb toward nirvana.

Simon pinched my nipple, forcing me to arch my back, to offer him more. "Come," he ordered, his dark eyes demanding the pleasure of seeing me in ecstasy.

My heart pounding with love, I submitted to my needs and to his command, breathing his name just as the little death arrived to make its exalted claim.

I flowed with soft screams, fighting to keep my eyes open. Meg pushed her fingers in deeper, her mouth firming on my little nub, her sucking relentless. Simon watched proudly, victoriously, as my body bucked and churned in its attempt to cram Meg into my cunt.

In the end, it was his pleasure that brought me the greater contentment.

"You're right, sweet as honey," Meg confirmed when, having removed his clothes, Simon returned to join us on the bed.

Meg and I unwound from each other, making room for him to lie between us. Simon kissed and caressed in turns while our bodies took refuge in his masculinity. Leading Meg and me into our own private exchange of passion, he slid lower to bury his face in breasts. His hum of delight echoed as he fondled and suckled, his efforts earning him even more tender and responsive nipples.

"Meg." Simon gently separated us. "Why don't you come sit on my face?"

Meg's eyes sparkled. She moved quickly to straddle him, on her knees, backward.

"Show it to me first," he requested. "Open it nice and wide."

She shifted to find her balance then carefully leaned forward, her rear lifting inches. Both hands reached back, deepening the arch of her spine, and ever so luxuriantly spread her cheeks.

"Oohhh, what a sweet plump pussy," Simon murmured

after a moment of silent observation, and then sniffed deeply. "All right, baby, go ahead and set it down for me now."

Meg lowered herself on his face, her drawn out moan at initial contact turning into a breathy sigh of accomplishment with the final seating.

I took Simon's powerful cock in my hand and gave it a little kiss, inhaling his familiar unique scent before swallowing what I could of him, with all the tenderness my hunger would allow. His balls cradled in my palm, I sucked hard, in the very way that I know pleases him most.

Meg interrupted with a touch, desire in her countenance. She brought her head down, mouth open, anxious. Her moan rang of gratitude when I placed Simon's swollen tip between her lips. She suckled it preciously, then took it deeper, shifting her hips from side to side, opening herself wider for him.

As I carry a constant, insatiable need to pleasure Simon, I could not pass up the opportunity when it arose. Positioning myself between his bent legs, I licked and pampered his sac of skin while Meg continued to ravish his cock. Together, we created a lovely chorus of moans.

When still it was not enough, and I ached to provide more, I forced Simon's legs wider apart and reached lower, knowing just how much it pleasures him to have his anus tongued.

It took little time for Meg's breathing to grow heavier with her approaching climax and I returned to their side, to aid and participate.

"He loves cunt juice; smear him good," I whispered in her ear. She heeded my advice and, grunting, tackled the task with more gusto.

I gently squeezed one hand under the curve of her womanly tummy for support. The other, I sucked wet the middle finger then reached for her backside. My penetration into her tight passage was all the incentive she needed, and she toppled into sweet oblivion with a guttural roar. I pushed in all the way. Simon pressed her hips down from both sides; she crushed him hard.

"Yesss, baby, rub your pussy against that hot tongue," I urged over Meg's muffled screams, her feminine form convulsing in its pleasure while she valiantly rode the crest of insanity. "Feels so, so damned good."

Meg slowed at last, but continued to feed on Simon. "Yeah, he eats pussy real good, doesn't he?" Stroking her hair, easing her return, I gauged her satisfaction by her hungry suckling and muted whimpers. How well I know that profound need that always plagues me afterwards. Yes, sweet Meg, suck his cock, feed your soul.

I waited for Meg to fight her way back through the haze and straighten, then I straddled Simon's hips and slowly lowered myself onto his quivering shaft. Meeting Meg's smouldering gaze, I drew her to me for a taste of those provocative lips. What they tasted of was cognac and cock. I savoured the combination, and then left her to recover while I nourished myself from her ripe nipples and swayed upon the rock-solid penis that stood buried within me.

My breast fetish for the moment appeased, I let Meg slide off Simon, and then I came down into his loving arms. Her scent was strong on him, and now I licked *his* lips for Meg's own alluring taste. Our kiss was brief, but fiery.

Simon rolled me onto my side and re-entered me from behind. He knows my needs so well. A strong hand snaked over my hipbone and experienced fingers seized the slippery kernel of my clit for manipulation. The other arm lay in an arc, a supporting cradle, underneath my neck. Meg, for her part, took charge of my needy breasts. Coordinating her ministrations with Simon's languid strokes, the two joined forces and teased me relentlessly.

As I grew more responsive, my back curved into a pliant arch that allowed Simon deeper penetration. For that, he rewarded me with a more solid thrusting.

My orgasm suddenly upon me, Simon pushed in to the hilt and wedged his thumb through my lips and into my mouth. I exploded with a growl, my nerves alive. Simon pinched my clit with his working hand, my outer labia affording him a firm grip, and rubbed his fingers against one another. Meg bit one nipple and squeezed the other none too gently, adding a pleasant pain to my pleasure, only to have the scream of jubilation stick in my throat, as I sucked on Simon's thumb like a cock.

I relished the precious ecstasy for as long as I could freeze time. With the tension slowly ebbing, Simon and Meg, as good lovers do, held me tenderly, lulling me back to sensibility at the dictate of my own sweet time.

I returned from the bathroom and found Meg on her back and Simon on top. Her legs were wrapped high around his waist, in the age-old fashion that a woman opens herself to a man. He was thrusting into her, his balls slamming against her bottom. I climbed between his legs to watch them do so.

My affectionate caress of Simon's manly buttocks slowed him, curbing his thrusts into sensual grinds. I took his drawn out moan as a request. My mouth replaced my hands for a wet massage of his cheeks, stopping briefly to tantalize the small sphere of nerve endings before continuing lower to his scrotum, where I could taste and smell both Meg and me.

"You've got a great arse, Meg." I heard Simon say. "Do I get to fuck it?"

Her whimper of consent came without hesitation, and I reached for the jar I had brought back with me. As my greasy finger circled and taunted Meg's anal entrance, I continued to lave Simon's testicles with my tongue. He and Meg kissed while I took time to lubricate her, to prepare her for pleasure.

Ready, Meg turned over, laid her head down, and raised her rear high.

"That's nice, baby, that's just how I like to take it."

Simon took his place behind her on his knees and I took mine beside him. Unhurried, fanned fingers squeezed and moulded Meg's lush flesh, as much a posturing of their dominant and submissive roles as foreplay.

Meg purred, waiting docilely, straining to deepen her spinal arch.

Eyes glazed, Simon groaned with manly ego and spread her arse cheeks more taut for a better display of the oiled sphincter that was now at his discretion.

"Mmm, looks nice, babe." He tore his gaze away to thank me for the preparation, a thorough kiss that left me sizzling.

Meg's moans rose when Simon's hips pressed forward and the weight of his cock-head lay teasingly against the puckered entrance. Her moans rose higher when, taking hold of his thick shaft, he began to rotate it around the small circle, lubricating that same head in a blend of pre-come and grease to ease the penetration of her tight canal.

"You ready to give it to me, Meg?" Simon tapped gently then butted his swollen tip against her little ring.

"Yesss," came her soft, anxious reply.

I watched, riveted, as the darker resistant skin first indented slightly, then slowly began to give way against steady pressure.

"That's right, baby, open up your arse so I can fuck it."

Meg gasped, and I let out the breath I did not know I had been holding when elasticity prevailed and the bulbous head suddenly penetrated in partial then came to a halt.

With Meg's rubbery anus stretched forcefully to accommodate his thickness, and purple veins straining against the pink flesh of his shaft, Simon allowed her a brief respite. Then he resumed the invasion, taking an inch, returning two, conquering slowly, prolonging the exquisite sensations, sensations that I am gifted with often.

Meg moaned and whimpered, urging him to take her, to be swift in delivering them both to the height of ecstasy. Simon listened in silence to her exasperation – to what I know is symphony to his soul. And when her neediness grew into the very advantage he sought, on the next outward slide, he withdrew completely.

Meg lamented, her rectal muscles contracting reflexively, pleading for his return. Simon watched; triumph and pleasure etched on his face. Then he started the sweet torment anew, inserting ruthlessly slowly. Giving little; taking a lot. By the time he sank to the hilt, I was trembling, desperate for a release of my own.

Simon's hands fell away from Meg's hips, and he grew still. Meg cried in protest, gliding back and forth on his slick cock in her urgency, her coaxing strokes exposing the full length of the rigid shaft in one direction, then swallowing it back into the snugly-fit glove down to its base. When her efforts failed to raise a satisfying response, her strokes became more demanding, and grew into feverish pumping.

Meg's need successfully nurtured into a serving tool, Simon's attention turned to me. "Come here, babe."

I shuffled forward on my knees obediently, positioning my crotch above the open palm Simon held out at hip level. Knowledgeable fingers began to move, to stimulate. I might have collapsed from sheer exuberance, had my body not been already wracking itself into oblivion.

"Look at me!" Simon's commanding eyes bore into mine while he shoved a finger in as substitute, and continued to massage my bursting clit with his thumb.

Through the storm of rapture, I whimpered, "Simon," his wielding power once again granting me solace in the sweet submission that belongs to me by nature. "Ohhh, Simon . . ."

My husband, my love, the man who keeps my blood boiling and my heart thundering with life.

Having brought me to a swift completion, Simon held and cooed me through recovery, his patience great, his tenderness heartfelt.

Breath finally caught, libido appeased, I moved to kneel behind him, then reached for the lubricant.

For Simon, I used two fingers, inserting deep. A groan expressed his pleasure and he reclaimed Meg's hips, forcing her frantic pumping under control, hushing her pathetic mewling.

"All right, baby, you get your turn too." His hand slipped over the curve of her lush hip, disappearing under her abdomen, his own hips on the move to meet the mating call. I wrapped my free arm around his waist and held on tight.

Thrills vibrated in Meg's wail at the onset of orgasm, her body tensing first then shattering into convulsions. Simon's gentle thrusts grew more arduous, driving Meg harder and harder into the pinnacle of pleasure, then slowing with her downward spiral, only to pick up pace again and require more of her. She reached a second orgasm, bucking even more violently on his cock, her cries of ecstasy drowning his growls of satisfaction.

Following the peak came the desperation, the need for that all-consuming powerful thrusting, essential to completing a woman's satisfaction, an act catering to her primal need for domination, for possession.

A man well versed in women's needs, Simon obliged, pumping hard and fast, dousing the intensity. I pinched his nipple for their mutual gratification and braced myself. With Meg primed to his taste, smouldering and whimpering like a puppy, Simon pounded her arse for the final conquest.

"Take her, my love," I whispered, prideful of my man. "Fuck her."

And he did.

I woke to a knock at the door. "Who's that?" I demanded, disoriented. My eyes focused on the small clock on the night-stand and I saw it was past two.

"Thought you two might enjoy a late night snack," Simon offered, rising from the bed.

Meg and I shared a sleepy look, shrugging our shoulders, then sobered quickly at "Come on in" and, in a panic, scurried for the covers.

In stepped our favourite bartender, a familiar bottle in his hand and a cheeky smile that told all. "Cognac, ladies?"

The glance Meg and I exchanged this time was of delight and a fully alert one. Suddenly two pairs of arms shot out in wide welcome. "Yes, please," we called in unison.

The Mating

Edita (Toronto, Canada)

I have this dream, a fascinating dream. Too perfect to be thrown away. I rest on a smooth, spongy meadow filled by rabbits – hundreds of shiny, sleek black ones and fluffy, creamy white ones. They frisk round me, their noses twitching, their tails bobbing. Soft and cuddly, warm and vibrant. A deliciously familiar rabbit-hutch smell. They climb all over me and cover me with their downy fur until they knit me into a delicate bed of rabbits. Gradually we all join – me and the rabbits, to become one huge rabbit, that itself changes too, into Larissa Logan, and she holds me and loves me and . . . then I wake up. Fuck!

Christ, I'm horny. I have a pain right through the middle of my belly. Jesus, I don't think I can work unless I do something about this rampant hard thumping against my cunt. I'm sure the sheets have to be soaking. Fuck! I should get up and make an early start. With Brenda off ill, it means that I'll have to help out in surgery as well as do my own work. I hate helping in surgery. Particularly on a Saturday, it seems like a kind of sacrilege to have to work so hard on a Saturday.

Damn her! Three times I have had this dream about her. Three times she's been down on me and I've, in turn, been down on her, rabbiting around, rooting in her cunt, smelling, licking and sucking. Yes. I will have her. I will take her to me and make her mine. Bastard. Dream on, sunshine. I'm only the student seeing practice in summer and she's the lord almighty veterinarian, the boss lady, the superior one. Oh, come on, I knows that she's an icicle, hard as a rock. But below that mask, that disguise, for sure there have been some indications that she wants me, needs me, lusts after me, sure she does. Right! Like not! In each dream we are some sort of animal. She's as beautiful as she is in life – sleek, strong, muscular. Her huge eyes are the eyes of a cow, then a horse or, in this one, the eyes of a rabbit. I ache to rub my hands through her thick black hair, to nibble her tiny ears, to run my hands over her dense skin. I am a hormonal teenager with these hot, wet dreams of my boss.

In the shower, I continue with the fantasy. She's there, on her knees sucking me, licking me, swallowing me. She is on her knees, her ass to me and I have lubricated her asshole and am ramming my finger into her. I finish desperately on this note, my clit tiny and spent by making love to Dr Larissa Logan.

I arrive early, clear yesterday's files, pack kits into the auto-clave, set-up the operating room, take the dogs out and clean the cats. I look for things to keep myself busy.

For once we finish the office on time and start on the surgery. Cat spay first. Routine. I inject the dose as instructed by Dr Logan, tie the cat, shave it, disinfect the skin, and drape it. Dr Logan only has to make the incision and remove the ovaries and uterus.

If only it was one of the other veterinarians who was on today and if only I didn't have to help out in the operating room. I have tried to keep my distance from her, but it's nearly impossible in these cramped rooms to be anything but touch-ing. I would like to be in the other town, not two inches from her, my thigh touching hers, my hand brushing hers now and then. I can almost feel her breath on my face. God, I'm hard, so hard that it's like being a teenager, worse than when I was a teenager. I have never lusted quite as badly as this. I push myself right up to the operating table. I'm melting with desire for her. Every near brush or touch is like an electric jolt through my body. Damn! One minute I want her and the next I could kill her.

"Shit!" she says.

"What's wrong?"

"This is the one that's pregnant. You should have reminded me."

"Yes?" I say softly. Don't look for trouble so early in the day; don't reply in an equally aggressive way.

"Do you remember from the mists of your classes that there's an extra risk of haemorrhage?"

I ignore this. She isn't capable of speaking to any of her staff politely, particularly not me. Particularly not now. It's as if she resents a woman being a vet.

She curses again, but gets on with the work and sutures up the wound. The ovaries and uterus lie in a kidney dish. The uterus is distorted and looks as if it's filled by a string of marbles. I'm fascinated by those marbles. Can't take my eyes off them. "They're alive," I say. "Of course they are. What did you think?" She doesn't look up from her stitching.

For a second she looks up at me and there's a look on her face which could be disgust. Her lips curl down and her eyes are cold. Arrogant bitch. I wonder if the antagonism is because I'm a woman. No, that's really insulting. No, her attitude is just because she's a bitch, plain and simple. "Take the cat away and bring the next patient in."

"It's a shepherd – Lemour's one – the one that had a go at you last time when it was in for its ears."

"You frightened of it or something?"

"I didn't say so. It would be better if we brought it in together. You could sedate it."

"Now you're telling me my job."

I shrug and untie the tapes holding the cat on its back and take it into the recovery kennels. Carefully I place it on its side and check to see the tongue's out.

The shepherd is in one of the large bottom kennels and squints at me with glinting red eyes. His mouth twitches, exposing huge teeth, the tail vibrates a warning.

I return to the operating room and clear the table and put the instruments into the sink in the prep. room for later cleaning. Once everything's ready for the shepherd, I peep round the door of the office and Logan's there, feet up on the desk with her head buried in a paper, making a show of ignoring me.

I go to the kennel and open the door casually, as if the dog is a tiny, hand-licking poodle, and talk to him quietly. I slip my hand into his collar. The dog raises his lip enough to show red gum.

"Good dog. Good dog." I stroke his chest and the area behind the ears that drives most dogs into an orgasmic trance. He walks beside me as gentle as a lamb and goes limp when I put my hands under him to lift him onto the table.

Logan is in the pharmacy next to the operating room. I call to her, telling her that the dog's ready and she comes in and looks around. "Is the Cavitron set up?"

"No. Sorry."

"You knew that it was to be a scaling and extraction."

"Sorry. I forgot."

"Well, hold the vein and get him under and then set it up fast."

The morning goes in the same way – snipe, niggle and childish complaints. I should leave this office. Nothing about me is right. Nothing. I will never fit in, not with this hard on, throbbing between my legs. Damn my dreams of sex, sex and Dr Larissa Logan, Larissa, all the time.

As we finish the last case of the morning she says, "I want to do that dobe next. She's just right. The stud's coming in at twelve."

The dobe bitch is as sweet as the rabbits in my dream. Soft and silky and female in every way. I can almost smell her femaleness. Its body, like Logan's, is without an ounce of fat, and is streamlined to an efficient, beautiful machine. Its coat glistens with health.

And, by god, the bitch is ready. She rubs her back end on the floor, she pushes it against the wall, she does anything to get some sensation to her bright red, swollen vulva.

The male arrives. He's huge, and as male as she's female. Big-boned, tall, well-covered, silky and lithe.

I stroke him and bend down to talk to her. The dog licks my face. In fact, this male is as gentle as the female, a wuss, a big cuddly bear.

The two dogs are introduced and sniff and then go to their respective owners and place heads on laps. The owners and Larissa Logan and I sip coffee. Both dogs ignore each other. I pull the male's collar and drag him to the bitch. The bitch smells me and nuzzles me and he lifts his head and looks at the ceiling. Big deal!

The humans have some more coffee. The dogs stare into air.

I have seen males like this in my dad's kennel. They just need a bit of prodding, something to get them going. My dad used to joke that they are like men in their sixties, married to the same woman for forty years. I stroke him and pat him and whisper to him. "Come on, come on, boy."

The dog licks my face. Big sloppy kisses.

Ah, no, it's not the dog I am teasing but Dr Larissa. She wants me, she needs me. I am here for her.

I rub the edge of the bitch's vulva and wet my finger in her juices, I then touch the male's nose with my finger, covered in blood. He sniffs. I let him lick my finger and place my hand almost right into his mouth. He licks again and sucks my ear. If the dog could be as affectionate to the bitch as he is to me, then things would be just perfect.

Oh, this is Larissa I have here, on her knees. I have my finger in her cunt. I have her juice on my hands. I taste her in my mouth. It is she, here before me, waiting for me.

I stroke his penis through the prepuce. Back and forward I massage the organ under the skin. It pulses under my hand. I wet my finger in the bitch's vulva again and let him lick it.

Now, Larissa has my finger directed against her clit and it's soaking against it. I suck it and sniff it.

The penis is now sticking out of his sheath, bright and turgid.

My clit is so hard it's sticking out of my lips, almost hanging down like a baby penis. It's exposed and vulnerable.

The bitch backs into me, her vulva flagging, red, ripe, juicy.

The dog sniffs and half-heartedly attempts to mount the bitch. He loses interest when it seems too difficult.

God, I am over Larissa, doggie fashion, my cunt grinding into her soft, silky arse, my hands on her breasts, pulling on her nipples.

I again massage the penis until it throbs, and finally the dog, as if saying to himself, "Oh, hell, if I must, I must," mounts panting and pawing frantically, shagging ferociously. He's in her and tight, so tight, right in there, his arse muscles pumping and pushing. He thrusts into her, rams his penis right into her, rams it in, pumps himself into exhaustion and they are tied together. He tries to extract himself and can't. They turn. They are tied bum to bum, like a double-headed monster. The bitch is panting, a smile on her face. He is quiet, dazed.

Larissa and I, sixty-nine, me on top, she panting, panting, screaming, pushing gyrating up to me, stretching her legs until it's as if she would split into two. This is it. This is what I want and dream. My legs crossed, leaning against the wall, I come silently, violently, without moving a muscle.

When the bitch is gone and the office is cleared up for the weekend, I make myself some coffee and open the paper to catch up with the world. So much for Larissa Logan.

This is my time. This is . . . my eyes are heavy. I want her again. I know she'll be in Mario's for her Saturday lunch. I have to mind the shop. My finger slides down my pants. It curls round my panties.

Now, I order her here. She is to be here to service me.

She stands at the door. "None for the boss?"

"Didn't say you wanted one."

"Could have offered."

I make her a coffee and take it into her office.

"Is there anything wrong with having it with me?"

"No." I return with my coffee and sit across the table from her. I will not sulk. Actually sulking was the last thing from my mind. The show of the bitch and the male have made me hotter for her. I have decided to call Maria and take her out for dinner tonight. Anything to get this woman off my mind. When a woman wants a shag, she has to have a shag.

She reaches in the drawer and pulls out a half bottle of Chivas Regal. "Want one?"

"Why not?" Now what? One minute she's the bitch from hell and the next almost civilized. What's going on now? Do I really need to know? Hell with it. Go with the flow.

"Why not, indeed? It is Saturday."

She pours a good slug into both mugs. The heady, aromatic, full, heavy spirit burns its way down my throat. I feel my face flush in response to the heat.

"I dream about you," she says. "It makes things difficult. Try not to let it interfere."

"I know. Me too."

"Yes, twice I have a dream about you." Her face is soft, tender, dreamy. "Such rich dreams. Dreams . . ."

"Me too."

"Never."

"Sure I did. Dreams about you. Such passionate dreams." Her hand is over mine. I think I'll die. I will explode. I smell that vanilla, sweet smell of hers. The smell of her skin and her cunt. That heavy, loamy smell some women have.

"That's so strange."

"What were your dreams about?"

The phone rings. It always does in dreams, doesn't it?

"Damn it," she says. "Let the service get it."

"My dreams were . . . rabbits and you in a field. A field full of rabbits."

She moves her chair closer to mine. "Mine were of you on a swing and you were going up and down, up and down. A swing made of red rope, velvet rope. You were naked. And, as the swing came down, your legs . . . sorry."

"Go on." She could not stop now. I have to have more of the detail. "Come on."

"I walked up to you. And as you came down I was between your legs. Between your legs and you would have your legs right up to my face. So close I could smell your musk. So close and you smelt of honey and clover. Rich fresh clover. I kept the swing right up to my chest. Bent down to you and smelt you. Put my face right into your sex."

"Yes?"

"Yes. So close and your legs were round my head and my face . . ."

"Yes."

I knelt before her and started to undo the small buttons of her blouse so it hung forward. She wriggled her shoulders and the blouse came off in my hands.

Reaching behind her, I unclipped her bra and let it fall off her shoulders. Her nipples stood, proud, heavy and turgid. Golden and red at the same time.

First I sucked one and then the other, on my knees, kneeling as if I were praying. Paying homage at the altar of my idol, my goddess. Sucked each in turn until they both shimmered and glowed as if they were lit up from inside. She has enormous nipples. The kind with a knobbly area around them, little bumps, themselves the shape of tiny nipples.

I stood up and drew her up in front of me. We kissed. Her lips so . . . so very wet, as wet as a spring of fresh water. I sucked her juice, my tongue searching every part of her mouth. My sex hard against her thigh. Her skin was all that I had imagined, her taste the taste I had created over and over in my mind.

Desperate and panting, she fumbled with my trouser zip and undid it, then pulled the trousers down. I stood in my panties. They too were pulled down. Her face was buried in them, she breathed in deeply as if drinking the smell of my cunt.

"Yes," she said. "I have wanted you."

"I have . . . wanted this for so long."

Her sweater was the next item to come off and then her bra and they were both dropped on the floor.

Her gaze was fixed on my sex. I looked down. My thick blonde thatch stood proud and luxurious.

She went onto her knees and soaked the tip of my clit, her tongue licking and red, red and quick round it. Then her mouth engulfed me.

Jesus, I could not bear this.

I pulled from her and sat down on the chair. I was not some horny teenager to come the first second she touched me. No, cool down, buddies, cool it. I pulled her skirt down and with it, her slip. I then hooked one hand round her panties and pulled them down. I buried my face in the crotch, my tongue tipping her clit. My body turned into a river, into a pumping waterfall. I have never feasted on such a sugary, opulent cunt. It was jasmine and vanilla and honey.

Her legs were open wide, exposing everything for me to examine it. A smile lit up her face, her skin had a deep rich blush.

I opened her lips and ran my tongue down from her clit into her hole. Up and down. Licking like a child licks a popsicle.

She moaned and leant back. Her eyes were shut.

I wet my finger and circled her clit until it popped up to meet me. Yes, now. I bent to her and ran my tongue round it, round and round, and circled and teased it. I wondered if I should pinch myself to make sure I was awake. Or was this just another variation of the dream I have been cursing?

"Jesus, Christ. I can't bear this." Her eyes were shut tight and her lips a thin line. "It's too much. Too fucking much. I have to come." Her hand came to her clit and a finger worked it round and round.

Yes. I stopped and watched her for a moment, wondering how long she could go on. My own finger found my clit and worked it just as she worked hers.

"Smells of heaven."

"So do you."

I pushed her onto her back and opened her legs. I buried my face in her pussy, licking and sucking. One finger deep in her heavy, mysterious cunt. I felt her begin her orgasm, felt her tighten onto my finger. I rolled her over, rolled her onto her back. "Now."

"Yes now."

I was above her. My cunt to her cunt. She fingered me and I fingered her. God, I was right inside her, making her come. She had her hand round my back, her finger in my arse, rolling the finger round and round. God, this was more, much more than I believed possible. Impossible.

I ground into her and no . . . no . . . wait until . . . until . . . I teased her, feathered her and then focused my activity, not stopping, she became rigid for a second or two, then her body grasped me and a volcano erupted, as she panted, and moaned, "Yes, fuck me, for Christ's sake, fuck me. Shag me silly, come on, you bastard."

If that was what she wanted, that was what she would get. I pumped into her as if I was working out on the track, as if I was pumping for my life. And shafts of pain, pain and agony, and oh, such ecstasy, such a high in my clit, a charge from my clit right into my brain, a bolt of lightning exploded in my body. I kept pumping, thrusting and ramming into her long after I was finished.

She bit my ear.

I bit her arm.
I heard the door from the outside open.
I licked my finger.
She stood at the door.
"Everything all right?"
"Everything is just perfect."
She turned her head and smiled. "Better than dreams."
"Yes, much better than dreams. Even the best of them."

Men in High Places

Jessica (Berkeley, USA)

I come from a fairly conservative Catholic background. My parents didn't say a word about sex to me, except when my mother gave me a scientific facts-of-life talk when I was nine. I didn't really discover sexuality – what a marvellous thing it could be – until I met my very open-minded and very loving husband. We've been married for eighteen years and have two beautiful children.

My husband travels a lot for his business and the other day I read that most videos rented in hotels were porno and the average length of play was thirteen minutes. I told my husband and he laughed and said, "That sounds about right." But for me it's very different. I wonder if it's a gender thing or if I'm unusual, but I love to lose myself in long, elaborate fantasies, keeping my body just aroused enough so that it feels like I'm floating above the bed with images and words swirling around me like caresses. When I have a morning to myself, I can spend hours this way before I finally let myself climax.

My fantasies tend toward exhibitionism, although in real life I am very modest and proper and never wear anything you'd call revealing. I think people would be shocked to know what goes on in my head! Here are two of my recent favourites.

In my first fantasy, I've volunteered to be interviewed for a new study on female sexuality. The interview takes place at the office of a researcher at the local university and it's funded by a prestigious organization – in fact I learn of it from the ladies I work with at the library, who assure me it feels good to do something for the advancement of science. At the researcher's office, everything is very proper and professional at first. The female assistant gives me consent forms to sign and promises my identity will be protected.

Then the doctor comes in for the interview. He is older, mid-fifties, and very sure of himself, the type of man who looks down his nose at ordinary folk without an MD and at least two PhDs to their names. But, as is proper protocol with a subject, he is very cordial and smooth as he asks me questions about my sexual history, how old I was when I started masturbating, how I lost my virginity, how often I climax with my husband. At first I'm shy but, as I warm up, I begin to tell him things I've never told anyone before.

Sometimes, when I have a few hours free for this fantasy, I focus on all the details of the question-and-answer period, the way the doctor's eyes begin to glow in spite of his serious expression, the way he shifts in his chair as if he might be arranging something in his pants. Other times I move quickly to the special section of the interview. After I've answered all the questions, the doctor tells me I've been so cooperative, he'd like to invite me to participate in an extra "laboratory" phase of the study.

He leads me into a dimly lit room. In the centre of the room is a comfortable reclining lounge chair upholstered in a feminine, floral print. The doctor tells me to lie down and relax. He then disappears into the shadowy corner of the room. He snaps on a warm, golden light that illuminates only my body on the chair. Then he explains in measured tones that I will be providing very valuable data for his study if I agreed to allow him to film me masturbating.

I blush bright red and am about to jump up and stalk out, but his voice stops me, like a huge, warm hand pressing me back down in the chair.

He explains that I can take this at my own pace and end the session any time I begin to feel uncomfortable. "You're in charge, Mrs C," he says. "Just imagine you are in your own home with some private time and you've decided to pleasure yourself. We will make it impossible to identify your face on the video. This is all for a good cause and will promote a greater scientific understanding of female sexuality."

Finally I consent, but for a while, I lie very still in the chair trying to psyche myself up to do this for a good cause, just as my colleagues at the library must have done before me. At last my fingers creep up to unbutton my blouse.

"Wow, look what she's doing!"

I squint into the shadows and see that there are actually three figures over in the corner: one crouching behind the video camera that's set up on a tripod, the doctor with his clipboard and another taller young man in jeans. The last one is the source of this enthusiastic exclamation.

I realize the doctor lied to me. This is a show, not science. But the truth is this is my fantasy, to be watched while I'm masturbating, not only for the advancement of science but for the personal education of three curious men.

I pull my blouse over my shoulders. My bra opens from the front (as if I'd known this would be convenient when I dressed for the interview) and when I unfasten it, I hear another sigh from the darkness. My breasts fall free into the cool air.

"Awesome tits."

Then comes a harsh whisper, "Jeremy, Jr., I'm going to have to ask you to leave the room if you can't restrain yourself from making unprofessional comments."

I begin to tease my breasts. My nipples are highly sensitive – my husband calls them my "on buttons".

"Look at the expression on her face," the excited voice declares, heedless of the scolding. "She's turned on already."

He's right. My mouth has already fallen open in that "oh" of arousal and my chest is all flushed with a pink rash. I pinch my nipples and roll them between my fingers. My pussy is swelling and throbbing with tiny electric shocks of pleasure. I arch up in the chair. I want those men – young and old – to see it.

From the corner I hear heavy breathing, footsteps pacing, another deep voice making rhythmic grunts of frustrated desire.

I pull my skirt up to my waist and work my pantyhose down around my knees, my thoroughly wet panties nested inside. I put a finger to my clit. I spit on my other palm and start rubbing it all over my chest.

A low moan comes from the corner. "Dad, she's touching herself down there."

The father shushes his son and clears his throat. "Ah, yes, Mrs C now is the time for the first question on our survey. Are you having any particular thoughts or fantasies at this moment?"

"I'm thinking about rubbing hot spunk all over myself," I gasp. "I love it when a man comes on my breasts. But my husband doesn't do it often. He likes to come inside me." I'm strumming frantically now and whimpering with need. "I'm wishing a horny guy has just shot his load all over me . . ."

With a cry, a handsome young fellow in his early twenties leaps out from the shadows. He definitely resembles the doctor, but the long wavy hair and earring give him a sweeter look. In an instant he's standing over me, jeans at his knees, swollen dick in hand.

"I'll help you, Mrs C," he says. Such a Boy Scout. He stands by the chair, aiming his tool at my chest. With the other hand he reaches toward me.

"Don't touch her," the doctor yells. "That's against medical ethics." But there's a hint of jealousy, too, because I'm smiling at the young man and praising his hard, beautiful cock and telling him I can't wait for him to spray all over me.

I think it's going to happen soon by the look of him.

"I'm gonna come," he pants. "Open your mouth, Mrs C. See how much you can catch on your tongue."

Junior's dirty game appeals to me, and I'm strumming myself furiously as his semen arcs over me. One shot hits the target, another my cheek, the rest dribbles onto my chest. I spread the slick, soapy mess over my breasts, moaning with delight.

"More," I whisper. I could come but I don't want to. I want to float forever in this marvellous world above the clouds.

"Hey, Mike, she says she wants more. Do you want to try? I'll man the camera for you. This lady's super hot."

A husky affirmative comes from behind the camera and another young man steps out, pulling a thick cylinder of meat from his pants.

This time I can't help myself. I lean up and take that swollen, red knob in my mouth and start sucking it. Mike lets out a groan of appreciation.

"You can't do that," the doctor fusses. "This is a study of female masturbation, not a porno film."

I have both of my hands clamped on Mike's muscular arse and he's all the way down my throat. I know he's going to shoot his load soon, he's getting so hard in my mouth. It's as if he's pumping his excitement into me and even though I'm not playing with myself at that moment, my pussy juice is gushing onto the chair.

With a shudder, and a series of rapid thrusts, Mike ejaculates in my mouth. I hold it there and swirl it around with my tongue before I swallow it down. I'm so turned on, it tastes nasty and sweet all at the same time.

Mike zips himself up, embarrassed now, and quickly retreats to the corner.

I still hear one man's laboured breathing coming from the shadows.

"Doctor," I call, "I believe it's your turn. I still need a little help to get me over the top."

He lets out a long sigh. It's those last shreds of cool professionalism evaporating into the steamy air. Reluctantly he walks over, pausing every few steps, like he's being drawn to me, a fish on a line. He stops at the bottom of the chair. I can see his huge erection through his pants and a little stain of wetness at the outline of the tip. He tosses his clipboard on the floor and fumbles with the chair. The footrest snaps down, and he yanks off my pantyhose and kneels between my legs, cock poised to enter me. Clearly he expects I'll have intercourse with him. After all he's the doctor, the real man, the grand prize.

I smile. "Oh, no, Doctor, I have different plans for you. I want you to eat my pussy while you pull on your peter like the naughty boy you are. Isn't that right, Doctor? All this talk of scientific research when really you just want to see ladies play with themselves so that you can watch the video later in your office and get off. The truth is, Doctor, you are nothing more than a dirty little masturbator."

He can't really answer because he's already buried his face in my muff, his nose poking out over my fur. He is doing a good job, though, very professional. His tongue makes little figure eights on my clit, so that I'm squirming and squealing like some kind of crazed animal. And of course his hand is down between his legs yanking his own tool, and that's when I come, thinking about him on his knees doing exactly as I've commanded. Or sometimes I wait a little for my satisfaction, until after he's come. I like to watch him wiping himself with his handkerchief and mopping the puddle of his own spunk from the floor.

My second fantasy is a little different, though I can spin this one out for hours, too. In this one, I've just been hired by a very prestigious company far away from my home and my fiance. However, the job has great benefits and bright prospects for my career and I can't turn it down. Because rent in the city is prohibitive, new employees are allowed to stay in furnished company apartments. I'm in a spacious one-bedroom place with a huge, soft bed and mirrors all around.

One day, late in the afternoon, I am called into the president's office for a private meeting. I'm nervous, thinking I must have done something wrong or my probation period isn't going well, but he's very cordial and offers me a sherry and asks with apparent concern if I'm enjoying my work at his company.

Then he says there's something important he wants to ask me, but first he'd like me to watch a few video clips. A rather blurry image comes on the TV he's set up by his desk. At first I can only make out a flesh-coloured form moving sinuously across the screen, but then it hits me what I'm watching. A movie of myself, naked. There must be some kind of video camera hidden behind the large mirror at the bottom of my bed. I've hardly gotten over the shock of seeing myself stripped and exposed, when I have to watch myself do worse. The me in the video starts squeezing my breasts and pouting at the mirror in my best porno queen imitation. Which is exactly what I was doing the night before because I was missing my boyfriend so much and pretending I was dancing for him, the way he likes me to. Now I have to watch again as I slowly sink down and spread my legs and frig myself to a frenzy. A quick cut to a night the week before: me straddling the edge of the bed and staining it with my pussy juice as I thrust and grind my arse into the mattress. This time the camera picks up my loud moans as I come. And then another night, the naughtiest of all, when I was so horny for my boyfriend's cock, I used a hair-brush to get myself off. At first I slide the handle in and out gently, but by the time I near climax, I'm jabbing myself with it and sobbing with delight. It's all on video, even me licking my own juices from the handle when I'm done.

I'm blushing fifty shades of scarlet and practically melting into the leather sofa with shame, but the boss puts his hand on my arm and says soothingly, "I didn't show this to embarrass you, Jessica. I think it's wonderful that you are a very sexual woman who knows her own body and how to pleasure it." He tells me he has a proposal for me. An important part of his business strategy for his clients, especially international clients, involves a special team of attractive employees, mostly female, but there are a few males to allow for a variety of tastes. He would like me to join this team. It involves special training, but also very special bonuses.

I'm not sure if I'm being blackmailed, but I'm also curious and I agree. He tells me the first training session will be the next afternoon in his office. I should have workout clothes and anything I'll need to take a shower afterward.

I show up the next day with my gym bag and am met by the president and a handsome young woman in skin-tight exercise clothes. Her short black hair stands up in spikes and her body is lean and beautifully sculpted. I can tell she's used to being in charge. Even the president seems a little afraid of her.

"Jessica, this is your teacher, Mira," he says (sometimes I change the name, but usually it's Mira). "She is going to train you in the Technique."

With a firm hand, Mira leads me into a room that adjoins the president's office. It's like a dance studio with a mirror along one wall, some ballet bars and exercise mats and a strange apparatus that look like a barrel that has been cut in half. A set of handlebars is attached to one end and the rounded top is fixed with something resembling a saddle. In the centre of the saddle is a leather clip. I'm eyeing this weird object, trying to figure out what it is, but Mira is busy laying out some other devices, a set of small bubblegum pink barbells. The smallest is the size of a pinkie finger, the largest a plump bratwurst. She explains that the company Technique is actually a form of strengthening "your most secret feminine muscles". Her dark eyes twinkle.

Before we start, however, she has to evaluate me. She tells me to lie back on the mat and pull down my pants and underwear. She puts some kind of lubricant on her finger and slides it into my vagina. "Squeeze me as hard as you can," she commands.

I notice the president is standing in the doorway watching. I squeeze.

"Can you do it any harder?" Mira asks.

I try, but I can tell from her frown she is disappointed in me.

"Well, it's a start." She looks over at the president. "She'll need a lot of work."

"I know Jessica has what it takes."

Mira then goes on to explain that the Technique involves using the vaginal muscles to milk a man's penis to orgasm in such a way that he doesn't have to move at all, just lie there and have the woman do it all. My muscles have to be stronger and I have to learn several other tricks first but, if the president is right about me, I'll make the grade eventually. The first exercise is to practise squeezing my muscles down there every day, with and without the barbells. Mira shimmies out of her pants and invites me to put my fingers inside her, to get an idea of what I'm working for. "No lubricant necessary," she winks.

Trembling with embarrassment and excitement, I slide two fingers into her pussy. The sensations are amazing. Her hot, satiny walls close in around me and begin to undulate, rippling and kneading with perfectly controlled timing until my finger is tingling and my shirt is damp with sweat.

Mira smiles and eases my fingers from her body. Then she informs me that the second exercise requires that I come into the studio after work. She glances up at the president.

"Do you have a friend for Jessica?"

"Oh, yes," he says apologetically. Mira obviously calls the shots in this relationship. He leaves the room and comes back with a box. Mira opens it. It's a very realistic dildo, the kind with veins and rubber testicles dangling down. She grins at me. "It's company policy to give these guys a name. What shall we call yours?"

I'm at a loss for words and blushing furiously. "Henry," I murmur. It's my boyfriend's name.

"Okay, Henry," she says cheerily to the obscene rubber tool. "Wanna go for a ride with your pal Jessica?"

I almost have to laugh. Mira is strapping "Henry" onto the barrel. Just then I remember where I've seen these things before. Long ago in my older sister's women's erotica magazine there was an ad for something like this, except in the picture there was a woman straddling the barrel, her head thrown back in ecstasy. The ad said you could buy your own device or get an instructional video. I always thought I'd like to try one or at least see that video, but of course I didn't have the nerve to order such a thing in the mail with my mum asking questions.

"We call this our 'horsie'," Mira says with a wicked smile. "It's a crucial part of mastering the Technique, which, of course, works best when the female is superior." The president clears his throat nervously.

Mira helps me onto the "horsie", I'm already quite wet and slide right down onto the saddle. "Henry" is just the right size for me, very close to my boyfriend who is about six inches. I realize that the front area, around my clit, has a patch of furry material, like a man's pubic hair. In spite of myself I start grinding against it.

"Good, good," says Mira. "It looks like our Jessica has had a little riding practice before."

Bashfully, I murmur a yes.

She reaches under the horsie and flips a switch. A small screen at the centre of the handlebars lights up. "This gives you your pressure reading. Squeeze those pussy muscles as hard as you can."

Again I try my best. A feeble "two point one" appears on the screen.

"For the Technique, you need at least a ten," Mira says and pats my naked buttocks, her hand lingering there a bit too long. "But you'll make it, my girl. Here's what we do. Every time I clap my hands, you squeeze. At the same time you ride up and down, very slowly."

She claps her hands and I squeeze. This time the reading's a little higher. She claps again and keeps clapping at a steady rhythm, although sometimes it's faster and sometimes slow and lazy. Before long I'm getting into it, and I imagine each clap is her hand coming down on my arse like a crop, urging me on.

"Concentrate, Jessica. Make those numbers go higher."

I try, but it's difficult and suddenly I'm coming and rocking on the horsie as I watch the meter numbers flutter with my contractions. The most I get is a lousy three point two.

But, as the president predicted, I am a dedicated student. I come to the studio every evening and even on weekends to practise on the horsie for hours. Within a few months I'm quite the accomplished equestrian and doing tens on a regular basis. After I carry off the Technique quite successfully on the president himself, Mira says I'm ready to go out on the job.

Actually the first part of the assignment is more of the same – practising on the horsie with Henry attached – but, this time, there's a client in the office outside. I'm told to leave the door open and make sure I have myself a very good time, which I do. Then, when a special signal light goes on, I get up, dress in a skimpy skirt and midriff top – no underwear – and walk through the office.

That's when the president invites me along to dinner. He always takes clients to dinner when they're in the middle of important financial negotiations. I look over at the client and smile happily as I accept the invitation. The poor guy is red in the face and has a huge boner because, of course, he's been watching and listening to my workout in the next room instead of paying attention to the numbers. After dinner we all go back to the office to continue negotiations, but this time I sit on the edge of the president's desk, with my legs open just enough to fill the room with my natural perfume and give the client a view of my completely shaved twat. By now the guy's sweating and trembling and he'll sign anything to get me back to his hotel. Both the president and I have indicated I'm up for a very personal celebration when the deal is done. Sometimes in my fantasy I take the client back to the hotel and ride him until he's a boneless blob of Jell-O on that bed, babbling about how I'm the most amazing fuck of his life. But usually I end up coming just as the guy takes the pen to sign, and he's gulping and his eyes are darting over at my bald pussy practically hanging out of my skirt and I can tell he wants me more than anything, even all the money in the world.

I think it's interesting that my fantasies start out with me being all shy and repressed, but as I get turned on, I take control and get the better of snooty guys in white coats and business suits. It's a form of pussy power, I suppose. I'd say in spite of the shame my parents made me feel about my sexuality, it's become a very positive force in my marriage. My husband and I have a great relationship, and we treat each other as equals. It's different out in the real world, though. I don't think women have an equal share of power in public life yet, but that's a nice fantasy to have, too.

Jessie's Girl

Jayden (Hancock, USA)

The lake wasn't crowded that day, even though the temperature hovered around ninety. And it was humid – a steamy, dripping scorcher of a day when the only thing that mattered was keeping cool.

There were small knots of people scattered around the lakefront. They lay unmoving in the sun as if immobilized by her rays, but the three of us opted for the semi-shade of a scrubby ash tree. We too were motionless, feeling the sweat wind and trickle down our bodies.

I felt a tickling as a bead of perspiration slipped from under my bikini top and trailed down my torso. Jessie reached over and caught it, then lifted his index finger to his tongue.

"You taste great even when you're well done, Jayden."

I turned my head to face him, laughing at his mischievous expression. Jessie grinned, brushed a lock of his shaggy hair out of his blue eyes, and spread his hand over my stomach.

Lang rolled up on his elbow. He watched Jessie's hand traverse the moist hills and valleys of my body and his face twisted into a mask of resentment. "I wish Crystal was here," he said. It was at least the twentieth time he'd expressed this sentiment.

I felt sorry for him. We'd been planning this picnic for weeks, then Crystal had called and cancelled at the last minute. Lang's disappointment was palpable, so Jessie insisted he come along with us anyway. He had, but he'd been brooding all day.

"I'm sure she's just as bummed out as you are," I assured him, rolling to face him, "and she can't be having much fun – spending a day like this sick in bed."

I stopped talking, because I saw he wasn't listening. Instead, he was staring at my chest. I glanced down and saw that the strap of my bikini top had slipped down over my shoulder, allowing one breast to nearly pop free of its narrow confines.

Lang's eyes were popping in a similar manner. "Anyhow," I continued, adjusting my strap, "maybe we could plan another picnic for next week, when Crystal's feeling better."

"Maybe," Lang agreed, but his eyes were still on my body. The undisguised lust in them made me a little uncomfortable but, in truth, I didn't really mind him looking at me that way.

I'd always found Lang exceedingly hot, with his curly dark hair, olive skin, and solid, muscular body, and I knew he was attracted to me, as well. Lang had a weakness for tall, willowy blondes and I was just his flavour, a fact which he transmitted by an occasional smoky flash of his dark eyes. He'd complain how Jessie had always gotten the best girls and tease us both, singing that Rick Springfield song from the Eighties, *Jessie's Girl*. "Where can I find . . . a woman like that?" he'd chant. I could tell Jessie got off on the fact that his buddy found me so attractive, but I sometimes wondered if he realized just how deep that admiration ran.

Of course Jessie had no reason to worry, not really. No matter how hot Lang and I found each other we'd never act on it, because Jessie was too important to both of us. Lang and Jessie had been roommates since college and close friends since childhood. They were different as night and day – if Lang was dark and mysterious as the night, then Jessie was the bright gold of day, with his long blond hair, quick smile, and lean swimmer's build. Each was intensely sexy in his own way, but it was Jessie I loved. We'd been a couple for two very happy years and I knew he was the one I'd be spending the rest of my life with.

Much as I adored Jessie, though, I couldn't resist indulging in the occasional naughty fantasy about Lang. Some nights when Jessie and I made love, the mere thought that Lang was in the next room was enough to send me spinning into a potent, savage orgasm.

The way Lang was looking at me now made me wonder if he'd heard me on some of those occasions. His dark eyes seemed to lap me up and I flushed, shifting back against the comforting solidity of Jessie's body. Despite the heat he readily spooned around me and I felt his crotch fit snugly into the hollow beneath my buttocks.

Jessie reached for the strap of my bikini top. "Leave it," he commanded, drawing it back down over my shoulder. "It looks good that way. Doesn't it, Lang-o?"

"It does," Lang agreed, his eyes once again on my partially exposed breast.

Jessie kissed my shoulder, his hand moving around my body. As Lang watched, Jessie's fingers surrounded the soft circumference of my breast and gave it a firm, deliberate squeeze.

Lang's eyes widened and I was shocked speechless. Before I could recover, Lang scrambled to his feet. "I'm going in for a dip," he said abruptly, heading for the water.

Jessie laughed softly and nuzzled my ear. Normally this melted me, but this time I pulled away and glared at him. "What was *that?*"

His blue eyes were wide and innocent. "What?"

"You *know* what!" I snapped, yanking the strap of my bikini back into place. "Why are you groping me right in front of Lang?"

He chuckled again and sneaked another quick feel. "I'm sorry, Jayden. I just couldn't resist. He's got such a hard-on for you he can hardly look at you."

"He does not," I insisted, but I felt the flesh twitch between my legs.

"Oh, yes, he does," Jessie maintained, his fingers stroking the underside of my breast. "Didn't you notice he was pitching a tent?"

As a matter of fact, I had, and I could see that Jessie sported a similarly stiff rod. "Lang is your best friend," I reminded him. "Doesn't it bother you, to have him check me out that way?"

"No," he assured me. "It doesn't. I can hardly blame him. I mean, look at you, babe."

His hand slipped lower and burrowed between my legs. I cast an uneasy glance over my shoulder. "Jessie, somebody might see . . ."

"No one's close enough," he whispered, his hand coaxing my thighs apart.

But one person was. Lang was no more than twenty-five feet away, standing in waist-deep water. His eyes were on us as he sank to his knees, the water rising to his chin.

"You know what he's doing, don't you?" Jessie asked softly. "He's jerking off, wishing it was *him* with his hand on your pussy . . ."

I could feel my vagina loosening, becoming slick. Jessie kissed me then, slipping his tongue into my mouth as his finger slipped around the edge of my bikini bottoms.

"You want to fuck him, don't you?" he whispered against my mouth.

My eyes widened and I shook my head, but Jessie pressed closer. "Tell me the truth," he urged. "You've thought about it, haven't you? Taking his big cock, sucking it," he continued, as his fingers probed the slippery crevice between my legs. "Fucking it . . ."

I couldn't lie, because he could feel how hot his words were making me. "Maybe I have," I confessed, "but I love *you*, Jessie. I would never . . ."

"But what if I said it was okay?" he said, stroking my swollen nether lips. "What if I said you could fuck him . . . if I could watch?"

I'm not sure if it was outrage or arousal that caused my sudden shortness of breath. "I couldn't do that," I said. "Jessie, I just couldn't! And what makes you think Lang would want to, anyway?"

"Because Crystal's holding out on him," Jessie confided, his index finger gently nudging my clit. "He told me. He hasn't gotten any in three months, not since he started dating her, and he's ready to explode."

I couldn't answer, suddenly suffused with the vision of myself naked in bed with Lang as Jessie stood over our intermingled bodies. I closed my eyes and pressed closer to Jessie as a spark of desire flared in my stomach and plunged downward, making me tremble as it ignited between my legs.

How would it feel to be the kind of woman who'd do something like that – have sex with another man while her lover watched? It would take a particular sort of woman, a wild, wanton creature who wasn't afraid to take risks.

And what about Lang? How exactly would one go about convincing him that he wanted to take part in such a thing? I wouldn't even know how to approach it with him, so I'd have to leave it to Jessie. Once that thought occurred to me the scenario suddenly coalesced into a real possibility, though, because Jessie is the most persuasive person I've ever known.

I knew that I'd be merely a prop, an observer who would watch, fascinated, as her lover seduced his best friend. He'd use my body to do it: drizzling suntan oil over my torso and massaging it into my flesh with long, sensual strokes; running his fingers over the small scraps of fabric covering my most private parts; making my nipples harden right through the cloth.

Lang might make a pretense of ignoring us, which will force Jessie to take more extreme actions. I suspect that he'll push my bikini top aside, far enough to entirely bare one breast. The angle of Jessie's body will shield me from the eyes of other beachcombers, but do nothing to conceal me from Lang, who won't be able to tear his eyes off my erect nipple.

As it gets later in the day, the sun will begin to creep down in the sky and her rays will peep beneath the cover of our tree. Jessie will notice and take this opportunity to drizzle more oil over me. "Don't want my girl getting burned," he'll remark, grinning at Lang. "Want to help me out here, buddy?"

Lang won't need to be asked twice. He'll take over my breast, kneading the oil into my hot flesh as Jessie's hand slips into my bottoms. Jessie will attend to my clit as Lang teases my nipple, pinching and rolling it between his oiled fingers, his breath coming in short, hard gasps.

I moan softly when Jessie takes his hand from between my legs. He shifts closer, slipping his thumb into the waistband of his shorts and drawing it down, just far enough to free his cock. I feel its silky head glide over my stomach, lubing itself on my oil-drenched flesh.

Lang lets go of my nipple and grips his own crotch with urgency. He is visibly trembling. "God, you're killing me," he groans, fumbling at the front of his bathing trunks. "I gotta

. . . man, lemme . . ." He tugs and his dick springs out, stone hard and oozing clear juice.

They press against me, one on either side, and as I close my hands over their cocks I feel the differences between them. Jessie's shaft is an elegant wand – long, sleek, and graceful. Lang's is shorter but twice as thick, a solid, sinewy piston. They slide between my hands and buttery flesh and, when I let them nudge each other, I hear Jessie's swift intake of breath. That's when I realize that my man doesn't just want to watch Lang fuck me. He wants to fuck Lang himself.

When Jessie suggests relocating to a more private place, Lang doesn't answer, just jumps to his feet to gather up the picnic gear. We carry it to the truck and Jessie stows it in the back as I get into the cab. Lang is beside me in a second and he kisses me for the first time, his mouth rich with beer and passion.

Jessie gets into the driver's seat and kisses the back of my neck as Lang is kissing my mouth. I can feel Jessie's fingers untying my top and it falls away, then Jessie is cradling my oiled breasts, lifting and offering them up for Lang's mouth.

"Such beautiful tits . . ." Lang's voice is hoarse. "Gimme those big, beautiful tits . . ."

Lang buries his face between my breasts, squeezing them together to suckle both at once. Jessie tugs at my bikini bottoms, so I raise my arse and he peels them down to my knees, then pushes my thighs apart. My cunt yawns open, glistening wet and quivering, and Lang plunges his hand between my legs, to grope and squeeze greedily.

"When we get home," Jessie tells him, "I'm going to watch you fuck my girl, buddy. That okay with you?"

"Yeah," Lang breathes. "Just hurry, man. I can't wait to fuck this." He slides a finger inside me, then two. "Christ, this pussy is wet . . . wet and ready . . . shit, man, *hurry!*"

It takes about twenty minutes to reach their apartment and Lang fingers my wet cleft the whole way. I'm squirming, my naked arse wriggling against the vinyl seat as his busy fingers tease and fondle my clit. Jessie concentrates on driving, a small smile on his face, but I can see that his dick is so hard it seems about to rupture his shorts.

By the time we pull into the driveway, I've come twice; short, sharp bursts that I know are only hints of the delights to come. Jessie doesn't give me a chance to put my bikini back on, just grabs the beach blanket and swathes it around my near-naked body then hurries me inside, calling for Lang to bring in the beer cooler.

As soon as we get through the door, Jessie tosses the blanket aside and lifts me onto the kitchen table. "Did you get a good look at his cock, babe?" he whispers, kissing me deeply as his hands strip away the scraps of my bikini. "Are you hot for it, that stiff, thick cock?"

I moan my assent as he pushes me back and lifts my legs high. "You look so beautiful, spread wide and ready to be fucked . . ." he murmurs, burying his face between my legs. I shiver when his lips wrap around my clit, sucking it like a warm, wet vacuum.

And this is how Lang finds us when he comes inside a moment later: me stark naked with my heels pointing at the ceiling, Jessie's hands cradling my arse while he devours my pussy. Lang stops dead and drops the cooler with a clatter.

"Holy fuck," he sighs, bracing himself against the table with one hand and gripping his crotch with the other. "Shit, that's hot. That's so fuckin' hot . . ."

Lang reaches out but, before he can touch me, Jessie wrenches his mouth away and pulls me to my feet. "The bedroom," he urges, his voice syrupy with desire.

A minute later I lie across the bed, groping for a condom while Lang rips off his shorts. Jessie slips one into my hand as Lang crawls on top of me. He grabs my legs and hooks them over his shoulders, humping impatiently as I unroll the condom over his rigid cock.

When he is sheathed, I point him into my hot, wet cunt. "Fuck me, Lang," I beg.

"Yes, fuck her," Jessie urges and when I look up at him I see that he too is naked, his hand wrapped around his own stiff pole. "Give Jayden what she wants, buddy."

Without further preamble, Lang's thick cock plunges into me, impaling me up to the hilt with one jab. He fucks me with short, hard strokes and it's good . . . so damn good that I catapult into an immediate orgasm, heaving and moaning from the powerful waves of pleasure coursing through my body.

"Fuckin' hot pussy," Lang puffs. "This is some sweet, hot pussy." He inches my legs up around his neck and my back bows as his hands lift my ass even higher.

"Do it harder," Jessie encourages, and I see that he's stroking himself in time with Lang's thrusts. "She likes it fast and deep . . . so fuck her hard, buddy." The movement of Lang's hips accelerate, his cock pistoning like a jack hammer, and I can feel his balls slapping my arse as he rams into me.

I squeeze my eyes shut as I begin to come again, moaning and sobbing with the intensity of it. I ride the crest of my orgasm and, as I wind down, feel a silken touch on my cheek.

I open my eyes. Jessie is kneeling over us, his cock hovering near my face. "Suck me, babe," he urges. "Suck my cock while Lang fucks you."

I arch my head back, open my mouth wide, and take Jessie's long cock down my throat. Lang is still pumping, obediently fucking my pussy while Jessie fucks my face. Watching me suck Jessie's cock seems to turn him on even more and he voices his approval while he fucks me: "Yeah, baby – suck that cock. Take it all, Jen, swallow it down . . ."

Jessie slides his cock nearly all the way out of my mouth and pauses, lingering just on the tip of my lips. I am well-attuned to what he likes and so I give it to him, my lips sucking and nibbling the so-sensitive spot just below the dome of his penis. Lang fucks me in a slow and steady rhythm, and one particularly firm thrust causes me to lose my lip lock on Jessie's cock. It rears up, striking Lang's face and he recoils, but Jessie groans out loud and I realize then what my man wants most.

I take hold of Jessie's cock, suckle gently, then slip it from between my lips and switch my attention to Lang. I kiss him deeply, sensuously, then turn back to Jessie's cock. I nuzzle it, suck it, and kiss Lang again.

I keep it up, alternately kissing and sucking, and I can hear Jessie moaning, feel his cock throbbing between my lips. This time when I draw Lang close for another long, passionate kiss, the tip of Jessie's cock is still in my mouth.

Lang's body stiffens in surprise, but I writhe beneath him,

my tongue darting back and forth between his mouth and Jessie's cock. I swirl my tongue faster and faster, caressing Jessie's hard prick and Lang's soft lips at the same time.

I'm on fire, my hips rearing up against Lang's cock with utter abandon while my mouth gobbles Jessie's cock. "Come on my face, baby," I plead. "Come on my face while Lang comes in my pussy. I want it so bad, Jessie. Please . . . Lang, come on . . . help me . . ."

Then Lang's mouth opens and we're sharing Jessie's cock. It glides between our mouths, our tongues mingling around it, and I can see wonder in Lang's eyes, and heat.

Jessie's hand grips the back of Lang's neck and he's groaning, animal sounds that tell me he's close. I see his balls tighten, retract, and jets of heat explode across my face. One . . . two . . . three spurts, his thick cream streaming over my mouth and chin.

"Shit!" Lang shouts. "Shit, me too, man! Me too . . . " He arches his back and heaves against me, his body spasming with the power of his orgasm.

For a moment, all of us are motionless: me with my legs locked around Lang's back and Jessie's cock against my face; Jessie poised on his knees above us, leaning against Lang's shoulder; Lang with his cock buried deep within me, his eyes wide with surprise.

Jessie reaches down, scoops a bit of milky cream onto his finger, then feeds it to me. I lap it up dutifully, murmuring. With his other hand, he strokes the back of Lang's neck.

"Everybody okay?" he asks.

Lang is watching me lick the cream off Jessie's fingers. "Oh yeah," he whispers and kisses me, his tongue reaching into my mouth for a taste of Jessie.

We lie side by side in the darkening bedroom. The temperature has dropped along with the sun and a soft breeze wafts through the open window, fresh and cool against our damp bodies. We don't speak, each lost in our own thoughts of what has passed between us.

Lang is in the middle, so quiet that I wonder if he's asleep. I hear Jessie stir and, when I look over, I see that he's stroking

Lang, exploring his body with the gentle fingers I know so well. Lang remains still, his eyes squeezed shut.

Jessie touches his nipples, caresses them, and my own hands move to canvass the dense area between Lang's legs. Lang's breath tightens, proving that he's awake after all, and, when Jessie puts his mouth to a nipple, I see Lang's cock twitch.

I reach for it as Jessie's head descends. His mouth leaves a wet trail as he follows the thin line of hair that tapers down Lang's abdomen. Lang's cock is lengthening, stiffening in my hand. I offer it to Jessie and, when he takes it in his mouth, he wears a rapt expression. I watch his lips surround the velvety head, watch him take it deep in his throat, so deep that his nose nudges Lang's pubic hair.

Lang opens his eyes then, sees who it is sucking his cock with such reverence. "Dude, I don't know about this," he says, although his hips are moving back and forth, responding to the ministrations of Jessie's talented mouth. "Jess, I don't know . . ."

Jessie lifts his head. "Relax, buddy," he whispers. I take Lang's throbbing cock in my own mouth while Jessie moves to his balls. He kisses and fondless them, his finger tracing a slow, sensuous path over and behind the twin sacs. I can't quite see what Jessie is doing back there but, judging from the volume of Lang's moans, it's something extra special.

When Lang's cock rears up hard enough to make me gag, I pull my mouth away and move for a better look of what Jessie is up to. I see that he's caressing Lang's anus, stroking and gently prodding the tight ring of flesh.

Jessie slips a finger inside his arse and Lang moans, spreading his legs wide. Jessie's finger burrows deep, his tongue tracing the same trail his finger has blazed. When Jessie's tongue snakes into Lang's arse alongside his finger Lang goes crazy, thrusting and rearing and moaning out loud. "Shit, that feels good . . . so damn good . . . nobody's ever done that to me . . ."

Jessie gives him a gentle push and Lang rolls onto his stomach, his arse rising high in the air. I have to touch myself as I watch Jessie tongue-fuck Lang, have to caress my pussy as Jessie's mouth caresses Lang's anus. Lang humps his arse against Jessie's mouth and I can see that he's completely under Jessie's spell, ready to submit utterly to whatever he wants.

Jessie reaches between my legs, lubes his hand on my juices, then slips first one slick finger, then two, into Lang's arsehole. He holds out his other hand and I give him what I know he wants – a condom.

When Jessie withdraws his fingers to slip on the condom, I see that Lang's anus has opened – flowered – and is quivering with need. Jessie presses the head of his sheathed cock against Lang's arse, raising his eyes to me. "It's your turn to watch, babe," he tells me as he begins to work his penis into Lang's wet hole.

And I do watch, mesmerized, as Jessie takes him slowly, little by little, fondling Lang's genitals as he penetrates his arse. Lang grimaces, clutching the bedclothes with white-knuckled hands. "Shit, that hurts," he grunts. "Dude, it hurts . . ."

"It will stop hurting," Jessie whispers. "Just relax. Don't fight it." He strokes Lang's cock as he presses deeper into his arse, and he doesn't stop until he is fully submerged, his own balls flush against Lang's.

They seemed suspended, poised on the edge of something. Lang's body is rigid, clenched, his face twisted into a rictus of pain. It seems they are soldered together, then something gives and I watch Lang's body relax and sink back against Jessie.

Jessie begins to pulse his hips back and forth. Lang emits a long sigh and Jessie lengthens his strokes, releasing Lang's cock to grip his hips. Lang's body begins to move in tandem with Jessie's, and Jessie increases the power and depth of his thrusts.

Jessie's head is thrown back, his eyes closed and his mouth wide open, contorted with profound pleasure. Lang's face is buried in his arms, but the murmurs coming from his throat are unmistakable sounds of ecstasy. Between his legs, dipping and bobbing freely, is the hardest cock I've ever seen. It seems ready to burst: skin stretched tight and shiny, its tip leaking gobs of clear juice. I want to touch it, suck it, lap up those drops of slippery precome.

I reach for it, but before I can get there Lang flings his head back. "Oh, shit!" he shouts. "Oh, fuck! *Fuck . . .*"

His cock explodes, ropes of semen shooting across the bedclothes. Jessie tightens his grip on Lang's hips, plunging ferociously, and when he comes it is with a short, sharp cry and a final thrust of such force that Lang is propelled forward, his face disappearing into the pillow.

They rest together, Lang's face hidden, Jessie's still twisted in ecstasy. As his breathing slows Jessie withdraws, removes the condom and ties it off, then drops it to the floor beside the bed. He runs his hand over Lang's back – a luxuriant stroke that begins at Lang's shoulder and slides down his spine to linger briefly between his buttocks – then Jessie rolls over on his back and stretches out between us, mindless of the semen spattered on the blankets.

Lang lifts his head and contemplates Jessie with a peculiar expression. Jessie meets his eyes steadily, holding his gaze for an endless moment. Finally Jessie smiles, then rises up on his elbow. Lang stays very still as Jessie kisses him, the lightest, gentlest brush of lips against lips.

Lang sighs then, his body relaxing and sinking down in the bed until his head rests against Jessie's chest. It seems an incredibly intimate action, far more than anything that came before, and, watching them, a nameless fear takes hold of my heart.

I experienced a sudden pain in the pit of my stomach and felt inexplicably cold, despite the warmth of the day. I must have withdrawn physically, because Jessie gripped my arm and pulled me back against him. When I opened my eyes, blinking in the bright sunshine, he was watching me with tenderness and concern.

"I love you, Jayden," Jessie told me, drawing me closer to his side. "I love you very much. You know that, don't you?" I nodded and he kissed me, with the same passion and adoration I'd always known from him. I melted against him, reassured, then heard Lang come splashing out of the water.

When I looked up at him, he was eyeing me with the same lust I'd noted earlier. "Getting late," he observed. "Do you guys want to head home? We could pick up more beer and hang out, maybe watch a movie. Or something," he added, with a little smile.

I didn't reply. Jessie hesitated for a moment, then gave my waist a squeeze. "Not tonight, buddy," he replied. "We'll drop you off, then I'm going to head over to Jayden's place for the night."

I exhaled. The air rushed out of me and it wasn't until then that I realized I'd been holding my breath. A flash of disappointment crossed Lang's face, but he nodded. "Cool," he said. "Maybe I'll call Crystal, see if she's up and around."

"She'd like that," I assured him.

He shrugged as Jessie started packing up the picnic gear. "Maybe she would. Sometimes I'm not so sure she's the right one for me, though." I started to get up and Lang extended his hand. "I think I'd do better with a different kind of girl. Somebody more like you," he added as he helped me to my feet."

"Sorry, buddy," Jessie interjected, tossing the wad of towels at Lang. "Jayden's taken. You'll have to find your own."

Lang nodded and chuckled ruefully as he caught the towels. "I know. You always *did* get the best girls."

Jessie grinned. "Damn right."

"Where can I find . . . a woman like that?" Lang sang softly, and Jessie and I laughed as we gathered up the blanket and cooler. Then the three of us headed for the parking lot, the rays of the sun colouring the lake a soft pastel and the air beginning to cool as the day came to an end.

Home Study

Sabrina (Edmonton, Canada)

It was a quiet night on the train. My stop was a way away so I
sat on the cushioned vinyl seat next to the window and let my
mind wander as the scenery passed by me in a blur.

Usually the cars were crowded full of people reading books
or newspapers, consciously ignoring one another or simply
staring into space. Tonight there were only four others and
myself. I'd noticed them when they'd clambered onto the train
at the last stop like a group of rambunctious puppies. College
boys. Cocky as only young, good-looking and athletic college
boys can be.

"She wanted me bad," one said loudly. "I could tell just by
the look in her eyes. She was creaming her panties just wait'n
for me to ask her out again. Next week when we go back she'll
cream them when I walk in the door, I won't even have to talk
to her."

Laughter from the others signalled that not all of them
agreed with his assessment of the situation.

"Get real, Scott. She won't give you the time of day next
week. She works in a pub full of guys that hit on her every day
and girls don't like it when you lead them on like you did. She's
hot enough that she'll be onto someone else by the time you get
back there." This guy looked like the smarter of the foursome,
good-looking in a studious way with a quiet authoritative
voice. The type of voice that gave me orders in my dreams
and made me cream my own panties.

They didn't bother to try and be quiet so I closed my eyes,
laid my head against the window and let myself be entertained
by their conversation. They argued amongst themselves about

how much a woman would put up with if the sex was good
enough and just how good each of them was in bed. When a
particularly stupid comment was made I couldn't smother my
snort of laughter and they went silent.

Knowing that they'd heard me, I turned in my seat to face
them and give them something to think about. "First of all,
yes, a woman will put up with a lot if the sex is good. Second,
just because you can get it up quickly for rounds two, three and
even four, doesn't mean you know how to use it. It only means
you have stamina, which is a given at your age."

Their reactions, clearly stamped on their expressive faces,
ranged from surprise to anger to awe. My guess from this was
that girls didn't talk frankly to them and if they did they were
written off as ice queens.

"Yeah? And I suppose you're going to tell us what makes it
good, then?"

The challenge came from the loudest one, Scott. He'd been
the one boasting about the waitress when they'd stepped onto
the train. He was tall, well muscled, and obviously the self-
proclaimed leader of the group. I eyed him a second before
checking out the others – all with shaggy hair, young eager
faces, and hard bodies that my fingers itched to feel.

Making a spur of the moment decision, I stood up and faced
them as the train slowed near my stop. "I'll do better than tell
you. I'll *show* you. If you're brave enough to come with me now
and do everything I say, I'll teach you what pleases a woman."
I stepped off the train and began walking towards the stairs.

Seconds later footsteps clattered behind me and a voice
called out, "Everything?"

"Everything." I answered without a backward glance.

Pounding footsteps signalled them catching up to me. When
I felt their presence close behind me I stopped and turned
around.

Looking over the three that had followed me, anticipation
made my breath catch in my throat. They were eager students
and the power their willingness gave me worked as an aphrodisiac. My blood heated in my veins as it rushed through my
system and settled between my thighs. "I live just up the road.
Once we walk into my house you will act on your best

behaviour. Treat me with the respect you would any of your professors, for I am about to give you your most valuable education."

We walked in silence, each with our own thoughts. Once at the small old house I rented, we filed into the living room. "Make yourselves comfortable, boys. I just need to make a quick call."

I walked into the kitchen, picked up the phone and dialled automatically. When my roommate answered on the second ring I told her I had a special surprise for her and asked if she could make it home from work early. When I returned to the living room, the guys were all seated on the sofa, shoes and jackets off, talking quietly amongst themselves.

"Tell me about yourselves," I asked.

Tom, Nick and Steve were all on the university basketball team together. They also shared some of the same classes and were consistent B students as well. When I asked about career dreams I learned that their friendship had surpassed the basketball court to plans of becoming future business partners. "We know that not all of us can make a career out of basketball but we want to keep playing as long as we can."

They were so cute and earnest when voicing their plans for the future, I couldn't hold back any more. "Okay. First lesson." I walked to the big picture window that looked out on the street and pulled the blinds closed before continuing around the room lighting candles and dimming lights. "Set the stage, guys. Women, no matter what their shape, feel antsy the first time they get naked in front of a guy. Make the light the most flattering and they will feel comfortable. The more comfortable they are, the more uninhibited they'll be and then more fun is had by all."

I strolled over to the stereo and put on my favourite Enigma CD for some quiet background music

"In order for you to make her feel comfortable, you need to be comfortable as well." My body started to sway to the music and I began to slowly take my clothes off. I danced as if I was alone. Closing my eyes and running my hands over my breasts I continued to talk as I stripped. "You should know where she needs to touch you to please you and how she needs to touch you. Soft, hard, a lick or a bite." I pinched my nipples hard through my shirt. "If you don't know what pleases you, how are you supposed to know what pleases her?"

Soon I stood in front of them in nothing but a purple silk bra and matching panties. Lust and eagerness vibrated off my captive audience and arced through the air. It was clear they wanted me and all I had to offer, yet none of them reached to adjust the straining erections in their pants, let alone relax enough to pull them out for me to see.

They needed help.

I reached down and grabbed Steve's hands from where they rested on his knees and pulled him up with me. "Dance with me," I instructed. "And you guys need to relax. Get comfortable with yourselves. Pull out your cocks and stroke them for me. I want to see how you touch yourselves."

Steven pulled me close and we swayed with the music. His chocolate eyes stared into mine as we moved, his big hands roaming up and down my back. I brushed my body teasingly alongside his until he grabbed my arse and pulled my hips tight to his so that his cock thrust rhythmically against me. I unbuttoned his shirt as he kept our hips moving together. After pulling off his shirt, I stepped back.

"Continue the dance for me. Slowly taking off all your clothes," I whispered before turning back to the two on the sofa.

Tom's dick was short but fat, with an angry red head that made my mouth water. I licked my lips and eyed Nick's cock next. Long and thick, with drops of pre-come already wetting the tip, it made my pussy clench in anticipation of being filled. "That's it, guys. Get up and get undressed." I settled myself on the empty sofa and watched as they quickly stripped down to nothing. When all three stood in front of me with dicks waving in the air, waiting for further instruction, I smiled and gave my next command.

"Make yourselves come."

They looked at each other uncertainly.

"C'mon, now, guys. You need to be totally comfortable with yourselves first. No shyness allowed." To get their attention back on me and off each other, I slipped off my bra and fondled my own tits. Pinching and rolling my nipples around, I watched each of them reach for their cocks. Unable to help myself, I let one hand slide down my body and between my legs to where my panties were soaked. "The first one to come will be the first to move on to the second lesson. How to eat pussy properly."

I watched as they started pumping themselves. Hands fisted over hard cocks, hips beginning to thrust as they moved towards orgasms. It was a tight race. As I watched them pump and groan, my finger was flying back and forth over my clit. I knew that the fact they could see my hand moving in my panties, and not see my cunt opening hungrily was helping them towards their goal.

"Ohhh . . . uhmmm," I moaned as I pressed my thighs wider apart. I could feel my climax getting closer. My finger worked my clit harder . . . harder . . . there. Colours exploded behind my eyes and I felt my muscles tense and shake as small waves of pleasure rolled over me.

"Ughhh!" I opened my eyes in time to see Nick's eyes slide closed as a loud groan escaped his mouth and come erupted from his throbbing cock. Grunts from the other two followed closely as they too shot jism into the air.

"Well done, boys," came a soft voice from the entryway. "What has Sasha promised as a reward for those performances?"

I stood and walked over to the woman in the doorway. "I'd like you guys to meet my roommate, Emma. She's come home early to help me out with your lessons." I leaned in and gave her a soft kiss on the lips. "Thanks."

"All right, oh yeah," came murmurs of approval from over my shoulder.

My hand cupped Emma's soft cheek as I smiled into her eyes. "I promised you as the reward."

Reaching for her hand, I pulled Emma into the middle of the room where the guys surrounded us. "Oral sex is different for every woman. When one tells you they don't enjoy it, it's because they've never had it done by someone who really knows how to eat pussy." I walked in a slow circle around Emma, letting my hand run over her body, patting her fanny, cupping a heavy breast. Then stopping directly in front of her. "Whatever the case is, you need to get her going first – don't just dive between her legs, thinking that will warm her up, because it won't."

I looked deep into Emma's green eyes and saw the flames of arousal flickering to life. With sure fingers I unbuttoned her blouse before peeling off the rest of her clothes. I let my hands brush the curve of her breast then skim over the hard tips of her nipples. First my fingertips and then my lips trailed lightly over her belly, the backs of her knees, and finally the insides of her thighs. I realized that I was doing exactly what I'd told them not to and stood up again. Tangling my fingers in Emma's curls, I pulled her to me and opened her lush lips up with my tongue. Cupping a firm tit in one hand I reached behind her and fondled her plump arse with the other.

Tearing my mouth away from hers, I licked my way down to the tit I held and suckled at the nipple until it was rigid in my mouth and she was moaning softly into the silent room. With a final nip at the little morsel, I let go and led her over to the sofa.

Kneeling between her legs, I spread her thighs as wide as I could. "Look at that. A sight to behold." Using my thumbs, I opened her crudely and leaned forward to give a firm lick up the crease of her pussy lips. "Firm strokes with your tongue, boys. First you poke around a little, licking, maybe a nibble or two, avoiding the clit."

I demonstrated with them watching over my shoulders, my fingers keeping Emma's thick pussy lips spread so she was totally exposed. Her scent was strong and musky, her taste a mixture of sweet and tart. Once I could feel her tunnel grasping at my thrusting tongue, I backed away and urged Nick into my place.

"First prize, Nick," I whispered in his ear. "I want you to give her multiples. All you need to do is stay at it nice and steady. Firm strokes, a nibble here or there and then, when you know she's almost there, suck on her clit. Use your fingers, tongue, and teeth. Anything goes when you're in this situation. Listen to her moans and read her body's signals as to what pleases her most."

I turned and pulled Steve over to stand behind me as I

leaned over Nick's back and braced myself on his shoulders. I pulled off my soaked panties and nestled my arse backwards until Steve's prick rested between my arse cheeks. I pulled one of his hands around me, and placed it on my own pussy. Needing no further encouragement, he began to explore between my thighs, his thick fingers parting me and sliding into my hole, thrusting in and out briefly before his thumb found my clit and he began to work me over good. Not wanting to be left out, Tom stepped in closer and began to massage my tits, pinching and rolling the nipples around as he watched his friend eat Emma's pussy.

I kept whispering words of advice into Nick's ear, occasionally taking a nibble of my own on the side of his neck. Emma's cries were getting louder, and getting all of us hotter. I reached down between Nick's legs and grasped his rigid dick firmly. He grunted and his tongue hesitated in working Emma for a second.

"You can't get distracted, Nick. She's almost there."

So was I. I spread my legs wider and arched my back, pushing against Steve shamelessly.

Emma's hands reached down and she laced her fingers through Nick's hair, pulling him tighter against her. I could see her hips moving and heard the whimpers I knew signalled an oncoming orgasm.

"Don't stop," I called out. Both Steve and Nick followed my instructions. "Keep it gentle for a minute. There, that's it, she's coming, I'm coming, harder now, harder, yes, there, that's it. *Yess.*"

"Yesss," echoed Emma.

"Stay there, Nick," I commanded breathlessly. "A little push and she'll come again."

Nick tickled a finger lightly over her anus and he sucked her clit into his mouth. Sure enough, Emma's cries filled the room again.

I shifted my hips a little, and Steve read my silent instruction perfectly. Swiftly entering me with his cock, he moved both hands to my hips and began to pump me full from behind. I bit my lip to keep from moaning aloud. With one fist still pumping Nick's cock, I pulled Tom over so I could suck his cock into my hot mouth at the same time and be surrounded and filled by hard cock.

The pre-come flowed steadily from Nick's cock head over my fingers and I knew he wouldn't last much longer. The throbbing of Tom's dick in my mouth testified that he was close as well. I closed my eyes and revelled in the sensations assaulting my body from all sides. A soft hand stroked under my chin and I opened up to let Tom's meat slip from between my lips.

Opening my eyes, I saw Emma urge Tom to straddle her on the sofa, where he began to fuck her mouth. From where I was I could see his buttocks clench and release with each thrust between Emma's lips, but Nick's view of this act was the breaking point for him. I heard a guttural moan rise up from his chest and felt his come rush through the veins of his cock and shoot into the air.

I pulled my hand away from his shrinking dick and placed both my hands on his shoulders. With Nick resting his head on the sofa between Emma's thighs, watching Tom shaft her mouth, he was still well positioned for me to brace against Steve's thrusts.

My head fell forward and I arched my back for deeper penetration. A whimper of pleasure escaped my lips as Steve's cock hit deep in my womb. He grunted and picked up the pace, his cock hammering into me as he watched Tom pull out of Emma's mouth and spray jism all over her tits.

"Oh yeah, Steve," I urged. "Let go, fuck me. Fuck me hard."

His hands gripped my hips fiercely and he panted loudly and fought to hold back his own orgasm. My belly tightened and I felt my cunt clutching at him. Then the tremors started. From deep inside I could feel my orgasm building. "Yes, that's it. Harder! Yes. Fuck, fuck, fuck," I chanted until I felt my pussy walls spasm and juices run down my spread thighs in release. A few hard thrusts and I felt Steve's come shoot into me hotly before we both collapsed onto the floor, only to stay there in a languid heap trying to catch our breaths.

I must've drifted off to sleep because then I heard Steve's voice from a distance as his hand gently shook my shoulder.

"Excuse me, Miss. Are you okay?"

I smiled up into his polite gaze, his polite distant gaze. Confused, I looked around at the near empty space surrounding us and realized I had drifted off to sleep . . . on the train!

Heat flooded my cheeks and I scrambled for my bag on the seat beside me. Mumbling thanks and apologies, I dashed for the exit before the doors slid shut, not caring if it was my stop or not.

It wasn't my stop. It was one stop past where I usually got off, but that was okay. Placing one foot in front of the other, I started off for home, a smile slowly spreading across my face as I felt the wetness between my thighs. My sojourn into fantasyland had prepared my body well and I wondered if Emma was home from work yet. After I tell her about my dream, it shouldn't be too hard to convince her tonight would be a good night to go on a manhunt.

Skirts and Shoes

Lydia (New Orleans, USA)

As the Italian-looking shoe salesman slips a sleek red heel on my right foot, I see him look up my skirt. I feel an immediate rush and do my best to pretend I don't notice.

Wearing a navy blue mini-skirt, my foot up on the stool and my knee high, he has a clear view of my crotch. He blinks, looks at the shoe he just slipped on my foot, then looks back up at my crotch and says, "How does it fit?"

"Fine." I feel nice and hot as I switch feet, lifting my left knee now, my skirt climbing even higher. I run my hands through my long brown hair and lean back. He takes another look at my panties. I can see the top of my thigh-high stockings, so I know he's getting a great view.

According to two ex-boyfriends, my legs are my best feature. But the shoe salesman isn't looking at my legs. My panties are extra sheer, skimpy white panties, with enough of my dark pubic hair sticking out the sides to make it interesting.

At thirty, I'm several years older than the salesman, who's brazen enough to *stare* at my crotch as he finishes slipping on the left shoe.

I stand and walk around, catching the attention of a heavy-set man who has been dragged into the store by his equally heavy wife. He stares at my legs as I step around and watches me sit.

I point my knees in his direction so he can get a look. I cross my legs like a man, knee outward, and toy with the shoe's instep. Then I lean back and let the shoes salesman take off the shoes and slip on a black pair.

A very skinny man, passing in the mall, stops and pretends

to look in the windows at the shoes. He watches me as I lift one knee and then the next. With my knees this high, he can't help but see my panties, even at his distance.

My shoes salesman looks as if he's counting pubic hairs.

The black shoes don't fit and I thank him and grab my purse. He smiles and puts my blue heels back on, taking his time, taking another long look.

He's the fourth salesman I've flashed today. Standing, he adjusts his crotch as I leave. Two men follow me as I head down the mall. I love it, turning them on. I slow, but pass the next ladies shoes store. It's one of those where you have to try the shoes on yourself. Without a salesman's face a few inches from my crotch, what's the point?

The last store in the mall has no customers. I spot the shoe stools, so I know the salesmen help you here, so I go in. A short, balding man comes out of the back and smiles at me. I ask to try on a pair of white heels, give him my size, then sit facing the mall.

As the bald salesman arrives, and I lift my knee, I see the skinny man is back, looking in the window. My bald shoe salesman doesn't seem to notice at first, but I catch him stealing a peek as I switch legs.

Two pair of shoes later, I walk out, my crotch damp now. The skinny man shadows me, but leaves me as I walk out to my car and drive off. On my way home, I fantasize about driving over to New Orleans next weekend. I'll visit the ladies shoe stores on Royal Street. In my fantasy, I don't wear panties. I hope I'm brave enough.

In a white blouse and my extra-short, red mini-skirt, I wear thigh-high stockings again and red heels. I feel the summer breeze on my bare arse as I move down Royal Street from the Monteleone Hotel. I'm dolled up, extra make-up, crimson lipstick, my hair curled with the wet look. As I pass an antique shop window, I catch my reflection. I have "fuck me" written all over.

I stop outside my first shoe store and see the mandatory stools inside and two male salesmen. On my way in I see the police station is across the narrow French Quarter street. Two young cops give me a long look.

The two salesmen each ask if they can help. Both in their forties, the white one is dapper in a blue suit. The second is dark, African-Latino looking. He needs a haircut and his white shirt is dishevelled.

"Size six, please," I tell the dishevelled man as I pick up a white high heel. He smiles at me and eagerly goes to fetch the shoes.

I move to a row of chairs facing the street, subtly pushing the stool closer to the chair before sitting to face the street. Draping my purse across the seat next to me, I cross my legs to remove my shoes. I roll my hips to either side to tug down my skirt, which does little to hide anything. As soon as I uncross my legs, my entire crotch will be in view. The two cops are still across the street, still looking this way.

The dishevelled man moves to the stool, lies two shoe boxes next to it and sits. I put my right foot up on the stool, my knee extra high because the stool is closer than normal. The man digs out a shoe and starts putting it on. The top of his head rises slightly and I know he's getting a full bush shot.

His hands tremble. I reach for my purse and pretend to look for something in it. He finishes with my right foot, so I throw it over the side and bring up my left knee, my legs open for a second. Then again, with my left knee high, my pussy's right there, about a foot from his face.

The man in the blue suit moseys over in front of me and takes a look as he passes. I close my purse and sit back up and then rise and walk around with the new shoes.

"They're a little tight," I say as I sit again, my knees pointed at the dishevelled man.

"I have a half-size larger," he says, digging into another box.

I kick off the shoes, lean back and put my right foot up on the stool again. Leaning back opens my crotch even more. The blue suit moves back. "They're Parisian," he says, pointing to the shoes.

He's getting a nice look at my French-American pussy, but I don't say anything. I dig into my purse again and pull out my lipstick and mirror. The dishevelled man finishes with my right foot and I throw it over the side as I open my mirror. I take a second before lifting my left knee, my knees open wide for them.

I reapply my lipstick as the man takes his time with my left shoe. Peeking around the mirror, I see both men leering at my bush. When I stand up to walk around, I have to pull my skirt down, it's risen so high.

"No," I tell them. "I don't like the look, actually."

"What about these?" The man in the blue suit shows me a different shoe.

"No," I tell them as I slip on my shoes and leave them panting, maybe not on the outside, but I know I got to them.

The cops are gone. I shrug and continue down Royal Street. The breeze flows up my skirt and I'm damp already. The next two shoe stores have women sales staff. I pass two more without the mandatory stools.

I almost miss a narrow one sandwiched between two art stores. No customers here, either, but the stools are there. As I step in, a young salesman steps out of the back. He's in his early twenties with straight dark hair and a nice square jaw.

"May I help you?"

I pick up a black heel and ask for my size.

Sitting, I pull the stool closer, kick off my shoes and wait. A blond-haired clone of the salesman comes out of the back. Square-jawed too, he smiles at me, moves around and glances at my crossed legs.

"It's beautiful out there today, isn't it?"

"The weather's gorgeous," I tell him as my salesman returns with two shoe boxes.

As soon as I raise my knee, they both look and their silence is exquisite. It takes a second for my dark-haired salesman to get started. These guys are too young to be subtle.

They try small talk. More about the weather as I open my knees to switch to my left foot, then lean back to give them a clearer view. Smiling at one another as I stand and walk around, they watch me – captives of their hormones.

I like that in a man.

I sit and cross my legs like a man again, playing with the shoe's instep, my legs open. They stare at my bush. I wonder if they can see pink.

"Do you have this a half-size larger?"

They both nod. My salesman reaches for the second box without looking at it as I sit in front of him again. Leaning back, I raise my right knee. As he slips on the newest shoe I reach down and start working my stocking up.

"These things always slip down," I say as I pull up the stocking, my fingers rising higher and higher until I have the elastic between my fingers. I open my leg slightly to pull the stocking all the way to my crotch.

Both of them let out a little gasp.

Switching to the other stocking, I open my legs more to pull the elastic all the way up. Looking up, I see they are staring at my bush, as if mesmerized. I'm so hot, I feel my chest rise.

I throw my right foot off the stool and raise my left foot for the second shoe. The salesman lets out a long sigh and says, "Wow."

"Y'all enjoying the view?" I say languidly, as I lean back.

"Oh, yeah," the salesman says to my pussy.

I look up at the blond man, who pulls his gaze away to smile at my face.

"Come on now," I tell them. "I'll bet y'all see a bush or two every day."

The man with one hand on my left calf and one on the left shoe he's easing on to my foot shakes his head slowly. He lets go of the shoe and brushes his hair out of his eyes, his left hand still on my calf.

"We talk about what it'd be like trying shoes on a naked woman. But it's all a fantasy."

I bite my lower lip and nod toward the door. "Lock the door and maybe your fantasy will come true."

He looks up at me with those wide brown eyes and smiles. The blond needs no further instructions. He hurries and locks the door and draws down the door shade. Anyone stopping on the street to look in the window will still be able to see my back, but I tell myself, *let the show begin.*

"Take off the shoes," I tell my salesman as I start unbuttoning my blouse. He pulls them off and leans back as the blond pulls a stool up next to him to sit on. I hand him my blouse.

I unhook my bra and pass it to the dark-haired one, freeing my breasts. They stare, as if hypnotized by my nipples. Taking in a deep breath, I reach back and unbutton my skirt and work the zipper down. I have to close my legs in order to pull my skirt down. I stop when I get to my knees.

"You wanna take it the rest of the way?"

They both reach, hesitate and then carefully pull my skirt off.

I lean back and open my legs.

"Why don't each of you take a stocking?"

They move forward and my dark-haired salesman is brash enough to let his little finger touch my pubic hair as they tuck their fingers into the top of my stockings and pull them down and off. They leer at my body parts, looking at my tits and then at my pussy and then back again.

"So," I say, my voice deeper now. "You've seen me. I'd like to see a little skin."

They rise quickly and pull off their clothes in a rush, dropping them on the floor. A moment later I had two raging hard-ons in front of my face. Both point up like flagpoles. The blond's is taller and thinner, the other thicker.

I run my fingers across the front of my bush, touching the wet folds of my pussy lips, slipping a finger inside momentarily.

"Oh, I wish I had a camera," the blond says.

The dark-haired man grabs his dick and I point to it and say, "I'll take that one first."

Spreading my legs, I shimmy my arse forward as he moves to me. Resting his hands on the chair's arms, he presses his dick forward. I grab his hot crank and squeeze it gently and guide it to my wet bush.

I feel its tip press against my pussy lips. I gasp as he works his hips forward and his thick cock slides into me. I shudder and crane my neck up to kiss his lips. He shoves his tongue into my mouth as his cock sinks completely in me.

And he fucks me right there, with his partner watching and who knows who peeking in the front window. We rock back and forth, his sweet, delicious cock screwing me good. I feel myself come inside and he keeps banging away, his balls slapping my arse. I keep rising, keep getting hotter and when he spurts inside, in long, deep gushes, I come again deeper and hotter.

As soon as he slips off, the blond is there, sliding his cock in me, reaching his mouth down to kiss me and I'm off again to another good fucking. He slows twice but I keep bucking against him and pull out his come as he gushes inside.

I don't hear the tapping until he slides off me.

The dark-haired salesman stands half-dressed facing a front window. The blond lets out a worried gasp as I see two cops looking in. One taps his knuckle against the window while the other points to the door.

Lying there with my legs open I watch the salesman nervously let the cops in. One is black and the other white. Closer to my age, they look so cute in those baby-blue police uniform shirts and dark blue pants.

Both stare at my body as they step up.

The white one says, "Y'all have something to cover those windows?"

"No," one of the salesmen croaks.

"Y'all have a back room?"

"Yeah."

The black cop moves forward, takes a long look at my open, sopping pussy and then reaches down and scoops me up in his arms in one scoop.

"You, OK?"

I nod.

"You wanna file a complaint . . . or . . . would you like to feel a real man fuck you?"

I lean forward and kiss his wide lips and he tongues me and carries me to the back room. His partner has moved ahead of us and clears a space on the carpet. The black cop lies me gently on the carpet and stands over me. He hands his gunbelt to his partner and then his shirt.

His partner steps out into the store and I hear him telling the salesman to get dressed and keep the door locked.

The black cock is bigger and thicker than any I've ever seen. He kneels between my open legs and climbs on me and mounts me. I'm wet as hell but it still takes a minute to work that big cock into me. It fills me completely and I cry out as he starts worming it inside me.

We kiss and bounce against one another. He grinds and I grind back. He fucks me long and hard and I come twice before he fills me with his African come. The second cop is already naked and gives me a quick fuck. Smaller in stature, he sucks my tits as he screws me and I come once again before he spurts inside.

Rising, he dresses quickly.

The black cop steps back in completely dressed. He sits next to me and asks if I'm OK.

I nod and smile at him.

"We got a car around the corner," he says. "We can drive you to your car. Unless you want us to leave you here."

"I could use a towel and something cool to drink."

He grins at me.

One towel and one Coke later, the two cops help me dress and walk me out the store and around the corner to their car.

"We spotted you as soon as you started down Royal," the white cop tells me.

"I know," I say, then tell them my car's parked in the lot across from the Monteleone. On the way, the black cop looks back at me and tells me I have a great pair of legs.

As I climb out, my legs are wobbly, so I lean against their car. The black cop gets out and asks if I'm OK again.

"Yes, actually. Just a little wobbly." I have to laugh at myself.

"You do this often?"

I shake my head.

He passes me his business card and says, "Next time, give me a call and I'll arrange a great flashing, great fuck-a-thon for you, Baby."

So that's what the police call a gang-bang. A fuck-a-thon.

New Orleans – my kinda town.

Conduct Unbecoming

Nola (Toronto, Canada)

When he asks if he can fuck me every day, and I nod yes, he smiles. But, when he asks me if *I* will fuck him every day, and I say, "Yes, every day," – he comes – and I am one step closer to taking everything I want from him.

I'm a dominant woman and I want my man submissive. I want to be the top to his bottom; always. As a policeman, his daily life is filled with decision-making and a sense of being in charge. Quite simply, he spends a lot of time telling other people what to do, why they should do it, and when to do it. I want all of that to change though when he walks through the front door at home and faces me; I need to be in charge here. I want this.

Toronto is a big city with a lot of places to hide and I will give him the extra task, as he drives around his division, of finding a secluded spot where I can visit him while he's working. I see myself waiting in my car, seat tilted back. Dusk has just turned to night and, although I can't see anyone else, the buzz of the city is near enough to touch. I'm wearing high heels and a loose-fitting dress, nothing else. High heels because he is taller than me and they will give me the extra few inches I need; loose dress because underneath I have my strap-on harness cinched tightly. It's the one with straps that secure around my upper thighs, leaving my pussy fully accessible. While I wait I play with the double-ended rubber dildo that I will fit in the O-ring when he arrives. But, for now, I fuck myself slowly with the end that I'm going to fuck him with.

I see the headlights of his police car winding slowly down the back lane that I am parked in. My car is backed in, the passenger side tight against the ivied cement wall. I watch him pull in to a side drive then back out again and reverse silently down the lane and stop beside me. I told him to leave an extra few feet behind his car because I want him there, outside. Stories abound of officers trapped in the back of their own cruisers while *searching* an arrestee; fodder for the guard room rumour mill. He turns off the engine and turns to look at me. I bring the black rubber cock to my mouth and make a great display of sucking both ends before slipping it out of sight and under my dress. I ease his end through the O-ring and slide the other inside myself. He can see me push down in my car seat and knows that I'm enjoying the hard fullness my pseudo-cock provides me.

I get out of my car and walk behind his police car, my dress tented and bobbing in front with every step. He watches in his rear-view mirror as I lift my dress and start to lube the rubbery length. He gets out and, like every good policeman, puts on his hat and threads his nightstick through the loop in his belt before strolling back to meet me. This is a reverse search though and he assumes the position over the trunk of the car when I tell him to turn around. I tell him that there's been a complaint to the station about him and I'm going to have to question him, take appropriate action, and discipline him if necessary. I undo his belt and unzip his pants and, with the combined weight of his nightstick and gun, they fall heavily to the ground. As instructed, he is not wearing any underwear, so at some point during his shift he has managed to go back to the station change room and take them off. Good. I reach around and undo the buttons of his shirt and pull up his undershirt to expose his nipples to the cooling night air. I pinch and roll them between my fingers, testing his ability to keep quiet until asked to speak.

Distant sirens fade away and the car radio blares with a constant traffic of persons and vehicle checks. DOB's and Foxtrots, Bravos, and Tangos, noisy parties, and unwanted guests. All for neighbouring divisions, but I know that he still has one ear tuned in case the dispatcher calls his radio ID.

I tell him to bend over and place his hands on the car trunk in the usual spread 'em position. I waste no time and reach between his legs to grap his balls and give them a good squeeze. My hands are cold and I can feel them tighten dramatically before falling back down as they heat under the gentle but insistent pull and push that I apply. I spread his cheeks and lubricate his arse as I work a finger, then two, in and out. He will start to have second thoughts just about then, and begin to protest out loud that this is not a good idea and that we might get caught. I take it as my cue to convince him otherwise and enter him in one thrust. We both gasp as the forceful action pushes both ends home. It feels too good this way to even withdraw and I stay pressed up against him grinding ever so slightly, each forward motion causing a deepening of the low groan that escapes him. I cannot maintain this non-movement for long and begin to thrust in earnest, fucking myself as I fuck him. The heels of my shoes sink very slightly in the packed drive but still provide me with the height and leverage needed to ride him hard. His bulk and authority is taken completely away by the rubber phallus that splits his arse. He is not in charge, I am, as I ride him and force him to accept that at any time he will give me what I want, how I want it. I withdraw the full length then bang back in; yes, I am rough with him. Noise brings attention, attention means I will stop, so he does not call out. The O-ring rides my clit as I ride him and brings me rapidly closer to coming, so I stop briefly with both ends buried deeply in their respective homes. With one last burst, I bring us both off. Me against the O-ring and his arse, him with me in his arse, and the hand he has brought down to jerk his own cock with. His come flies in a stream over the trunk and onto the rear window, and he collapses forward, breathing heavily. It comes then: the call on the radio, the Sergeant is looking for him.

I withdraw and walk back to my car. I unhook the harness and throw it onto the front passenger seat of my car. I slide in, adjust the seat, start her up and pull away. A last look back shows my officer still behind his car leaning slightly forward, hat still on, but off to the side a bit. I know he hasn't moved and his pants are still around his ankles, his arse will still be shining in the early moon light from the lube that is by now smeared across it and down his thigh. I don't wave goodbye.

I will go home, to our home and I will wait for him. When he comes home I will meet him just inside the front door. Other people take off their coats and shoes; when he comes home he will take off his clothes. I buckle his leather studded collar around his neck and attach his leash. He bends over and I insert a plug in his arse; not too big, but shaped in such a way that it will not come out on its own. I lead him downstairs and into my room. Some would call it a dungeon, but I call it my room. It is there that I re-establish the hierarchy of the house.

There are times when he comes home all pumped up from a car chase or big arrest and he needs to be taken down a peg or two, paddled even, hung up and penetrated. There are a number of devices that I can attach him to, depending on my mood, and I am still feeling aggressive after fucking him at work, so I decide to paddle him and bend him over the sawhorse. I kneel in front of him and attach the weighted nipple-clips; they will swing back and forth each time the paddle meets his arse. Before I take up my position behind him, I put my fingers inside myself and let him suck the juice off each one. I give him five strokes a side and he does not protest; ever.

I let him get up and make him crawl up the stairs ahead of me, which he will do, nipple-clip chain clinking on each step, leash dragging behind him. He will crawl all the way to our bed where he will sit obedient and quiet, plug pushed deeply inside. I will unlock the chest that sits at the end of the bed and let him select a dildo. This is the only decision he is allowed to make inside these walls, and he chooses carefully lest that privilege be taken away. I wait patiently; it's the least I can do.

He chooses a pink tapered plug, not much wider or longer than two fingers, but I will let him do this as I've ridden him quite hard already tonight. He lubes it himself, leans back on the bed, pushes out the ball-plug and slides this one inside himself. I tell him to show me and he spreads his legs, knees up so I can watch as he slowly slides it in and out.

I hook the leash over the bed post and adjust the length so it is taut but not pulling, letting him know that he is not in control, nothing has changed. I kneel between his feet and force his knees wider and I tell him to look at me and fuck himself. I ease one knee up against his arse cheeks, forcing the plug deeper. I place his hands on his own knees and lean forward to remove first one clip then the other, sucking the painful freedom from pressure into my mouth and never easing the weight of my knee as I lean into him.

I lean to one side and ease down on to the bed, replacing my knee with a hand and work him with the dildo as you would fingers in a pussy. I tell him that he is my pussy. I bite him, suck him, lick him, kiss him, and he lets me; he wants me to fuck him again. I want him flat out on the bed underneath me and ease him round, face down, making him hold in the plug as I crawl behind him. I know the angle that I need to take up to keep it inside him; he knows it as well and spreads his legs to allow me between them. He is much larger physically than me, muscled and toughened by too many nights on the streets, but he gives it up to me here.

He knows that I don't want to fuck him because he is weaker than me, more feminine; I want to fuck him this way because he is stronger; I want to fuck him like I'm fucking a man and the noises I want him to make are the deep grunts and groans of a man taking it. I lie with my full body weight on him, forcing his hardness into the twist of bed sheets underneath.

I can't reach his hands but am able to pull his arms to the sides and pin them out, cross-like, and here, unlike at the back of his police car, I can take my time with him and it is my pleasure to do so. I grind into him increasing the pressure and speed until he grunts in time with each thrust, until he forgets his day and the world is no bigger than this room, this bed, me, this fuck. Until his world right now is his arse, that it is full of me, that there are no choices or decisions to be made, he is being fucked relentlessly, and he will take it until I decide I am done. He will always come this way but fight it as if the fact that no hand is touching his cock when he does is different. I bring him through his orgasm, slow the pace enough to allow him to catch his breath and think that I'm done. I'm never done. I'm not done now, but I slide off and he turns his back to me and I curl behind him, plug still in place.

I let him rest and he does not protest when I ease him onto his back. Protesting will never work; I will fuck him again and harder, he knows that. I grope through my toy chest for a slightly bigger dildo and lube it well. This one is realistically shaped and I know that he will feel each ridge as I work it in. I kneel between his thighs, take him in my mouth and lick and suck him until he hardens again. When I release him, his hips strain, pointing his bobbing cock upwards, and I lean in and close my tits around it. He reaches down to hold them himself, squeezing them tight and pinching my nipples between his fingers. He strains hard enough that on the upward thrusts I am able to lick the slitted head.

But I stop him, forcing his hands down and under his ass and he knows that he must leave them there. I begin to slide my rubber accomplice inside him; tightness becomes acceptance, the head disappears and his arse clenches rhythmically around the stem. I suck him into my mouth to the same depth. The more he takes, the more of him I take. He begs for more mouth but must take more rubber as well. Even I don't think I could really synchronize this movement at real cock-sucking speed, but I will try until one action overtakes the other. I will either penetrate him deeply and suck him off or penetrate him repeatedly and let him come in my mouth. Either way, he will come again, because I want it.

This is what I want; this is the way I want our life to be and I am working towards it. He has spent many years on the road and, every day, every shift he works is full of decisions and he's tired of making them. I don't have my room, yet, but I will and it will be equipped with hooks for hanging and ropes for restraining, paddles and whips, collars and clips. I want everything at hand and accessible, not hidden away. I do slide my fingers up his arse when he comes; he only said he didn't want that the first time I did it and when I'm using three fingers I tell him it's only two. I do have a rubber cock that he helps me fuck myself with but I really picked it out for him. I talk to him as I ride him and I tell him that I'm going to do all these things; I'm going to make him crawl naked down the hallway, I'm going to follow behind him and when I tell him to stop I will mount him from behind and fuck him, make him crawl some more then mount him again, and again, and again. I'm going to collar and leash him; when it is warm, that is all that he will wear. When he comes home he will, in front of me, grease himself and insert his own arse plug which he will wear until I tell him he can take it out. He will cut the grass, walk the dog, wash the dishes, and watch TV – always plugged.

I'm going to blindfold him, tie his cock down and string him up in the basement, toes barely touching the cold floor. After I have reddened his arse with a paddle I will line it with my most delicate whip. I will lick each red raised welt then stand on a stool and fuck him.

I will meet him after work when he goes out with the boys for a drink. He will go to the men's room and insert the plug I've brought with me and come back and sit on a stool and chat and laugh with all his friends. I'm going to fuck him before he goes to work, and fuck him again when he comes back home. I will not take out the cock when I'm done and he will have to learn to go to sleep with it inside and if I wake in the night I will ride him again. In the morning, if I want, he will allow me inside him again.

I am going to have an extra strap-on in the garden shed that I will use on him midday while the neighbours pull weeds in their vegetable patch. While they have afternoon tea, I will hang him naked from the crossbeam in the shed. I will spread his legs, weight his balls and while they nibble on tiny sandwiches I will take his cock in my mouth and eat him. At night he will get down on his hands and knees and I will ride him on the back lawn under the starry sky. I tell him that he will let me finger him whenever I want; that he will let me stroke his cock till he comes; suck his cock when I want; that he will masturbate for me when I tell him to. I tell him these things now and I see in his eyes that he wants it that way – he wants me to take everything, leaving him just whatever he is allowed or made to do – and I want to make him do all of it.

Work Is Play

Karen (Albuquerque, USA)

When it comes to real-life sex, I'm about as straight-laced as my Minister's united running shoes. But when it comes to fantasy sex, I'm a girl gone wild! I see a guy or gal that turns me on, and right away he or she becomes a character in one of my wicked sexual imaginings.

Take, for example, a colleague of mine at work, a leggy Latina by the name of Vanessa Sanchez. When I first laid eyes on her, was when the first of my fantasies featuring her took shape in my subconscious. There's nothing more exciting than combining business and pleasure, in my book, and when I tossed Vanessa into the erotic mix I concocted one heck of a sexual fantasy to keep me motivated on the job. The only problem was, Vanessa actually caught me in the middle of my super-hot daydream.

Well, here's how that most satisfying day at work played out:

Vanessa tentatively approached my desk, unsure of herself and what I wanted. I was sure, though, very sure.

"You wanted to see me, Ms Williams?" she said in a soft voice. A voice soft enough and warm enough to suck into your mouth and swallow down.

Easy, I told myself, easy. You don't want to scare her off. So I nodded in a businesslike manner, stood up, walked past her, and shut the door to my spacious, well-appointed office. Then I turned to face her. Her green eyes briefly met mine, then dived down into the thickly carpeted floor.

She was dressed in a simple black skirt and white blouse. Like any one of a million other office workers, except that the skirt was short and the blouse was tight. The skirt showcased her large, round, firm arse, and her long, toned, supple legs. Her dancer's legs were sheathed in glistening, black, sheer stockings, all the way from her high-heel-encased toes to somewhere just above her short, short skirt. Her large, full, blatant breasts pressed against the thin, see-through fabric of her blouse, and in the air-conditioned office her dark, erect nipples were clearly visible through the flimsy material – big and hard and begging to bust free. Her hair was chestnut, with red highlights, and her face was delicate and doused a golden brown, advertising her sultry, sexy Spanish heritage.

"Yes, Vanessa," I said briskly. "Have a seat, please. I wanted to discuss your performance evaluation. Your three-month probation period is up today, as I'm sure you know."

She sat down in a comfortable leather chair in front of my large antique desk, while I stood before her, leaning against the desk. I watched her cross her slender legs, fight with the ever-rising hem of her skirt. I felt my pussy go wet and my face get warm, as I stared at those long, lithe legs. I could now plainly see the bronze flesh of her right leg, between her skirt and her stocking. My eyes journeyed on an erotic course from that hot starting point, down the sculpted length of her leg, past her fleshy thigh, her rounded knee, her muscular, moulded calf, her slim ankle (narrow enough to easily wrap my fingers around), and down to her foot – a foot dramatically displayed in black, imitation leather stilettos.

"Yes, I do . . . know," she mumbled. She leaned forward to nervously grasp her knee, interlace her fingers around it, her nails flashing silver. Her bountiful breasts almost tumbled out of her over-stretched blouse as she leaned over her legs, and I could see and appreciate the warm, deep cleft between her two magnificent mocha mounds.

But I was a leg-woman from way back, from the days of ballet lessons and summer vacations at the beach and gym classes, and so that's where my eyes returned, and lingered. "You've been doing a good job, Vanessa," I intoned. "Everyone thinks so. However, I've had a couple of complaints about your . . . business attire – the way you dress."

She squeezed her legs and her emerald eyes flashed angrily

at me, her blood boiling instantly. "Who's . . . I mean, what are these complaints about – specifically!?"

That was a good question, since I'd made them up. I stared off into the fiery jade depths of her eyes, momentarily lost. "Well, take your skirt, for example," I said, making up policy on the fly. "Our company dress code states that skirts cannot be more than four inches above the knee." I reached back and picked up a metal ruler off of my desk. "Stand up, please, and we'll see just how far above the knee your skirt is."

She rose from the chair, tugged down her skirt. "I think it's petty of people to complain about their co-worker's clothing . . . behind their backs. They're probably just jealous," she added saucily.

"They probably are," I agreed inadvertently. I flushed and swallowed hard as I gazed at her stockinged legs – legs that seemed to go on forever; then I licked my lips with a wooden tongue and dropped down in front of her, in front of her silky legs. I could smell the faint, sweet, warm scent of her body spray, and perhaps even the musty, beginning dampness of her pussy. She was a passionate girl, easily aroused. She jumped when I cupped the back of her right leg with my left hand. My fingers lingered on the soft sheen of her stockings, surreptitiously caressed the fine, black material, and the hot, brown flesh that it covered.

"Okay, here we go," I croaked. I grasped the back of her thigh more tightly, and then placed the cold, steel ruler against the bottom of her skirt, on the front of her leg. A quick glance told me that her hemline was a good six inches above the knee, but I'd known that much from a mere visual inspection. To an experienced leg-watcher like myself, hem-length is all important. I pressed the ruler firmly against her leg, and then slowly slid it up underneath her skirt, until the tip of the metal touched her burnished flesh.

"Oh," she gasped, her emotions running quickly from anger to pleasure, hot to hotter.

I kept on sliding the ruler up her leg, until it touched the edge of her panties, while with my left hand I began openly caressing the back of her leg, stroking up and down from her thigh to the vulnerable spot at the back of her knee, and then back up again – higher and higher each time, slowly and sensuously. My hand slipped underneath her skirt, touched the top of her stocking, felt the rounded flesh that led up to her big, beautiful buttocks.

"Oh, Ms Williams," she breathed.

I reluctantly pulled my eyes away from her lush, luxurious legs and glanced up at her face. Her eyes were closed, her red, pouty lips open, her body quivering with excitement, her big chest heaving with mounting desire. "Call me, Karen," I said, for lack of anything poetic to utter. My mind was muddled with the brazen leg-heat of the young, Latina hussy. I sensed that we were well beyond words, anyway, and that's exactly where I wanted us to be.

I slid the edge of the ruler underneath her panties, rubbed it against her ultra-sensitive skin, firing her pussy, while my other hand caressed and squeezed her butt cheek, revelling in its firm over-fullness. "You've got beautiful legs, Vanessa," I whispered, mesmerized by the feel of her soft, smooth, super-heated leg flesh.

"I've seen you admiring them, Karen," she confessed quietly. "And wondered when you would take matters into your own hands." She stared down at me, her emerald eyes misted over with lust, her nostrils flared with passion-heavy breath. She slowly began to unbutton her blouse.

I dropped the ruler and quickly moved directly between her willowy legs, squatting in front of her, gripping her legs with both of my loving hands. I began stroking her legs, running my hands up and down her thighs, down the back of her legs, the front. Her knees buckled slightly and she gasped, but I kept right on fondling her gorgeous legs. I couldn't ever get enough of them, but I'd die a blissful death trying.

She tore open her blouse, peeled it off her shoulders, and threw it aside along with her inhibitions. The Venetian blinds on my floor-to-ceiling twentieth-storey office window were open, exposing our wanton desire to the great, big world beyond, but neither of us cared. My own world had shrunk down to the busty young woman's long, stocking-clad legs, and the wet, smouldering pussy that I knew lay at their apex.

Vanessa frantically unfastened her chaste, pink bra and

tossed it away. Her big, beautiful tits spilled out into the open. They were huge – round and heavy, peaked by thick, long, dark-brown nipples that were already fully engorged as a compliment to my preliminary leg work.

"Take off your skirt," I said in a choked voice, my hands never taking a break from groping her stunning legs.

She fumbled with the fastener on her skirt, her hands shaking and clumsy, until, finally, she succeeded in unhooking it, and the skirt puddled at her feet.

"Yes," I murmured, as I stared at her satiny, black panties. The contrast between her skin's deep, rich brownness and the sleek black of her stockings was simply and utterly breathtaking. Her panties were damp at the front, at the bottom. "Sit on the edge of the desk," I ordered, and she obeyed.

I stood up, turned around, and reached out and slipped my quavering fingers under the top of her right stocking, and began to carefully unroll it from her leg. She lay back on the desk and stuck out her leg, moaning softly as I unrolled her stocking. I tore off her high heels and pulled the stocking from her foot. As I did the same with her left leg, she began to play with her tremendous tits, squeezing and kneading them, gripping their heavy thickness in her small hands. She rolled her inch-long chocolate nipples between her fingers and groaned.

I had both of her stockings in my hands now. They were still warm from the heat of her hot, hot legs, and I rubbed them together, rubbed them against my face, drank in the silky sensuality of the heavenly garments, smelled the sweet smell of young womanhood in them. Then I placed them to the side and grabbed up the fleshy reality of her bare legs. They shone brown and smooth in the light, and I held them by the ankles, and pressed them together. I began sucking on her toes.

"Yes!" she hissed. "Make love to my legs!"

That had been my intention all along. I held her feet together and sucked on as many toes as I could cram into my hungry mouth at once. Then I pulled them dripping wet out of my mouth and flicked my tongue up against them, against the underside of her feet. Her legs jumped in my hands, but I held on tight. I swallowed two of the toes on her left foot – sucking on them, tugging at them with my mouth, playfully biting them. My tongue coated them with saliva, bathed them with my grateful admiration, my mouth worshipping them. I put her feet back together and sucked long and hard on both of her big toes at once, then licked at the soles of her feet again, lapping at the sensitive skin in long, slow –

"Karen! Hello! Karen!"

I gave my head a shake. "Huh, what?" I looked around. Ms Sanchez was standing next to my tiny desk, looking down at me, a stern expression on her face. "Yes, Ms Sanchez?" I asked. I'd been day-dreaming again. And judging by my boss's angry face, she didn't know and didn't care what a big role she had played in that dream.

"Karen, I'd like to see you in my office. Right now!" She abruptly turned around and walked away, my bleary eyes following her big butt, as it bounced underneath her tight, black skirt.

The other girls in the typing pool were looking at me and smiling. I grinned stupidly, got up, straightened out my skirt, and stumbled away from my desk and after Ms Sanchez, knowing that I was going to catch hell – again.

"Yes, Ms Sanchez?" I said glumly, when I'd arrived at the door of her spacious, well-appointed office.

"Come in and shut the door, please, Karen," she replied briskly. "Have a seat."

I did as she said and sat down in a comfortable leather chair in front of her large antique desk. She stood in front of me, staring at me with her big, green eyes.

"Karen, your three-month probation period is up today. And this is the fourth time in the last three months that I've caught you day-dreaming when you should have been working." She held up my personnel file, and continued in a businesslike manner, "What are you thinking about when you're supposed to be working, anyway?"

I blushed scarlet and looked down at my hands.

"Do you have some personal –" She was cut off by the phone ringing. "Just a minute," she said, and walked around her desk and picked up the phone.

I sucked some cool air into my overworked lungs and made up my mind. It was now or never. I stood and walked over to

Vanessa, picked up her hand in mine, pulled her from her chair, and walked her in front of the desk.

"What are you doing!?" she asked, startled by the bad, bold look in my baby-blues. "I —"

Her words caught in her lovely throat when I bent down in front of her and began caressing her legs. "This is what I've been dreaming about," I confided, feeling up her legs with no intention of taking no for an answer.

In a matter of a few fleet minutes that seemed like sexually charged hours, I had her flat on her back on the desk, her hands groping her tremendous tits, polishing her jutting nipples, while I sucked on her slender toes. I sucked both of her big toes into my mouth at once, and my head bobbed up and down on her toes as if I was sucking a rock-hard cock. I licked the soles of her feet, my tongue tracing trails of fire on the bottom of her delicately arched feet.

"Yes," she moaned, like I knew she'd moan, her body jumping each and every time that I licked her feet — and I licked hard and often.

I bathed her beautiful, bronze feet with my tongue, sucked on her toes again, kissed and nipped at her ankles, and squeezed her fleshy calves in my hands. Then I placed her sparkling feet between my legs, squeezing them with my knees, and quickly pulled off my stylish cashmere sweater and lacy, black bra. I lifted her legs back up and pressed her naked feet against my full, dewy, bare breasts. "That feels good," I murmured, rubbing her feet against my tits and chest.

"Let me do it," she said.

I let go of her and watched and felt her use her feet to massage my breasts. The sensual delight of her saliva-slick feet on my big, white tits and pink, engorged nipples made me weak in the knees, and the head. She rubbed my juicy globes with her feet, played with my rigid nipples with her toes, then took one oversized tit between her feet and squeezed and fondled and caressed it.

I closed my eyes, tossed back my head, and groaned, my long, blonde hair cascading down my naked back. The air in the office turned hot, my voluptuous body hotter. I felt loose and limp, and my head spun dizzily as my senses were rocketed unchecked along an erotic rollercoaster by that Latina vixen massaging my tits with her talented feet. I quickly found myself teetering on the brink of a catastrophic orgasm.

I grabbed onto her loving feet before I exploded in premature ecstasy, opened my eyes, and said, "I want your toes in my cunt."

She smiled up at me, then pulled her tit-buffers out of my hands, stood up, and brushed the unimportant business paraphernalia off of her desk. Her butt cheeks quivered with the effort, and I reached out and grabbed her big behind. She straightened up with a sigh, leaned back into me, and I wrapped my arms around her massive chest and held her close. She turned her head, parted her lips, and I pressed my wet mouth against hers. We kissed ferociously, longingly, our tongues fighting a frenzied battle in which there were no losers, only winners. I gripped her huge, tan tits and squeezed them, felt the incredible heated heaviness of them, pulled and primped her nipples, all the while mashing my mouth against hers – tasting deeply of her.

Finally, we broke apart. She pulled down her panties and stepped out of them, and I clawed off my skirt and my panties and joined her on top of the desk. Her pussy was slick with dampness, gloriously naked except for an inverted triangle of soft, brown fur at the very top of it.

"I want you to toe-fuck me," I hissed, as I sat back on the gleaming surface of the oak desk, facing her. I stuck out my left leg until my foot was only inches away from her beautiful face. She let me dangle there for awhile, like the toe-teasing scamp that she was, staring hungrily at my foot, her thick, pink tongue flicking out and brushing lightly against my toes. My leg began to quiver with the effort of holding it up and out, and the raw sexual anticipation of what her mouth would do to me, until, finally, she gently took hold of my foot and steered the outstretched toes into her mouth.

"Yes!" I cried out, oblivious to the strictly business setting in which we were pleasuring each other, and the staff working just outside the thin confines of her office-playground.

She fed on my toes. She sucked them, licked them, bit them. I closed my eyes and let the scalding waves of sensuality wash up from my leg and engulf my pussy. I shuddered as her mouth attacked my foot and her tongue slapped against my toes. She licked and kissed the bottom of my ivory foot, the top, my ankle, my calf. She was obviously an experienced foot-worshipper herself, as evidenced by her practiced, patient technique. I stroked my pussy, rubbed my swollen clit, shoved a couple of fingers inside my sopping wetness.

"No!" she exclaimed. "Not like that!" Her green eyes were blazing with lust.

I took my fingers out of my red-hot pussy, let her watch me lick the juices off. Then I pulled my foot away from her and spread my legs, extending her an open invitation to foot-fuck me.

"That's more like it," she said, smiling wickedly.

She held out her right leg and I caught it and sucked on her toes until they were good and wet. Then I steered her delicate foot down to my burning, blonde pussy and brushed it against my glistening lips. I was jolted with pleasure. She pushed her foot forward and her big toe pressed against my aching clit, and I screamed with unbridled joy. My body rippled as if with electric shock, and I knew that I would not last long with her toes in my pussy.

"I'm going to fuck you," she said, and thrust her big toe inside my pussy. She pushed farther inside of me, and I grabbed onto her tapered ankle and helped her plunge in and out of my volcanic pussy with her toe.

As she and I toe-fucked my cunny, she began rubbing her own steaming pussy with her hand. She shoved two fingers inside and frigged herself fiercely, all the time foot-fucking me with abandon. We stared fiercely at each other, at our sweat-dappled, heaving bodies, our eyes glazed over with suffocating passion and towering desire. The sight and smell and feel of that sun-kissed Latina goddess was rapidly becoming too much for my pussy to bear. I desperately hammered her foot into my flaming lovebox, her toes penetrating deeper and deeper and deeper – to my very sexual core, where lay mind-shattering ecstasy.

"I'm going to come!" I screamed at her.

Her lips were set in a grim, red line, her teeth clenched, her face contorted with the effort of staving off her own explosive climax until the very last possible moment, as she finger-fucked herself to the searing edge of all-out orgasm. She screamed, "I'm coming!" and her body shook, and her magnificent brown melons were jolted over and over again as powerful orgasms detonated inside of her and thundered through her writhing body.

My mind and sight went fuzzy, and my whole world disintegrated down to her foot and my pussy, my pussy and her foot. My cunt erupted, and scalding waves of supererotic bliss crashed down upon me and my body convulsed with the most intense orgasm I had ever experienced; once, then twice, then a devastating third time. I felt like I was going to pass out as I was rocked again and again and again by earthquake orgasms that had as their epicentre Vanessa's toes in my pussy.

Aftershocks of ecstasy tore our bodies apart as we desperately held onto each other – my hands clenching her foot, her hand squeezing my leg – until the last of the white-hot orgasms had coursed through us and dissipated. I raised her foot up out of my smouldering pussy, to my mouth, and licked my come off of her wiggling toes.

"I want a taste, too," she whispered exhaustedly, and I let her pull her limp leg away so that she could twist her foot into her mouth. She licked what I had licked and smiled a satiated smile.

My left foot reached out and began to fondle her soaking wet pussy, getting to know it a little –

"Karen! You're doing it right now, aren't you?" Ms Sanchez demanded to know, slamming the phone down angrily.

I grinned sheepishly. "Doing what?" I asked innocently.

Fortunately, I didn't get fired that day, just incredibly fired-up. It's my work-related fantasies, after all, that help pump up my morale, turn my ultra-boring joe-job into a so wicked toe-job.

The Gift

Dahlia (Berlin, Germany)

The martinis were stronger than they should be before 4 p.m., and lunch took twice as long, but it was my birthday, so I didn't really care. I've always been pretty good at not letting on how drunk I felt, and today was no different. Making my way back to my desk, a neat grin on my face, my feet methodically moving left, right, left, right in my pointy black patent leather heels, I slid gratefully into my seat and exhaled slowly.

All I had to do was keep staring at my monitor for a couple more hours and then I could leave early. All I had to do was stare and type a few words and no one would know that I was wasted off my arse. I just had to keep my mouth shut, my face focused, and no one would know the difference.

"Dahlia?"

I turned around.

"Um, someone left this at the front desk for you."

Michael reached forward and gently placed an artfully wrapped package on top of "To be Filed". I stared. I knew this package would impress me even if I wasn't seeing double – the bow was red luscious silk, the paper was as smooth as satin and as brilliantly red as my fingernails, and the box was big enough to cover my entire desk.

"Do you know who dropped this off?" I asked, turning around, but Michael had already gone back to the mailing room, leaving me alone with my oversized gift.

I glanced around the room but no one seemed to have any interest in me or my enormous red box. I debated for a second whether to open it now or save it for later, but knew that I couldn't resist, and so, with a sigh and a tingle of anticipation, I delicately slipped the bow off and ran my nails under the tape keeping the paper shut. With a satisfying hiss, the wrapping fell to the sides, and I stared at the white cardboard box.

I looked once more at the wrapping paper – no note, no explanation. Having no idea who would give me such a large present, much less deliver it to my desk, I opened up the box and peered inside, hoping the contents would provide some answers.

At first, all I saw was a neatly folded stack of black lace, underwire, and red ribbon. I looked around the room – no one was watching. Was this some kind of joke? Without taking the fabric out of the box, I reached in and lifted up the material. I groped with my left hand to see if there was anything underneath. My fingers found a slim metal chain – and nothing else.

What the fuck? I looked around the room again, but no one was watching, no one was snickering, no one was paying me any attention. Time to figure this one out, I thought.

With a quick sudden motion, I slid the fabric out of the box and into my briefcase. As I stood up, I reached into the box one last time, grabbed the chain, and dropped it into my suit pocket, before making my way, calmly and professionally, to the restroom, all traces of inebriation eradicated by curiosity and adrenaline.

The bathroom door securely locked, I placed my briefcase on the shut toilet seat and opened it. The pile of lace and ribbon eyed me suggestively. I shook my head, smiling to myself – this was definitely the most intriguing birthday present I'd ever received. When I lifted up the fabric, it took form and I laughed out loud. Barely enough material to cover anything worth covering. I knew it would cover enough to make anyone lucky enough to see desperate to know what was underneath – and I knew it was the perfect size.

Within a matter of moments, my suit hung neatly on the hook behind the door, and I was wearing a decadent mass of material – all criss-crossed and tied and finessed around my breasts – the underwire fitting perfectly under my cleavage, the ribbon wrapped around my waist and lacing up the back of the corset, the red silk creating a pattern of Xs against the sheer black lace of the rest of the garment. The box had also thoughtfully contained a pair of black thigh-highs topped off with an inch of red lace.

I didn't dare leave the stall to look at myself in the mirror, for fear someone would walk in, but I didn't need to – I knew it fitted me perfectly. Slipping on my heels, I leaned back and closed my eyes. Running my finger against the ribbon's smooth satin, I tried to remember how long it had been since someone had stroked me the same way. It had been a very long time.

My last boyfriend and I had split up almost a year earlier and between my work schedule and my distaste for bars and one night stands, I'd slept alone every night since, which made this gift all the more mysterious. No one had shown much interest in me in a while, and the only appointments I made these days were with co-workers and clients.

As I ran my fingers back and forth over the trail of red ribbon, eyes closed, breath quickening, I let my mind wander. By the time my fingers reached between my legs, I was all wet. With a rush of need and desire, I shoved first one, then two, inside, pressing along the curve of my body, breathing deeply as every inch of me focused on the hot wetness of my insides. I slowly started to push them in and out, my left hand making its way along the fine bone of the corset's underwire, cupping my breast and pinching my swollen nipple between my fingers.

The pain from my nipple, combined with the swelling of my clit and the pressure of my fingers, following a martini lunch, almost made me pass out. I slid back against the wall of the stall, falling into the corner, sweat glistening on my face, my hair in my eyes, as I pressed in and out, harder and faster, feeling every inch tighten, every inch beg for more, my clit craving the pressure of my fingers, my pussy craving the pressure of a cock. I alternated as quickly as I could – a few seconds outside, a few seconds inside, my fingers darting across the edge of my clit, back and forth, round and round, and then inside – quick, as deep and as hard as I could shove. In and out, round and round, back and forth, every motion of my right hand echoed by my left across my breasts.

Both breasts had long since been liberated from their lacy confines, and they swung over the underwire, quivering as my hips thrust forward and my entire body began to shake. I could feel myself starting to come – the hint of delicious pleasure teasing me on the edge of my horizons, a promise of what would come if I kept at it, if I didn't let up, if I shoved harder and deeper, if I pinched stronger and tighter, if my fingers moved faster and my hips pushed further.

Leaning against that damn bathroom wall, my hair around my shoulders, my breath heavy, my face flushed, my wetness leaking down my thighs, I kept moving – my fingers, my hands, my hips, until I could feel the sensation building and building and building and then – with one big rush, I exhaled as millions of tingling sensations rushed through me.

A huge grin on my face, I shoved my briefcase off the toilet and sat down. My chest was heaving, my head was spinning – and I felt amazing. I couldn't remember the last time I'd masturbated, and I certainly couldn't remember the last time I'd done it in a public restroom. It had been way too long. What a birthday present.

Ever since David left, I'd gone into autopilot. Getting close to someone else seemed like way too much work and way too much risk. It was easier to focus on my friends and my job and my apartment. Without anyone to run their hand between my legs, without being woken up in the morning by someone pressing up against me, it was easy to forget that my body served anything but clinical purposes.

The last ten minutes had been a delicious reminder.

With my clit still throbbing and my nipples still swollen, I unhooked my corset and stepped back into my suit. I'd almost forgotten the day wasn't over. I looked at my watch – an hour or so until I could leave without guilt. I bent down to pick up my briefcase when a loud clang startled me out of my daze. I glanced over to see a pile of silver chains against the edge of the toilet.

I smiled to myself. I'd totally forgotten. What the hell was that? Reaching over, I picked up the large circle at one end and lifted – it was a very delicate, very finely linked leash, the clasp attached to a matching very delicate, very finely linked collar. I smiled to myself. Whoever put this gift together certainly spent a lot of money, I'd never seen a chain so expensively made, and whoever put this gift together definitely knew how to pick things out. That outfit had fitted me perfectly, and my flesh already tingled at the feeling of cold metal against it.

Suddenly remembering a small make-up mirror in my bag, I fastened the collar around my neck, letting the leash hang down over my shirt. I couldn't resist. I opened up my mirror and looked at myself. I looked naughty. I couldn't remember the last time I felt naughty, much less looked naughty – and it felt good. I loved the way the chain looked against the collar of my white shirt, the metallic glitter of the leash against the sober grey of my suit. I ran my fingers down the metal and felt chills down my spine. Delicious.

I unclasped the leash from the collar and slid it into my bag. I kept the collar on. I wanted its cold reminder to stay with me for the rest of the afternoon. Doing my best to keep a straight face, I made my way back to my desk. I felt as if everyone must have heard my moans or at least noticed the excessive time I had spent in the bathroom, but no one paid me any attention, no one commented on my pinkish cheeks or my unruly hair. I patted my hair anxiously as I sat back down at my computer, realizing I had forgotten to check my appearance in the mirror.

"Um, excuse me?"

The meek voice came from behind me, and I spun around guiltily. The girl had long curly brown hair and huge brown eyes behind small tortoiseshell frames. I noticed her lips, which were large and seemed just slightly dry and cracked. For an instant, I wondered what it would taste like to lick them wet.

"I really hate to bother you, but –"

"It's no problem," I said reassuringly. "What can I do for you?" She looked vaguely familiar, but I couldn't think from where. I tried to remember if I owed her any paperwork.

"This is terribly awkward," she flashed a nervous grin, her hands anxiously twisting together, "but, you see," and then it all came out in one sudden rush. "I went out at lunch and I bought myself a present and I left it on my desk while I ran to answer the phone and the lunch receptionist thought it was for you because my name is also Dahlia and the regular receptionist told her it was Dahlia's box, and I don't know exactly how it happened but she told Michael and somehow he thought it was yours and then I asked him if he'd seen it and he said oh no, he had thought it was for you, and he gave it to you, and I don't know if this makes any sense, but I wondered if you knew where my box was?"

I smiled. Of course. Of course it wasn't for me. Of course not. How ludicrous. Only in my life. I smiled at her, at this darling girl with the dry lips and the nervous hands.

"Nice to meet you, Dahlia."

She laughed shyly, her hands resting for an instant against the edge of my desk.

"Why don't you have a seat?" I asked, motioning to my extra chair. She sat down and stared at me, clearly wondering what I was going to say next.

"The box is here." I gestured under my desk, showing her where I had tucked the package before my trip to the bathroom, "but the contents are in my bag. I'm sorry."

She looked at me, confused.

"I couldn't resist. I had to try it on."

She laughed again, a bit longer this time and a bit less shy.

I reached into my bag and pulled out Dahlia's outfit and slipped it back into the box. The leash I placed carefully on top, before handing it all to her.

"I'm really sorry about this. You must think I am terribly strange." Her eyes stared straight into mine, wondering what I thought of her.

I smiled back at her. "Not at all. I think you are wonderful. It is the best birthday present I have ever had."

"It's your birthday today?" she exclaimed in wonder.

"Yes, yes, it is." I couldn't help smiling at this delightful girl.

"Oh, God, I had no idea. Why, then you must keep this. It should be yours." She pushed the box back at me.

"No, no, no. It is yours. I got to try it on. That was amazing enough for me. It's your outfit. It belongs to you."

There was a pause while we both thought about what to say next.

"Please. I'd like you to have it."

I couldn't stop staring at her lips. "No, no, that's okay, it's

not really me, anyway. I like my underwear to be brighter than
the clothes I wear on top . . ."

She laughed again, this time the shyness almost gone, the
brown eyes seemingly bigger and browner than before, and I
began to notice little hints of gold inside them.

"You know," she leaned over to me and said, in a soft
whisper, "they have corsets in red and pink and blue . . ."

My first thought was that her lips were only inches from
mine. My second thought was that I'd never kissed a girl. My
third thought was that a pink corset might be the best thing I
could ever buy.

"Will you take me to the shop? I want to go."

"Of course!" she exclaimed. "If you won't let me give you
mine as a birthday present, perhaps you can let me buy you
another?"

"Only if you let me buy you a drink after?"

I couldn't believe it. I was flirting with a girl. I was flirting
with a girl also named Dahlia. I was sitting at my desk, flirting
with a girl with my name, and all I could think about was how
her lips would feel between my teeth.

"I would love it," she said as she stood up. "Shall I stop by
your desk at six?"

"That sounds great." I couldn't stop smiling at this creature.

She leaned over again, her lips inches from my face, and my
breath stopped. What was she doing? Was she going to press
her lips against mine, her tongue in my mouth, running against
my teeth, her breath mixing with mine? Was she going to kiss
me at my desk?

"You can keep the collar," she whispered, and then she
turned to walk away.

I closed my eyes, waiting for my heart to return to normal.
Two more hours to six.

Amanece's Story

Amanece (Puerto Rico)

I am Amanece, and I am a 50-year-old woman. Ever since I remember, I have had sexual fantasies of dominating a male. Being from San Juan, Puerto Rico has not helped develop that fantasy to fulfillment, although it has become an addiction since I was eight years old and masturbated to Robin Hood kneeling at having recognized King Richard, or Pedro Infante apologizing to his father. The earlier fantasies involved father–son, king or queen and military knight, but soon developed to woman dominating man, and from words and looks moved to sexual and conscious consent. The Internet has helped fulfill a lot of these fantasies virtually and has helped to fulfill some in real life, but what a woman develops in her fantasy world is hard to meet. Therefore my hands and my best lover, my mind, play an active role in my sexual life that maybe no man will ever satisfy, although I do not give up in my search.

My fantasy man is always the same one, a man I have never met and cannot describe the image of him, but I know how he is, how he feels, what he wants. He is sure of himself, with a lot of self respect and respected, sensitive, and all he wants is to live for me and fulfill all my desires, be my complete slave.

I have many fantasies with him; the one I am presenting now is one of my favourites as it shows him apologizing and grovelling. This one goes:

To be Mine

I call him from work and let him know that I am looking forward to getting home and finding him ready for me. I know that he realized the call was from me and he felt that slight tremor inside him, an excitement immediately recalling his submission.

"And, by the way, I need to talk to you seriously tonight."

"Yes, Mistress," he would whisper with a trembling note, knowing that that sentence meant that he must have done something that needed correction.

He would come home early and get himself ready and in position. Since we were leaving together he had to have his work done in time to be home before me. As I open the door he takes my briefcase, puts it away and follows me to the living room where he kneels, taking off my shoes, massaging my feet, my glass of wine ready. I breathe deeply and relax, letting his feeling of submission grow, feeling it in the intensity of his massage, in the way his whole body expresses it by the perfect form, correct position of his feet, the way he holds them and the veneration I feel as he lowers to suck my toes and continue with the massage.

I snap my fingers for him to stand for inspection. He stands, legs separated, straight, pushing his nipples out, hands on his head, face straight ahead. I like him to have a slight erection if not a full one. This evening it is a shy one, which makes him more nervous. He is trying to take sideways looks at me, checking for my anger, feeling humble.

He is totally shaved for me, from head to toes . . . all of him. I check for any hair on his body as he must keep himself this way. His balls are hanging with the clamp-on weights he has to wear; I want them to hang low. I make them swing a little, hearing him gasp. As I touch his nipples they harden quickly, as trained, and he is wearing his chastity belt. I move to his back and ask him to bend over. I put on plastic gloves which make a distinct sound and, lubricating my fingers, insert two; he is open and clean. I pick the butt plug he is to wear tonight and slowly push it in, it always makes his knees quiver but he knows that this is only in preparation for what is to come. He is ready. All my toys are out and easily available.

After I am done he places his hands on his back and, lowering his face, begins his apology.

"Mistress, I have done, or not done, something that has

upset you. Please will you correct me now or would you prefer later?"

I walk around him, letting the tension built up in him. His mind roams, looking for his fault, apprehensive about my next actions.

"I expected you to fall on your knees as soon as I got home and recognized your wrong-doing. It is understood that you must announce your misdeeds and ask for punishment. You have not even acknowledged your fault. I am very surprised."

He kneels. "Mistress, please forgive my lack, for which I have just increased your anger and my punishment; I beg to be told so I completely grovel at your feet, asking for your mercy. Please, my Mistress, correct your slave."

He is visibly perturbed and willing to be humbled and be called to his place, to stand corrected.

I love to hear my slave apologize; I have taught him a ritual. To recognize the misdeed, preferably explaining his own deficient thought that led to it, to confess and say how wrong it was, to ask for forgiveness and beg for punishment and atonement and then promise that it will not happen again. After the punishment he will thank me again and then we will have a tender moment by me taking him in my arms making him feel better, while he is still contrite and making up. He is mine and only my wellbeing counts.

"I am tired, had a long day today, but I cannot go on like this, cannot tolerate your lack of training! I was told that yesterday at lunch a lady came into the restaurant you were in, with a lowcut blouse and a very nice body. You seemed to have lusted after her, even bending a little on your chair and the chastity must have bitten on your erection. This I was told by friends that were there. If you are going to embarrass me in this fashion, I think you should move out of my house."

He prostrates himself to the floor.

"Amanece, Mistress, punish me hard. I will take all, but please do not tell me to leave. I did look at the woman and had a problem with an erection. Mistress, I have no excuse. I know you are very generous at taking me out of my chastity and letting me masturbate, even you doing it yourself, up to the point of almost coming, every day. I know I am only allowed to come, if you wish, every three months and that it has been two months and three weeks without coming; in this manner you keep me correctly aroused for your use. I know I must not look at another woman, and never in a lusting fashion. I should have averted my eyes, especially at this point when my penis is so out of control, as I am a week away from you permitting me to come. I promise you I will not embarrass you again. Please punish me harshly for this and let me display the marks, so that people will see that I was corrected. Please forgive me, permit me to atone. You are the only woman that matters to me. I know I should have remembered this and admitted it to you as soon as it happened; I have been wrong."

He was squirming like a worm on the floor while saying these words. He knew that I must be very mad.

"Get me the belt that hangs in the living room."

He crawled out and came back with the belt on his mouth and, prostrating himself on the floor, offered it to me with extended hands.

"Position!"

He got on all fours, shoulders to the floor and arse in the air, and received fifty strokes. Every stroke pushed the butt plug deeper, his face rubbing the floor. I have a strong hand and the belt was thick. I hit him on the arse and thighs and legs, so that when he wore shorts friends would see the mark.

"Stand."

I took off the chastity. His penis came to erection immediately it became free, in spite of the hurt. He started trembling, seeing me so close, feeling so humbled, wanting to appease me.

"You will hump the floor every night for a month without coming after I caress and excite you. Maybe this will let you know that what you must concentrate on at all times is to be able to stand the three months until I let you come. That this is my wish and, if you are mine, you are to obey me."

"Yes, Mistress, as you say."

I came close to him and started kissing him. He separated his lower body from mine so his erect penis would not touch and offend me, but I grabbed his arse and pushed him to me, rubbing against him. He moaned and I continued kissing and licking his neck, caressing his back, his nipples.

"Mistress, please, I am about to come. Please have mercy on me and let me back up so I do not shame myself offending you, please."

I pulled his hair, bending his head back, opened his lips with my fingers.

"It will be such a hard month, slave."

I separated from him, letting him quiver and forcing his desire to subside. I held him in my arms, caressing his hair, as he convulsed.

He was on his best behaviour after the correction; he served my dinner, walked along the beach with me although his basketball team was playing that night, without even mentioning it, came home and gave me a bath then a massage. He stood kneeling beside the tub while he bathed my body with a sponge, rinsing me later and, when I finally stepped out, drying me totally. His body was sweating and quivering from the excitement of having me so close and he was so aroused. I touched him briefly while letting him attend to me and during the massage my body relaxed in his hands. Whenever he came close to touching my nipples or my cunt lips, he would murmur: "May I, please?" before I permitted him.

"I want you to massage my cunt with your face and bald head." He closed his lips as he knew it wouldn't involve using his tongue until permitted, it was just rubbing, first the head, then lowering his whole face to his chin, back and forth, then letting his nose tease my clit until told to stop or to use his tongue. By then his face would be filled with my juices and my smell impregnated his head. Involuntarily he would start whimpering.

"You will wake me up in this fashion every morning and when I feel satisfied you will come to my side and lift a little your leg so I can play with your balls and penis. I will wear my strap-on, which is on top of my night table, and use your arsehole as a pussy, until I come. Then you would be left alone. I imagine your penis fighting the chastity with the erection, but you will be left wanting, in remembrance of all the women in the past that were used by men and then left, just like you will be left. Every morning, this will be your ritual."

His excitement only grew and he would fold over from the

pain and beg (I love to hear him beg). "Please, Mistress, may I offer you my insignificant balls so you can enjoy slapping them so my erection will subside. You will be so generous if you will permit me to relax by inflicting pain, please, I beg you. I know I deserve to be like this, doubling over in excitement at your feet, at your whim. It will be a very difficult month that I have earned with my reproachable behaviour, but I beg you, just tonight, let my balls and my penis relax. I beg you, wonderful Mistress, my only star, my Goddess, I beg."

"All right, I will grant you this, but I will tie you so you remain in place until I am done, yes?"

"Yes, Mistress, as you wish. Thank you, thank you."

I tied his wrists and ankles to the bed frame and made his head comfortable, as he would be jerking.

"Are you ready, slave?"

"Yes, Mistress."

"With your eyes open!"

I showed him my open hand and brought it to his lips; he kissed it tenderly and eagerly. His penis was still fighting to get our of its cage. I started hitting him in his balls in a constant rhythm and the slaps made him jerk and moan; his eyes watered but he mouthed "thank you" repeatedly. I stopped long after his penis had almost disappeared, bringing my hand again to his lips and this time waiting for his gratitude in a flourish manner. Crying, he did this. By now, he was exhausted. I untied his hands and took his balls and tied them, having both ends tied to where his ankles were. He knew what I was doing. Frightened, he begged:

"Please, Mistress, please, let my ankles remain untied; I am so frightened of moving and cutting my balls."

"Ah . . . but you won't, and tomorrow morning I expect good service, so you will untie yourself and begin before I awake. Good night, my love, my slave."

I kissed him gently but let him rest, afraid of arousing him again. He had gone almost three months and now had to wait one more. I remember when I used to masturbate him at least three times a day and made him come; now it was when I permitted, although his erection was a must and was his service. I had to have available at all times, a hard penis to mount, to tease, even to mouth, but one that knew there would be no relief until I wished.

I woke up in the middle of the night; he was fast asleep, carefully lowered so the rope tying his balls to the bed posts would not pull. I took off his chastity; he woke up and looked at me. I just had to touch his penis and it sprang hard in a minute. I smiled while I raised over his body. I brought my cunt to his face and lowered it, rubbing it up and down; his lips closed, waiting for my decision. I continued to lower myself until I was over his penis; just the head I got inside. He moaned loud, his balls were hard and he felt it tighten more around the rope as I moved up and down.

"Mistress, I want you so badly, I am so hot, as horny as a bitch in heat, please . . . have mercy."

I pushed down a bit more and continued humping him, making love to myself. He could hardly move with his balls tied.

"How much longer, my love? Tell me, how much longer do you have to wait?"

"Until you wish, maybe a month and a week more if I behave, Mistress, until you say."

"Yes, much better. You know where you are standing and what is good for you, right, slave?" I kept talking while I continued to make love to myself using his hard rod.

"Oh yes, my Goddess."

"I am feeling oral."

I moved out of him and lowered my head to his penis. Feeling my cold mouth tighten around his hot penis made him scream with pleasure.

"Mistress, please, I cannot take it. I will come. Please".

"How dare you say this. What are you supposed to say when this happens?"

"Yes, yes, Mistress. Please, Mistress, I beg you to slap my hurting balls so my penis knows that it just exists to pleasure you and he must be of service always. Please let my balls feel the pain of my lack of control. Please."

"Are you ready?"

"Yes, Mistress."

Again I played the ritual, the showing of my hand, taking it to his lips, his eyes closing to the surrendering of what was to come and the slapping. This time, just twice, as I wanted to continue playing.

"Please, Mistress, I am ready to be used. Thank you for not letting me shame myself again."

The next morning, he untied his balls and enticingly and softly climbed up to me, I quivered in my sleep and let him continue to caress me as told, careful not to be abrupt, attentive to every movement I did. As I opened my legs to him he let his head fall and caressed me with it. He was careful not to hurt me as I had used him for so long last night, stopping several times to correct his demanding erection but continuing with my pleasure. He knew my lips must be sore, so he was delicate.

"You may lick."

His tongue became wide and hard as he softly passed it over my whole cunt lips and, as he felt my tension, it narrowed so it would flick on my clit, never allowing any saliva to make me wetter, just keeping the right moisture, which was my moisture only.

"Again, just your face."

His mouth closed and he moved his head only, slowly bringing his nose, checking to see if the action was approved before going further with masturbating me with his nose.

"Sweet slave, sweet."

He pressed his mouth to my cunt and vibrated with sounds.

"Keep on." He must have done this for some time before I asked for his tongue again. He became just my toy machine, my vibrator but not only to me, especially to him. He knew and became a perfect toy, my perfect slave.

"Enough."

Slowly he left the bed and went to the kitchen while I lingered more in bed, thinking of what a wonderful and useful slave I have.

Debt Collecting

Liza (London, UK)

When my husband tells me he's taking me out tonight, and that
I should wear the clothes he's laid out for me on the bed, I
really don't pay it a second thought. He will often book tables
at nice restaurants as a treat for me, and buy me a new outfit to
wear for the occasion, and it's a while since we've spent any
quality time together as he's been so involved with his work.
Perhaps he's realized he's been neglecting me and this is his
way of saying he's sorry. So I take a long bath, cream my body
all over with lotion, wrap a towelling robe around myself and
walk into the bathroom to see what he's chosen for me.

At first, I think he's playing some kind of practical joke.
Instead of the designer label cocktail dress and slinky lingerie
I've been expecting, I see clothes which, frankly, are better
suited to a Soho streetwalker: a tight white crop top in some
shiny material, a denim mini with a frayed hem which appears
to be less of a skirt and more of a belt, a black push-up bra and
matching thong panties, made of scratchy artificial lace. No
tights or stockings, just white stiletto-heeled shoes.

"I can only find some cheap, nasty stuff on the bed," I call
down the stairs to my husband. "Are you sure you haven't
made a mistake and brought the wrong bag home from the
shops?"

"There's no mistake," my husband calls back. "Put it on and
I'll explain in the car. Oh, and put your hair in a nice, high
pony tail and make sure you're wearing lots of red lipstick and
black eyeliner."

By the time I've finished dressing and applying my make-
up, I look and feel like a tart. The bra, which is clearly visible

through the thin top, thrusts my small breasts out provocatively, and the miniskirt is so short that if I bend over or stand carelessly I will be displaying the cheeks of my bum, separated by the chafing lace of my thong. I go downstairs, tottering a little on the three-inch heels, still wondering what this is all about. My husband just nods his approval curtly, and leads me out to the car without letting me grab a coat to cover my slutty outfit.

I wait for him to give me an explanation, but he says nothing. It's only when I realize that he is driving away from the high street, towards one of the roughest estates in town, that I finally ask, "What the hell is going on here?"

At last he breaks down and confesses. First of all, he says, he loves me and he always will. He's been keeping things a secret from me because he wanted to protect me, but now everything has gone beyond that point. For the last year or so, he tells me, his business has been in financial trouble. For a while, he tried to forget about his problems, and carried on spending money he didn't actually have, treating the company's funds as though they were his own personal bank account.

As the debts began to mount, in order to keep up the lavish lifestyle we had become accustomed to, he decided to borrow money to cover the shortfall, but when the bank refused to give him a loan because they deemed him to be a bad credit risk, foolishly, he turned to the most notorious money lenders in town, the Lee brothers. He knew they were supposed to be involved with all kinds of criminal activity, but he was desperate. Of course, despite his promises to repay the money, he hasn't been able to, and their threats of what will happen to him if they don't get at least some of it back have been getting more and more vicious. Finally, he has come to a solution which is acceptable to them: he is going to pay a portion of his debts by giving them unlimited use of my body for the night.

I can't believe what he is telling me: it's the most outrageous thing I've ever heard, and I demand that he turns the car round right now and takes me home. There is absolutely no way I am going to let these strangers have sex with me. My husband tells me he has tried everything else, but the two have seen the photograph of me he keeps on his desk in his office, and they want me. And what the Lee brothers want, the Lee brothers get.

We pull to a halt in front of a rundown tower block. The walls are plastered with graffiti, a mattress and a broken fridge have been dumped on the concrete forecourt and a couple of the street lights don't work. I can't help thinking that the car will probably have lost its radio and maybe even its wheels by the time we return to it.

We take the lift, which is in semi-darkness and stinks of urine, up to the ninth floor. My husband raps on the door of one of the flats. It is opened by a man who must be a good six foot four in height, with a lean, powerful physique. I have to admit he is not unattractive, but he looks rough and ready, his dark eyes hard in his tanned face. He eyes me slowly up and down, and his lips curve upwards in a feral smile.

"Very tasty," he mutters. I almost expect him to haul me inside the flat and leave my husband on the doorstep, but he doesn't. Instead, the two of us follow him into the living room. It's small and cramped, with a stained carpet and a three-piece suite with torn beige covers, and it smells of mould and boiled cabbage. I can't believe the Lee brothers actually live in this squalid little place, given the amount of money they're reputed to have made from all their dodgy dealings, and I suspect this is just the place they use when they want to give someone a working over – though not usually of the type they're clearly planning to give me.

The other brother is lounging on the settee, but he gets to his feet as I enter the room. He's about ten years younger than his sibling, slightly shorter and stockier, with blue eyes and spiky, highlighted blond hair. They don't look anything alike, and I suspect they have different fathers. The one thing they do share, however, is a look of undisguised lust as they stare at me. Their eyes seem to be stripping me naked, and I feel vulnerable but also suddenly, shockingly excited. What do they want to do to me? Will they expect me to perform sex acts I never have for my husband? Will I be able to say no? And, more importantly, will I want to?

Without being told, my husband goes and sits on a wooden-backed chair in a corner of the room. The dark one – I haven't been given any kind of introduction, nor do I expect one – unthreads the thin leather belt from his trousers and uses it to fasten my husband's wrists securely behind him, binding him to the chair. There are beads of sweat on his brow and a panicked look in his eyes as he realizes he's helpless. Whatever these two lowlifes decide to do to me from now on, he can't prevent it.

The blond comes to stand behind me. He grabs hold of my honey-blonde pony tail, and twists my head round to face his. Though his features are softer than his brother's, and I suspect he probably has the nicer nature of the two, I'm acutely aware of how much bigger and more powerful he is than me, and a strange mixture of fear and anticipation shudders through me.

He presses his mouth to my neck, and I think for a moment he's going to kiss me. Instead, his teeth nip my skin, just enough to bruise, and I realize he's leaving his mark on me with a love bite. I wriggle in his grasp, but he holds me tightly. I can feel his cock beginning to stir in his jeans, the hard length of it pressing against my backside.

"Cute body your missus has got," he says to my husband, "and I can't wait to see it naked."

As he speaks, he is pulling at the midriff-baring top I'm wearing. The stitching in one of the badly finished seams gives way, and he casually tears the garment off my body.

"Not got much in the way of tits, has she?" the older brother says, and my face flushes with embarrassment at being discussed so crudely.

"I dunno," the blond replies, squeezing my breasts through the push-up bra. "I reckon there are a couple of nice little mouthfuls here."

"Well, get them out, then," his brother tells him, and the blond reaches into the cups of the bra and scoops my breasts out. The nipples stiffen under a combination of his touch and the greedy gaze of his brother, and I almost want to thrust my chest out further, as if to prove to them that I've got something worth looking at.

I've almost forgotten that my husband is sitting meek and immobile in a chair, and then I glance over and meet his gaze. He looks away, ashamed, but I have seen the size of the bulge in his trousers and know that having to watch what is being done to me is turning him on.

The blond is still playing with my nipples, and I realize how much I want to feel his mouth on them. His brother has other ideas, though.

"Strip the rest of it off her," he says. "I want to see her cunt."

Again, my cheeks burn: my husband has never called it that in all the time we've been together. Sex with him is gentle and tender; not rough and crude. There's nothing but roughness and crudity about these two, so why do I find what they're doing so exciting?

The blond does as his brother asks, unzipping the miniskirt and letting it drop to the floor. Then he tugs my panties down and off. I'm standing there in nothing but bra and high heels, nipples hard, pussy damp. I can smell my own arousal, and I'm sure they must be able to, too.

The older brother thrusts a hand between my legs without ceremony, finding me wet. His thumb settles on my clit, rubbing it hard. It normally takes very little of this type of treatment to bring me to orgasm, and despite myself I am panting with desire when he abruptly withdraws his fingers and orders me to my knees.

I comply, and am rewarded with the sight of him unzipping the fly of his jeans. He wears nothing beneath them, and the dark arrow of pubic hair that leads to his groin comes into view, followed seconds later by the hardening length of his penis. Even partially erect, it looks big, and I shudder with guilty pleasure at the thought of being made to take something that size in front of my husband.

His brother follows suit rapidly. His cock, almost fully hard from where he's been rubbing against me, is not particularly long, but is thicker than any I've ever known.

"Suck me," the blond commands, pressing his helmet to my lips. I open my mouth and take the fat purple head inside. He tastes sweaty and a little sour, but the intensely male aroma of him has its own power to arouse me, and I begin to lick him with an eagerness which surprises me. I lap briefly at the little slit in the tip of his cock, inducing it to weep a tear of salty juice into my throat.

A hand suddenly grabs hold of my pony tail, yanking my head back painfully. Not wanting to be left out, his brother is now demanding that I pay him the same attention. He thrusts his erection into my mouth, causing me to gag as the blunt glans nudges against my soft palate. He does not want gentle strokes of my tongue; instead, he is keeping tight hold of my head, thrusting hard between my lips and effectively fucking my mouth.

The blond soon grows tired of his brother monopolizing my mouth, greedy for the touch of my lips and tongue on his cock once more. As he urges me to blow him again, I take the initiative and grasp a penis in each hand, proceeding to suck and nibble on each one in turn.

I can't help wondering whether I will be required to suck them both till they climax. Will they make me swallow their loads, or will they spray my face and hair with their come? The question is rendered irrelevant when the dark one pulls right out of my mouth.

Is he going to fuck me now? Suddenly, more than anything, I want to feel that huge cock powering into me. I'm sure that, as far as he is concerned, size is all that matters and technique is an alien concept. To my shame, the thought of being treated as little more than a sex doll by him excites me intensely.

"You take her cunt," he tells his brother, as though this is an arrangement they make on a regular basis. "I'm having her arse."

This is something I'm not prepared for. My husband has suggested anal sex on a couple of occasions in the past and I've always turned him down. I certainly don't want my first time to be here, like this – and yet I can't help wondering what it would feel like to have this man penetrate my forbidden hole.

"You've got no problem with me fucking your slut of a wife up the arse, have you?" he calls across to my husband. There is no answer, but the damp spot which is darkening the front of my husband's trousers tells its own story. What he has already seen has been enough to make him come, without even touching his cock.

"Do you want us to get her nice and wet first?" he continues.

"Yeah, I'm sure he wants to watch that," his brother replies.

"What do you reckon? I'm having her cunt, so I'll lick that. You want her arse, so you lick that."

The blond lies on his back, before ordering me to kneel above his face, my rump raised in the air. In this position, my bottom is easily accessible to his brother, and it is his tongue I feel first, snaking out to touch my tight little rosebud. I groan as the blond joins in, licking my crease with rapid strokes of his tongue. In truth, I am in very little need of his attention, my sex already flooding with juice, but I give in eagerly to the feel of two hot mouths working me front and back. I feel the hard tip of a tongue press at my anus, the muscular ring relaxing enough to allow it to penetrate me a little way.

At this point, the two men seem to reach an unspoken agreement, deciding I am ready to take them both. The blond swivels round underneath me, so that now it is the head of his cock that waits at the entrance to my moist channel. Holding my sex lips apart with my fingers, I lower myself down on to the solid column of flesh, feeling it push my rippled walls apart. Once I have taken as much of him as I can comfortably manage, his brother presses his helmet against my other hole. I am aware of a swift pain as my sphincter tries to fight against the unfamiliar intrusion, then he is inside me, stretching my back passage as widely as his brother is stretching me in front.

I have never been so full of flesh, only a thin wall of muscle separating the two cocks. As I begin to ride them both, awkwardly at first, but then beginning to find a rhythm, I give a wild cry, trying to accustom myself to the bizarre new sensations I am experiencing.

As I expected, there is no finesse, just hard, deep thrusting. I reach down between my own body and that of the blond, seeking my clit where it is hidden in the damp folds of my sex flesh and stroke its head in the rapid, circular motions that are guaranteed to bring me to orgasm.

It is the blond who comes first, his long thighs tightening beneath me and his buttocks bunching before he shoots his semen deep inside my pussy. It is enough to trigger my own orgasm, my muscles clenching around the softening cock in my vagina and the still solid one in my anus. His brother follows quickly, unable to resist the pressure of my spasming passage. I can already feel their seed leaking out of me as they slide their softening pricks from my body.

They release my husband from the chair, and tell us we are free to go. They insist on keeping my wet panties as a souvenir, and my husband drapes his jacket round my shoulders to save me having to walk back to the car in just my skirt and bra. As we are leaving the flat, the older brother says, "So we'll take that as a down payment on what you owe us."

"Yeah," his brother laughs. "Call it a deposit."

We drive back to the house in silence, unable to talk about what's just happened. I have been thoroughly, disgracefully used, but sexually I have never felt so alive. And what my husband doesn't need to know is that I am already planning to visit the Lee brothers again, to see what other depraved things I can do for them to pay off our debts . . .